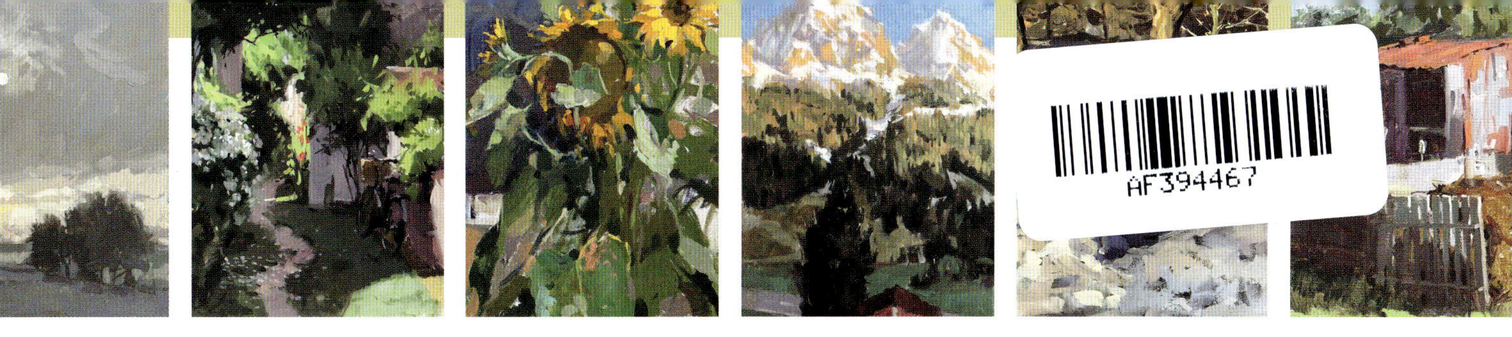

PLEIN AIR PAINTING
with *Oils*

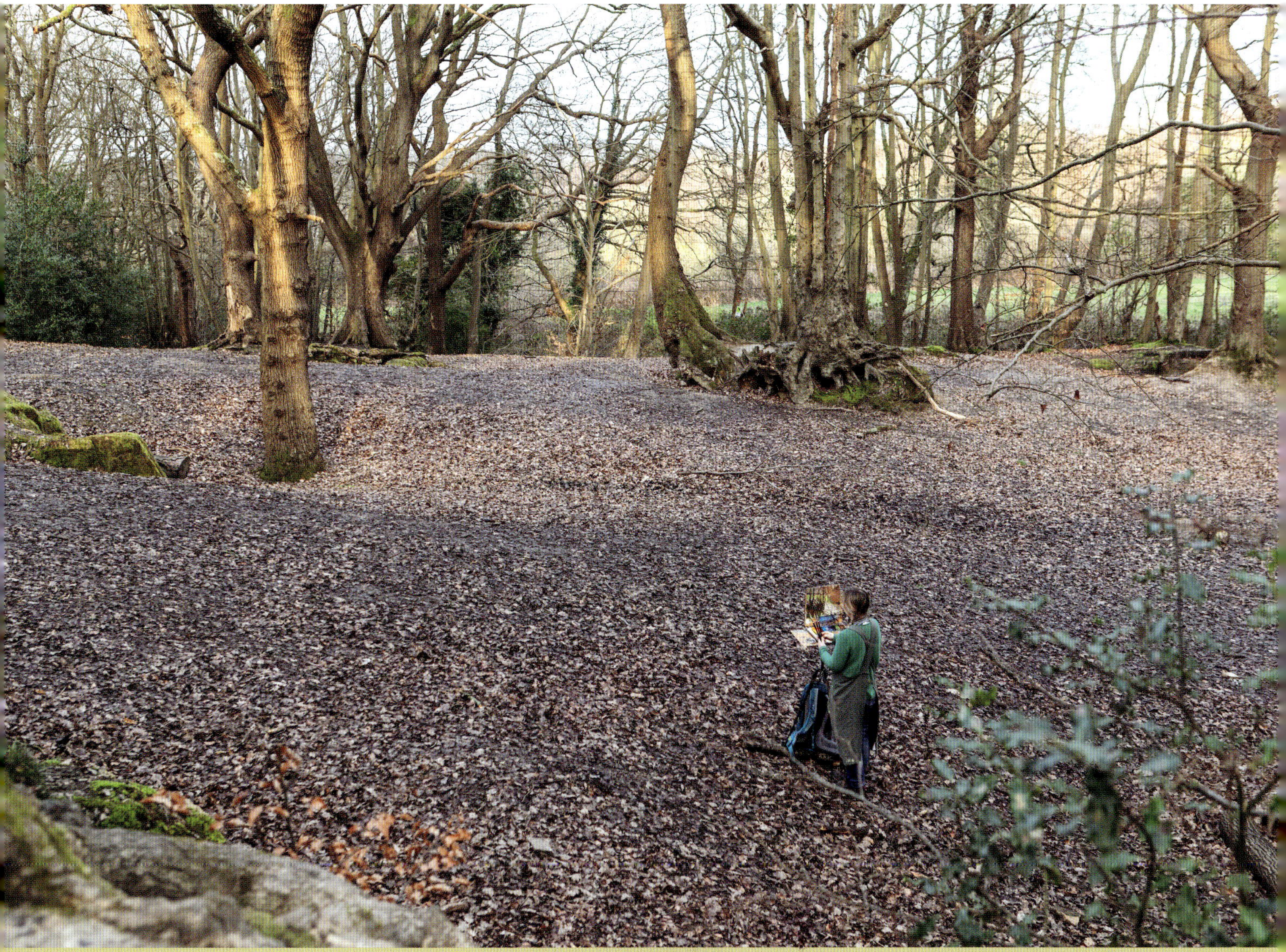

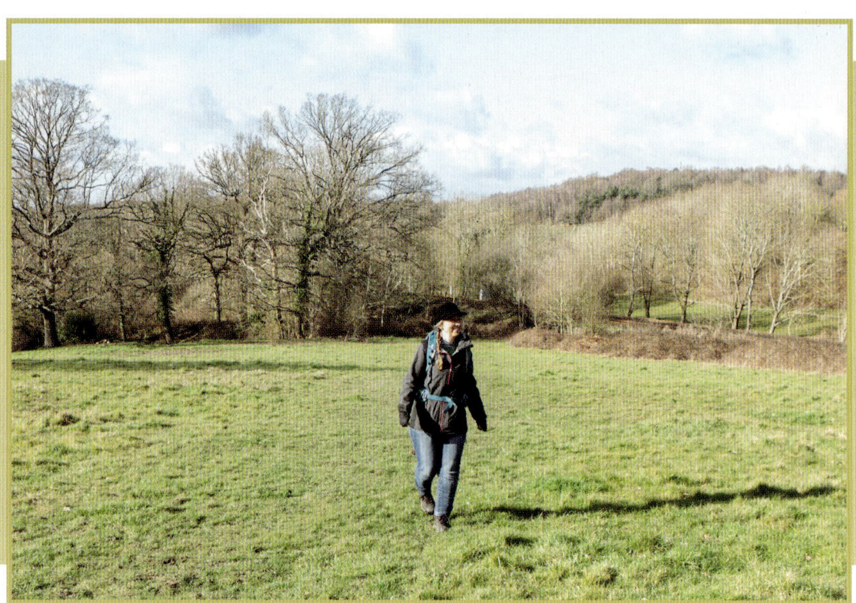

DEDICATION

I dedicate this book to all the friends I've ever painted with, and the plein air painters I am yet to meet.

...and especially to my squad, the Northern Boys.

'We few, we happy few, we band of brothers.'

PLEIN AIR PAINTING *with Oils*

A practical & inspirational
guide to painting outdoors

HAIDEE-JO SUMMERS

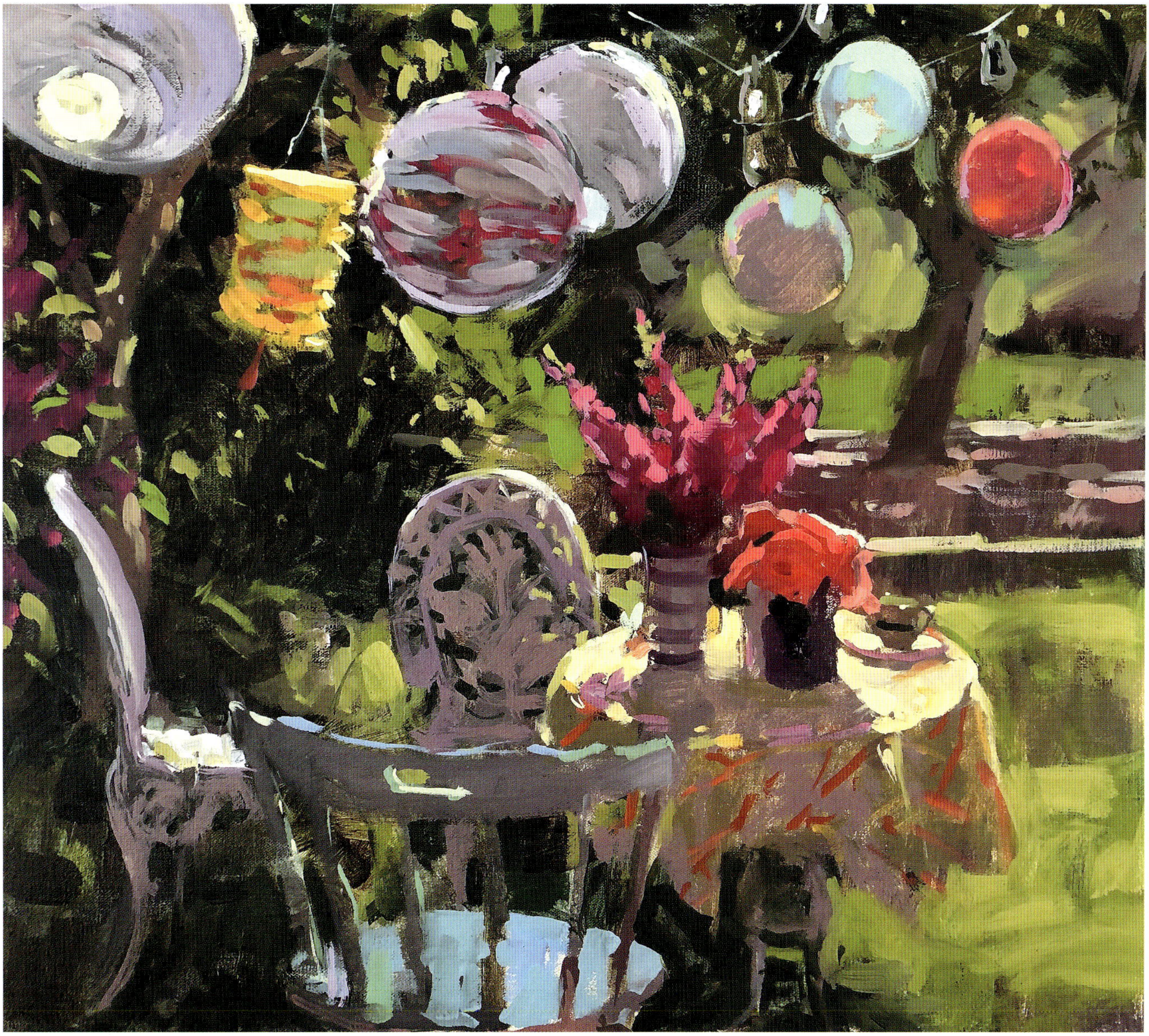

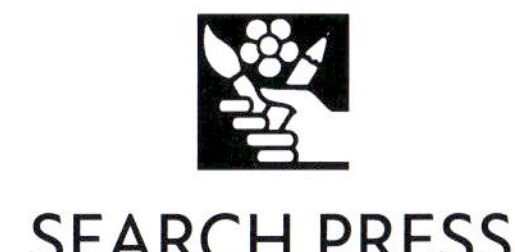

SEARCH PRESS

First published in 2022

Search Press Limited
Wellwood, North Farm Road,
Tunbridge Wells, Kent TN2 3DR

Reprinted 2022

Illustrations and text copyright
© Haidee-Jo Summers 2022

Photographs by Mark Davison at
Search Press Studios and on location, except
for this page, author's own; page 10, by
Susanna Heath; and page 15, by Kate Gabriel.

Photographs and design copyright
© Search Press Ltd. 2022

ISBN: 978-1-78221-876-0
ebook ISBN: 978-1-78126-845-2

The Publishers and author can accept no
responsibility for any consequences arising
from the information, advice or instructions
given in this publication.

Suppliers
If you have difficulty in obtaining any of
the materials and equipment mentioned in
this book, then please visit the Search Press
website for details of suppliers:
www.searchpress.com

You are invited to visit the author's website:
www.haideejo.com

ACKNOWLEDGEMENTS

I'd like to thank Search Press for giving me another
opportunity to share my thoughts on painting in this
book, and especially to my endlessly patient editor,
Edward Ralph, who makes it all a pleasure rather
than a chore.

Thank you to David Curtis ROI RSMA for his unending
encouragement and friendship; and to all the artists,
past and present, who inspire me to do better.

To my family and friends for your constant love
and support – and putting up with me when I've got
a bit too much on my plate.

Finally, special thanks to all those who collect my
paintings, you allow me the freedom to lose myself
in this wonderful obsession.

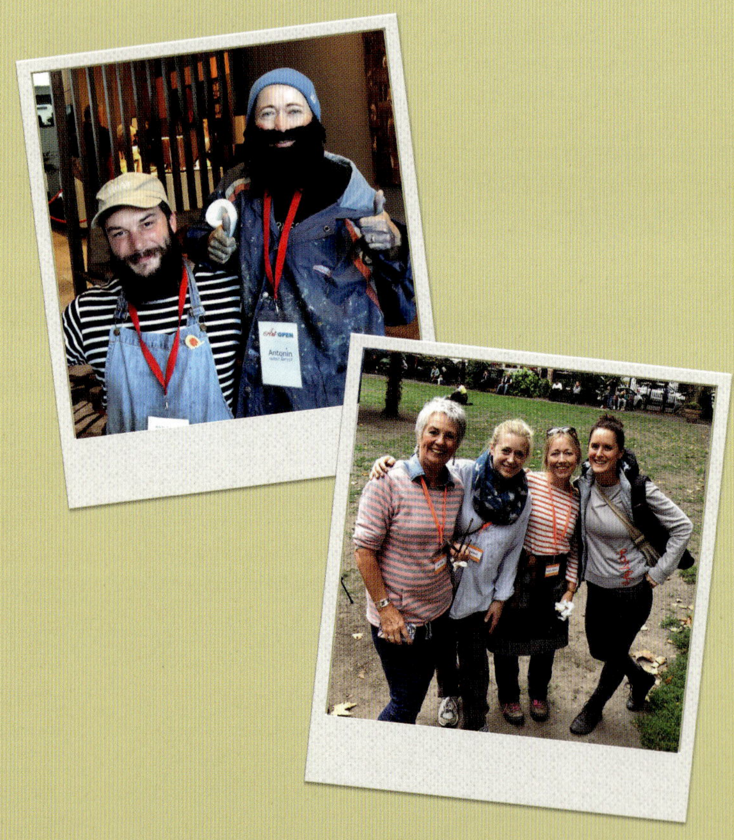

Dressing up fun with French artist Antonin Passemard
at Art in the Open in Wexford, Ireland.

Image of group painting together – Artist
friends Mo Teeuw, Valérie Pirlot, Haidee-Jo and
Melanie Harrison painting together at a British
plein air painters' meet up event in London.

Contents

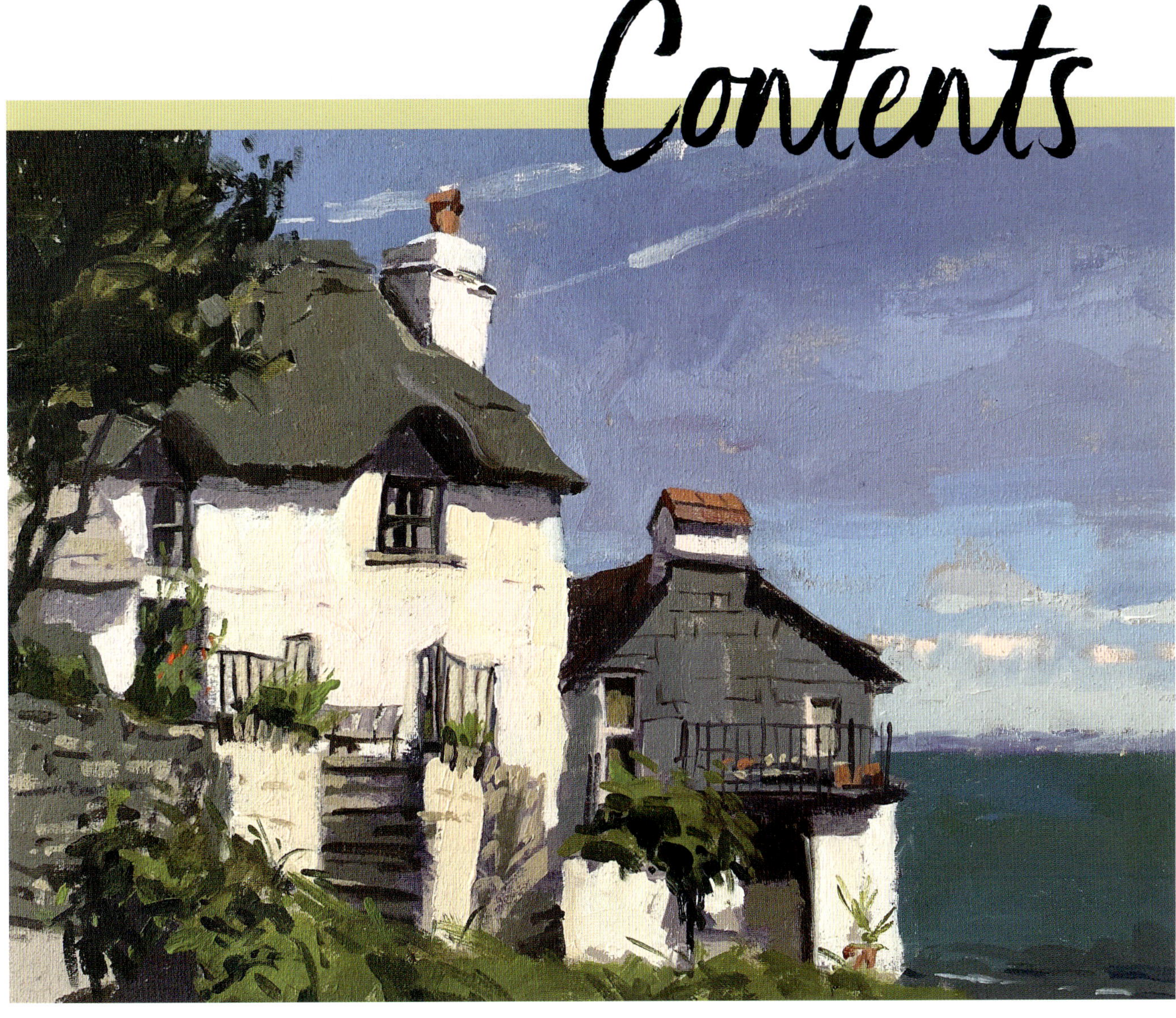

Foreword

There are two really annoying myths about painting. The first is that it is relaxing; the second that you have to be patient. They both imply a passive engagement with the process. Nothing can be further from the truth. Haidee-Jo, however, does not help our plight in trying to get this over. It's not that she finds it relaxing, or that she has particularly unusual reserves of patience, but she does give us that impression: the impression that it is easy. Of course, often those at the top of their game do so, whether it be Picasso or Matisse making seemingly effortless lines with a stick of charcoal, or Ken Howard laying down blocks of colour with his hog-hair flats.

People often talk about the decades of learning and practice that lead up to the moment of applying a brushtroke, but it is in fact the seconds immediately prior which are critical: the looking, the assessing, the mixing of the colour. That is the point of most intensity, concentration and indeed anxiety; where a plein air painter such as Haidee-Jo is at their best or worst.

I have seen Haidee-Jo paint; witnessed her looking, laying down colour, standing back and assessing. The impression she gives is one of peace, belying what is actually going on in her head. We know this because we see the results. We see her 'nail it'.

Haidee-Jo's facility is unquestionable but that is just one part of what she does. She also has the unerring ability to spot paintings in the everyday – to see poetry and beauty in our back yards.

As a painter, one of the great motivators is in seeing what your colleagues are doing. Every now and then they give you a right kick in the guts. While I was flicking through Instagram recently, a recent painting of Haidee-Jo's did exactly that. It was a gleaming greenhouse with sunlight bouncing from the angled panes of the roof. Firstly, she spotted something that many of us would not have noticed or, if perhaps we had, would not think it either worthy – or maybe even possible – to paint. Having 'seen' the greenhouse, she was able to analyse and portray it through another type of seeing: a more intense noticing, a series of assessments, decisions and questioning of those decisions that renders one exhausted after an hour or two. The resulting painting was able to hand on her initial gasp of seeing that light to the viewer, when they see it perfectly distilled in oil paint.

I feel that Haidee-Jo is the master of painting the thing that first brought her attention to the subject. Her paintings arrest us in the same way we would be arrested when we walk past that old shed, that snowman or that flower stall. She captures it. She sees it, covets it, steals it and then represents and shares it with us all. Thank you, Haidee-Jo.

Peter 'Pete the Street' Brown NEAC
January 2021

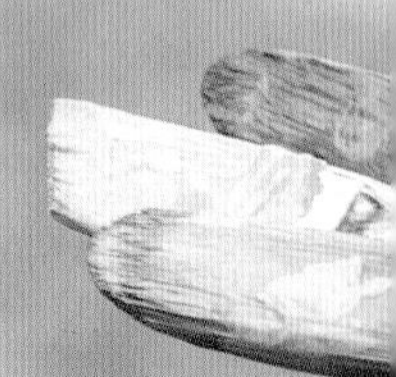

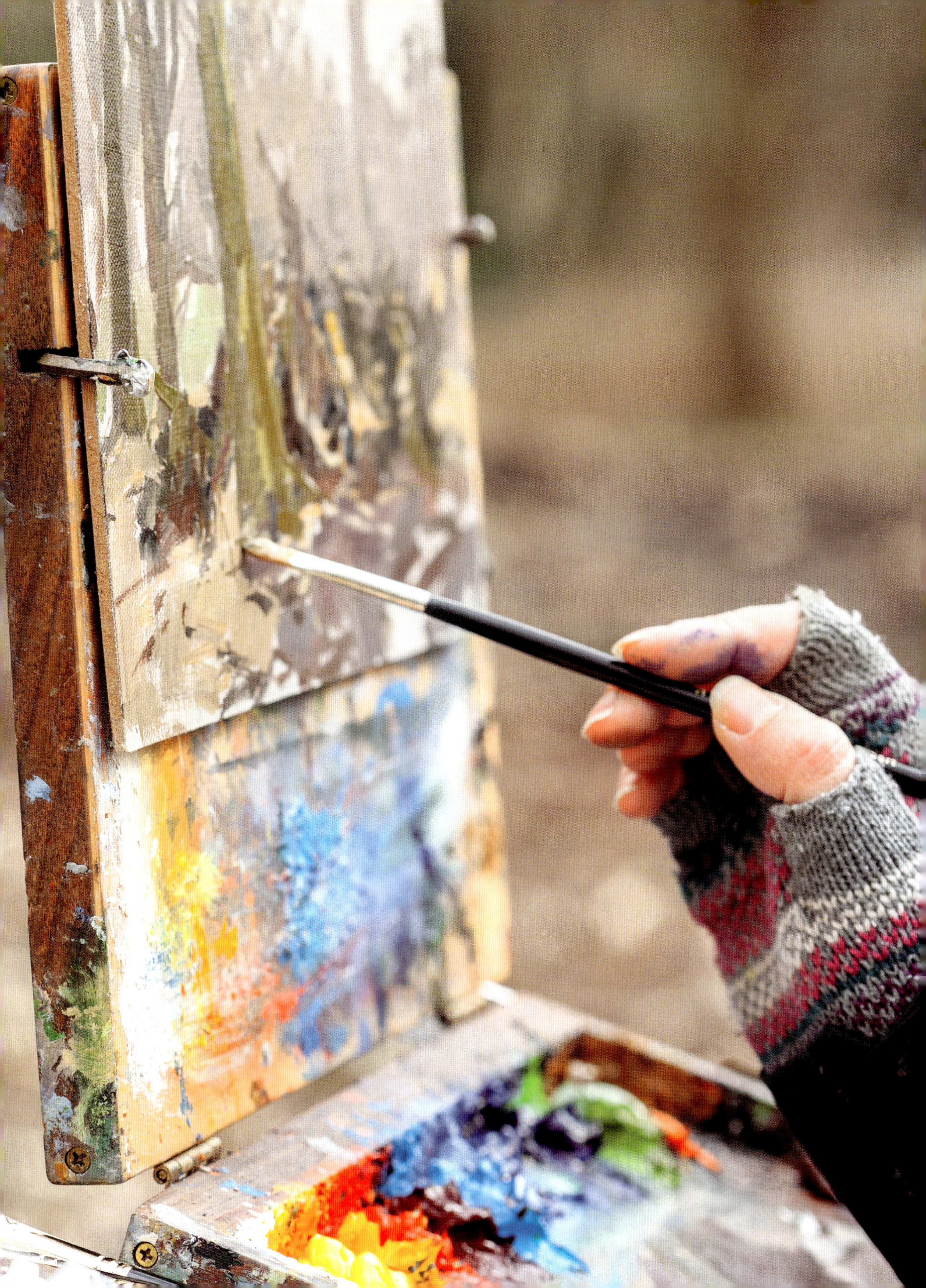

An introduction
to painting outdoors

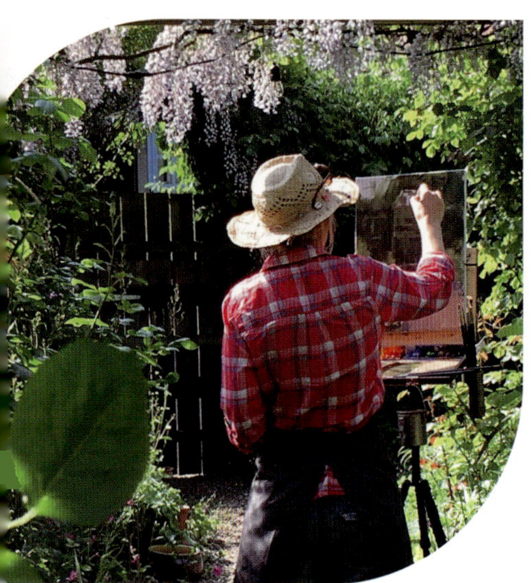

Louise Treacy, plein air painter
1954–2020

You may not have heard of John Goffe Rand, an American painter who lived during the nineteenth century, but we all owe him a debt of gratitude, as he is credited with being the inventor of the collapsible metal paint tube for artists.

John Constable pioneered painting the landscape in the open air in the early nineteenth century, but it was without doubt the commercial availability of tubes of paint from the 1870s onwards that made painting out in the landscape possible for the groups of artists who followed. Not least amongst these were the French Impressionists. Indeed, Pierre-Auguste Renoir is quoted as saying: "Without paint in tubes there would have been [...] nothing of what the journalists were later to call Impressionists."

The term *'en plein air'* is a French expression that simply means 'outside'. Painting outdoors is absorbing and comes with a whole host of health benefits. The benefits of mindfulness for reducing stress are well known, but you don't need to sit cross-legged and meditate in order to achieve this state of paying attention to the present moment: the activity of plein air painting is a great way to get there. More often than not, plein air painting helps me experience a flow state – that feeling of being at one with the task in hand, fully absorbed and focussed; where time seems to slow down.

Painting outside combines the captivating practice of painting from life with all the physical and mental health benefits of being out in the fresh air. Getting enough daylight is a key factor in the regulation of circadian rhythms – our internal body clock that governs every major organ in the body. Modern life can make it challenging to keep these rhythms in sync, and over a long period of time this can cause major health problems. Spending time outside absorbing blue light is becoming widely recognized for its health benefits, and having the sun's ultraviolet rays on our skin helps us to produce vitamin D.

The Japanese have developed a nature therapy called *shinrin-yoku,* or forest bathing. Studies have found that spending time in nature can provide emotional healing, decrease blood pressure, reduce stress and improve a person's sleep-wake cycle. Researchers from a University of Essex study found that as little as five minutes in a natural setting – whether walking in a park or gardening – improves mood, self-esteem and motivation. As plein air painters we reap these benefits at the same time as honing our craft – a win-win situation.

Plein air painting broadly means working outside in front of the subject, but there are a whole host of different interpretations of that theme. Some artists always work from life outdoors, but even then they vary as to whether they give the paintings a tidy-up or final 'tickle' in the studio before framing. Others prefer to sketch and take ideas from the natural world and then explore and expand on those ideas in the studio, exhibiting only the studio work as the end product. Still others will use plein air work solely as an exercise to hone their skills and enjoy the health and social benefits, with the resulting paintings or studies bearing no relation to their commercial artwork – much as a landscape painter may draw from a life model to keep their eye and hand trained. I don't think that labels really matter too much, except to say that 'plein air painting' represents a broad church of artists and it is one that we can all feel we belong to.

That brings me on to one of the biggest benefits of plein air painting, the social aspect. Plein air painting groups, events and competitions are popping up everywhere and, thanks to social media, we now have a thriving worldwide network. From local painting groups to large painting festivals such as Art in the Open in southern Ireland to huge international events such as the annual Plein Air Convention in the USA, organized by the publishers of *Plein Air* magazine, you can join

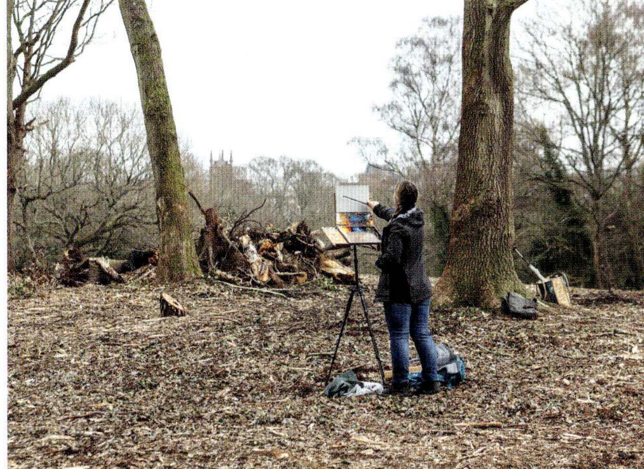

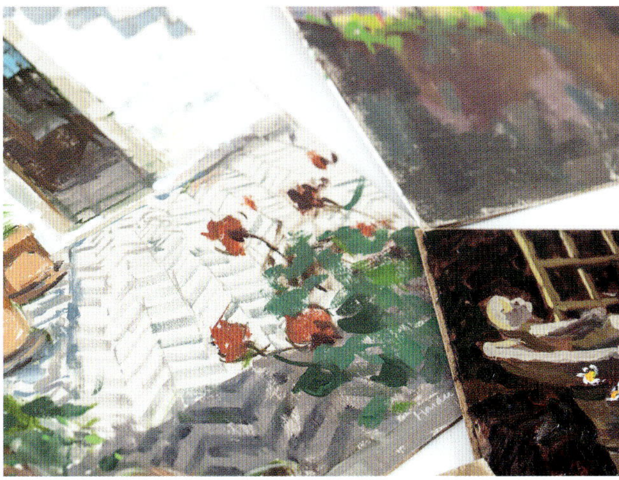

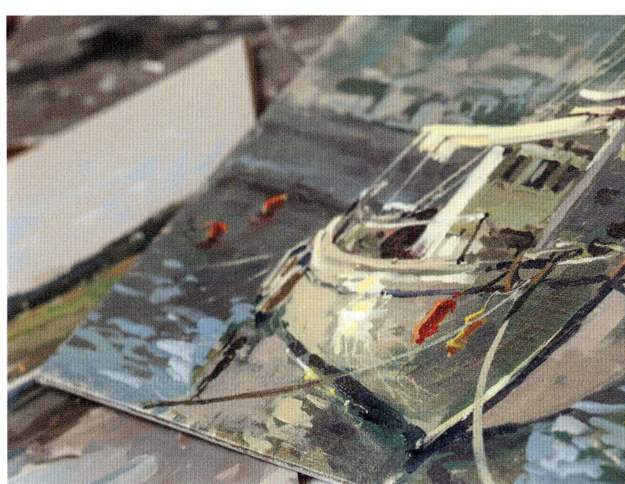

in with as much or as little sociable painting activity as you like. Painting in a group can really help with confidence, energy and just the commitment to get out there – and, of course, it's always fun to 'talk shop' with like-minded folk.

Besides the social and health aspects, what about the resulting work itself? Because of the challenges of working from an ever-changing subject, plein air paintings are characteristically looser and more spontaneous in style, highly desirable qualities for painters who feel that they have a tendency to fiddle and overwork – and also for collectors of art.

I won't pretend that it's easy. I've always said that to feel a whole gamut of emotions during the course of one painting is not unusual; taking you from elation to despair and sometimes back again! The challenge, however, is thrilling; the difficulties that you overcome, the obstacles you work through, the engagement of all the senses, the encounters with people you wouldn't ordinarily meet… all serve to keep you coming back for more. You will have so many memorable

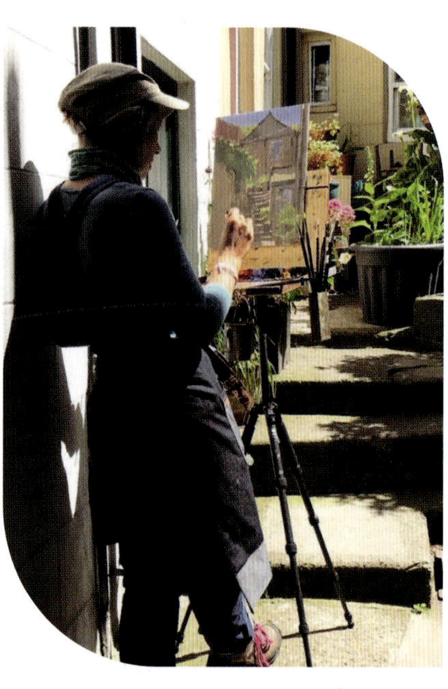

meetings and stories to tell that you just won't experience if you stay shut away on your own in the studio.

In this book I share some of my tried-and-true techniques and approaches for different aspects of plein air painting, and also some ways of working which were new for me – exploring these gave me my own broader look into the subject, and in doing so expanded my own horizons. In that spirit, I hope that you use the ideas and exercises in this book not as processes to copy by rote, but as an inspiring springboard to propel you into an exploration of your own ways of plein air painting, using your own personality, experiences and unique eye onto the world.

I firmly believe that we each have something special and original to say. Putting in the commitment to hours of practice and the exploration of new ideas – while critiquing your own work and noticing the direction it is taking – will lead you to find your own voice.

More than anything, I hope that this book helps you to enjoy your plein air adventures, and the people you meet along the way.

Opposite:
Cottage Steps and Shadows, Staithes
28 x 35.5cm (11 x 14in)

Above you can see me at work, immersed in the painting on the opposite page. Tucked away as close to the wall as possible to allow people to pass, I loved every minute of painting this one. It has all my favourite ingredients – but it was the sunlight, of course, that made it so special.

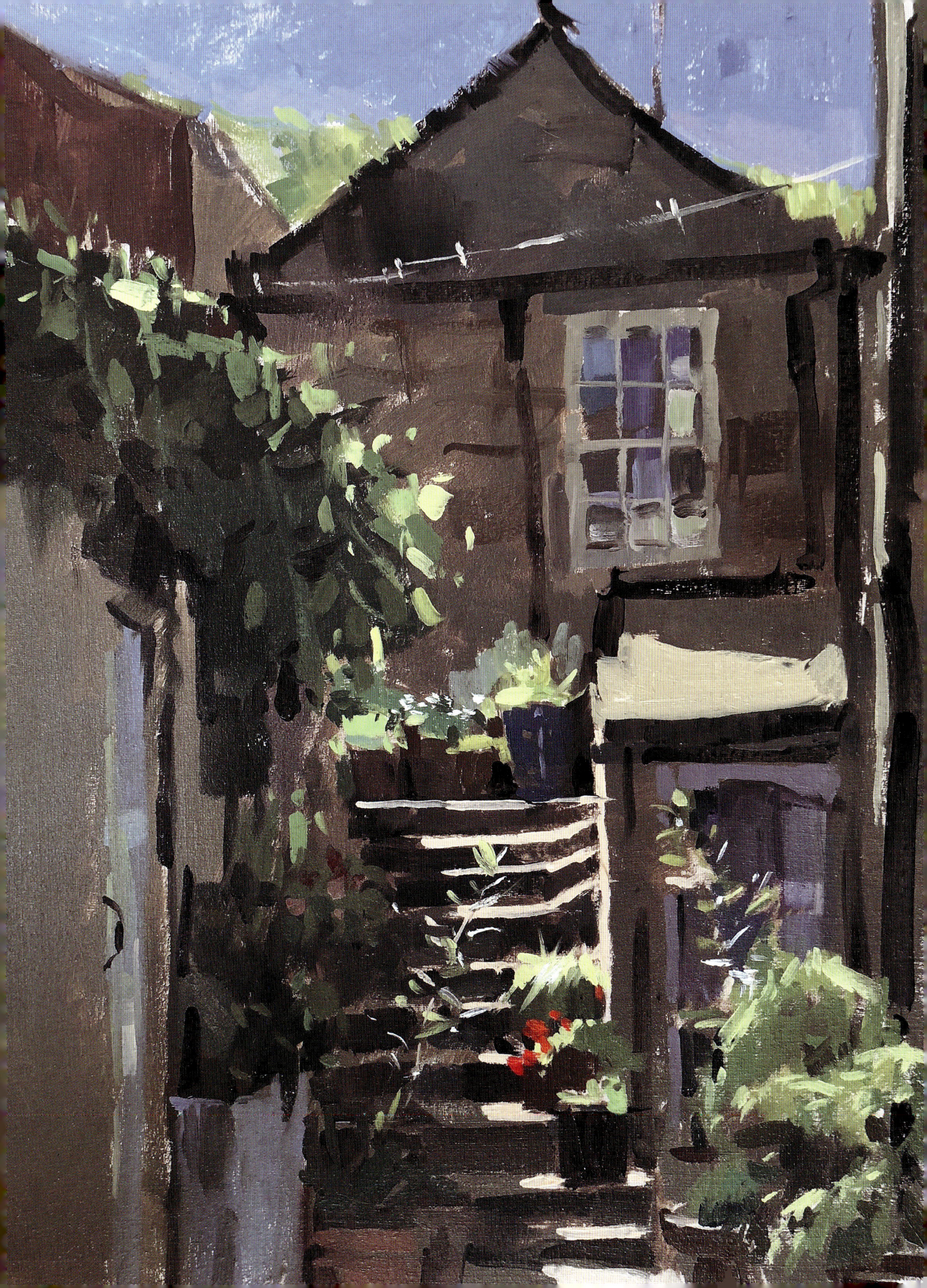

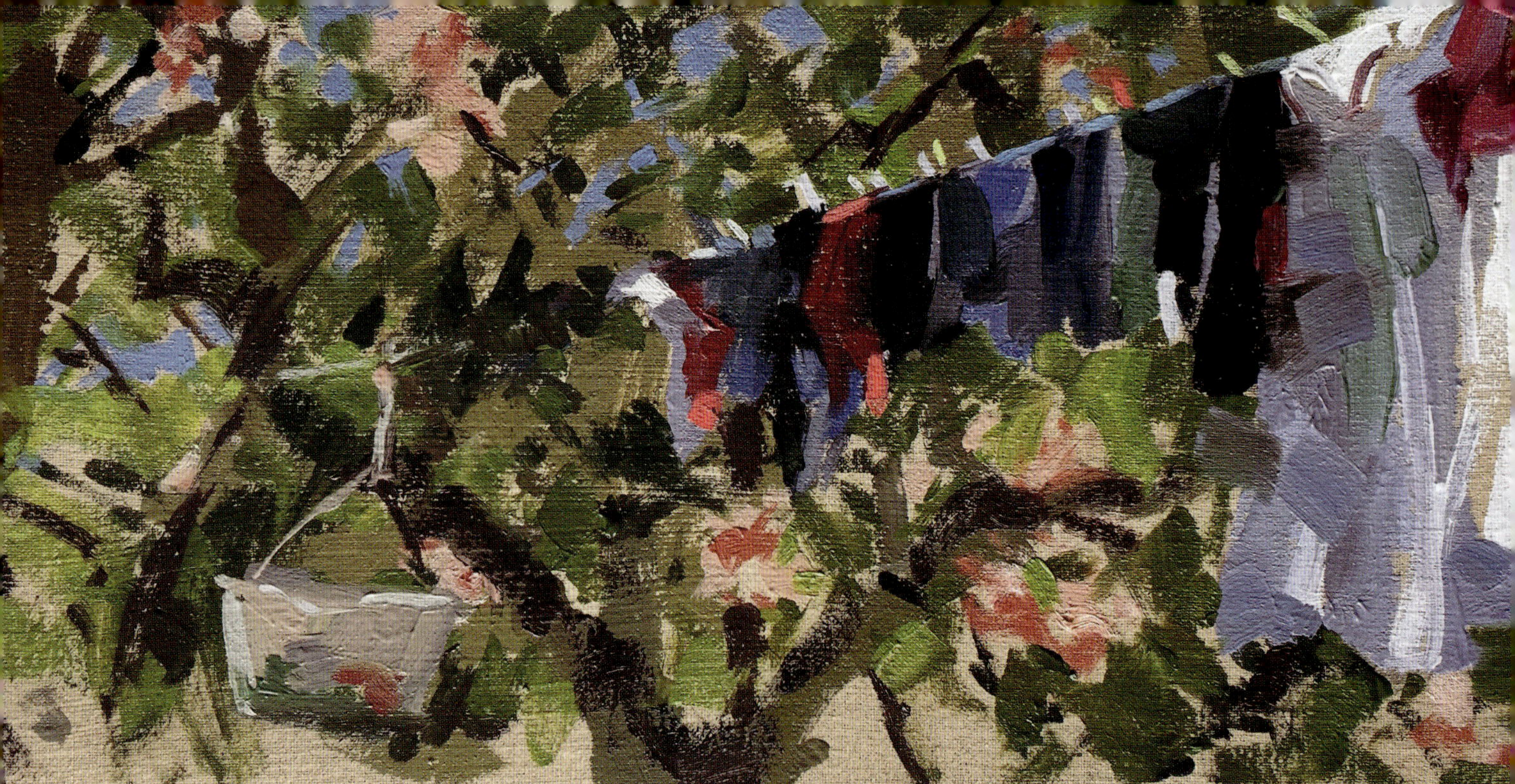

Choosing a subject

Let's get straight down to business. You can read all the theory in the world, but what's actually going to make you a better plein air painter is getting out there and having a go – and making it a regular practice to do so. It's surprising how many self-made obstacles can pop up in our heads to stop us actually doing it, so I just wanted to say a few words first about choosing a subject and getting started.

I often think that the hardest part of plein air painting is crossing the threshold of your own front door with your kit. We're judging ourselves before we even start; imagining that others will be critical of our efforts. We tend to feel self-conscious about the prospect of being watched by onlookers and, before you know it, procrastination has set in.

Some artists are big on planning and spend weeks honing their equipment, writing lists, watching videos and reading books (like this one). There are great benefits to be found in learning and planning, but be careful that you're not doing so much of it that you're avoiding taking action. The more times you get outside and paint, the easier it will be to overcome the anxiety around setting off and being seen painting in public. Once you have taken the first steps, you build momentum.

Besides the psychological barrier, practical factors can come into play to stop you actually getting some painting done. I've certainly turned up at a location with my paints only to find the weather throwing a curve ball;

Start small and start local. You don't need a grand landscape to make an interesting painting.

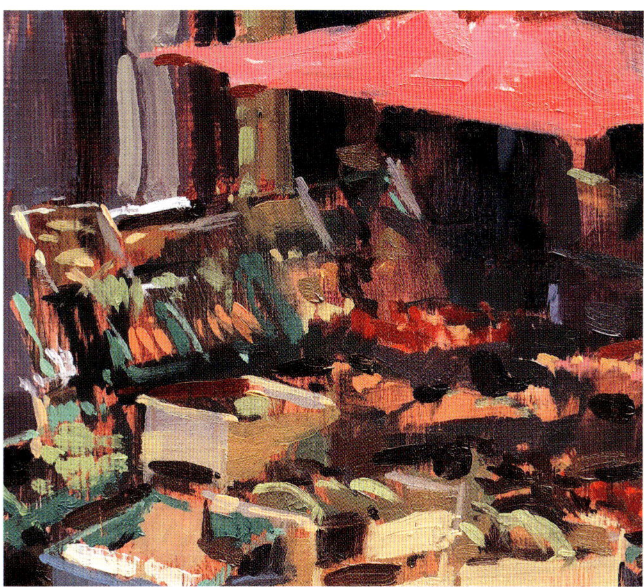

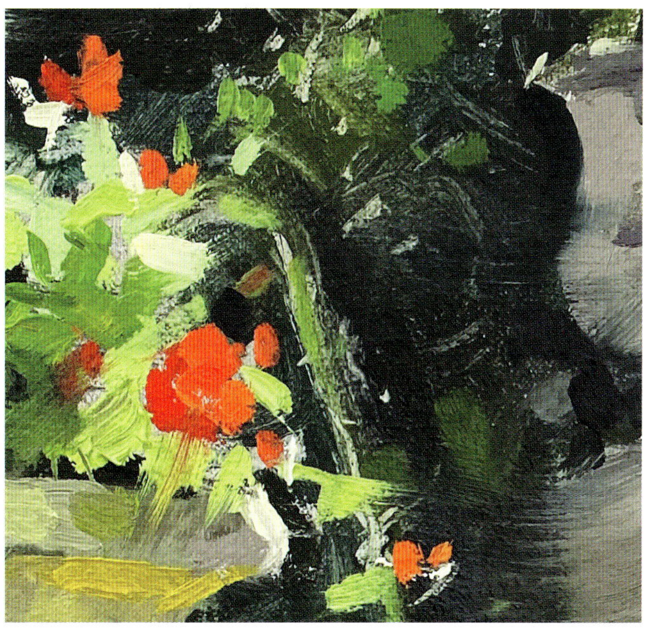

or simply not finding any of the kinds of subjects I was expecting to see there. Sometimes it's simply difficult to find something that makes you feel inspired. In these instances you can waste hours dragging your equipment round and round, getting increasingly frustrated and despondent.

Rest assured that these things happen to all of us, and for that reason it's a good idea to avoid setting out with high expectations. Set out to produce a study, not a finished piece; the sole intention being to learn something from the exercise.

If this is your first foray into plein air painting, start small and start local. You definitely don't need a grand landscape to make an interesting painting. I'm always interested in trying to spot something that would commonly pass unnoticed: the seemingly smallest and most insignificant subject can make a striking painting. Your own street, garden or yard is the ideal place to begin. Painting at home has many obvious advantages – you needn't worry about forgetting any supplies and refreshments are readily available.

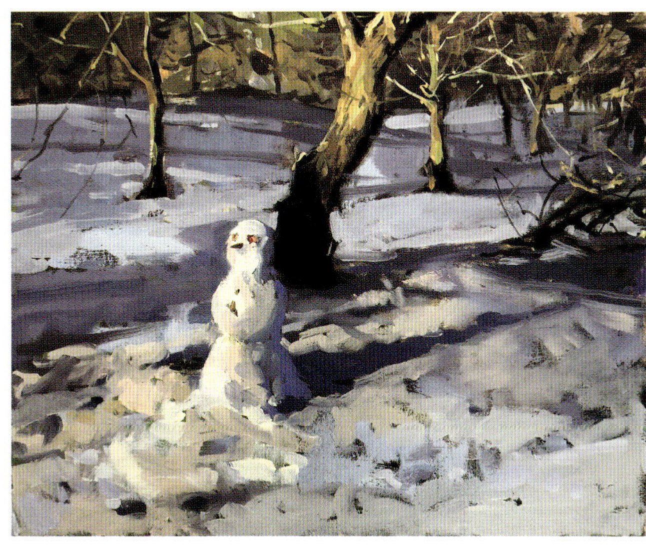

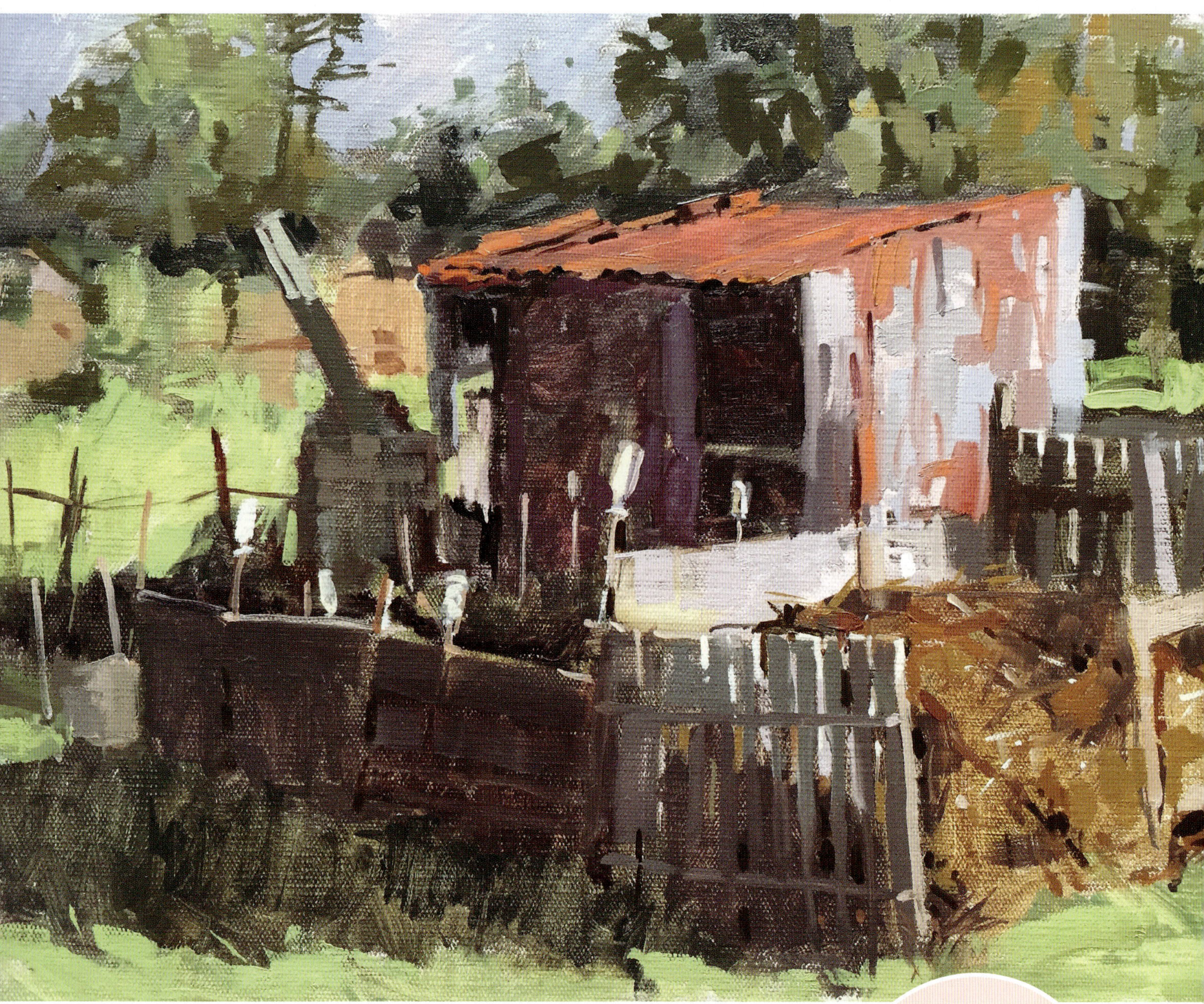

Rusty Shed at Holt Allotments
40.5 x 30.5cm (16 x 12in)

This rather dilapidated old shed held great appeal for me because of its intrinsic quirky character, but it was the particular effect of the light at that time that made me want to stop and paint it. I knew it would work well as a dynamic painting because of the underlying abstract pattern of light and dark shapes.

' Faith is taking the first step even when you don't see the whole staircase. '

Martin Luther King Jr, 1929–1968

Looking through artist's eyes

Before you decide on a viewpoint and composition you need to start looking at your garden or street through your artist's eyes, observing areas which have an interesting abstract arrangement of shapes and colours. It pays to be selective, and consider taking just a small section of what you choose as a subject. Sometimes we get an attack of 'visual greed' and are excited by so many aspects of a place that we are tempted to take on too much. The result can be an overcrowded painting with a weak and confused message. Ask yourself 'What is this painting about?' and 'Am I biting off more than I can chew?'

As a guide, look for a main focal point. If you are identifying three or more areas of specific interest within your subject, perhaps you are trying to paint three paintings in one – which rarely ends well.

When I'm in this situation, I promise myself I'll paint the motif with the strongest pull first, and then start a second painting with the next most interesting arrangement of shapes. It isn't always the case that I do start the second painting, but the mere promise of it is always enough to calm the 'monkey chatter' in my brain and let me get down to work.

Don't expect to be comfortable, but instead learn to embrace the challenges. Painting en plein air isn't an easy option, but I promise you it's invigorating and you'll feel like you've really achieved something after battling with the elements and coming home with a painted memento, however sketchy and unfinished.

Why not make a start right now? There's no time like the present. You can come back and read more when it's dark.

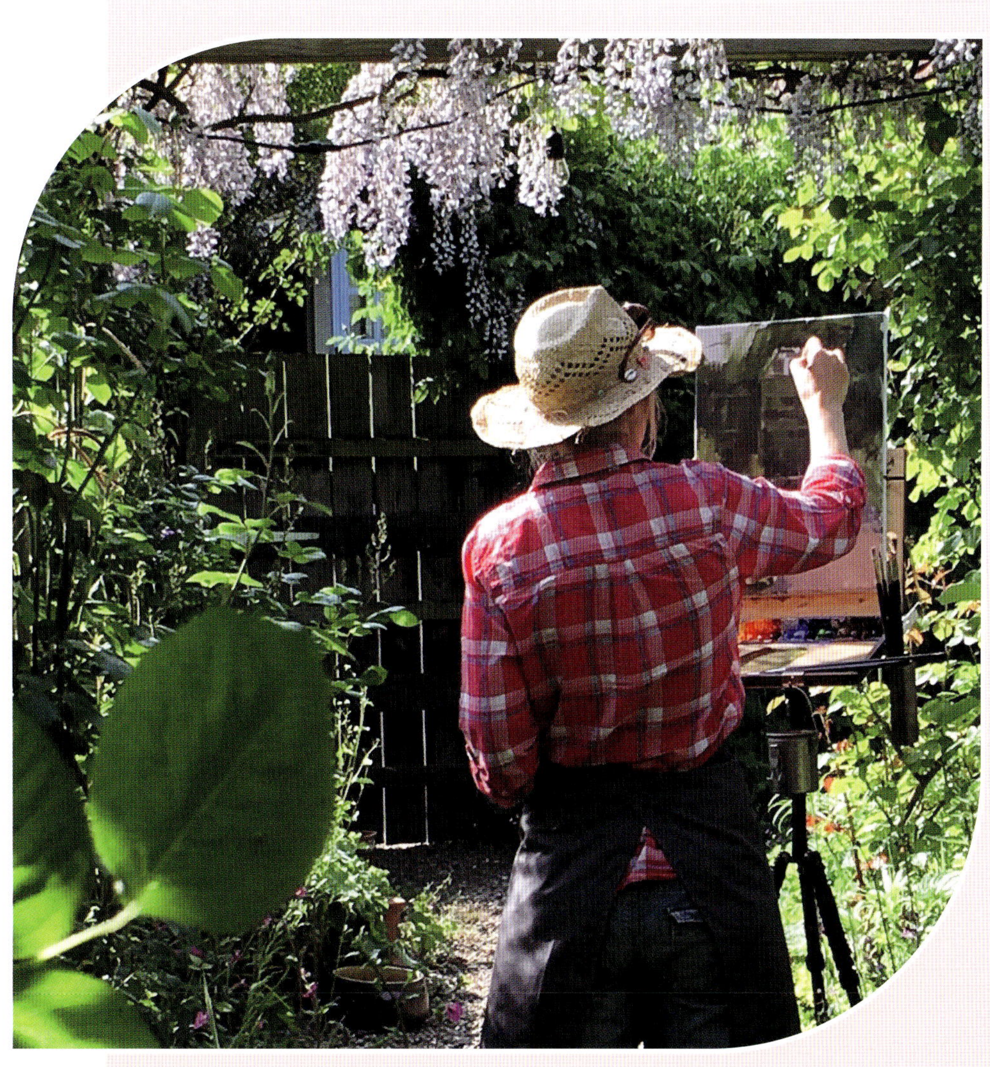

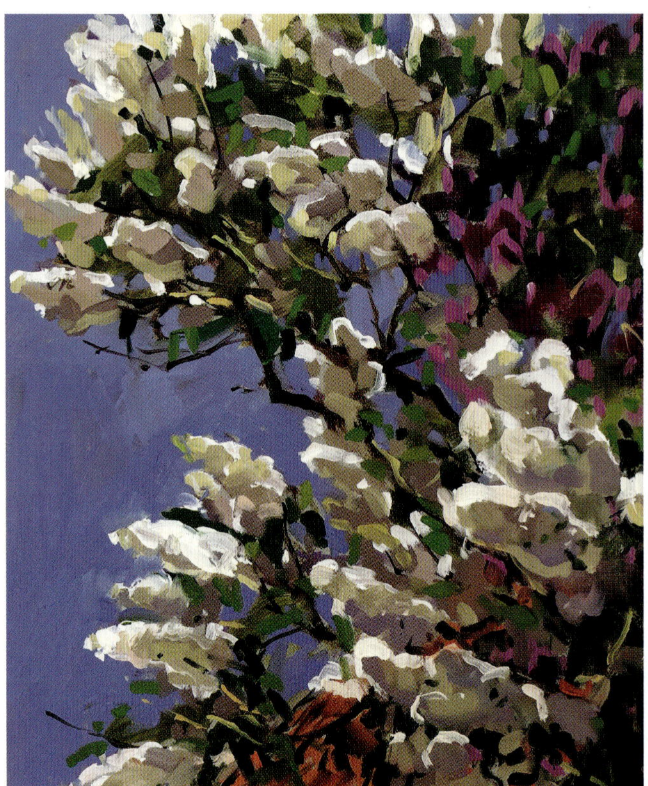

White Lilacs, Blue Sky
28 x 33cm (11 x 13in)

Finding a way in

Blossom on a tree is one of the most enticing subjects in spring but it can be very difficult to know where to start. The abundance of delicate petals, branches and unfurling leaves can be a dizzying prospect to paint. The secret is to take a broad view of the shapes and masses, ignoring the small details completely. With slight adjustments, these principles – of looking for shapes and masses – can be applied to every subject. It's a key lesson to bear in mind when working en plein air.

First of all, take time to observe the way the individual blossoms clump together, the general shape these clumps make, and how they attach to the branches.

- How distantly spaced are the groups of flowers along the branches?

- What shape does their silhouette or contour take against the sky?

- If it's a sunny day, identify from which direction the light is hitting the groups of flowers. Are there some branches and flowers (perhaps lower down, perhaps further away from you, perhaps overshadowed by another tree or building) which are not receiving direct light from the sun?

- Half close your eyes to help you identify the larger light and dark value shapes, so that you can simplify them as you paint.

- Look for the relative value of the sky. Is it lighter or darker than the sunlit blossom? How does it compare to the blossom in the shade? Sometimes it's a surprise just how dark these pale pink or white groups of flowers can look against the sky.

- Does the sky colour that you can see around the tree graduate as it comes lower down towards the horizon, or is what you can see of it a fairly even colour and value throughout?

Opposite:
Pink Cherry Blossom
28 x 33cm (11 x 13in)

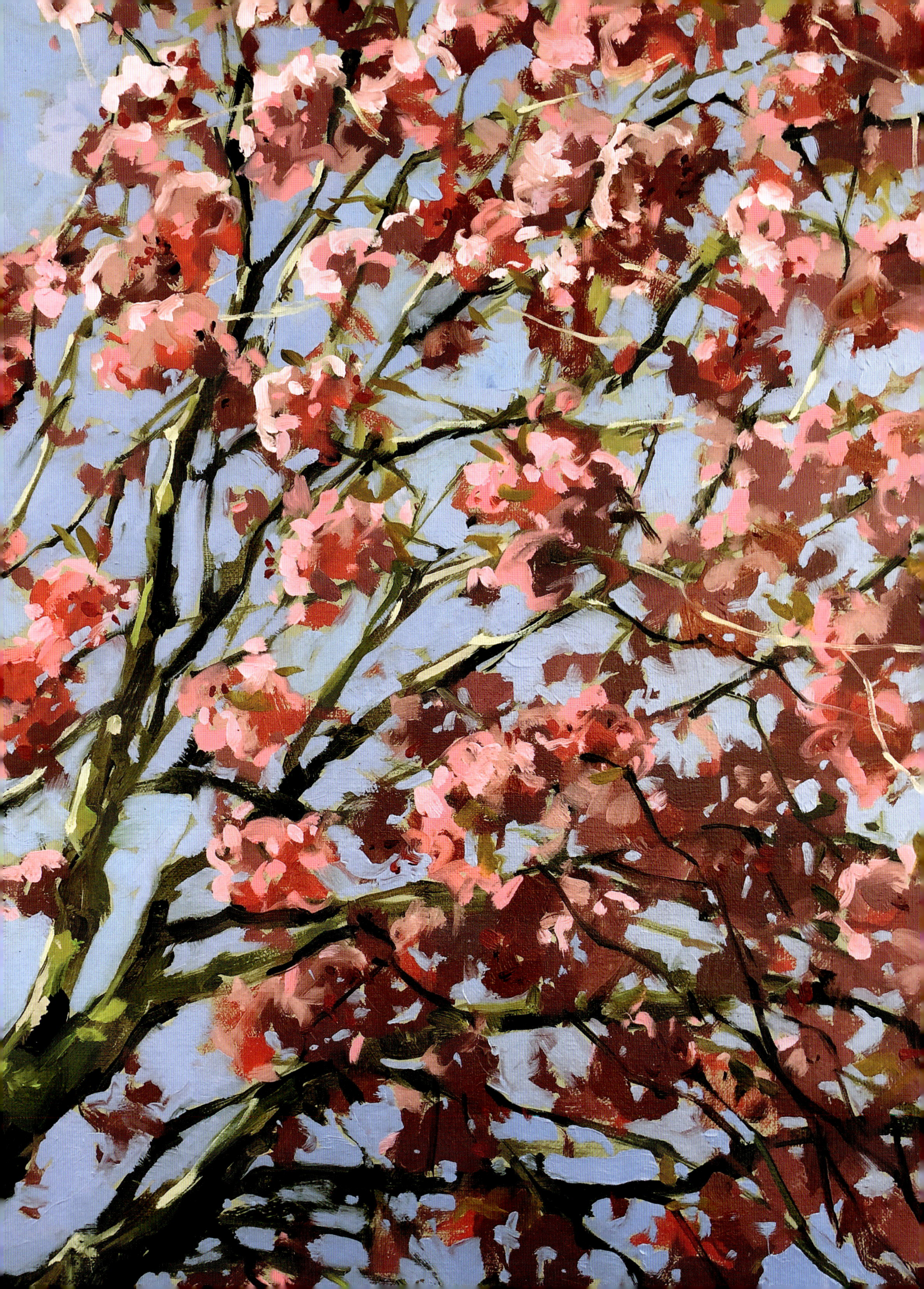

Getting outside:
equipment and supplies

One thing that will quickly start to concern you as a plein air painter is the portability of your equipment. It is no fun to arrive at your painting spot hot and exhausted because you are carrying too much gear – particularly if you end up not using some of it.

There is plenty of choice of easels, pochade boxes, tripods and panel carriers on the market. When you're looking to invest, do give proper consideration to the size and weight of each option. As you gain experience in plein air painting, you will probably find that you want to hone your equipment list down to the bare essentials. Take a look at the kit I carry, as an example.

A Prepared panels and holder I can carry small panels in my rucksack in a simple panel holder. The pictured panels measure 30.5 x 23cm (12 x 9in). If I need larger panels or canvases, I carry them separately. See page 26 for more on carrying panels.

B Bamboo brush roll These inexpensive wraps work really well for keeping my brushes (see page 20) safe. Cotton and leather brush rolls are also available.

C Small bag of paints This is a make-up case with a zip. If I'm really cutting down on weight, I only take the primary colours plus white.

D Carrier bag An essential for bringing home used paper towels and any other litter.

E Flask of coffee or water This is self-explanatory – I certainly regard coffee as an essential!

F Apron There's no getting away from the fact that oil painting can be messy, so an apron is very useful. One with a pocket is great for storing oddments.

G Metal turps pot This needs to be properly sealable, as it is filled with low-odour solvent.

H Medium I currently use the Michael Harding brand of oil paint medium, which is a mixture of stand oil and turpentine.

I Rucksack A good, well-fitted rucksack can make your kit feel much lighter. Mine has wide padded shoulder straps, a hip belt, sternum strap, range of pockets and a rain cover which tucks away.

J Palette knife In addition to its use as a paint applicator, this can be used to scrape excess oil off your palette, ready to store at the end of a painting session.

K Pochade box or easel Measure your box to ensure a good fit when choosing your rucksack. This box is a 30.5 x 25.5 cm (12 x 10in) Open Box M palette. Wet paint remains safely inside the box when it is closed. See page 21 for more on pochade boxes.

L Seasonal clothing Whether you need gloves and hat to stave off the cold, or a peaked cap and sunglasses (and sun cream) to avoid the dazzle, prepare accordingly.

M Smartphone A smartphone is great for taking reference photographs for later use in the studio, or for experimenting with compositional options. It's also handy in case of an emergency – just be careful not to be distracted by it.

N Brush holder This brass brush holder attaches to my pochade box, making swapping between brushes while painting quick and easy.

O Tripod I mostly use a carbon fibre tripod which folds down to an extremely small 34cm (13½in) in length, and weighs less than 1 kg (2lb).

Additional items

In addition to the pictured items, you will need kitchen paper and wet wipes for cleaning your hands, brushes and palette.

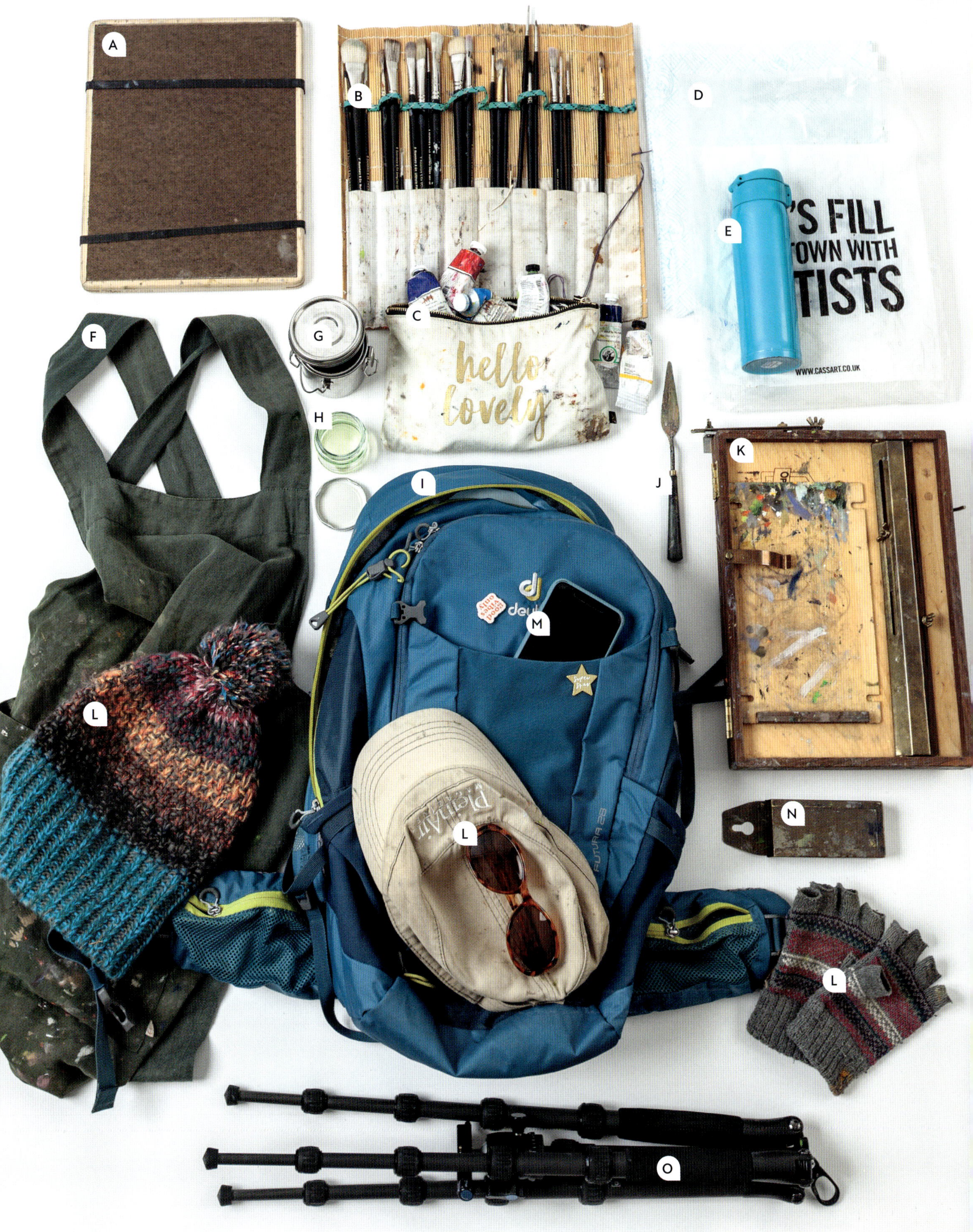

hello lovely
'S FILL
TOWN WITH
TISTS
WWW.CASSART.CO.UK
deuter

What paints and brushes?

While trying to save weight with your main equipment, it follows that you may want to streamline the rest of your kit too, taking a minimum of brushes and colours with you. There is a balance to be struck. Having a handful of similarly sized brushes means that you can swap between them to keep colours clean and bright. The precise size doesn't really matter; I tend to take around a dozen flats and filberts in the size 6–10 range. Note that manufacturer's sizes vary, so look for those between 6mm (¼in) and 20mm (¾in) across. I also take a few small rounds in sizes 2–3 for details.

I buy small tubes of paint where possible, but since some of the brands I favour don't make anything smaller than 40ml, I buy empty 14ml tubes and fill them from the large tubes in my studio. Having a pochade box which has space for the lid to close while paint is on the palette is a great advantage because you can put your paint out on the palette before you go and not need to carry any tubes with you, apart from perhaps a spare tube of white.

Each project in this book lists the paints I used, usually based on an 'extended primary' palette, which is explained on page 73. If you are an experienced artist, however, you will likely have your own preferred palette of colours. Rather than throw you into uncharted waters with strict lists of paint colours, I encourage you to react to what is in front of you with your own choices. That is the way to develop your vital observational skills – and to enjoy yourself.

My key colours

A   **Titanium white**

B   **Bright yellow lake or cadmium lemon**

C   **Cadmium golden yellow or cadmium yellow deep**

D   **Cadmium orange**

E   **Cadmium red light**

F   **Alizarin crimson**

G   **Phthalo blue & zinc white**

H   **Kings blue deep or violet-grey**

I   **Cobalt blue**

J   **Ultramarine**

K   **Raw umber**

L   **Transparent red oxide**

M   **Blue-black**

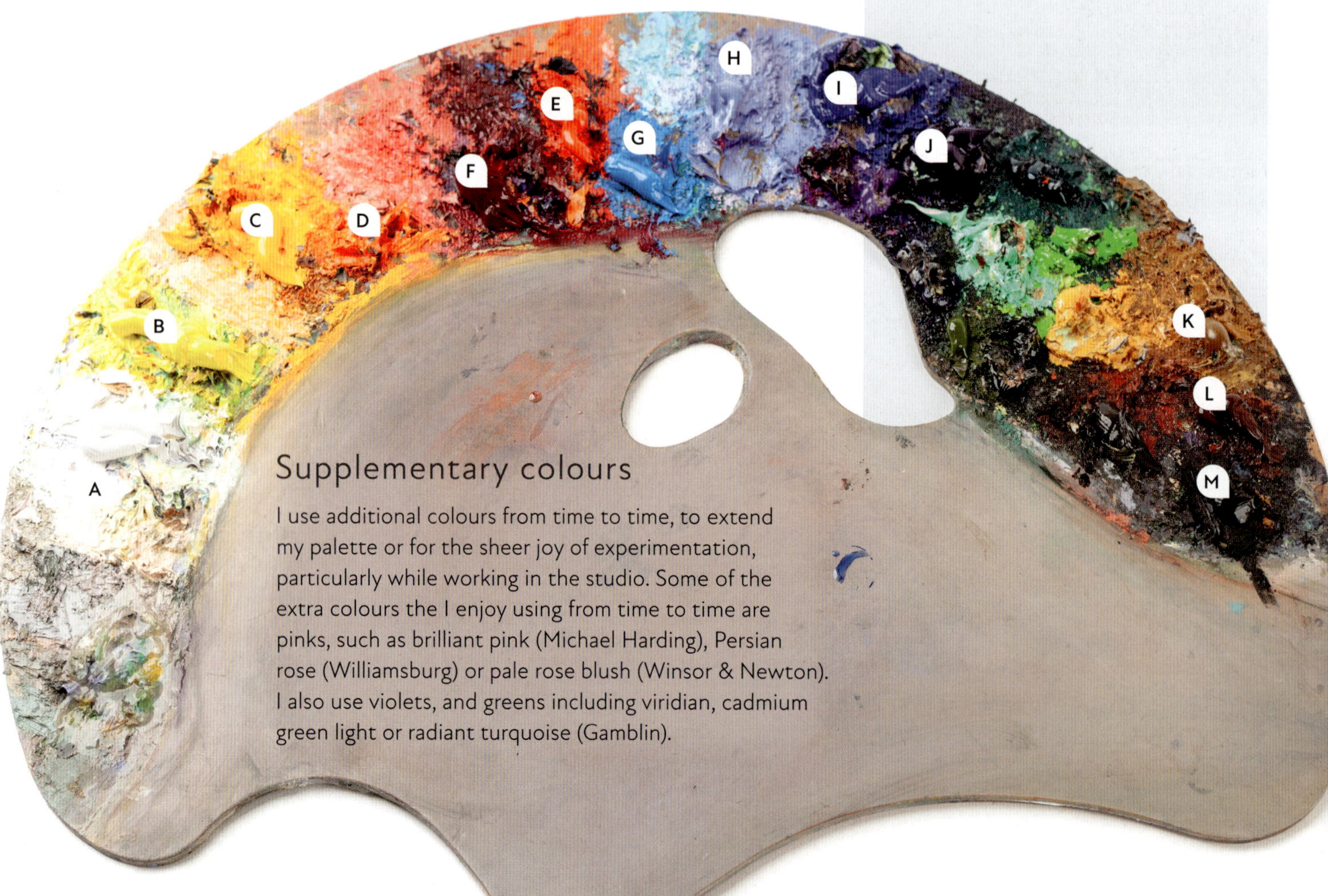

Supplementary colours

I use additional colours from time to time, to extend my palette or for the sheer joy of experimentation, particularly while working in the studio. Some of the extra colours the I enjoy using from time to time are pinks, such as brilliant pink (Michael Harding), Persian rose (Williamsburg) or pale rose blush (Winsor & Newton). I also use violets, and greens including viridian, cadmium green light or radiant turquoise (Gamblin).

Pochade boxes

Pochade, pronounced 'posh-ard', comes from the French word *poche*, meaning pocket. It refers to a sketch or piece of equipment small enough to fit into a coat pocket. A traditional pochade box is a small wooden box with a hinged lid which rests at an angle to enable the box lid to be used as an easel. Most also include a palette which fits inside the box. Many have a thumb hole underneath so the artist can stand to work, resting the box on top of the non-dominant hand, with the thumb inside the box providing a grip. Some include an attachment for a camera tripod, leaving your hands free to paint. Some provide storage underneath the palette, but of course this makes the box heavier.

It is fairly straightforward to convert your own little box, such as a cigar box, into a painting box and there are many suggestions online for how to do this. Alternatively, there are many different pochade boxes available to purchase commercially. Some are beautifully crafted and quite a significant financial investment, so it's worth having a good think before purchasing one about how you will be using it and what features you require. If you're on the lookout, this checklist will help you to decide which one would suit you best:

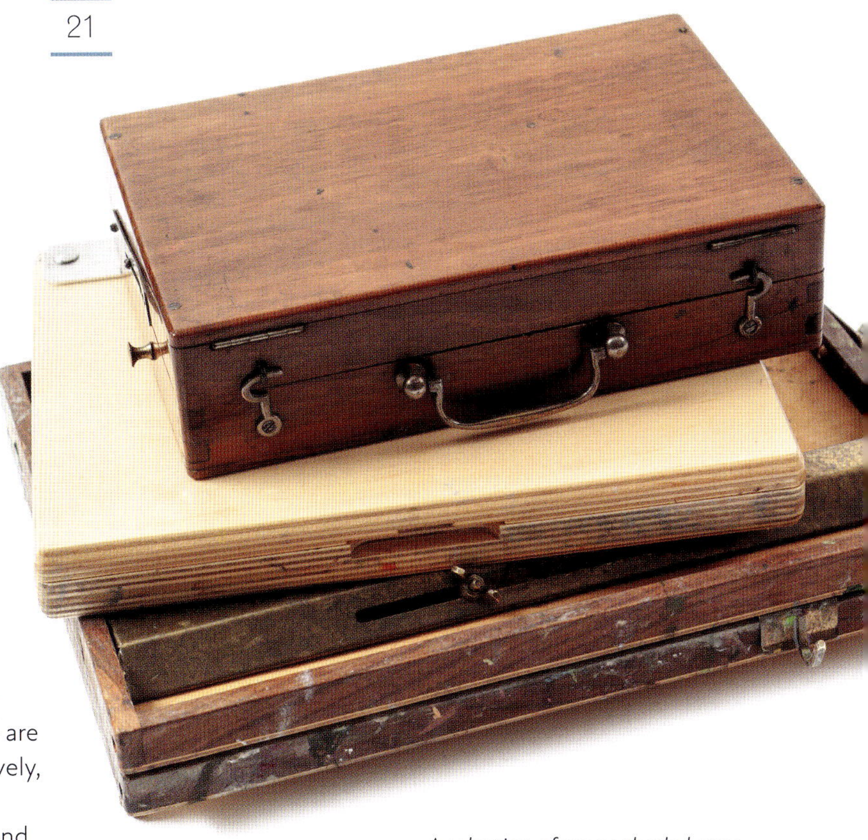

A selection of my pochade boxes.

Weight and size Does your pochade box need to be lightweight? Consider how and where you plan to carry it.

Panels Does it hold only one size of panel or can it adapt to different sizes? If so, what are the largest and smallest dimensions that it can accommodate? What thickness of panel does it hold and could it also hold a stretched canvas? Will it work with your usual painting support? Does it also store wet panels and, if so, how many?

Palette What's the minimum size of palette that will work for you? Can you get additional side trays for extra mixing areas if you need to? As for the palette itself – is it a colour you are happy to mix on? Will it be easy to clean? Is it removable? Are there alternative palette options available such as glass, coloured glass or Perspex? Can you close the lid of the box with wet paint still left on the palette or will you need to clear it immediately after each painting session?

Storage Does the box also have a storage area for paints and brushes? My preference is for a slimmer box using separate storage for panels but you might prefer to have everything contained within.

Tripod Does it have a fitting for a camera tripod so that you can stand? If not, can you attach your own tripod adaptor bracket? A small camera tripod is a useful addition if you like to stand, but I think the real beauty of the small pochade box is the option to sit and work at a table, too.

Brushes, boxes and being discreet

I like to have short-handled brushes with me when using my smallest boxes, because I am often seated while doing little sketches. If working inside a café or a busy building, I find that being seated is much more discreet and attracts less attention.

Easels

Pochade boxes are a small, light option, but you might prefer to try a traditional French box easel. An easel is a sturdy and reliable accompaniment to the plein air painter, but I wouldn't choose a full-size one unless you like a good workout. Half the width and weight, a half-size box easel does everything the full-size version will.

Box easels typically include a folding palette and slide-out drawer – very useful for resting the palette upon while you work. The top and bottom bars for holding your painting should be fully adjustable, making these easels suitable for a whole array of sizes, and allowing you to have your painting surface upright or tilted. Box easels have a carry handle and often a shoulder strap, and you can put your wet painting back on the easel to carry when it is closed.

Below are shown a selection of box easels and pochade boxes for easy comparison.

A Half-size French box easel This has a folding palette and a drawer for holding your materials.

B New Wave u.go This pochade box has a glass palette. It attaches to my camera tripod.

C Open Box M palette This has unique spring clips to hold the painting surface in place. Again, it attaches to my camera tripod.

D Antique pochade box A neat and conveniently small box, this incorporates a thumb hole to hold it while you work. It holds one particular size of panel.

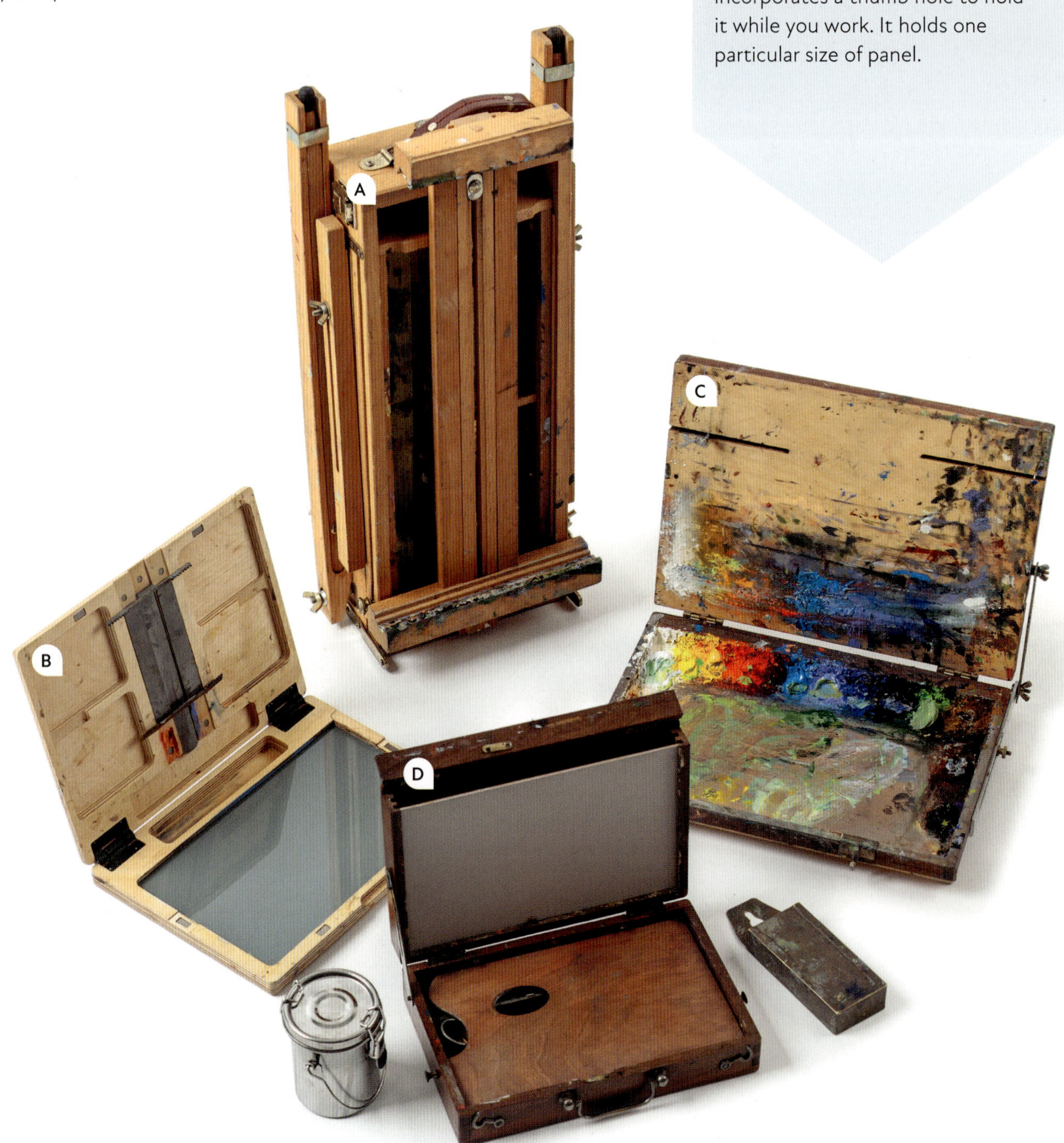

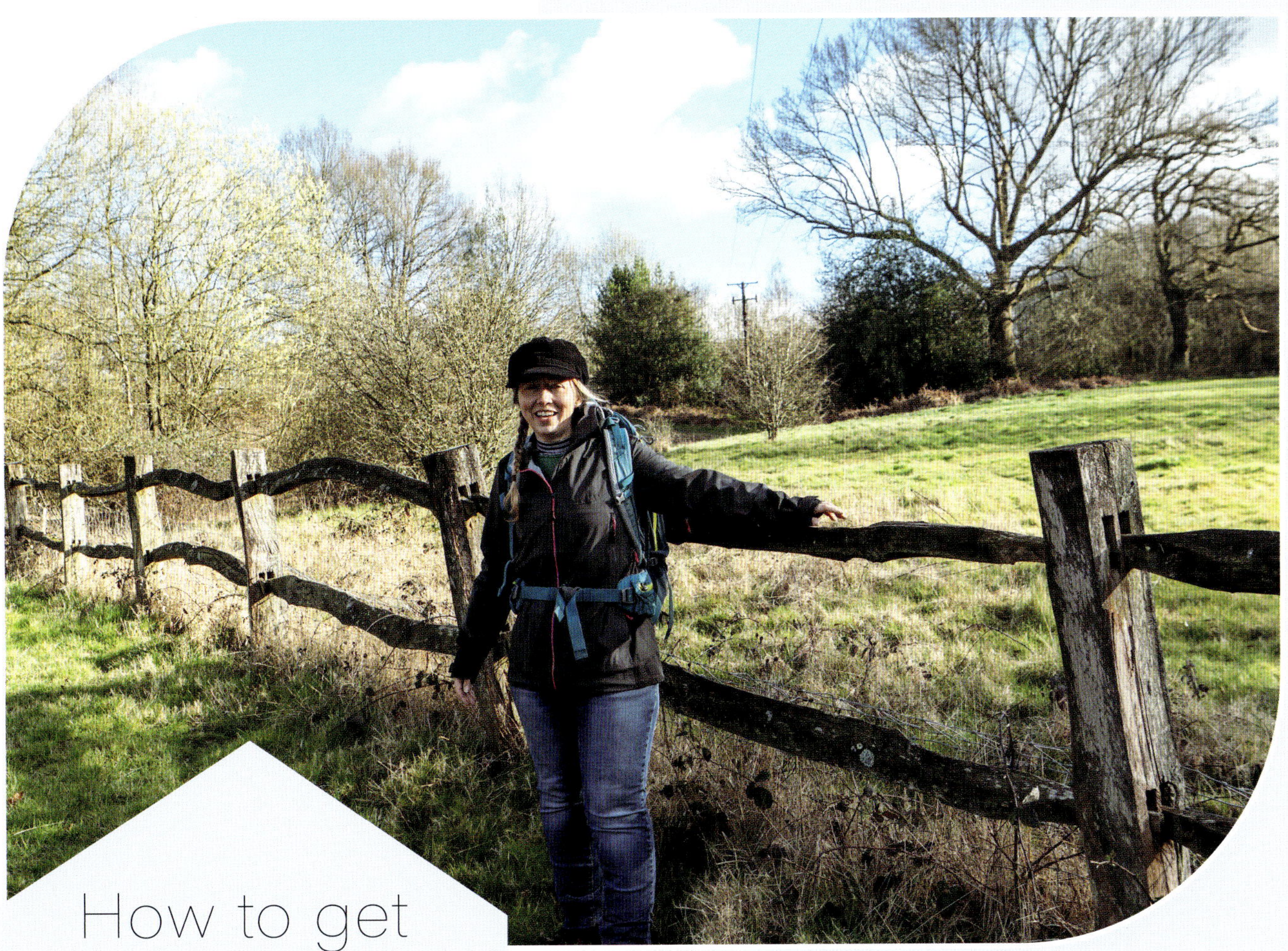

How to get around with everything you need

I tend to use a rucksack because it's convenient for most occasions, but there are times when you might prefer not to carry everything on your back. A shopping trolley bag with large wheels is a good option, except if you're going to be walking on uneven terrain or a sandy beach.

I separate most items into bags within my rucksack, it makes finding what I need easier and keeps everything cleaner. My paint tubes are in a zipped cosmetics bag, brushes in a brush roll and I keep the solvent and medium in a resealable plastic food bag so if there is a leak it won't cause any major problems.

Travelling abroad

When flying abroad I pack my painting panels in my hand luggage to avoid taking up space and weight in my suitcase. I pack my pochade box, tripod, brushes and paints in my hold luggage. Note that you can't fly with solvents, so you will need to source those at your destination or take a solvent-free alternative.

I make sure the paint tubes are well wrapped and placed inside a couple of clear plastic bags, to avoid the risk of leaks contaminating my clothes! If I'm flying long haul I attach the following note to the package of paints explaining what they are to any airline inspectors in case the suitcase is searched:

This bag contains professional artists' pigments made with vegetable-based oils. Please take care when inspecting to prevent pigment getting on your hands or clothing. The TSA defines flammable liquids as those with a flash point of 140°F or below. These supplies conform to TSA allowable standards with a flashpoint above 550°F, contain no solvents and are not hazardous. Please do not discard, these pigments are expensive.

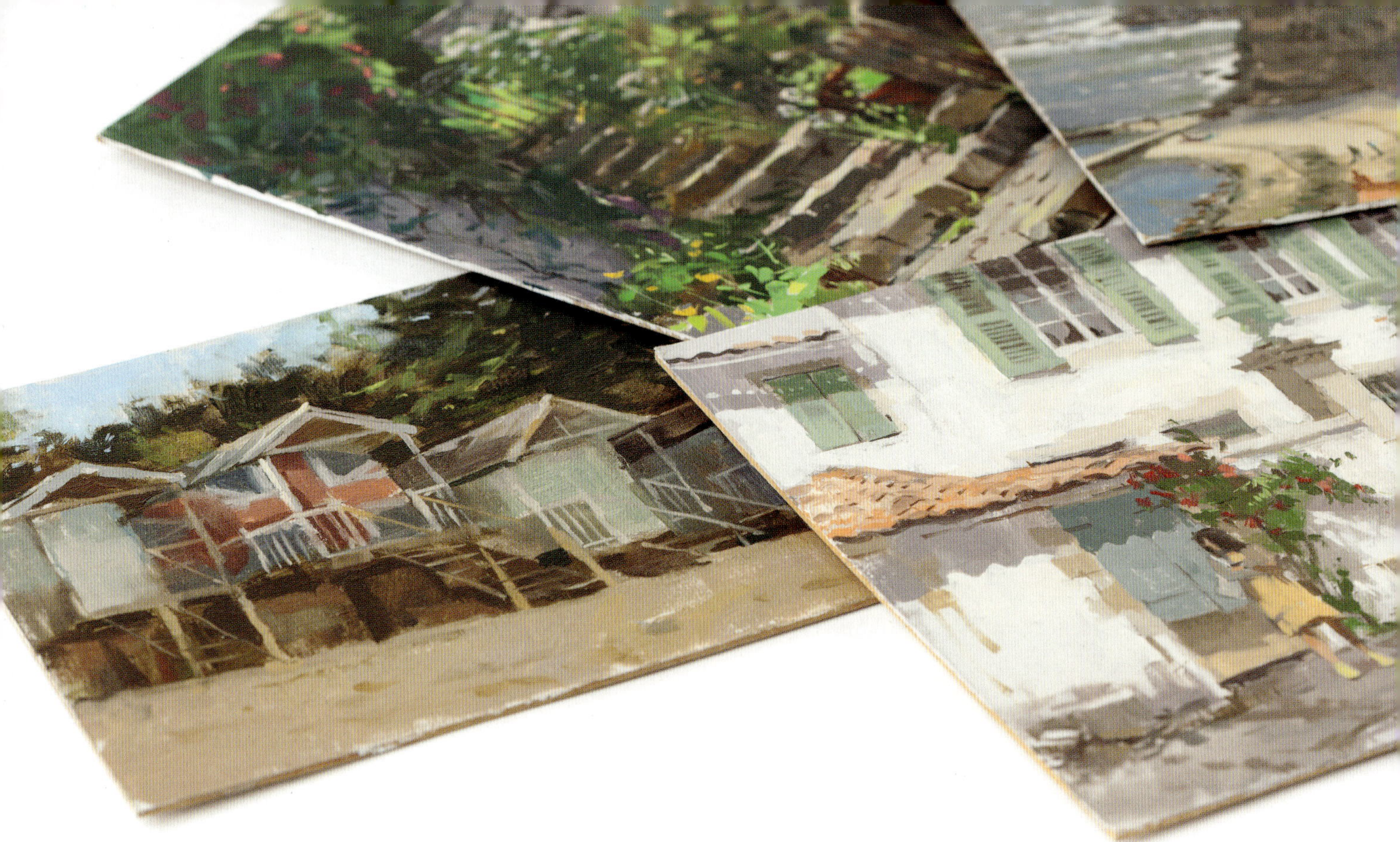

Canvas panels

Advantages of pre-bought

There are many commercially available painting panels
which vary in quality and price. The choice of substrate
upon which to paint includes cardboard, MDF or plywood,
birch, ultra-light foam board through to PVC composite –
even aluminium. Surfaces can be smooth or canvas-
textured, oil-primed or universal. I'm afraid the only way to
find the type that you prefer is to ask for recommendations
and try as many different types as you can. My preferred
pre-bought panels are oil-primed fine linen.

The disadvantages of buying ready-made panels is
that they can be quite expensive and they only come in
certain standard sizes. In the UK it gets harder and harder
to buy anything but metric sizes now, which is a shame I
feel: I prefer to think in terms of inches as those are the
traditional formats, and with which I'm more familiar.

Appeal of doing it yourself

Making your own panels is an economical option, but the
main reason I do it is so I'm not restricted to standard
sizes and formats, allowing me to experiment with square,
almost square, and long thin rectangles. I have MDF boards
cut to size for me at a woodyard.

It's perfectly fine to paint gesso primer directly onto
the boards, but because I like a canvas texture I use the
method shown opposite. A slightly faster option is to buy
ready-primed linen canvas and glue it to the board.

Making your own canvas panels

If you'd like the flexibility of having any size of panel – great for unusual shapes or a pochade box that requires a particular size – these steps will walk you through. I paint my panels with a neutral grey ground to take away the stark white surface, but you can tone it any colour you choose. You can use a combination of any red, yellow and blue paint to make a neutral mix; the precise hue is not important.

COLOURS

The three primary colours – red, yellow and blue

OTHER

Muslin fabric, 3mm (⅛in) MDF board, 7.5cm (3in) large household brush, gesso primer, craft knife and cutting mat

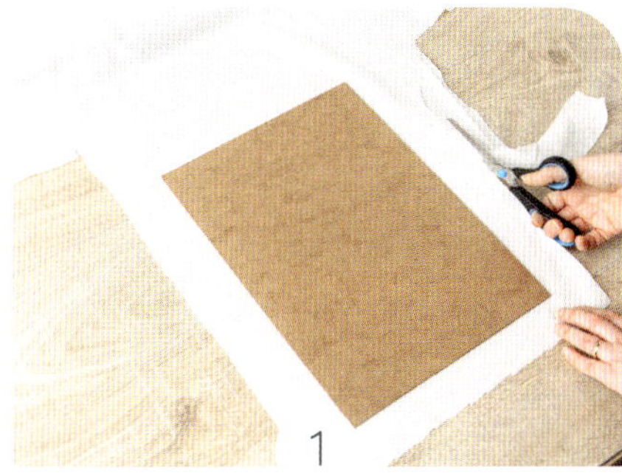

Cut the fabric with scissors, leaving a border of roughly 5cm (2in) around the board (3mm/⅛in MDF).

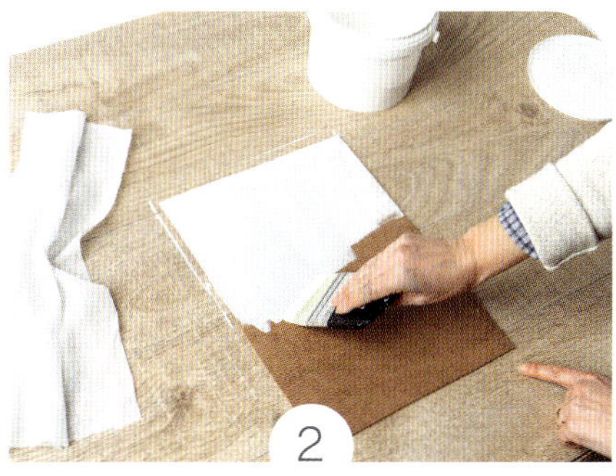

Use a 7.5cm (3in) large brush to apply gesso primer across the whole board.

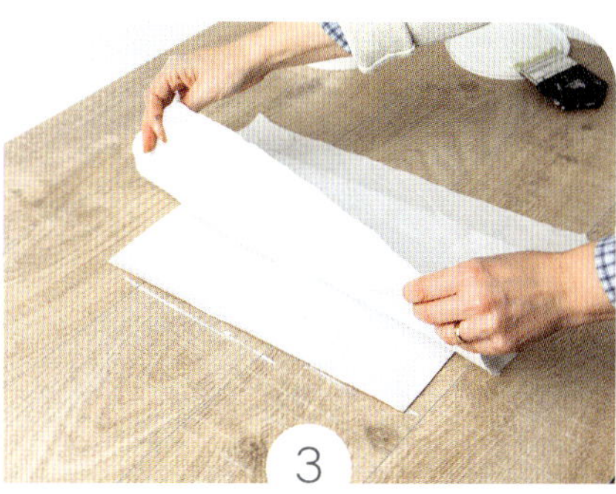

Lay the fabric over the wet gesso.

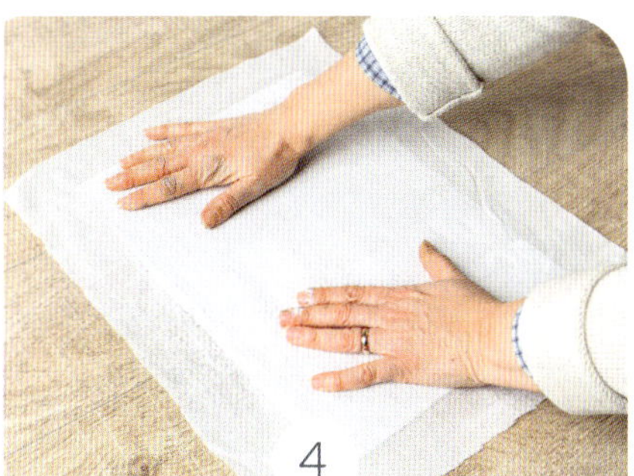

Smooth out the fabric with your hands.

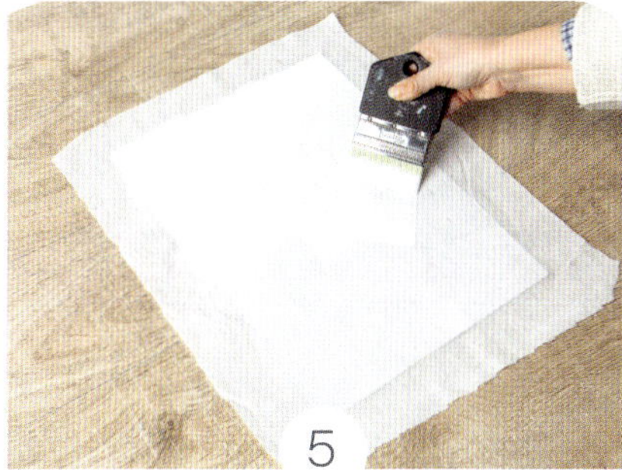

Immediately start painting another coat of gesso on top, pushing it well into the fabric with the brush.

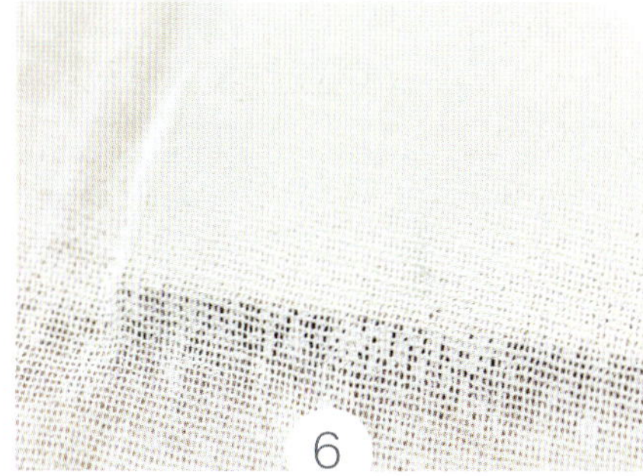

Once dry, the surface will appear slightly patchy.

Apply another layer of gesso.

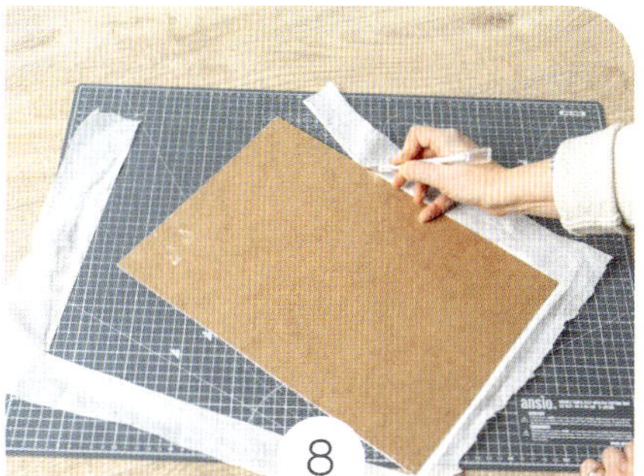

Once dry, use a craft knife to trim away the excess fabric.

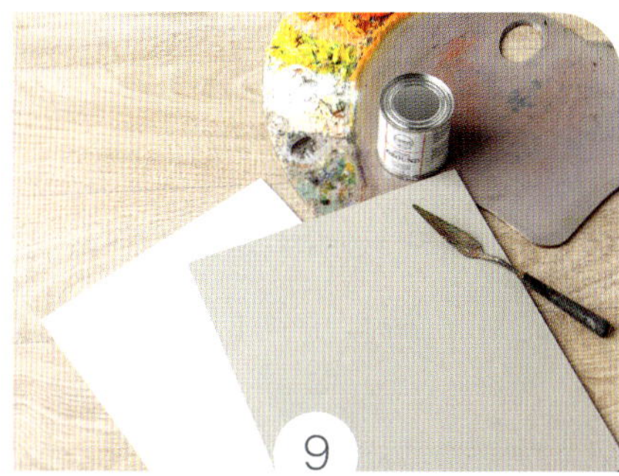

For a final coat of primer I use an oil ground mixed with any three primary colours to make a mid-grey.

Transporting wet oil paintings

Oil paints take a long time to dry, so you need a practical way of getting them back from location without smearing the paint or otherwise damaging them. Here are a few different options for you to try.

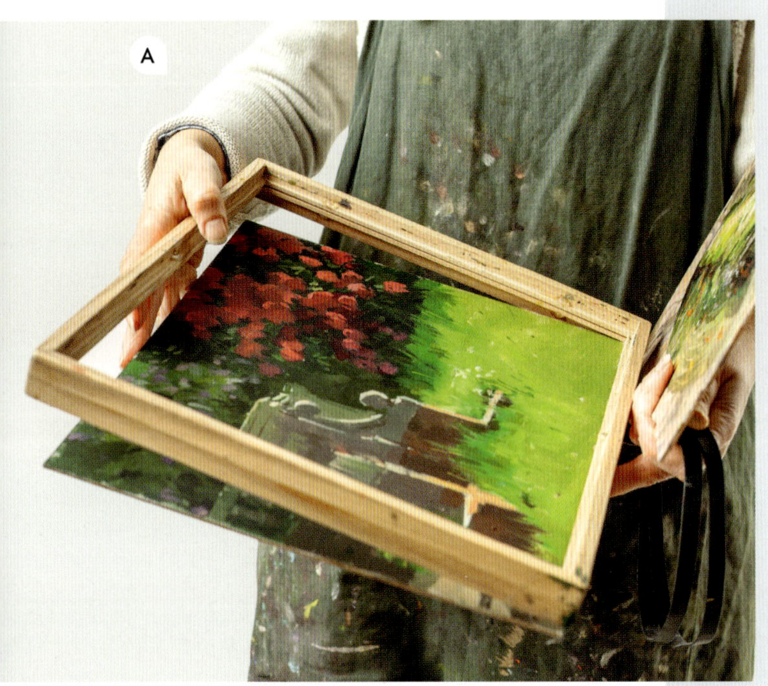

A – Frame-style panel carriers This simple approach involves having two panels of the same size facing each other, held apart by a wooden rim in the centre and secured around the outside with large elastic bands. You can make one of these at home by gluing two standard-sized slim wooden picture frames face to face. The panels are held in place against the rebate of the frame. I ask my picture framer to make bespoke frame-style panel carriers for me, to suit my non-standard painting panel sizes.

B – Matchstick spacers The matchstick method, as used by Ken Howard RA. Glue a matchstick close to the edge in the centre of each side on the back of your painting panel (see detail opposite) and allow it to dry. This allows you to stack together as many paintings of the same size as you like – you just need one dry painting or clean panel for the top of the stack. Keep them together with masking tape or strong elastic bands.

C – Raymar painting carriers Strong and lightweight, these are made of fluted plastic and incorporate a shoulder strap. They are designed to hold six panels back to back in a three slot track. The one I'm showing here is a multi-width carrier. It can take two panels 23cm (9in) wide, two panels 25.5cm (10in) wide and two panels 28cm (11in) wide. You can, of course, carry a variety of sizes in each slot. For example in a 25.5cm (10in) wide slot you could carry 20.5 x 25.5cm (8 x 10in), 25.5 x 25.5cm (10 x 10in) or 20.5 x 30.5cm (10 x 12in).

D – Canvas separating clips These are like double bulldog clips, with a raised lip in the centre to hold the wet painted surfaces apart. Hold two canvases facing each other and place a canvas clip in the centre of each of the four sides for a secure way to protect the wet paintings. It makes carrying canvases so much easier.

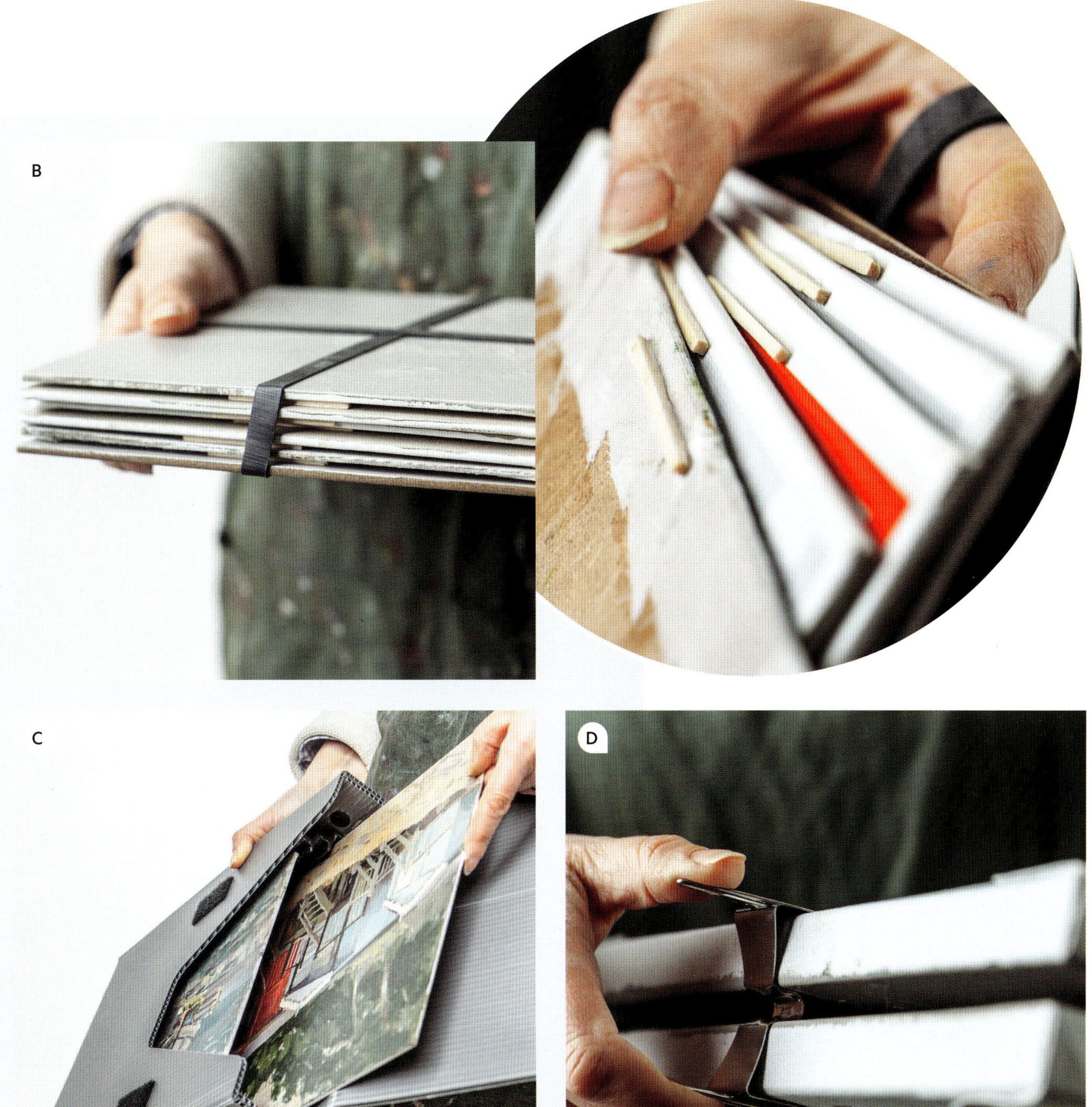

B
C
D

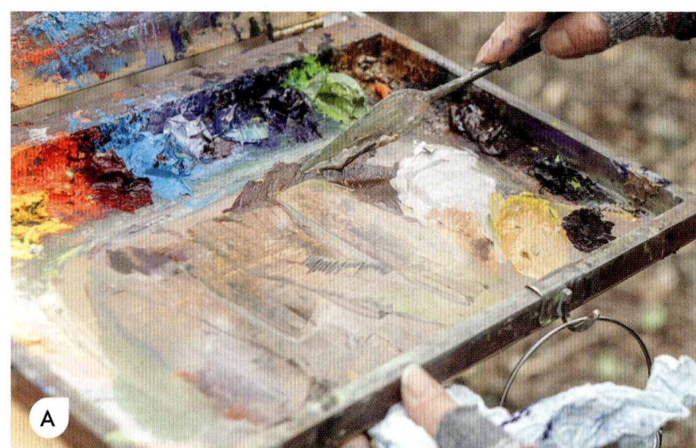

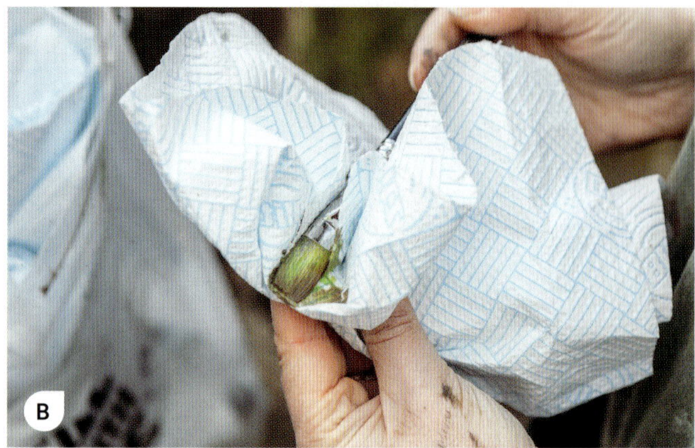

Packing up and clearing away

Once you've finished your painting session, make sure you pack up completely, and take away everything you brought to the site: materials, rubbish – and of course the painting!

A Scrape down the palette with a palette knife and then give it a quick wipe over with turps on a cloth.

B Use kitchen paper sheets to take any excess paint off your brushes, then swill them in the low odour solvent before wiping them again.

C Store your brushes safely wrapped in a brush roll; this helps to ensure the bristles stay straight.

D Spread your materials on the floor before starting to repack your bag. This will help to ensure that you don't miss anything.

E Make sure that everything goes back in the rucksack in a set order that lets you check nothing is left behind. Put all the waste into a plastic carrier bag and take it away to dispose of properly.

Useful checklist

Whether setting out or packing up, it can be handy to work through your plein air checklist to check that you have with you everything you need. Here's mine:

- Pochade box
- Lightweight camera tripod
- Finished painting, and any spare panels, packed securely in a small panel carrier
- Small paint tubes in a zip bag
- Sheets of kitchen paper
- Apron
- Stainless steel 'brush washer' containing low odour solvent and small jar of walnut oil or painting medium
- Palette knife
- Brush roll containing brushes
- Carrier bag for rubbish
- Pack of hand wipes
- Flask of coffee or bottle of water

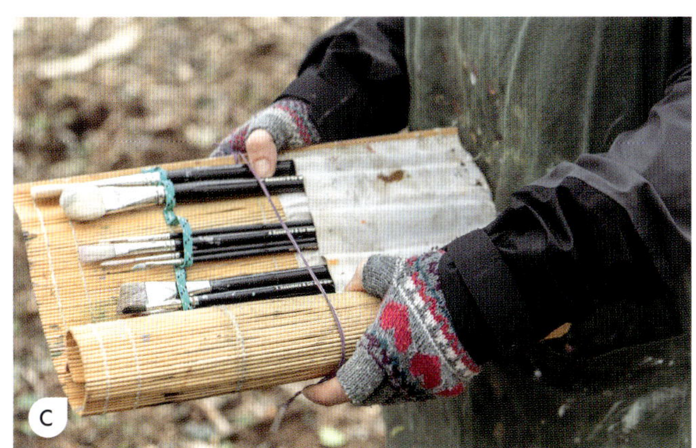

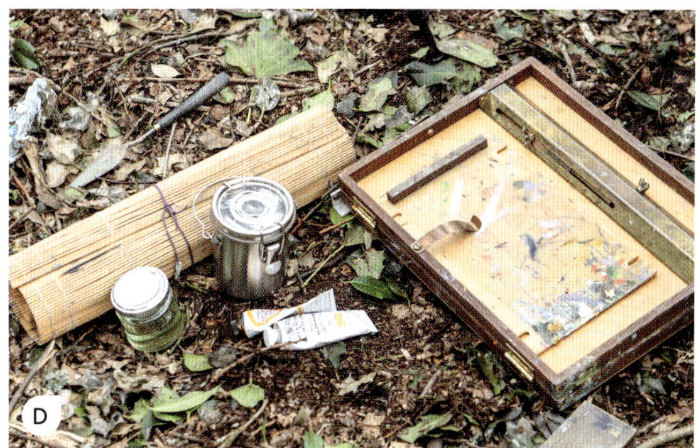

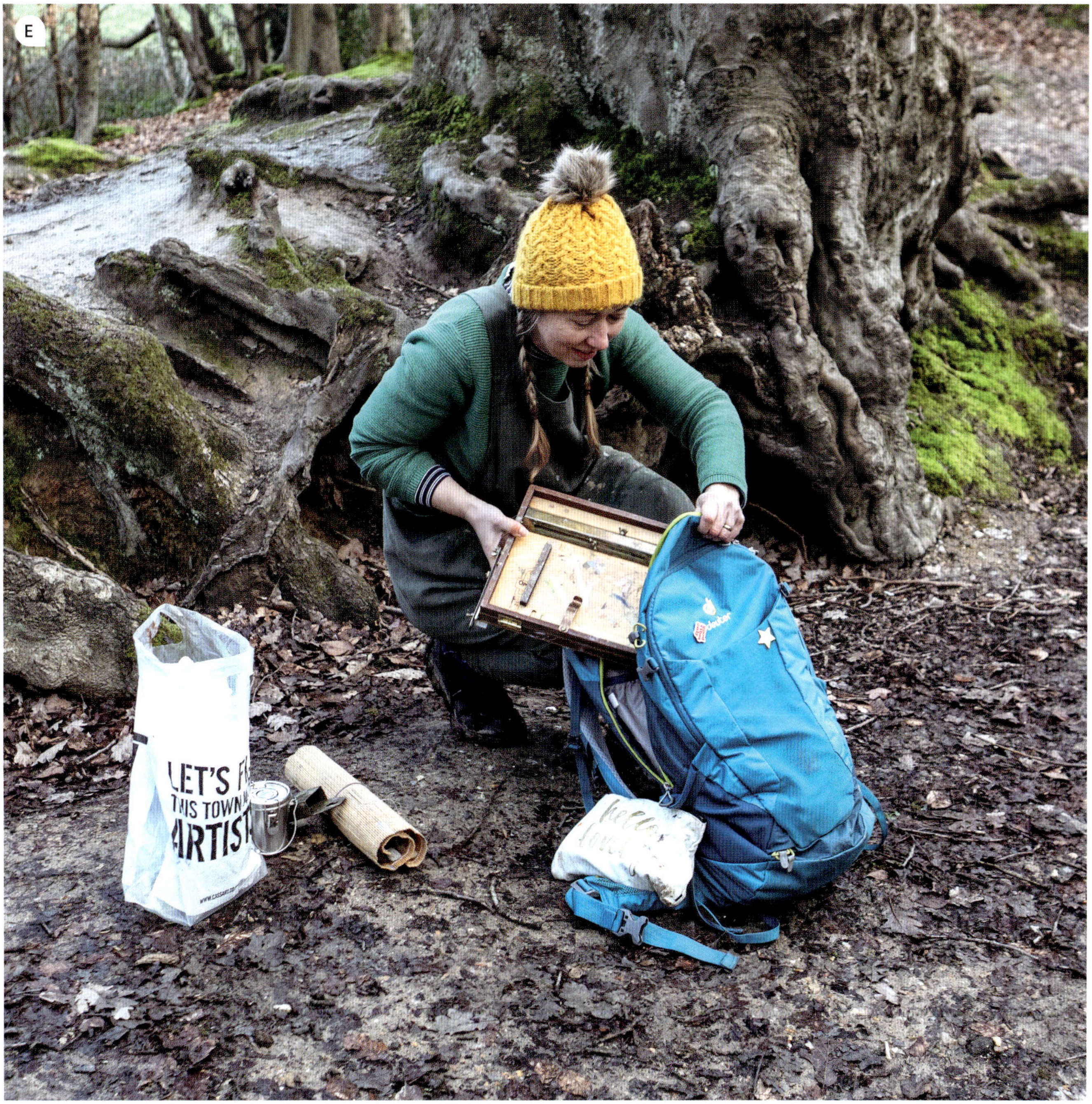

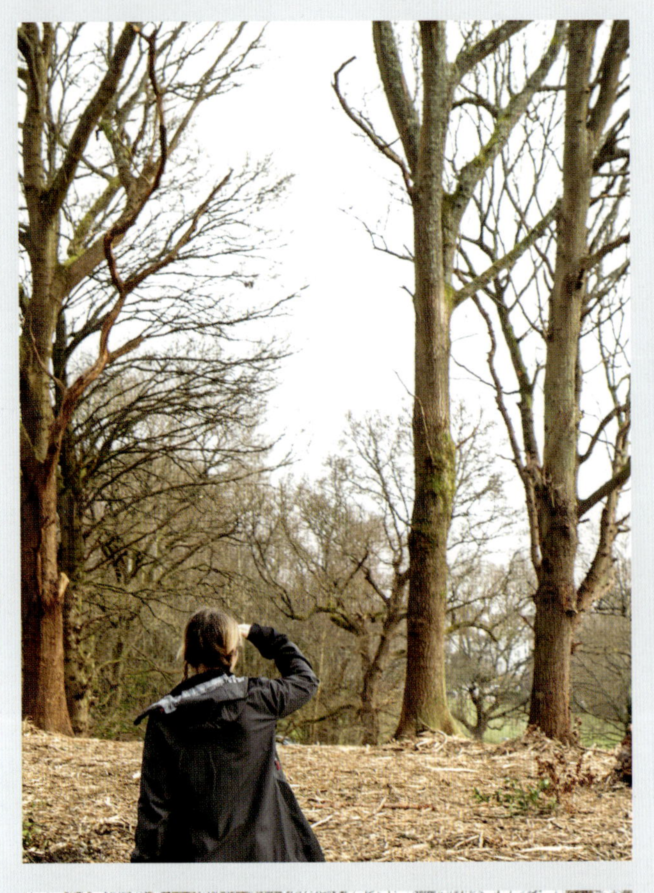
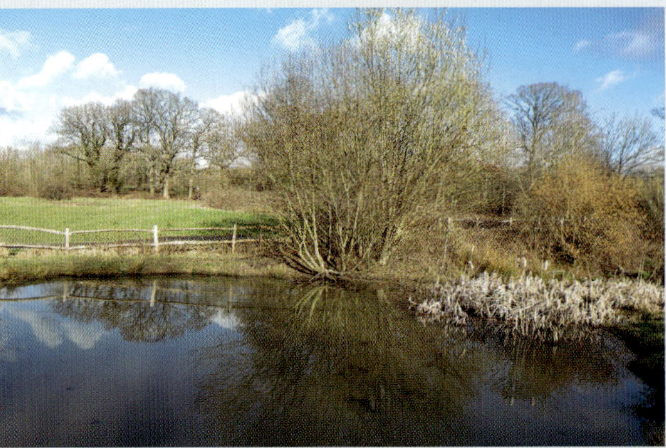
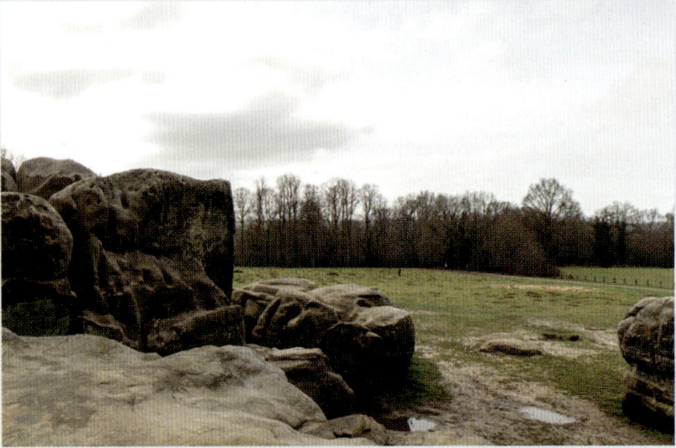
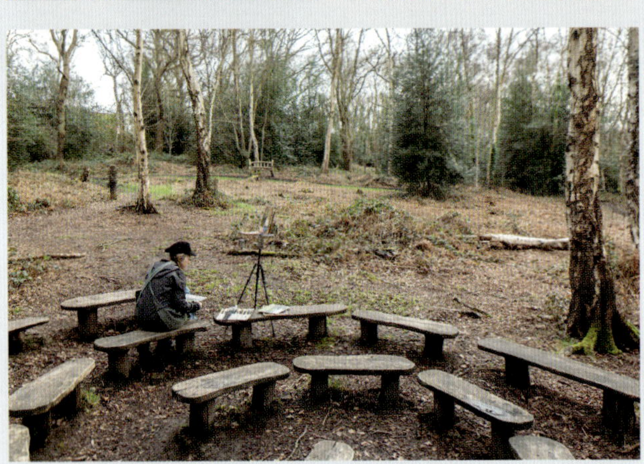
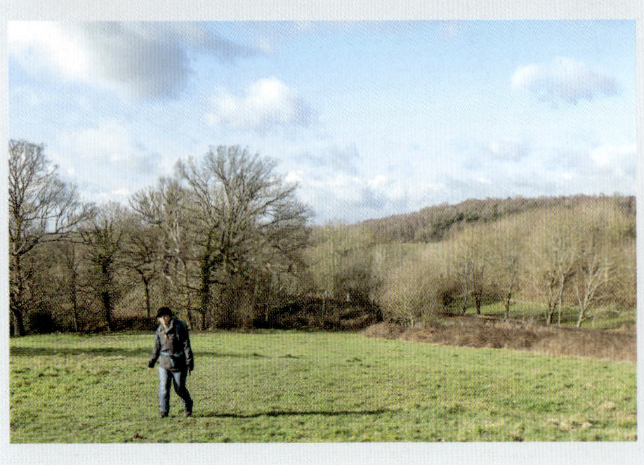
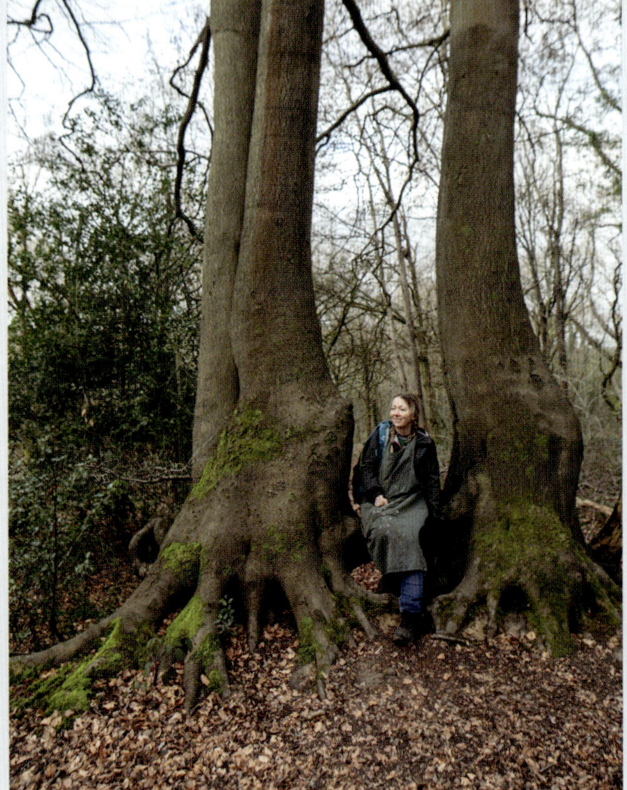

Finding inspiration

With all your equipment ready and bag packed, you're all set. It is now important to spend some time working out what you are looking for in a painting before you begin to hunt for a suitable place to paint. My advice is to avoid thinking about the precise nature of what is in front of you, and instead ask yourself: 'Do the ingredients have some potential to make a painting?' For example, rather than having a fixed idea of wanting to paint a beach scene or townscape, I'll look for a strong effect of light and an interesting variety of shapes. That way, whether I am at the coast or in a city, I will be able to find a subject to paint that satisifies my aims.

With this slightly more abstract approach, the exact location becomes largely irrelevant, and you'll discover that you can find inspiration wherever you are. On a cloudy day, I might instead look more for colour, atmospheric perspective, or reflections in water. You may be drawn to lines within the landscape, a dramatic sky or repeating patterns. You will soon come to learn which ingredients appeal to your sensibilities for – thank goodness – we are all different.

Scouting out a location and making choices

An experience that I'm sure is as familiar as it is frustrating is lugging your equipment round for miles in search of a better view – before ending up right back where you started, at the first scene which caught your eye. It's so tempting to keep looking for a better view just around the next corner, but the more tired you get, the more the desire to paint anything at all can wane. If this happens too often, it can become dispiriting. Avoid this by setting yourself a time limit for looking around and choosing a subject. If you have four hours to spend at the location, resolve to spend no more than an hour before putting paint to canvas. Consider saving your energy by leaving your equipment in the car until you've found your spot.

I'm getting better now at settling down to paint without wasting lots of time exhausting myself with a needless hike. Focus on the process of painting and trying to learn something each time you paint; treat the subject matter as of lesser importance. You will quickly find less time is wasted before you get down to business.

Short trips to visit new places are exciting, but can also be frustrating: you are just beginning to get your teeth into the scene when it's time to leave again. Many plein air painters will recognize that struggle of the first few days in a new place before you 'get your eye in'. For this reason, it's a treat, where possible, to return to an area to explore it in different seasons and weathers. If you have a lake, pond or woodland in your area do take full advantage of that.

Focus on the process of painting and trying to learn something each time you paint; treat the subject matter as of lesser importance.

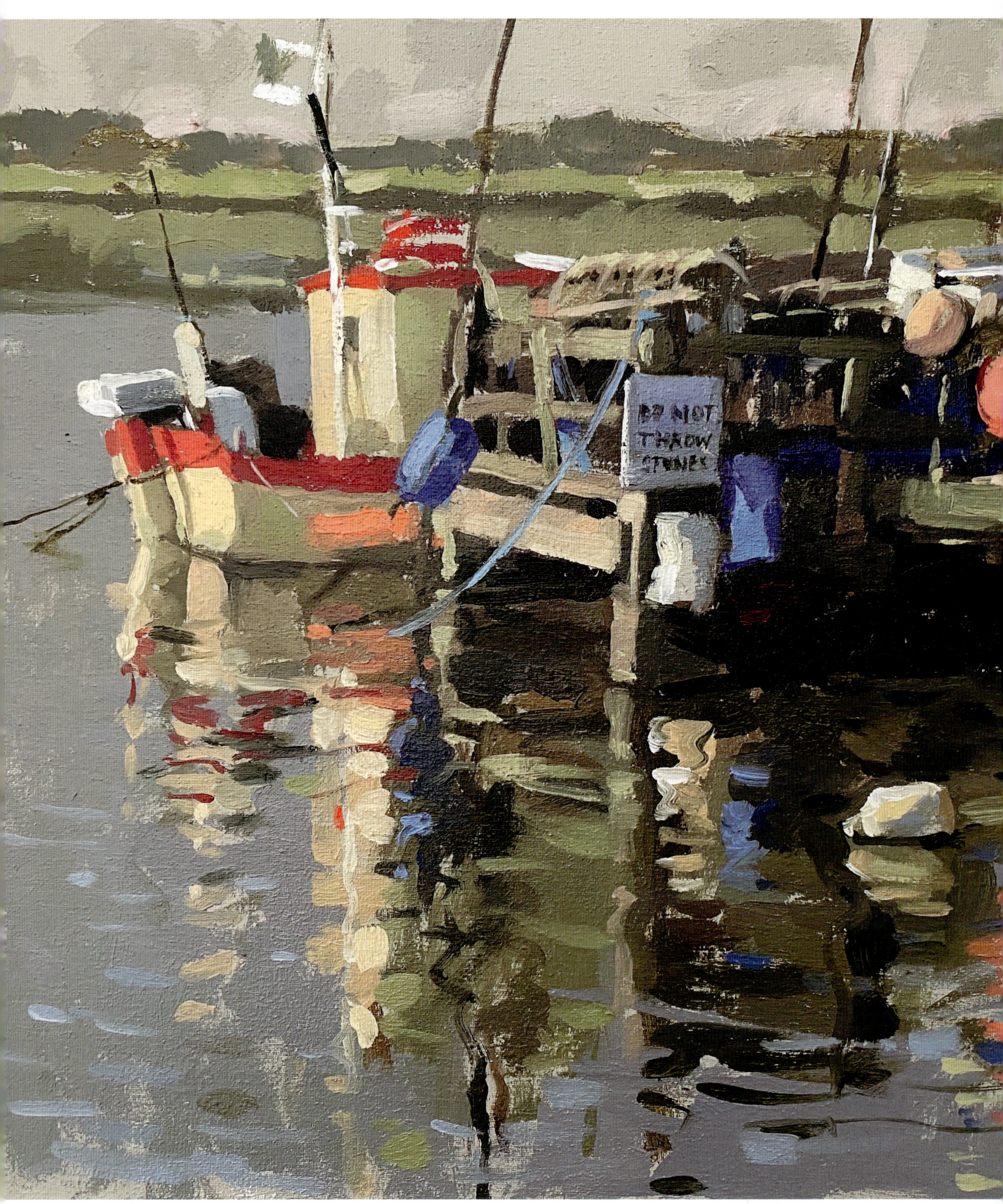
DO NOT
THROW
STONES

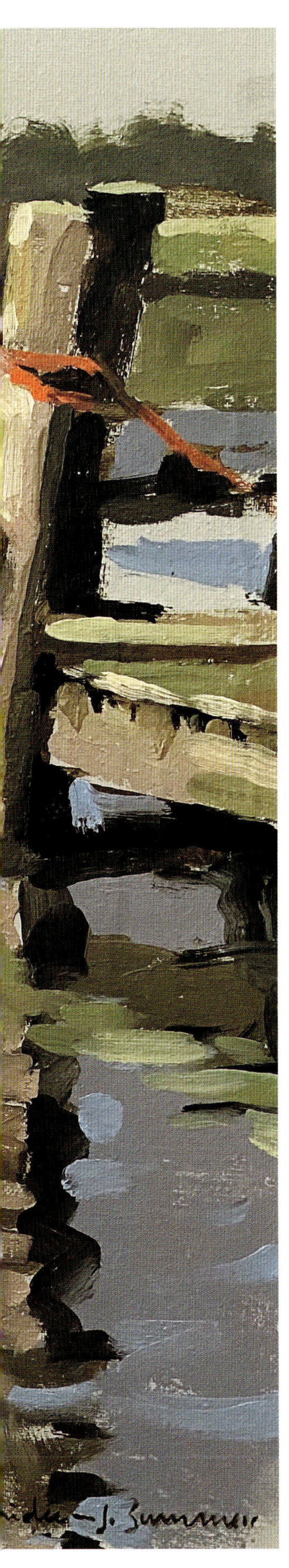

Painting outside: the bigger picture

Say what you need to say in the painting, then get out. There is no use chattering on after you have made your point.

Painting outside can be a little overwhelming at first. Even the most accomplished studio painters can find themselves struggling when faced with the onslaught of information and the speed with which everything changes when working from life outdoors. If there was just one pearl of wisdom that I could share with you to make your journey of becoming a plein air painter easier and more fulfilling, it would be this: keep a broad view.

Impressionism and realism

A thorough rendering of details will not necessarily give us a painting that has that all-important quality of believability – the sense that you could really be looking at it in three dimensions, rather than as daubs of paint on a flat surface. Surprising though it may seem, painting each leaf on the tree can leave the viewer looking at a lifeless pile of spots of paint representing leaves, without any real belief that this is a solid tree which exists in the landscape, being viewed from a certain distance through the moisture and dust particles in the atmosphere. This is fantastic news for those of us who want to produce a painting in a matter of hours, not months, so let that fact sink in and celebrate it.

This leads us to ask how can we capture the essence of the subject rather than saying too much? How do we obtain an impression of the tree in the landscape; get the message across about its particular tree-like qualities, along with a sense of place, while also showing something of the atmosphere and weather of the day? These considerations are probably enough to be getting on with before we muse over the extra dimension which is revealing to the viewer how you, the artist, feel about the landscape with the tree.

To address the questions above, consider this: if we don't need to render every detail about the scene, then we do need to simplify. We are bombarded with visual information when working outside and the longer we stare into any area of the subject, the more we see. Instead we must hang on to that first glance, the ability to see the whole subject at once. We must gauge how the various elements compare to each other from that, rather than letting our gaze linger for too long in any one area.

Blackshore Quay, Southwold
33 x 28cm (13 x 11in)

This was a busy marine subject painted in one alla prima (see page 44) session; it was important to keep things simple and avoid getting bogged down in detail. Fortunately, dark shadowy areas are easy to simplify. In this case I massed in a dark shape for the jetty and its reflections, and then picked out the sunlit shapes and edges on top of that. Anything else is left to the imagination.

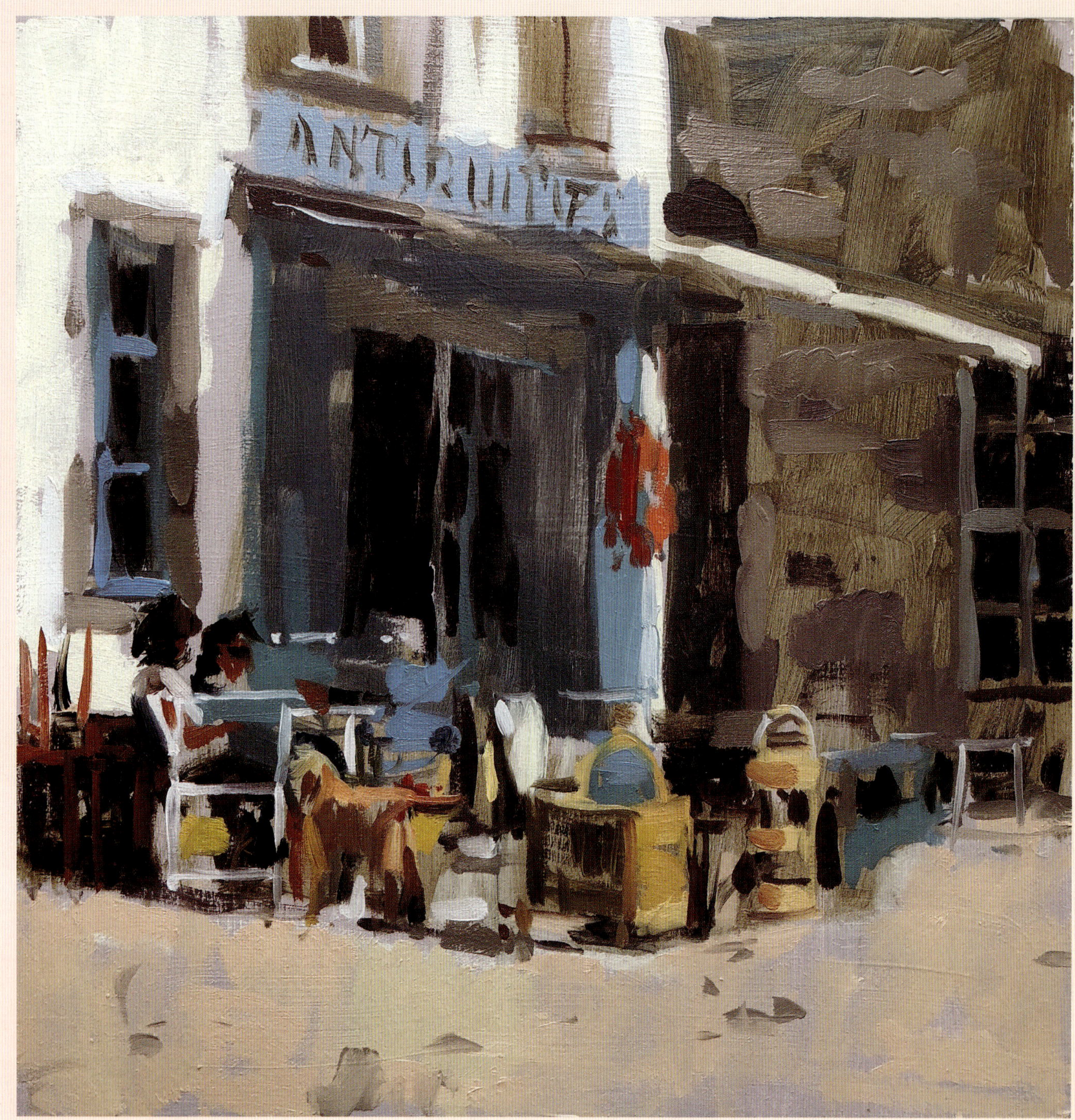

Antiquities, Saint-Martin-de-Ré
21.5 x 21.5cm (8½ x 8½in)

It is easy to get sidetracked by superfluous detail when painting a subject like this, a shop with lots of antiques and bric-a-brac outside. I wanted to convey a feeling of strong sunlight first, then a flavour of France, and finally the somewhat chaotic nature of the objects for sale. I picked out the major light and dark shapes and spots of colour, without trying to work out what the objects were: too much added detail would have taken away from the impact of the strong sunshine.

Find the essentials: simplify what you see

An impressionist, or painterly, approach is perfectly suited to painting a fast-changing subject. Try to get away from the idea that you are painting named objects. Instead, aim to see your subject only in terms of shapes, values and colours.

When I talk about shapes I'm not referring to individual objects, such as trees and gates. What I'm referring to are value shapes. One dark value shape could include a whole group of trees as well as the fence and gate, for example. Screw your eyes up to help you to see the large value shapes within your subject. If you get into the habit of seeing the big shapes first and moving down towards smaller shapes, you will soon learn how a simple but well-placed mark can convey a great deal of information to the viewer. Recognizing what you are seeing in these terms is half of the battle. Learn to observe in this way in order to paint and you are halfway there – before you have even picked up a brush or mixed a colour.

Even when you are not painting you can practise seeing the world in this way. Looking through half-closed eyes helps you to simplify what you are seeing into large blocks of colour and value, cutting down on superfluous detail.

If you want your painting to have a believable depth and make a strong impact, you need to crack the value relationships. Constantly compare one part of your subject to another – nothing is seen in isolation in real life and neither should it be in your painting. Have a value plan before you start and keep it in mind throughout. We'll be looking at this further in the chapter on design and impact on pages 84–107.

To start with, try very hard to match the colours and values that you are actually seeing, and not to let what you think you know about the subject get in the way. By isolating a small area of colour from what surrounds it, we are more likely to recognize it for what it is, rather than relying on our prior assumptions about the overall object's colour. A colour isolator can help with this: a simple piece of mid-grey board with a couple of holes punched in it. Looking through the hole at the area you want to identify will help you to recognise the value of a colour – that is, whether it is lighter or darker than the mid-grey value of the card itself – and the true colour hue. To ensure accuracy, hold the colour isolator at the same angle as your painting surface to get the same angle of light affecting both. If you don't have a colour isolator, you can simply curl your index finger around to make a small hole and look through that.

Blocking-in

Time is short, so any technique that gets both colour and tone in place quickly and accurately is valuable. Blocking-in helps to avoid over-focussing on details at the expense of the overall painting. Later on, the initial blocked-in shapes will help you to balance the final colours, as it provides something against which you can judge the local colours. The project overleaf shows this technique in action.

Café Scene

The aim of this exercise is to show you an example of how to break the picture into a few large shapes, allowing you to establish correct hues and values quickly across the whole painting area. When blocking in large shapes, don't look for the shapes of objects, but rather value shapes, which transcend the boundaries of objects.

Mix generous amounts of paint on your palette and apply the paint smoothly and with good coverage. When learning this approach, think about applying the paint in spots or patches of colour, laid side by side, that build up to a finished painting – in effect a little like creating a mosaic. Try to apply the right colour and value in the right shape in one brushstroke, so that you don't have to go back over the top with more wet paint. This will keep your colours cleaner. To keep things simple when working outside, try to keep the paint to the consistency that it comes out of the tube and apply in single strokes placed next to single strokes.

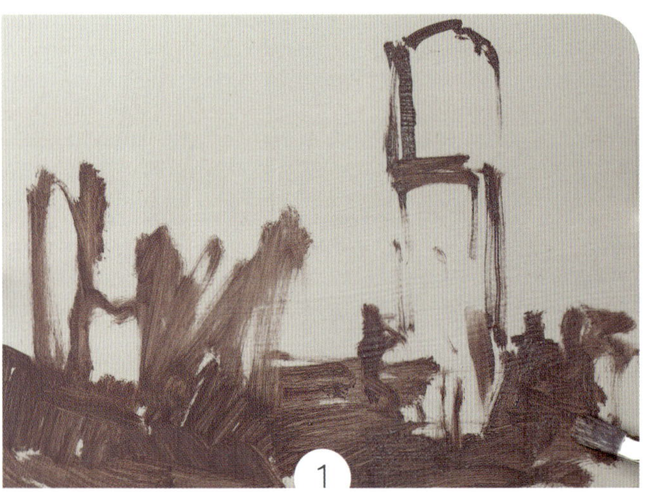

Start by identifying and painting the largest shape as a single block, using one of your larger brushes and a dark neutral mix. Screw your eyes up to see the large value shapes within your subject and mass values together to make larger shapes wherever you can. Generally I work from dark to light, so the first shape for me to block-in here was this large shadow area that encompassed the whole foreground, the shadows on the wall cast by the trees, and the shadow area inside the doorway.

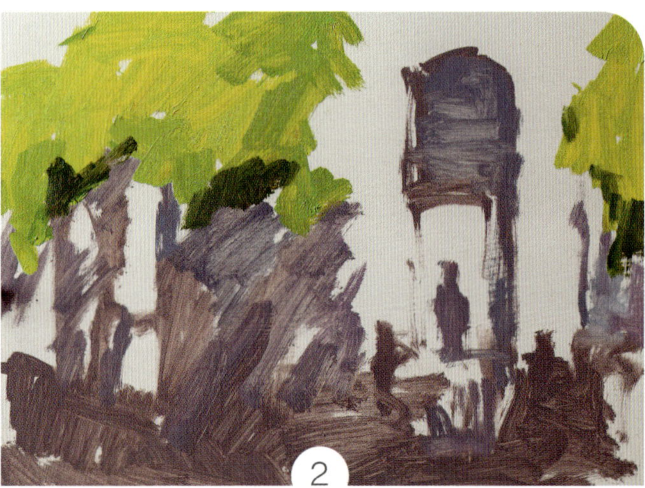

Move on to the next largest shape. Here, it is the foliage. When choosing a shape, squint your eyes to break edges or join objects together. Simplify the area and look for an 'average' colour; that is, one which will serve as the underlayer for as much as possible of the shape. You can of course vary from this while you work, touching in some varied tones, but try to cover the area and move on swiftly.

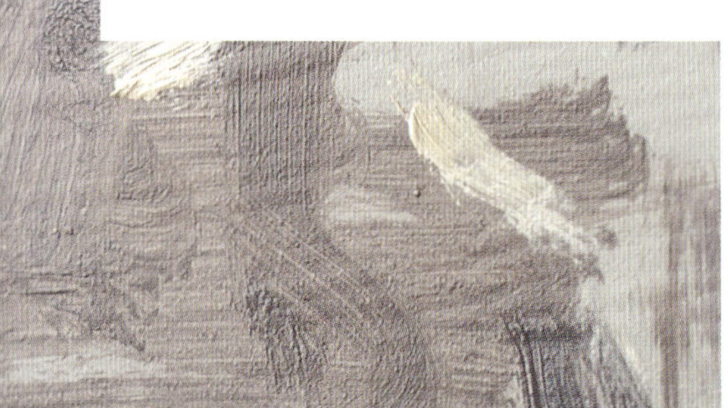

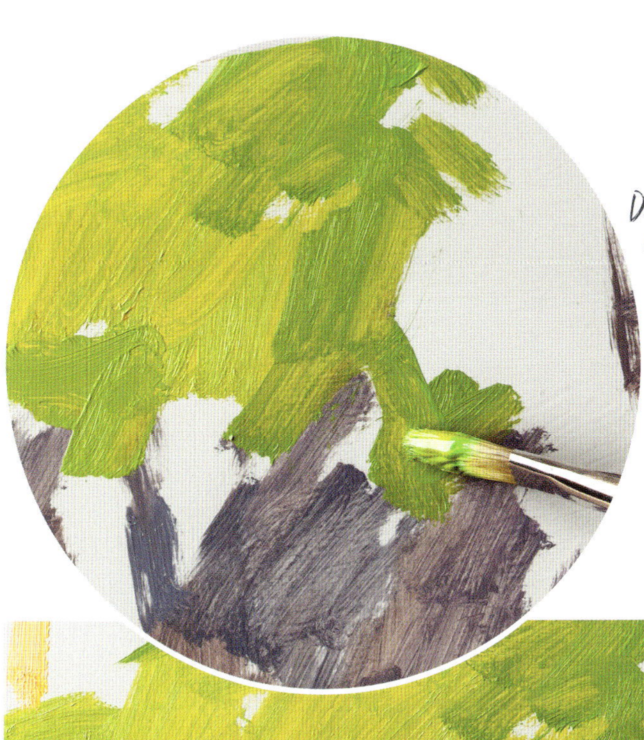

Deciding on an 'average' colour

For sunlit foliage, taking an average of the bright highlights and dark shades will usually give you something like a midtone green. The exact hue will of course vary depending on what you're painting. If an area is mainly one flat bright value, with tiny but extremely dark recesses, you should not find a midpoint. Instead, you might simply paint the whole area in a hue that matches the flat bright value. Simplify in the name of speed.

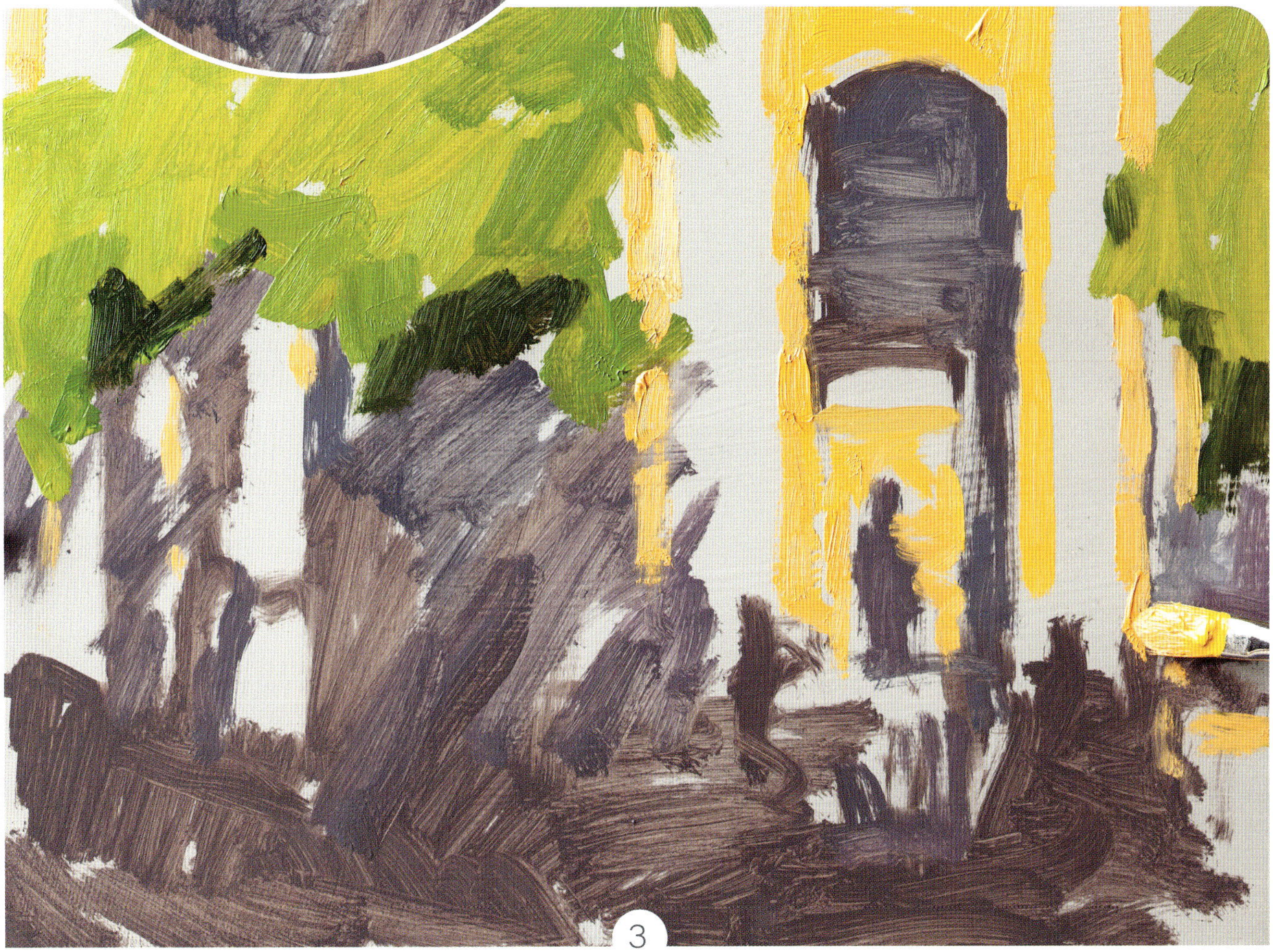

Continue to the next largest area – in this case the façade of the buildings – and repeat. Use your brushstrokes to evoke the nature of the area: compare the relatively straight marks used here with the looser, freer foliage and shadows.

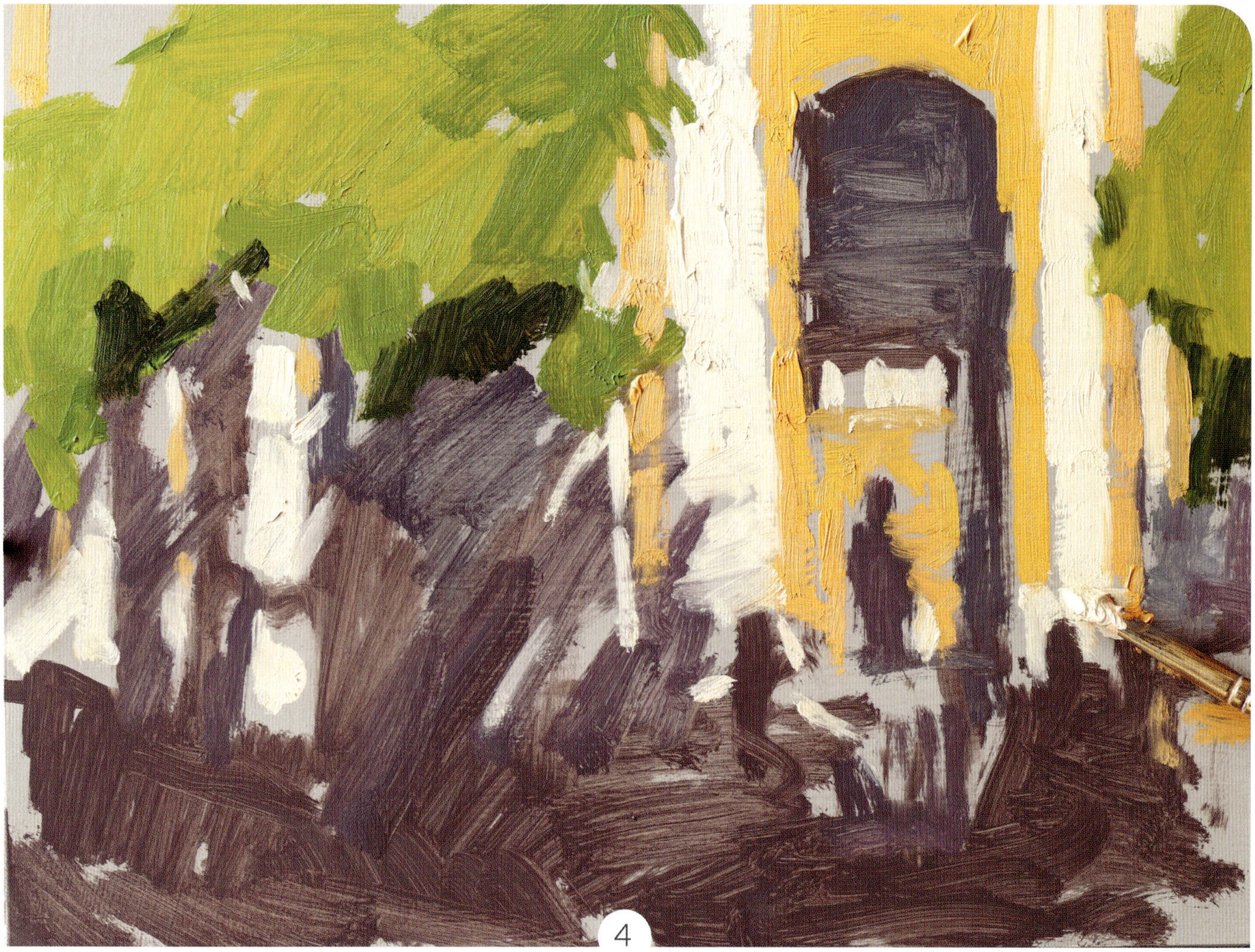

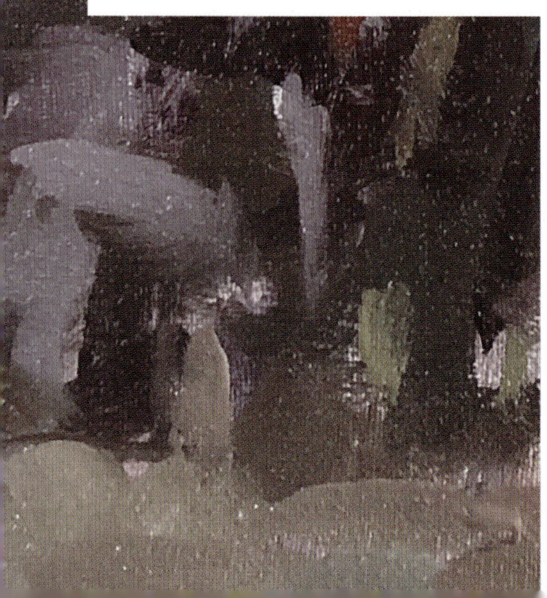

4

Continue the blocking-in process until the surface of the canvas is nearly covered. I've left the lightest value area to the last stage of the blocking-in process, because it can be a mistake to get white on to the painting surface too early: it can lead to muddy colours and confused tonal values. As a general rule of thumb, it's easier to make a too-dark painting lighter than to get darks back into a painting which has too much white in it.

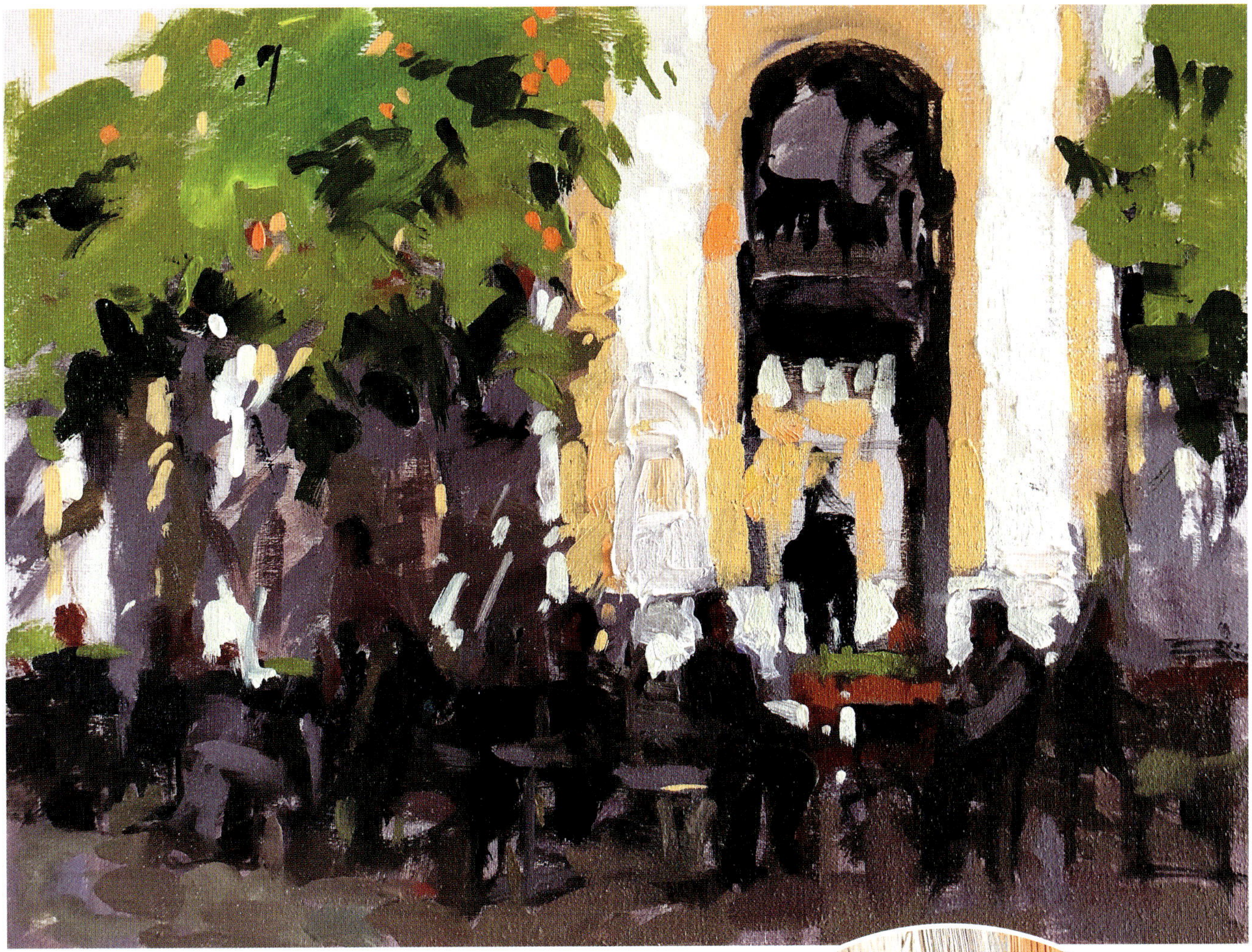

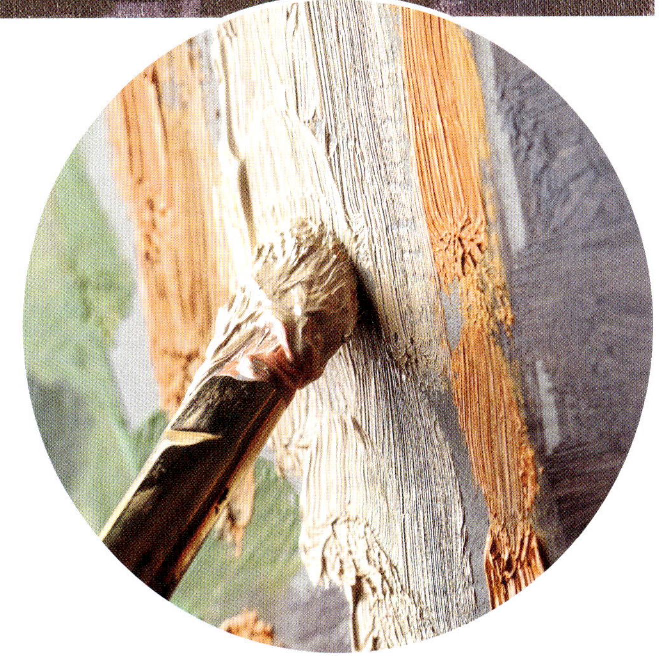

Finishing the painting

After the main colour/value shapes are placed with the blocking-in method, it's time to go back into them to refine them further. Move into progressively smaller shapes and tweak the colour where necessary.

Here, smaller darker shapes were picked out within the large blocked-in shadow shape to suggest figures seated at tables, and further decorative details within the doorway to the restaurant. Small spots of light made their way into the cast shadows on the wall to break these up and show that the light was dappled, passing as it did through the foliage of the tree canopies. A few small red-dark shapes suggested faces and the terracotta planters, and finally the small details of the growing oranges were added to the foliage.

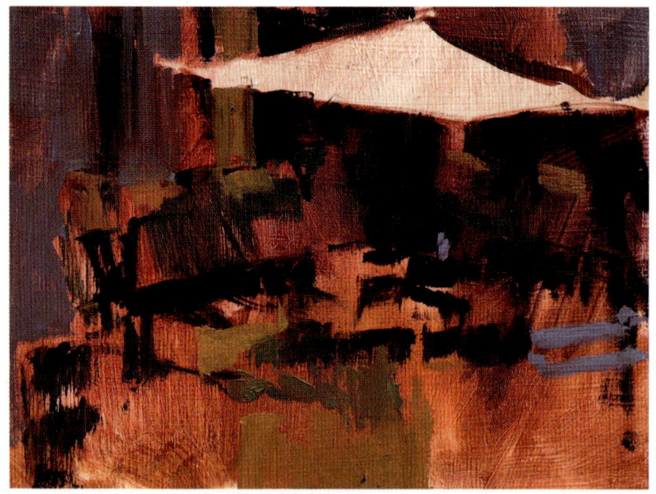

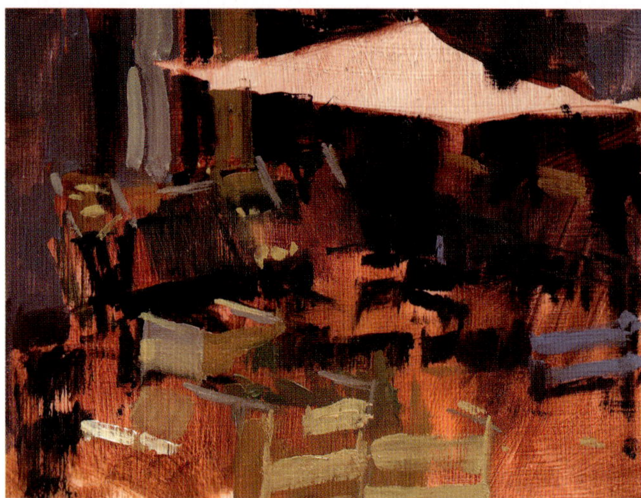

Details from earlier stages of Five a Day.

Using the blocking-in technique

I painted the artwork opposite, *Five a Day*, on a drizzly day in southern Ireland, with a small pochade box. The red parasol and the colourful produce caught my eye in the gloom. There are a lot of small details in a scene like this, so it can be tricky to work out how best to tackle it.

I decided to start with a patchwork of dark colours to act as a background over the whole surface, reserving the parasol shape because I needed that to be a light tonal value. I then suggested dark lines at approximate angles to pick out the dark sides or inners of the vegetable crates, as shown in the detail at the top of the page. I then started some lighter and mid-value short thick strokes on top of the darker underpainting. Again these suggested the sides of boxes, as shown in the detail below left.

With the basic structure of the market stall suggested, it was then time to add more of the highly coloured shapes and smaller details. It's always surprising what just a few brushstrokes can suggest to the viewer of the painting, and how little you need to tell the story. Seen against the dark wash underpainting, four small green blobby brushstrokes hovering just above three short orange dashes represents a box full of carrots.

Practise seeing your subject in its essential terms by making plenty of simplified colour studies. Using large brushes on a small board will help you to resist fiddling with extraneous details. Choose subjects to paint that have plenty of interesting shapes and a range of light and dark values. Block in just the large colour shapes and then, when you have covered every part of the surface, stop and move on to another study. Mass values together to make larger shapes wherever you can.

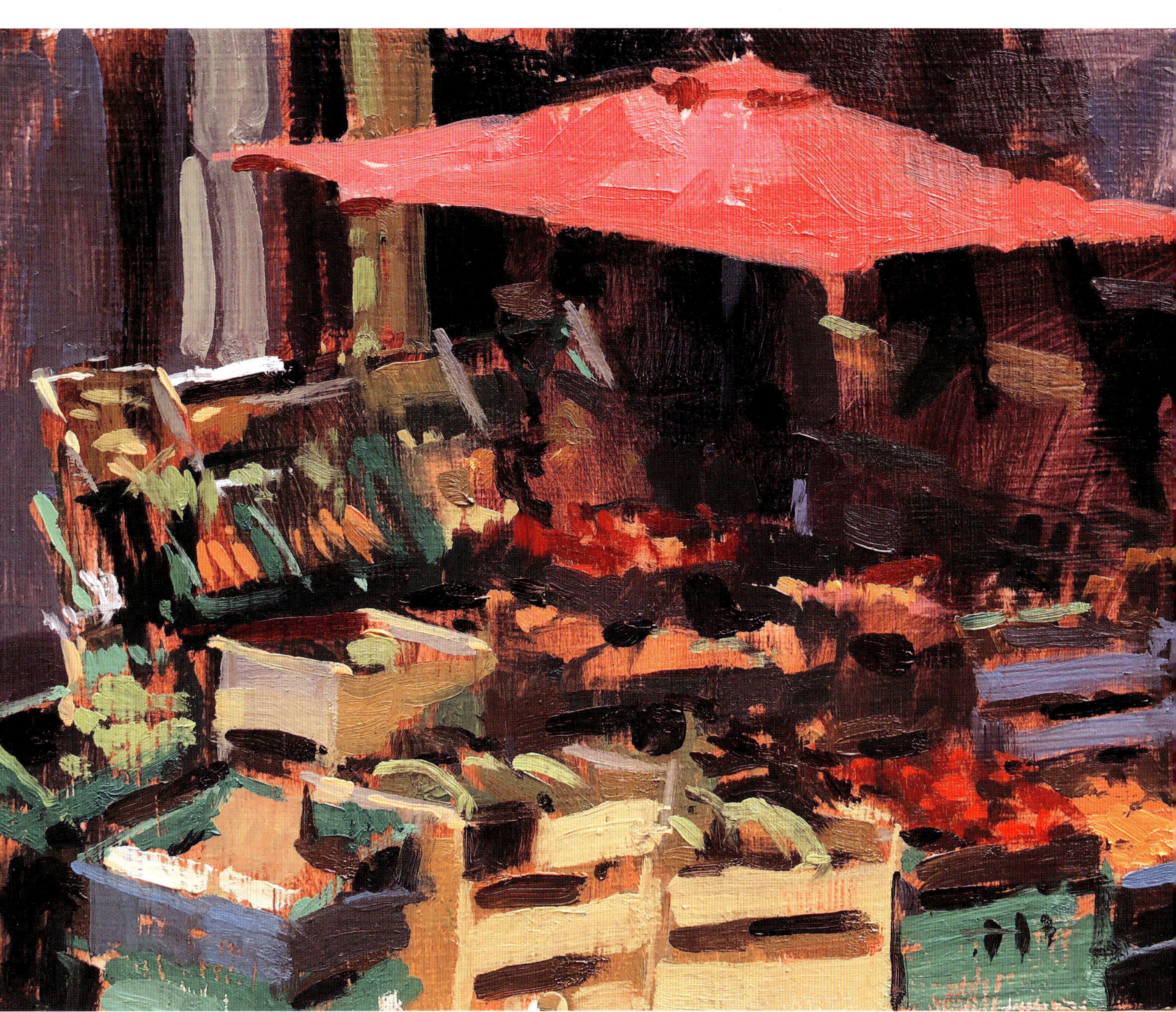

Five a Day
20 x 15cm (8 x 6in)

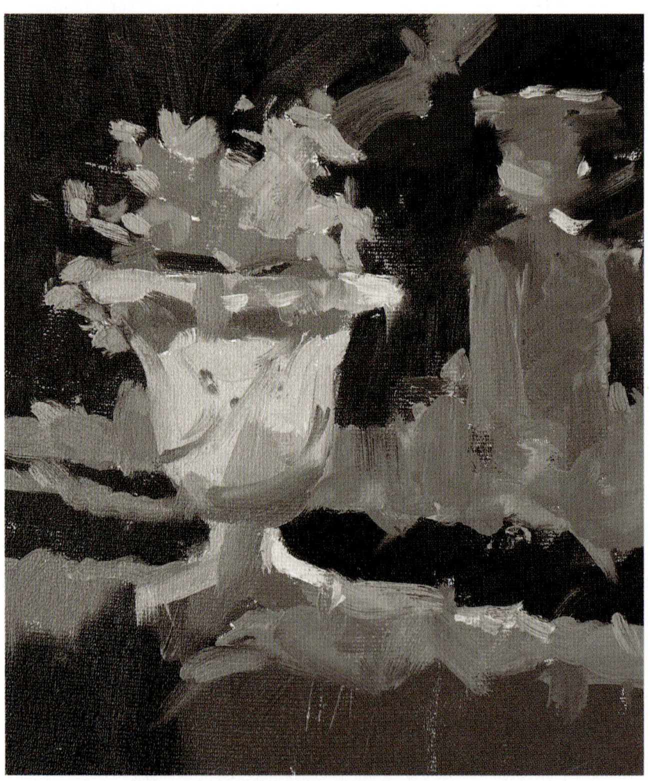

Another practice that might be of use is to take photographs of your painting as it develops. You can then look back on these and judge whether you went too far. Was it a stronger painting at an earlier stage? Did you add extra details that didn't benefit the painting? Did you overwork an area and lose the contrast between dark and light value shapes? By assessing your work in this way, you can try to avoid making the same mistakes again.

> **'Paint the melon before the seeds; the dog before the fleas. '**
>
> **Sergei Bongart, 1918–1985**

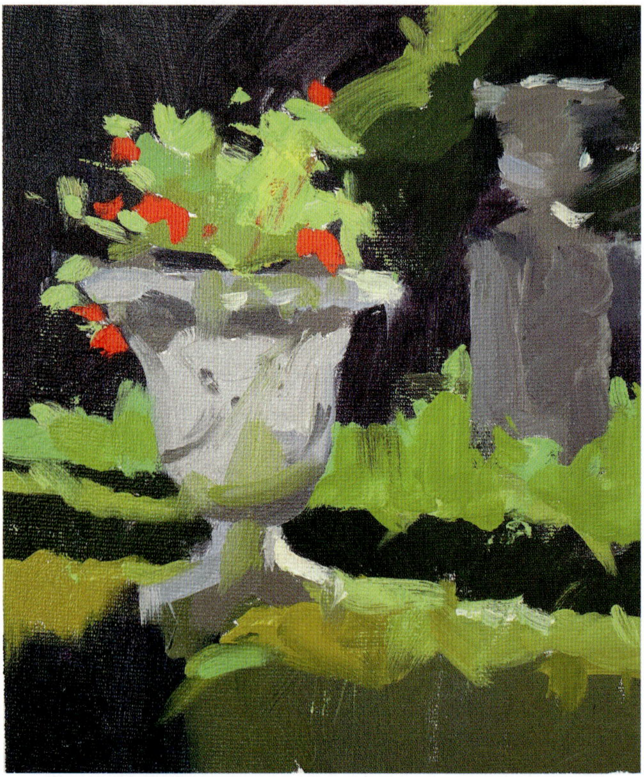

Shown on this page are examples of a subject seen in its essential terms (top) and painted as a simplified colour study (bottom), reduced down to its major value and colour shapes.

In the final version of the painting, opposite, the subject is painted with more nuance and refinement. There are slight colour temperature shifts, reflected light, smaller details and edge control. Crucially, however, you can still see the strong and simple colour/value shapes which together make the design of the painting. A strong design gives a strong message and leads to a painting with impact – a concept we will return to on pages 86–89. The smaller details and refinements are nice to have, but that underlying design, as seen in the simplified study, is essential to any painting, particularly one made en plein air, where time is of the essence.

Urn at Belton House

Immediately above is a simple colour/value study of the urn, made with a large brush. There is little to no detail in this study. The image at the top shows the study in black and white to demonstrate the tonal contrast.

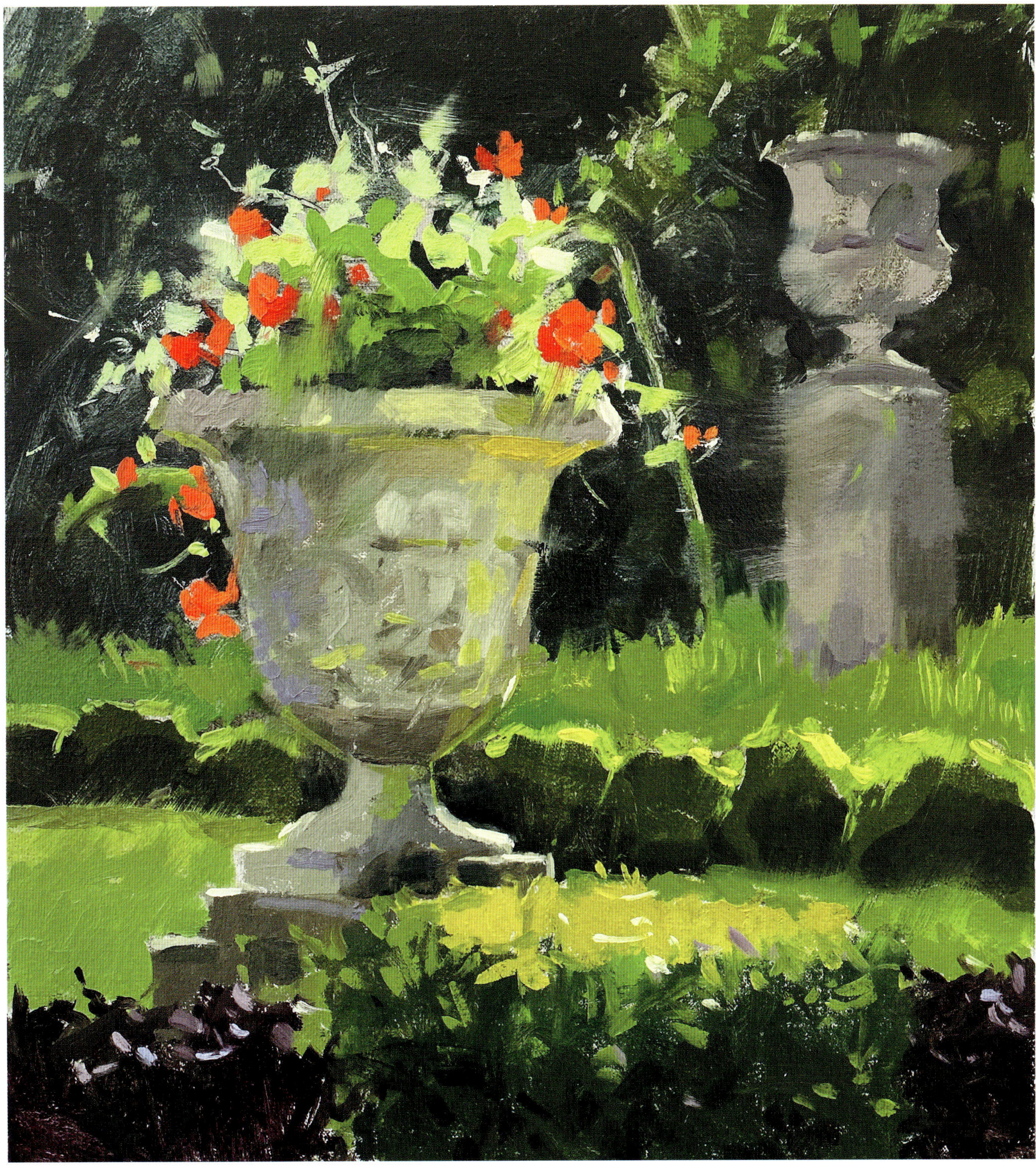

Urn at Belton House
25.5 x 28cm (10 x 11in)

Chasing the light: alla prima

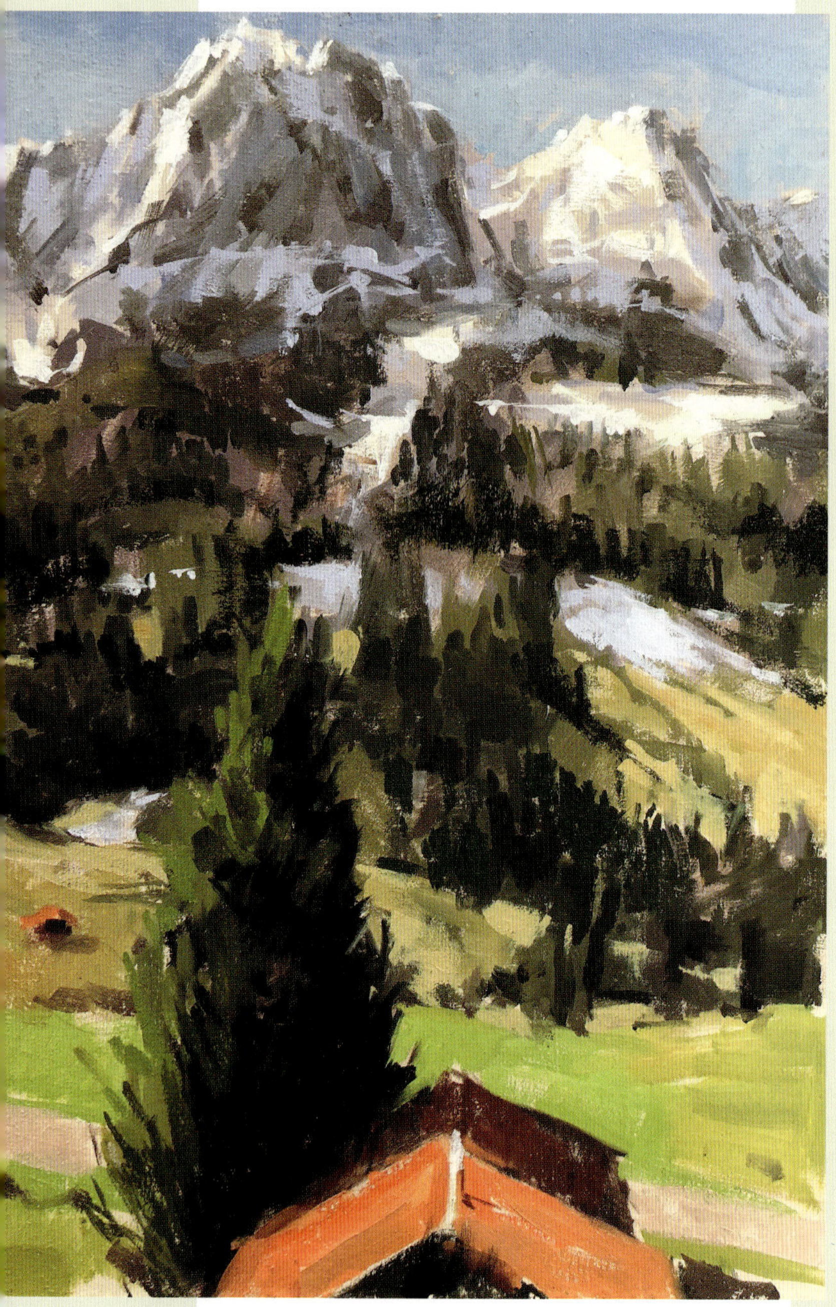

You'll have realized by now that the whole premise of plein air painting is capturing a scene that is changing as your painting session progresses. Nothing is static: the sun is constantly on the move, the weather changes, tides rise and fall, and inevitably an artist's view will be blocked by a large vehicle from time to time. Really, this whole book is about capturing a changing scene – you have to work quickly.

The title of this chapter is perhaps misleading; it could just have accurately been called 'not chasing the light'. The most difficult aspect of plein air painting is that our field of reference is constantly changing as the light moves. It's in our best interests to paint quickly and efficiently, getting the essence pinned down before we are looking at a completely different scene which doesn't relate to our painting anymore.

Trying to 'chase the light' in your painting means making reactive changes to the scene in front of you: the sun goes in, the sun comes out, the field is lit by the sun, a cloud has passed over, you mix a lighter colour, you change it to darker, and so on. How – and whether – to account for these changes is a common dilemma for artists working directly from life.

After several hours have passed the sun will be in a markedly different position in the sky to when you started. This will inevitably cause huge changes within your subject, so what can you do to avoid getting tangled up?

We look in more detail at painting over multiple sessions later on; but for now we'll focus on

Rougemont, Morning Light
25.5 x 35.5cm (10 x 14in)

It's a wonderful exercise to paint the same subject at different times of day in order to appreciate the many changes which the day brings. In this morning study I observed cooler colours on the mountain itself while the sun lit the foreground and that terracotta roof glowed warmly.

completing a painting in one session – a practice called *alla prima*, which comes from the Italian for 'at first attempt'. It's good to aim to complete a plein air painting in one and a half hours – or not longer than two. This general guideline may not sound like very much time but with practice you will get faster and – crucially – better able to make decisions under pressure.

Different times of day and different light conditions can be easier or more difficult to manage. For example, when working on an overcast day there are no shadows to worry over, and everything is being affected by the same colour of light in an even way across the subject. You can work for longer sessions on a day like this. By contrast, when working at sunrise or sunset you will see phenomenal changes in a very short space of time – these changes are not just taking place in the sky but are also affecting the colours and values within the landscape below.

Even with a fairly steady light source, you will face other changes within your subject, so it's always best to stay aware of time passing and keep focussed on the job in hand. I often set the timer on my phone to give me an alert after one hour – by which time I aim to have all the major colour shapes in the painting blocked in, so that I can see them in relation to each other. I will then often set my timer for another forty-five minutes, with the aim of being finished with the painting by the end of that time. I find that splitting up the painting session into two parts in this way helps me to concentrate and use my time efficiently.

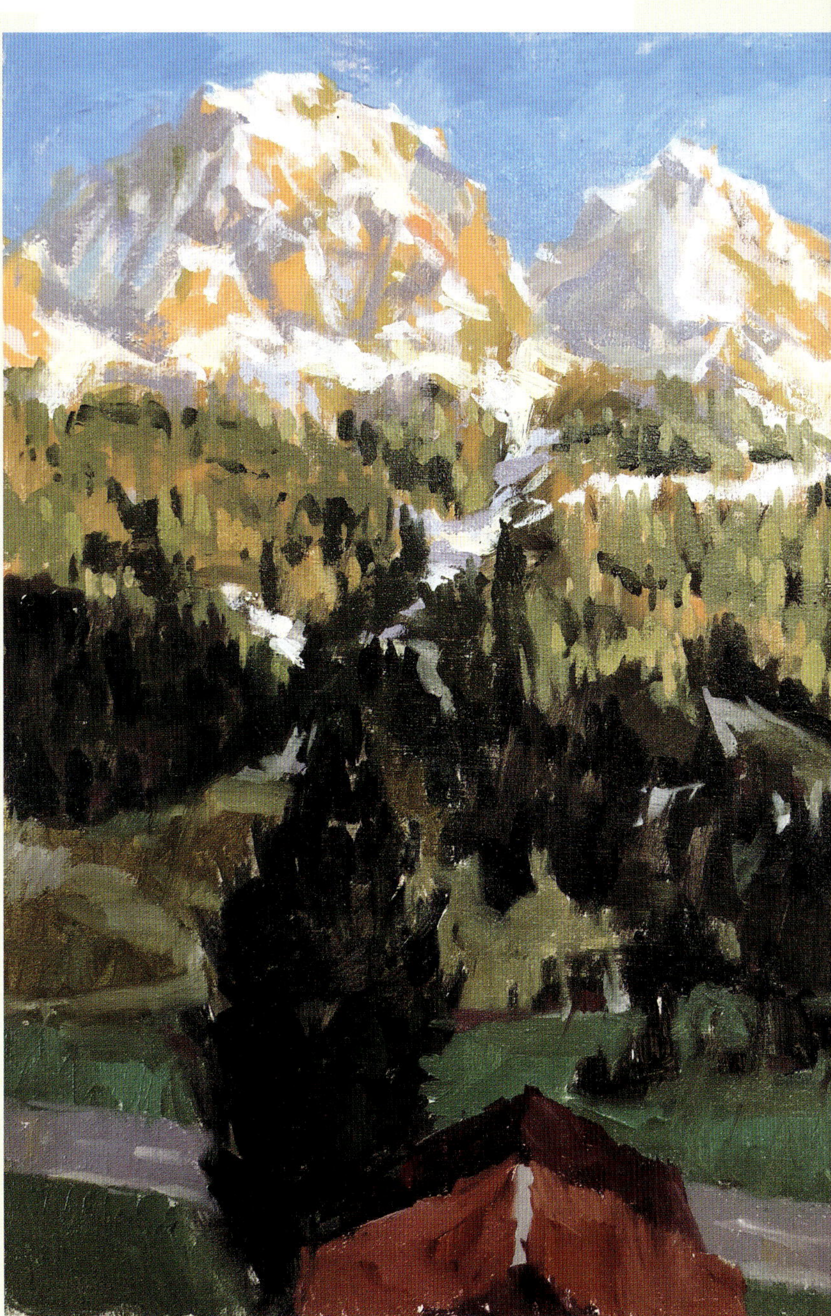

Rougemont, Evening Light
25.5 x 35.5cm (10 x 14in)

I painted again in the evening from the same position. Now the foreground was cool and shaded while the warm light lit the mountain top and the far trees with orange and gold hues.

I don't want to give you the impression here that you should freeze-frame in your mind's eye how the subject looks when you arrive and ignore all changes that occur from then on. Whether you are painting alla prima or over multiple sessions, one of the unique qualities of plein air painting is that, unlike a photographic snap, you're not capturing a single second in time. Your painting can encapsulate several hours of a particular day and tell much more of the story. For me that's part of the very appeal of plein air painting. Sometimes interesting characters, vehicles or animals might appear while you are painting, which you can use to enhance your composition or provide more interest. Stay observant and be receptive to making changes which will improve the painting, while keeping to a broad simplified plan or vision for the piece which stems from your first impressions.

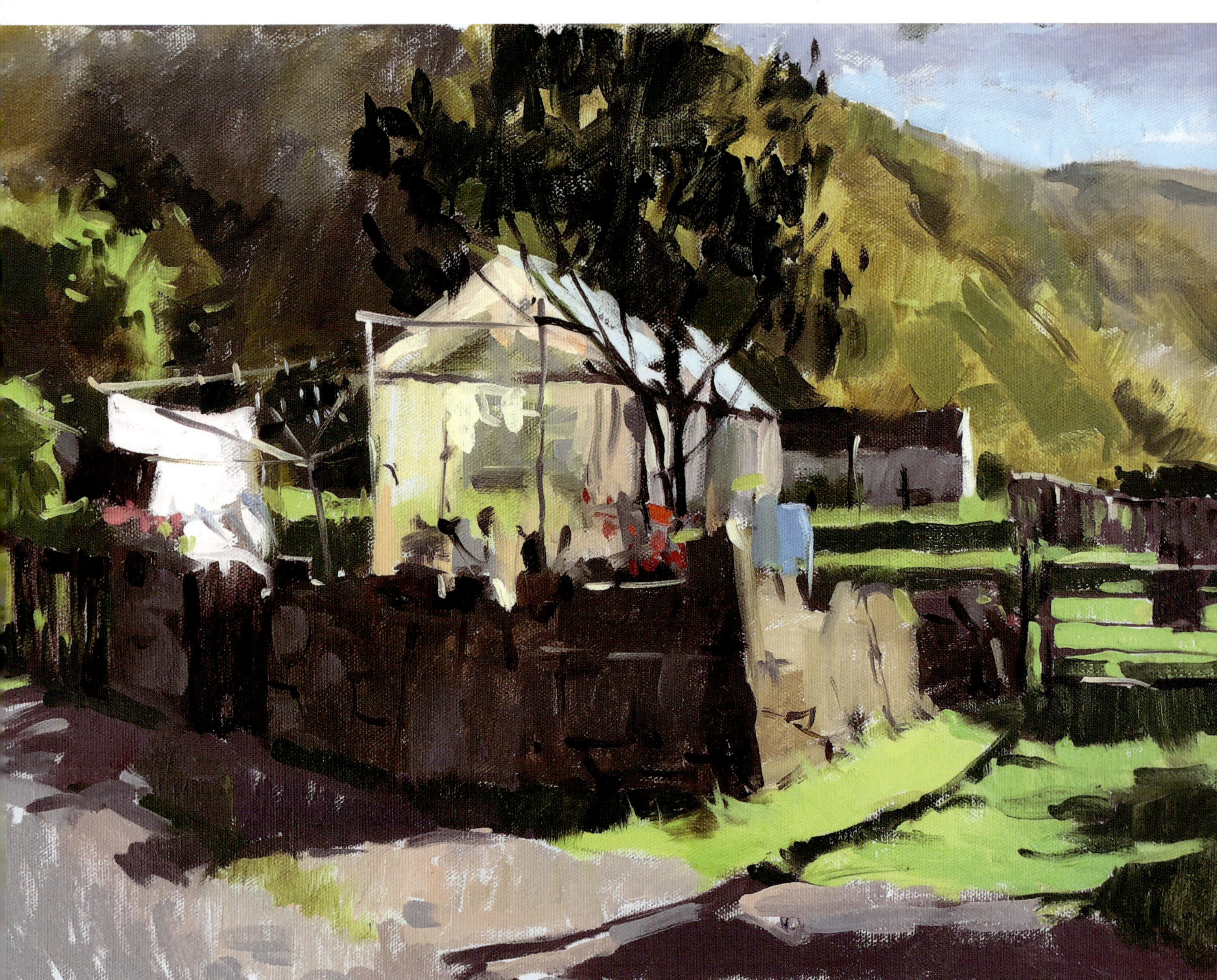

Greenhouse and Sheets at Solva
40.5 x 30.5cm (16 x 12in)

A painting about a strong effect of light towards the end of an afternoon, when shadows were long and the sun was going down. In circumstances like this I will rapidly mix a neutral colour to use for a tonal block-in at the beginning of the session. This allows me to get all those dark areas marked in – in this case the wall that's in the shade, the cast shadows across the road and field, the distant building and the bulk of the hill and trees behind the garden. As the shadows lengthen and weaken, this early framework allows me to continue working to the same value plan.

Trying to follow each and every change of light will undoubtedly cause you problems: muddied paint from overworking areas, loss of your clear value design and even shadows coming from different directions or some objects casting shadows while others don't. We can't stop the sun moving but there are methods we can use to help us stick to a clear message about how the light affects our subject; and to keep to that message throughout the painting process despite how it changes. We'll be exploring those throughout the book.

When going out to paint, I think the best mindset to have is to expect nothing to stay still or stay the same and then you won't be disappointed. Remember what you want to say in the painting, create a clear mental image, and work on developing a good short-term memory. This sounds difficult but you will quickly find that your visual memory gets better with practice – just like a muscle getting stronger. I've created a few exercises to give you a little extra practice in developing this skill. You can start using them in your studio, where conditions are more easily controlled.

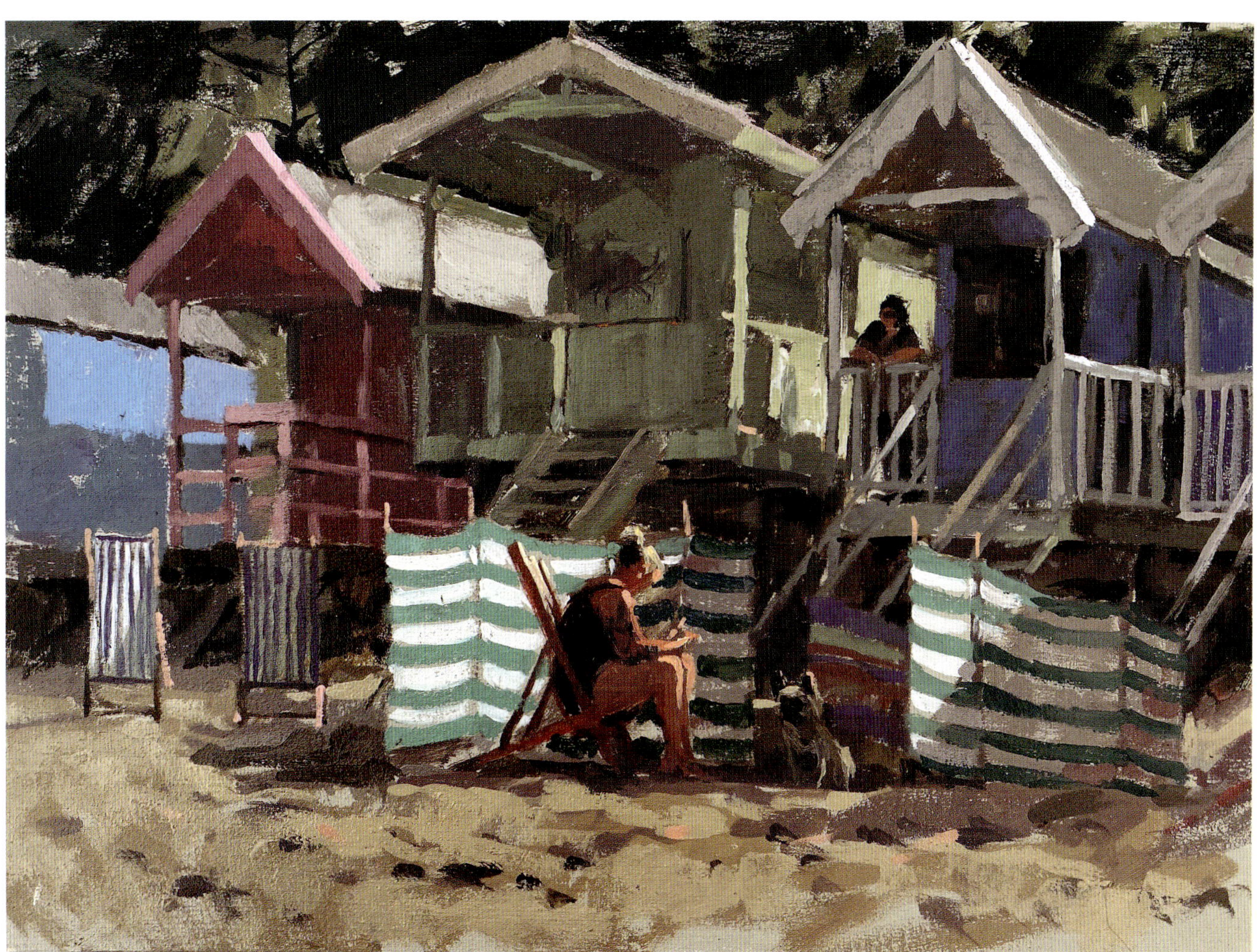

A Day at the Beach
35.5 x 25.5cm (14 x 10in)

Another fast-changing situation, in which I had to notice and remember which areas were in the light family and which in the shadow family. The shadows quickly got longer and the figure and windbreaks were no longer lit directly by the sun. I was fortunate to be back on the beach a few days later, so I was able to get this painting out again at the same time of day to check and redefine some of the areas that I'd missed during the first session.

Movement and rapid change

Later on in the book we tackle some of the major challenges of plein air painting; dealing with changeable light and weather, and various ways of fixing a memory of what you are trying to express using value sketches, under-painting or taking photographs. However, it's the continuous process of learning and evaluating which will improve your speed, decisiveness and memory. As the scene changes, so must your mindset.

Simplify as far as you can by cropping the composition or omitting/reducing elements of the subject. Use little vignettes to practise focussing on one part of the subject that interests you, rather than trying to make a complete painting. If you want to paint animals from life, do as much drawing as you can in sketchbooks, gathering information about their particular shape, habits and movements. Try to capture the gesture of a cat, cow or hen using only one line. With regular drawing practice you will develop your own visual language or shorthand.

Make life easier by using small panels and large brushes when painting moving subjects, then there's no chance of fiddling and getting distracted with small details whilst losing the essence of the motif.

More than anything, I want to encourage you to tackle your fears head-on. Choose those hard subjects that put you in a place of discomfort and challenge the heroic artist that resides within you. Don't impose limits on yourself because something seems too difficult to try. Give it a go anyway and focus on what you learn doing it rather than having expectations about the outcome. It's so invigorating to tackle something that you've never tried before, and you might just surprise yourself.

> ‘A person who never made a mistake never tried anything new.’
>
> Albert Einstein, 1879–1955

Charlie and White Daffodils
23 x 25.5cm (9 x 10in)

On a sunny spring day I was sitting on a low wall in the garden with my pochade box, ready to paint some of the plant pots and the white daffodils when our cat Charlie came and sat down right in front of my subject. Naturally I was delighted. The sunlight made his ginger hair glow, creating a striking contrast of colour with the bluish grey planter. Grabbing one smallish brush and dipping it into a neutral colour mix on the palette I sketched in an outline of his overall shape in seconds and then quickly roughed in the shadows within this outline and the cast shadow on the ground, making note of any strong highlights such as his ears and the curve of fur on his white leg. Of course he only stayed in this position for a few moments but even when he stepped away he was nearby, so I was able to look at him to check his colouring and patterns while continuing with the painting.

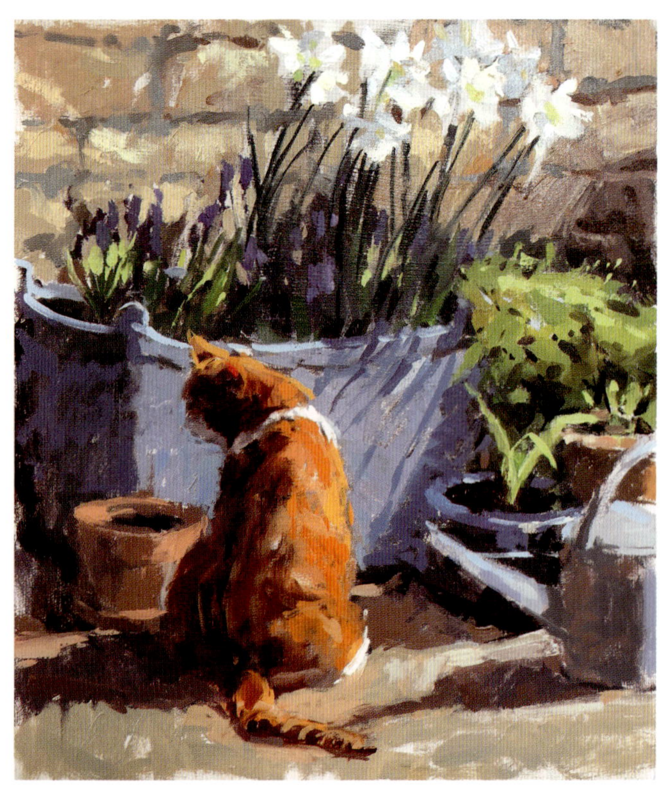

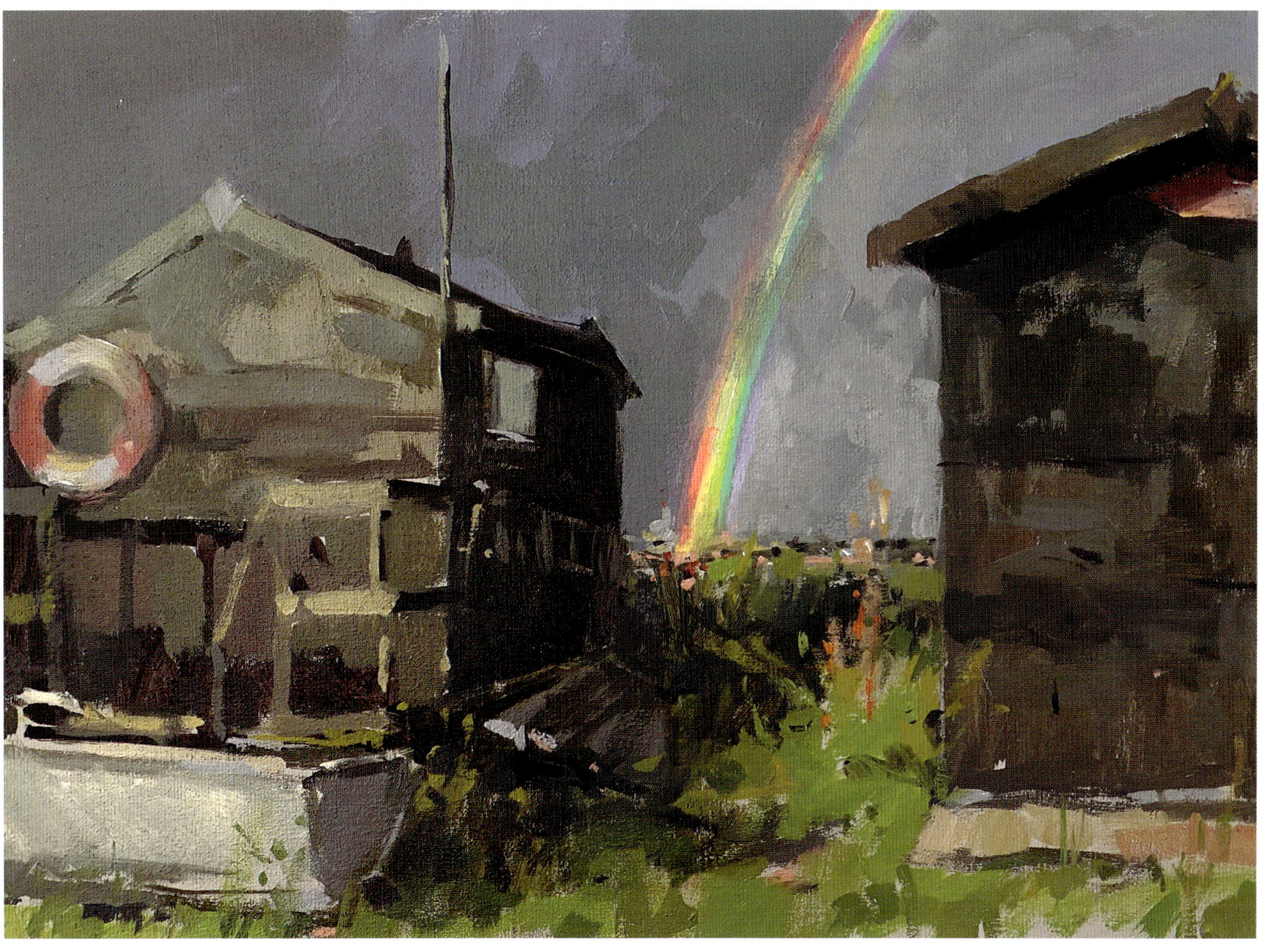

After the Rain, Blackshore Quay
25.5 x 35.5cm (10 x 14in)

*This was one of those serendipitous moments that happen only occasionally. I was
set up in front of this scene with my easel open, when something new and magical
appeared. With no time for second guessing or working out a strategy, I had an
opportunity to paint a rainbow from life.*

*Capturing the rainbow's brightness and vibrancy at the same time as its
transparency and transient nature was a great challenge. I worked first on the
rainbow because I knew it would be the most fleeting aspect of the subject.
De-saturating the colour in the sky (that is, lowering its chroma) was crucial
to enhancing the vivid, high chroma colours of the rainbow. Together with the
realization that the value of the sky wasn't as dark as it seemed to be (comparing
values across the subject and noticing how dark the shadow side of the shed
was in relation to the sky), this led ultimately to the painting's success. To me
this painting represents the sheer joy and happenstance that one can experience
when painting en plein air.*

Think ahead

Here are some useful pointers for dealing with change:

- As far as is possible, predict what's going to change the most dramatically, or the soonest, within your subject.

- Find out which direction is the sun going to move in.

- Are there clouds on their way that threaten to obscure the sun?

- If you're painting a coastal scene, is the tide coming in or going out? If you're attracted to a harbour or beach scene because of the water, do you need to leave working on the buildings and concentrate first on getting an impression of the water and boats?

- When painting animals, figures or vehicles, ask yourself where will they work best for your painting. If you're attracted to the scene because of them, consider from the beginning where they will fit into your composition and how you will get them marked down as soon as possible, in case they move out of sight.

- Work quickly and use larger brushes. When dealing with an especially fast-changing scene, aim to make a broad statement; a fleeting response. Forget about detail.

- Load up your palette with paint. The last thing you want to be doing in a fast-paced painting situation is wasting time finding the right tubes of colour and wrestling with those little lids to restock your palette.

- Look out for characteristic poses. A person or animal may not stay still for long, but if you have the opportunity to observe them for a while before painting, watch out for them repeatedly returning to the same position.

- Make it a game: try to represent the subject with the fewest visual elements you can.

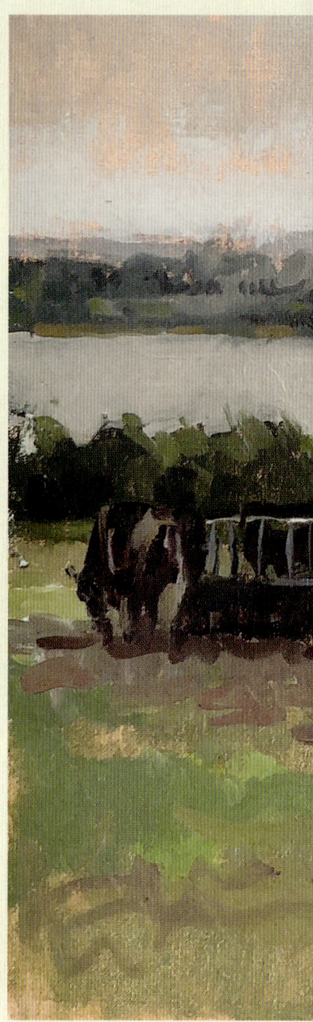

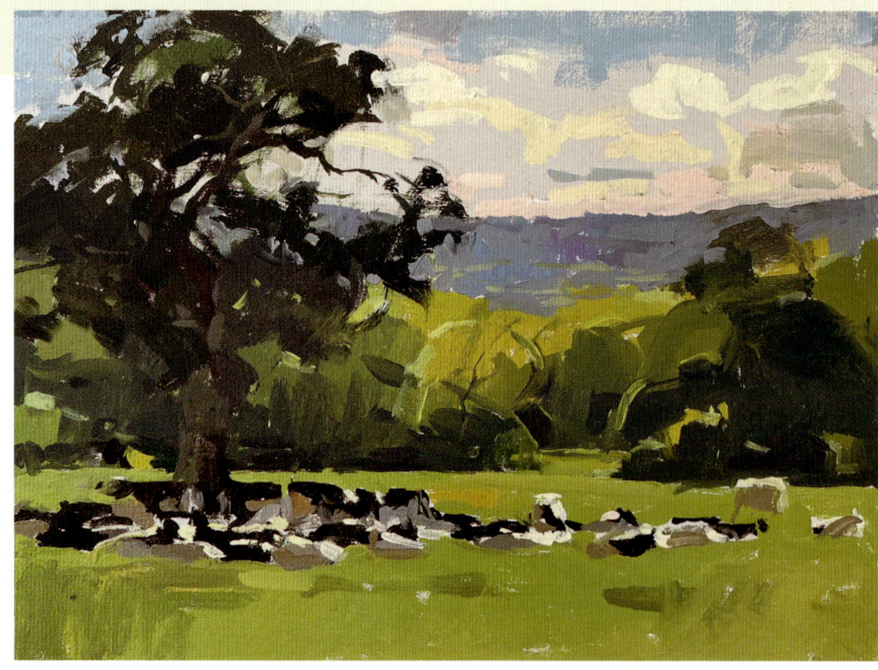

Cows and the Quantocks
30.5 x 23cm (12 x 9in)

A quick study of some distant cows resting under a large tree before being taken away by the farmer for milking. If you're painting animals, always assume that they're going to move. You need to prioritize painting them first.

By the time I finished painting the trees, grass and landscape in this example, the cows were no longer even in the field.

When painting cattle at a distance I screw up my eyes to see them as simple abstract shapes, a light and dark pattern. When they are grouped together like this it is even easier, as I'm looking for just one shape to describe the whole group. I worked quickly with three brushes and three different values; a warm white tint, a dark mixed version of black and a mid-value grey.

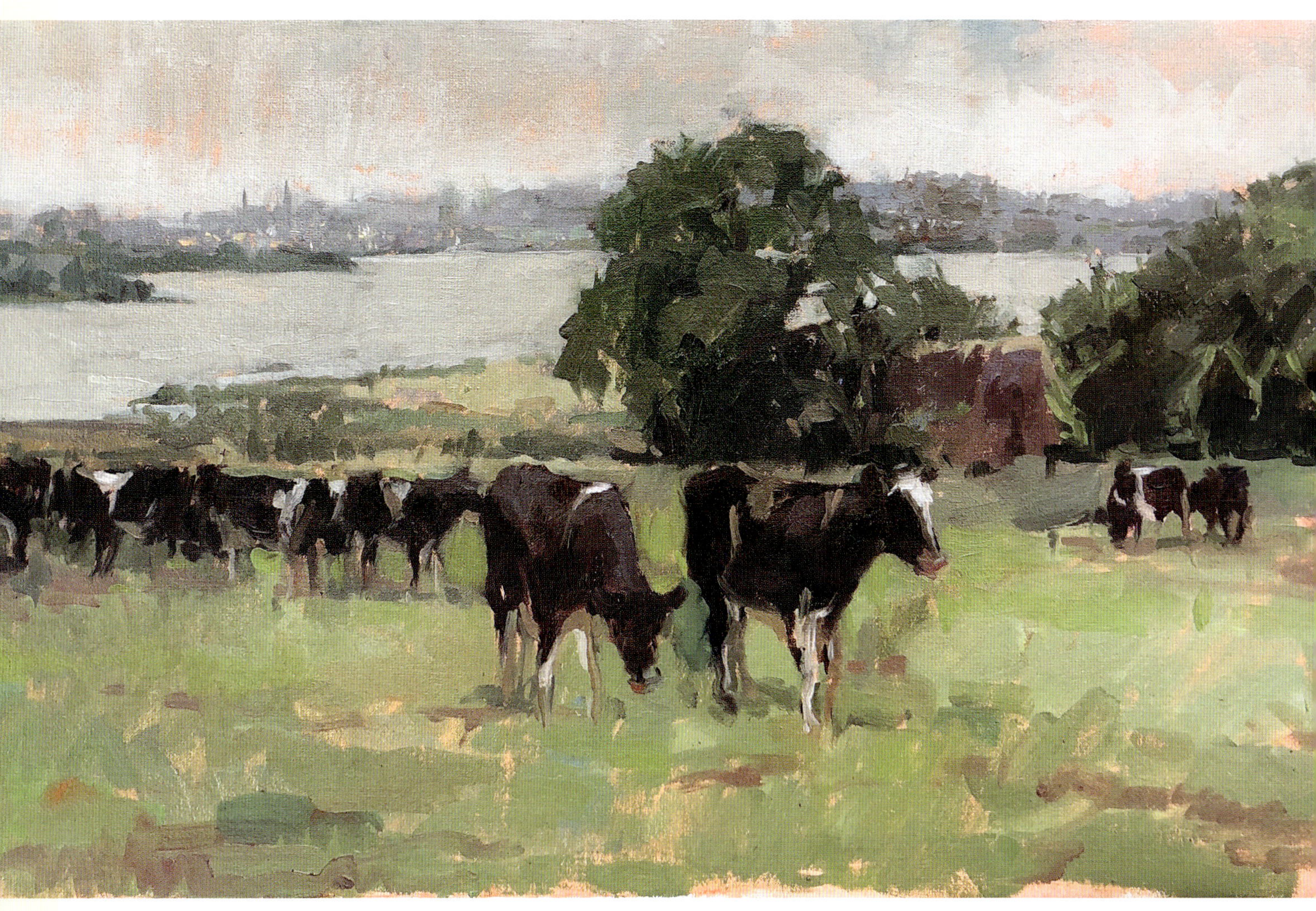

Dairy Herd at Artramon Farm
61 x 30.5cm (24 x 12in)

Another landscape with cows painted from life in Ireland. It's a good idea to spend time sketching cows before you launch into painting them. This helps you to get a basic understanding of their shape, which is especially important if they will play a larger part in your painting, as here.

They were on the move constantly around the field, but I thought if I set up near to the cattle feeder there was a good chance of them returning to that area, which they did. I tackled the group of cows as one dark mass joined together, then added a few indications of legs and white markings.

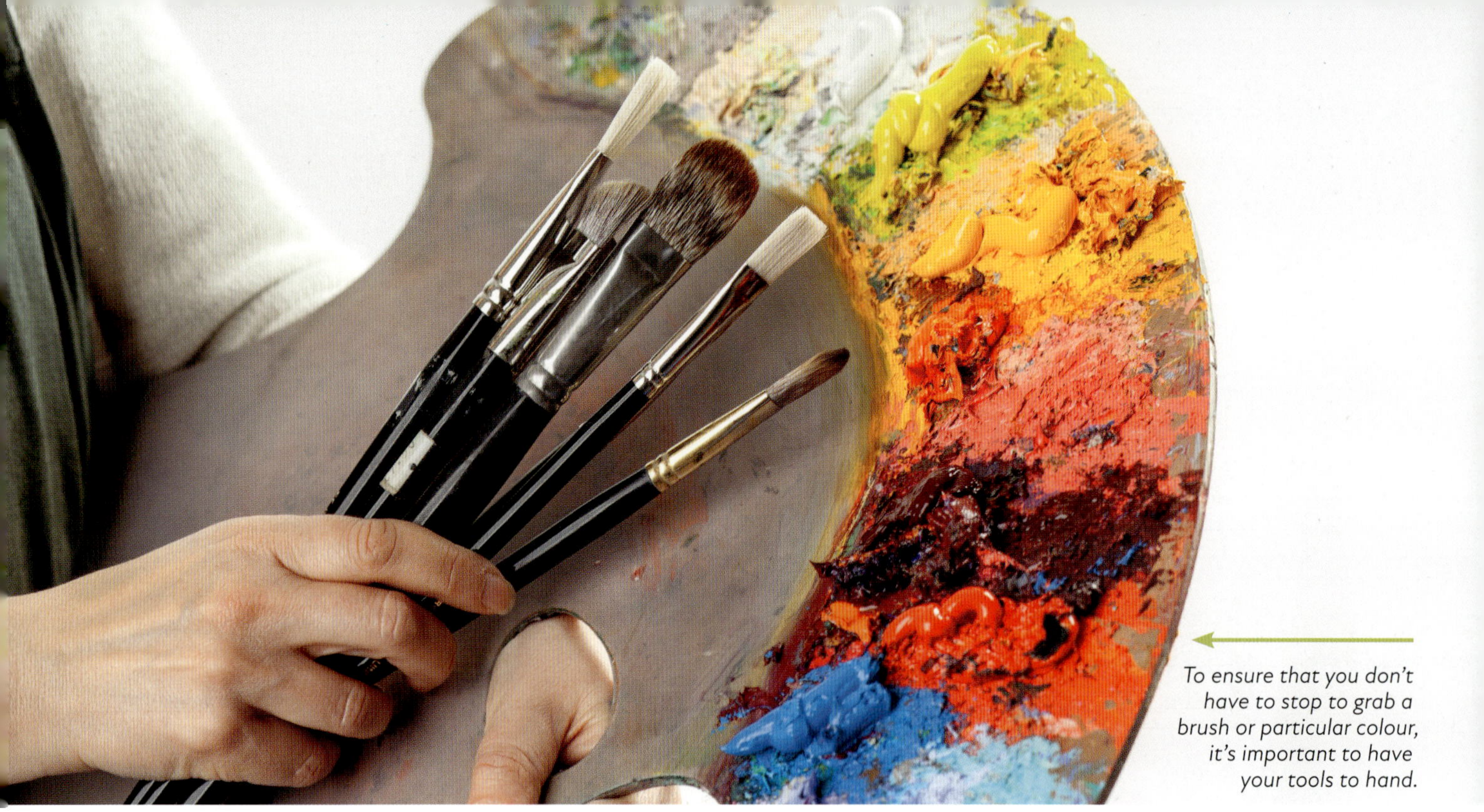

Improving your visual memory

This is a good exercise to practise in the studio to help to develop your short-term visual memory. When we are painting plein air, the scene before us changes so quickly that it helps if we can remember for a short while how things looked. For example, a figure who was only there for a few moments, or how the shadows looked before the cloud passed across the sun. This project also helps you to discriminate between what are the important shapes that you need to get down in the painting and what you can do without.

Finding your focus

To ensure you can put your focus on the structure of the painting, rather than precise hues (or worse, working out where a paint tube is) a little bit of preparation is useful.

- Have plenty of paint squeezed out on the palette and a good handful of brushes to hand.

- Look at the photograph and pre-mix five or six pools of colour which correspond to colours in the subject.

- Choose a panel or piece of primed paper or canvas that has the same overall ratio of proportions as the photograph; or use masking tape to mark out the correct proportions on the surface.

Premixing the correct colours beforehand, with reference to the photograph, ensures that you can concentrate on remembering shapes and form.

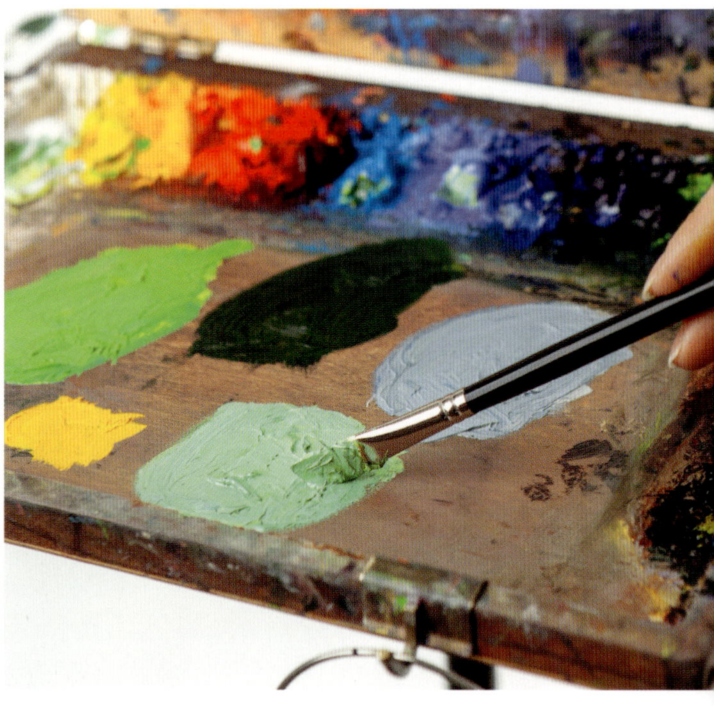

Getting familiar with the scene

Choose a photograph for this exercise that has a variety of interesting and overlapping shapes, but not too many little details. The one below is a good example, but I encourage you to use your own when you repeat the exercise. Study the photograph for a good ten minutes or so, aiming to identify key areas. The following points will give you some particular things to look out for:

- Look for the relative sizes and proportions of the shapes, the angles of lines and the distances between shapes.

- Imagine extending the boundary lines of the shapes outwards. Ask yourself where they would cut across the perimeter edge of the photograph.

- Picture the photograph divided into quarters and see which parts of the subject fit in each of the quarters.

- Half-close your eyes to study the value relationships of the shapes, noticing the overall value scheme and where the darks and lights fall.

- When you think you're ready, turn the photograph away and try the exercise overleaf.

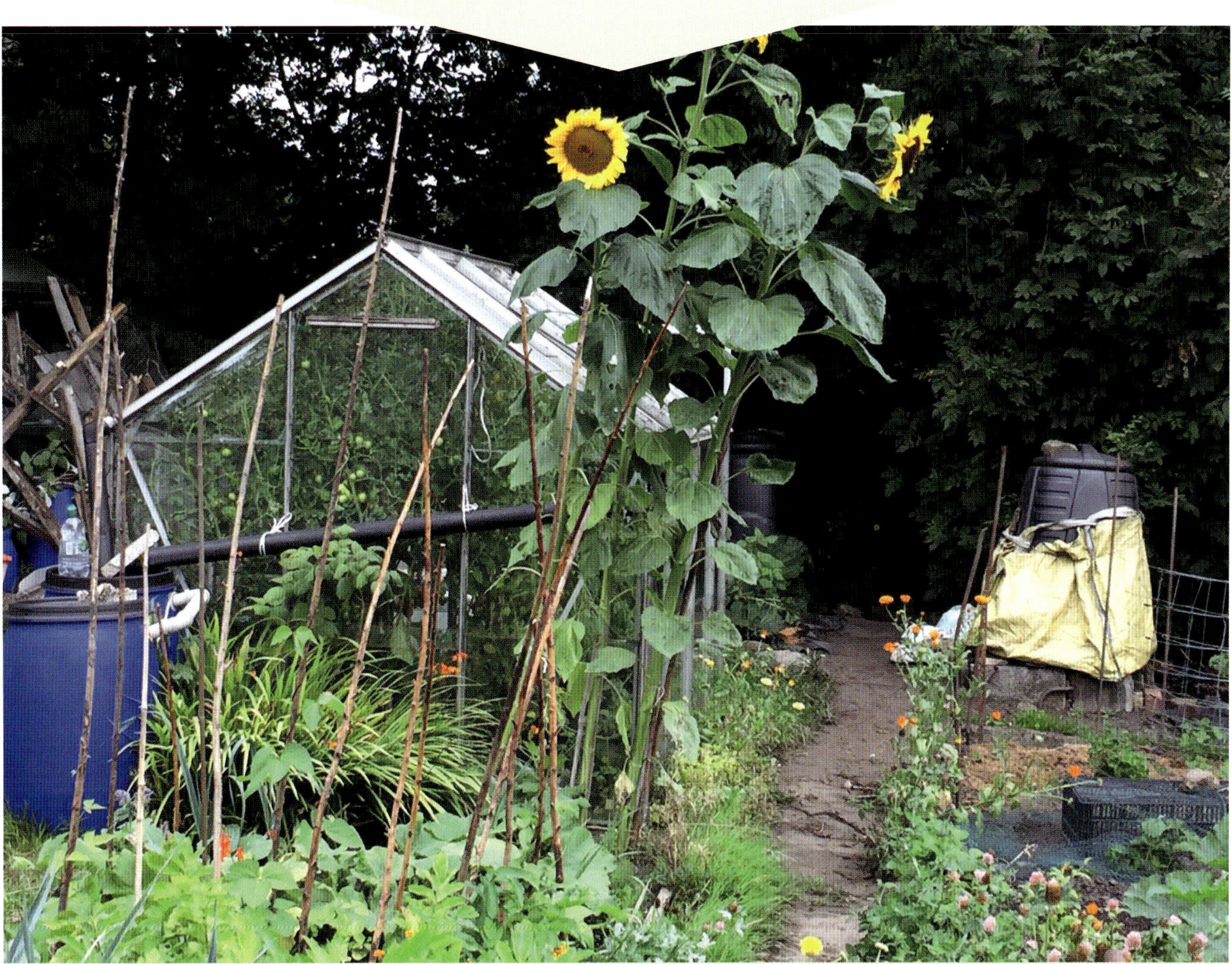

The source photograph

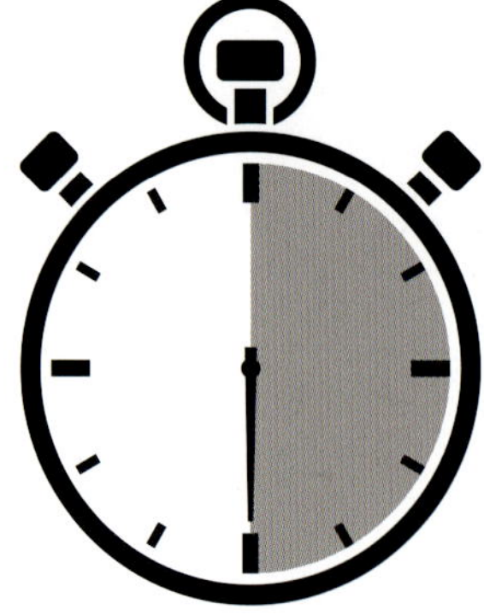

Half-hour painting from memory

With the photograph turned over, start as quickly as you can and resist the temptation to cheat by looking to check anything: just do your best with what you remember.

Work purely from memory, using the pre-mixed colours on your palette. It is hard to try to remember the colours and values as well as the shapes and how they fit together, which is why I suggest mixing pools of the main colours before turning away from the photograph.

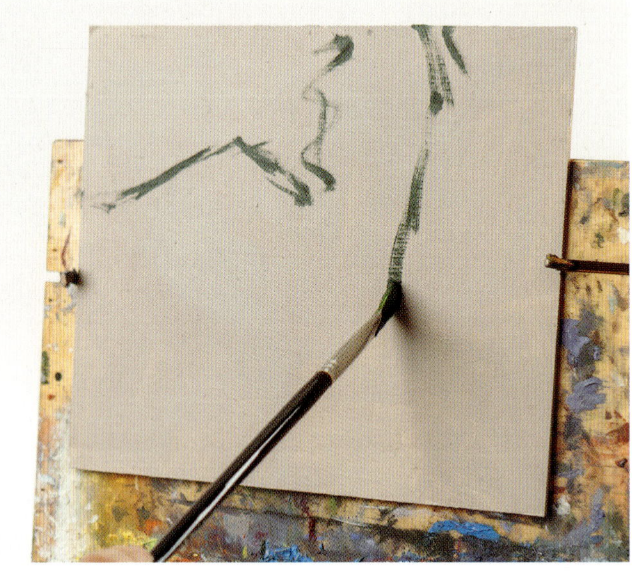

One minute

I start by plotting in lines where I remember the large shapes of the greenhouse and the clump of sunflowers to be.

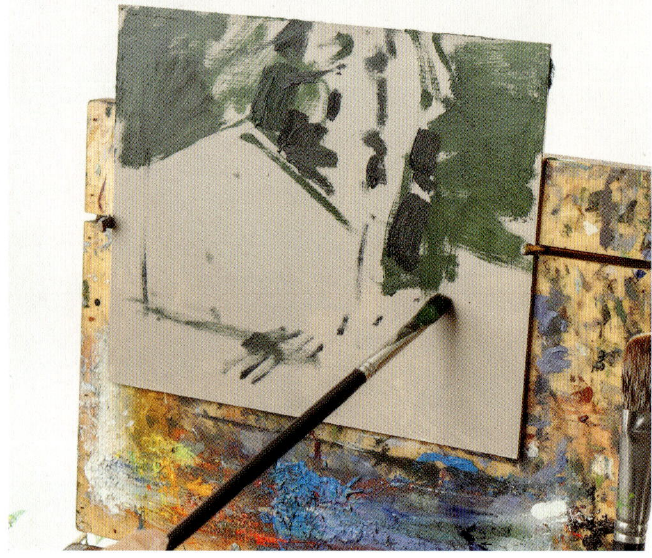

Five minutes

Working quickly, to keep the image in my mind, I then block in a large dark green area in the background.

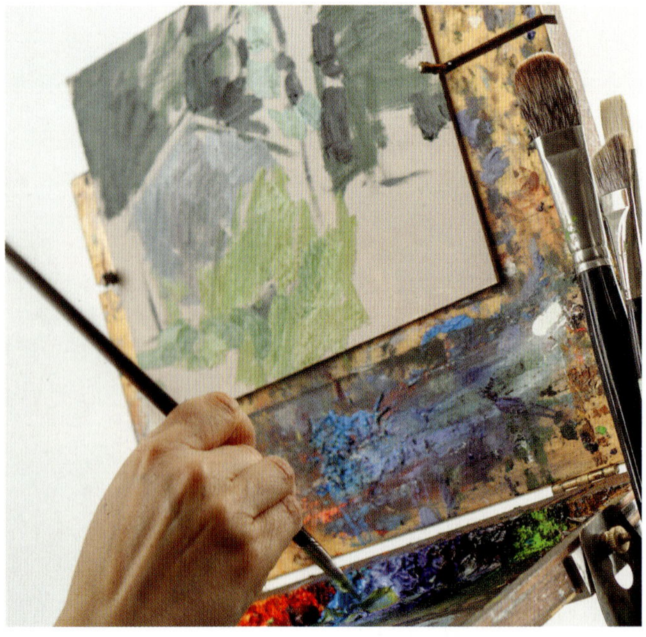

Ten minutes

Next I block in the pre-mixed approximate colour for the foreground foliage and grass, and a grey mix for the greenhouse glass.

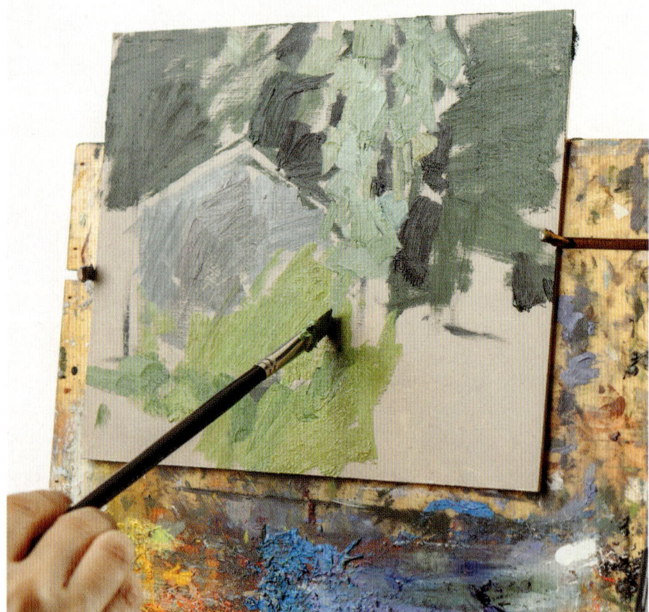

Twenty minutes

I adjust the green colour for painting in the leaves of the sunflowers, judging those to be a bluer-green with some added white.

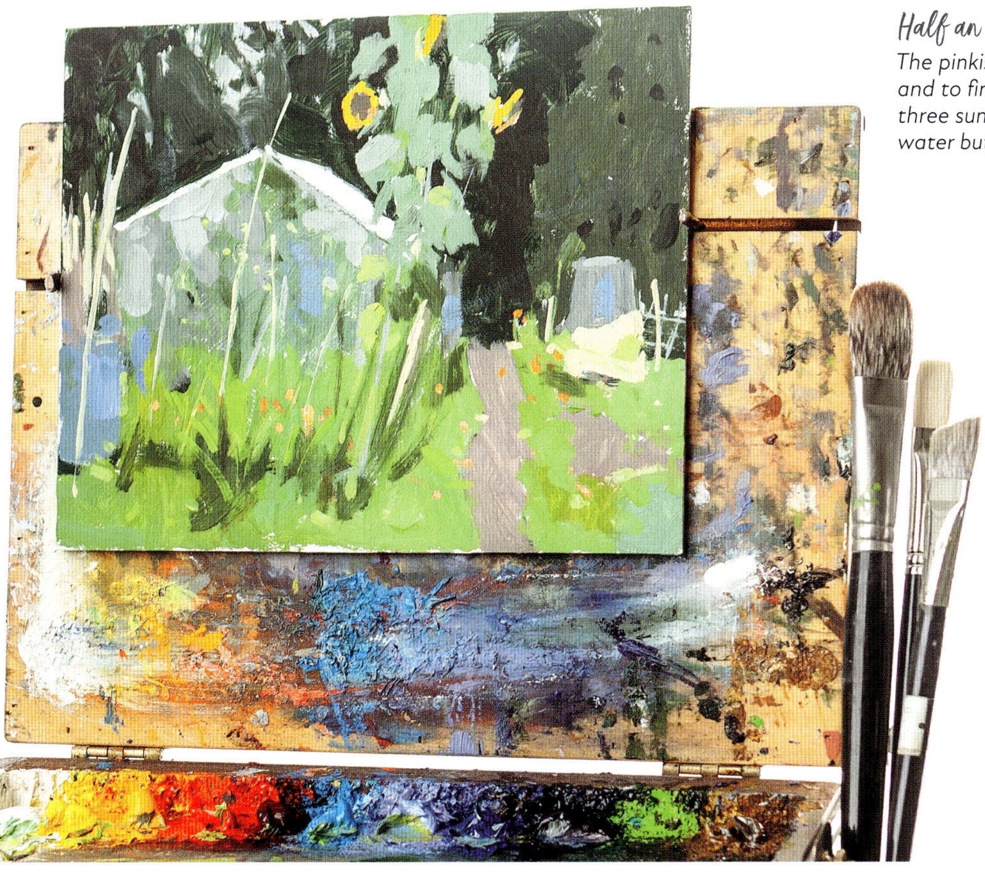

Half an hour
The pinkish soil of the path goes in next;
and to finish it's the smaller details: the
three sunflower heads, the canes and the
water butts.

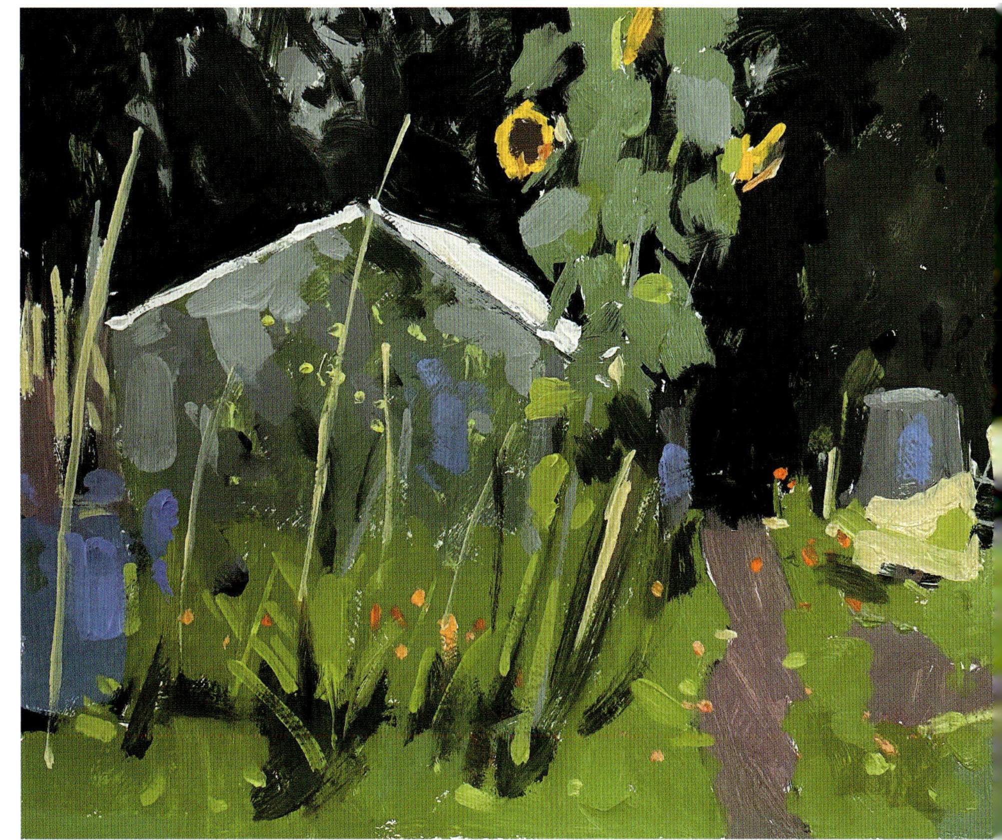

The finished painting
It's really interesting to compare the
resulting painting with the photograph.
What did you leave out or not notice? Did
you manage to make an overall impression
of the whole subject or did you have to
leave unknown blank areas?

The more you practise this exercise, the
easier it will become. It will help to train
your short-term visual memory and also
how to select the important elements
to take from a scene to make a fast
impression – a very useful skill when
working outdoors.

Painting against the clock

Going hand-in-hand with developing a good short-term visual memory, learning to paint faster will help to develop your plein air skills further. Everything about your subject is changing before your eyes, so it makes good sense to learn how to be decisive and get down the essential elements of a composition quickly and with the minimum of fuss.

To practise, work with a timer and set yourself challenges of different lengths. How much information can you get down in twenty minutes? How about an hour? 'Twenty minutes?' you say, 'Don't be ridiculous'. Yet there's method to my madness and it can be done. A strictly timed painting session forces you to make important decisions about the large shapes and key elements which make up your subject. Producing lots of small paintings in quick succession also gives you plenty of new compositional ideas.

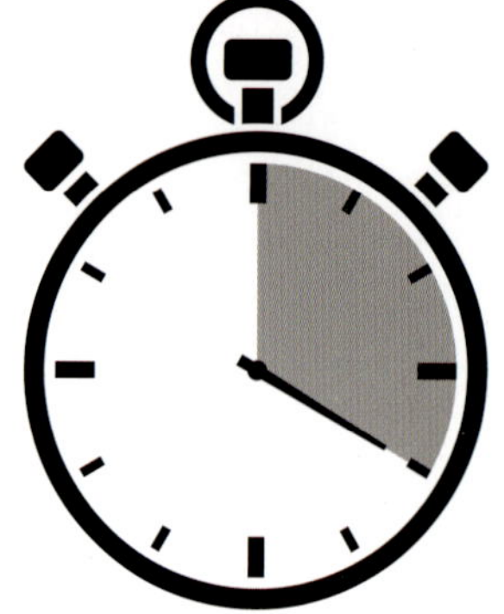

Twenty-minute paintings

You will need lots of juicy paint on your palette, a good choice of large brushes and a small panel. At first you may struggle if you're not used to working at this pace, but just try to get the whole board covered and not to have any expectations of the end result.

You may find these quick little paintings have a freshness that comes with bold brushmarks that you would most likely lose if you had more time to tweak them.

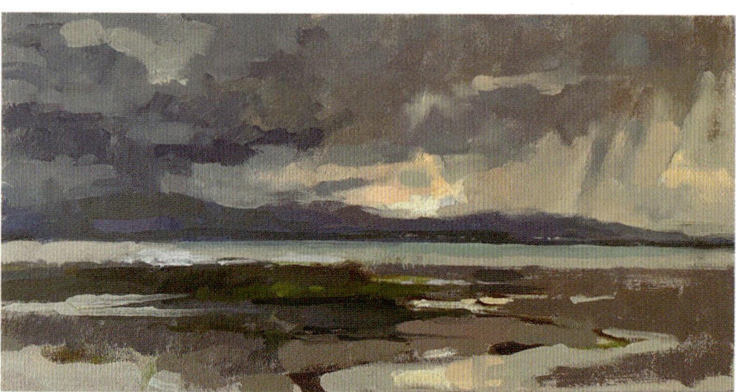

Evening, Morecambe Bay
30.5 x 15cm (12 x 6in)

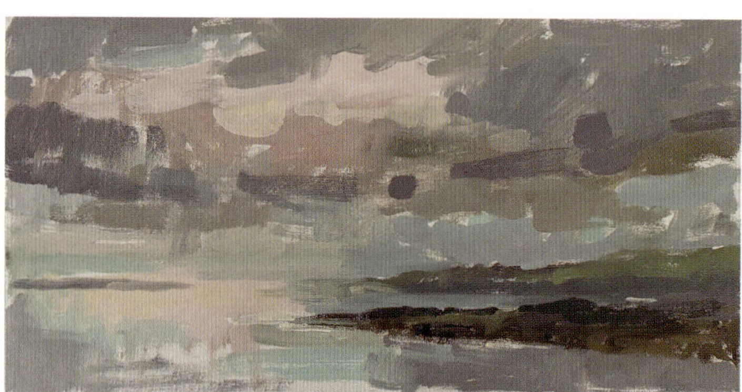

Evening sky, Appledore
30.5 x 15cm (12 x 6in)

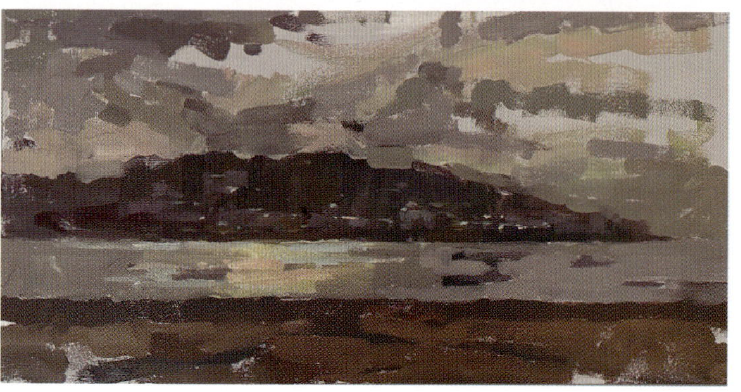

Towards Appledore, Evening Light
30.5 x 15cm (12 x 6in)

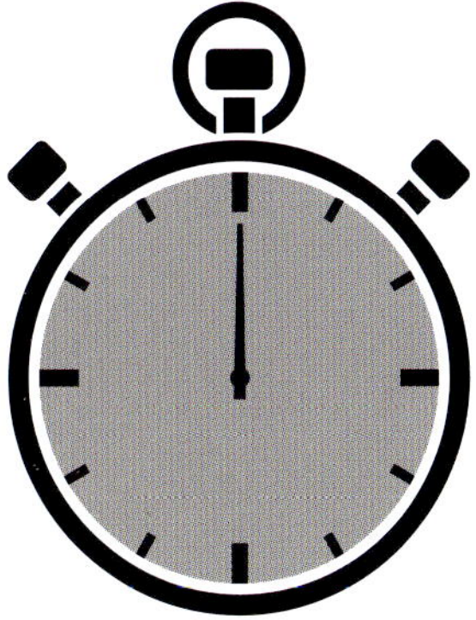

One-hour paintings

After a little practice, you will find that painting under time pressure does get easier – and after you've been doing plenty of twenty-minute paintings, an hour-long session will feel like a luxury.

Start with big shapes and swiftly get some paint on every area of the board. You can then refine the colours where needed and put down smaller shapes. Remember, paint the watermelon before the seeds, the dog before the fleas.

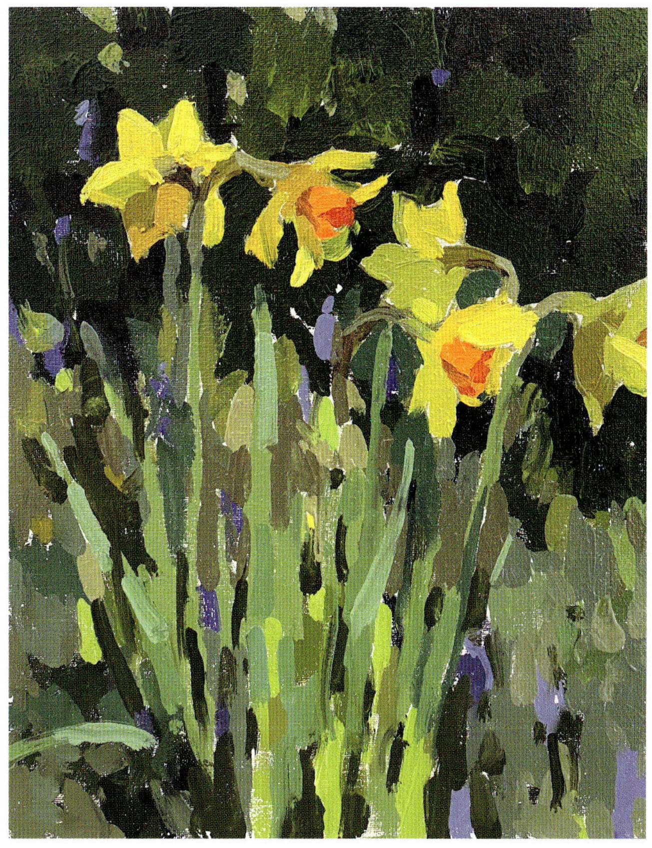

Daffodils and Muscari
15 x 20cm (6 x 8in)

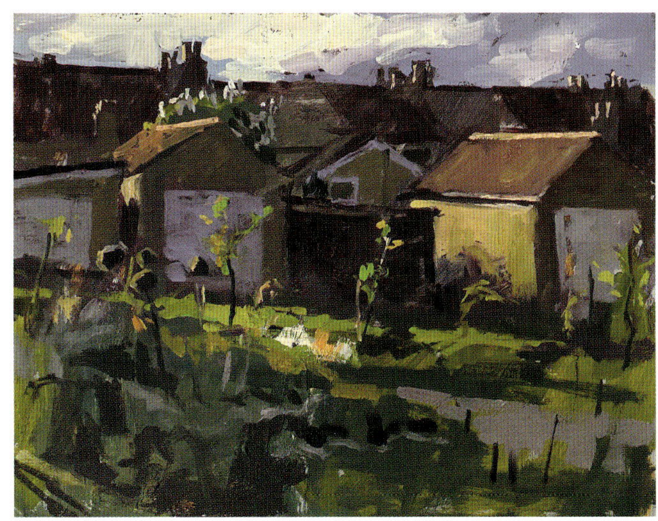

Evening Light, Garages in Bath
30.5 x 23cm (12 x 9in)

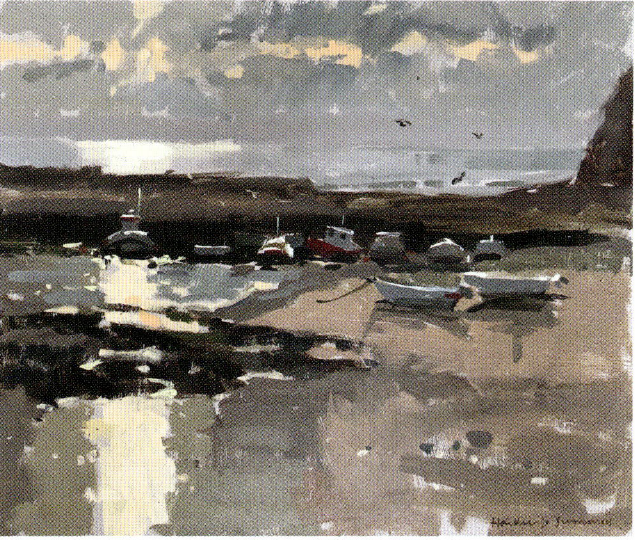

First Light in the Harbour, Staithes
25.5 x 20cm (10 x 8in)

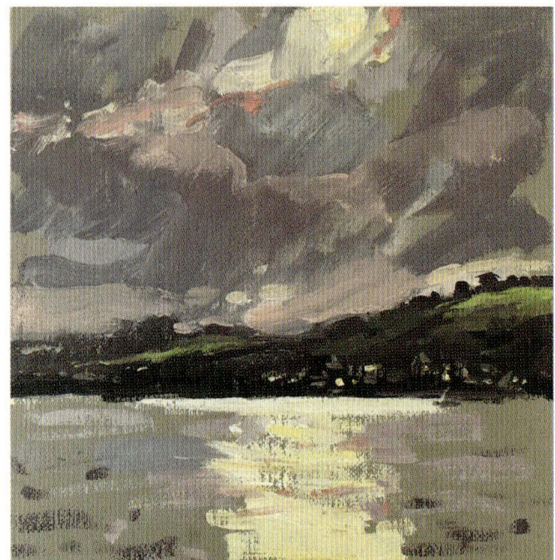

Number one 7.10–7.35am

Sunrise at Appledore. The clouds were moving fast, and the sunlight bouncing off the water. I got straight to work. It was invigorating trying to catch the dazzle on the water and the colours in the sky.

Number two 7.45–8.05am

It started raining, but fortunately I was standing under a bus shelter. I stayed exactly where I was but looked slightly to the left. The colour drained away and all became soft and grey. After about twenty minutes the rain was so heavy it was hammering on the roof of the shelter and bouncing up from the road. Why had I left my umbrella at the cottage? I was trapped here for a little while waiting for it to stop so that I could go back for breakfast!

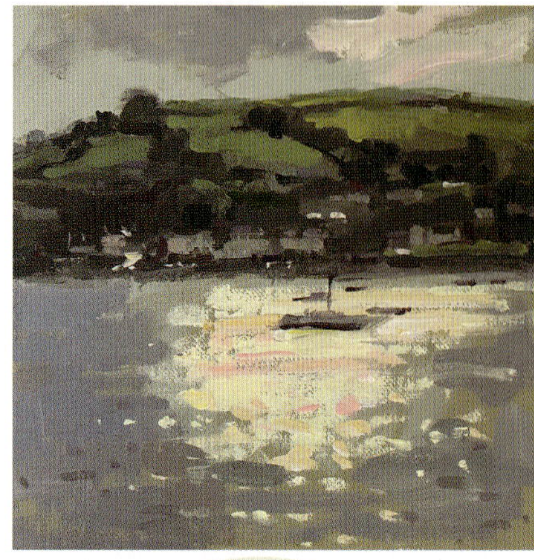

Number three 9.15–10.00am

After breakfast I returned to the bus shelter to see a beautiful band of light striking the water and hitting some of the rooftops in the village across the water. It was lovely to see the greens back in the hills.

Ten paintings in one day

There are other ways to pit yourself against the clock. I decided to set myself a challenge to paint ten paintings in one day, to really force myself into decisive action, and not to have the opportunity to overwork. I chose a day in May because of the longer daylight hours, and prepared ten boards of the same shape and size, 20.5 x 20.5cm (8 x 8in).

I squeezed plenty of paint out on my palette, began at 7 o'clock in the morning and ended with a nocturne at 10 o'clock at night. I used around twenty-five brushes during the day as I didn't stop to clean them. Although it sounds somewhat arduous – and I admit it was pretty tiring – I did make sure to take time out during the day to stop for meals. You can see here how I got on...

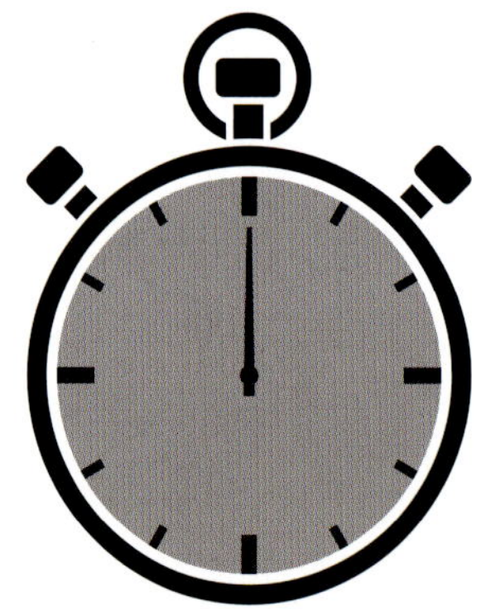

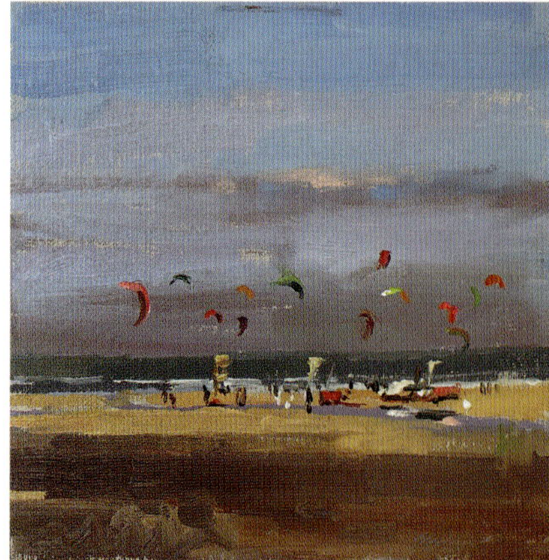

Number seven 3.15–4.00pm

For this one I climbed back over the ridge and down onto the beach – back in the wind again! I had spotted the kite surfers when I first arrived so was glad to have a chance to capture them. Usually I would only have painted one subject over three hours so it was thrilling to be able to take home three different studies.

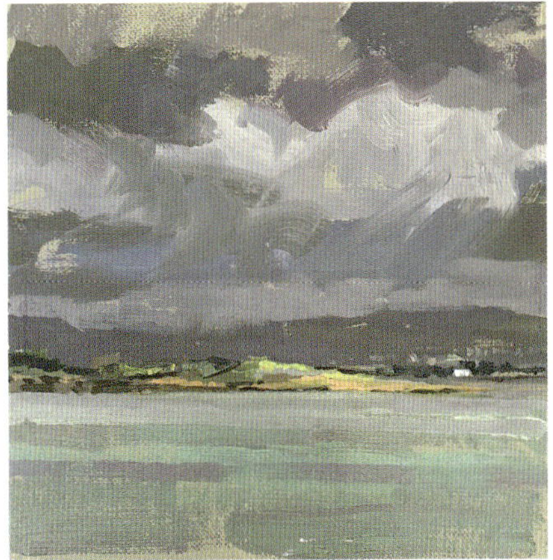

Number four 10.30–11.15am

A coffee break and another rain shower, and lots of thick clouds were swirling and gathering. Still looking from the bus shelter, a streak of light on a distant sand bank caught my eye, and the water changed to turquoise. I had really enjoyed finding different views from the bus shelter, but with four paintings under my belt I felt it was time to move on.

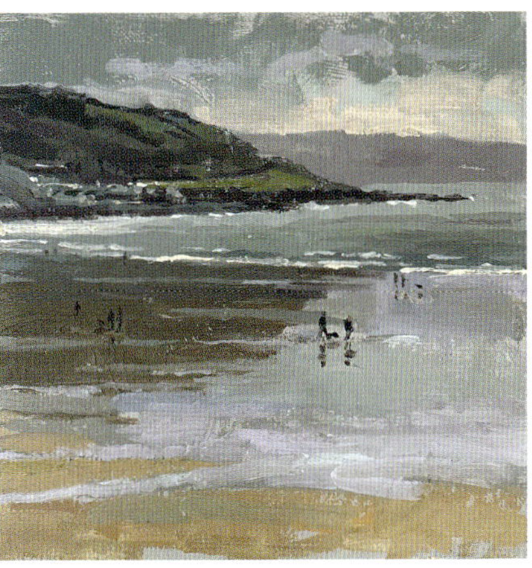

Number five 12.30–1.20pm

In the afternoon I set up to paint a short drive away at Westward Ho! From the top of the pebble ridge I had amazing views all round, but really strong wind. The tide was going out so I painted the wet sand and reflections, and added a few figures and dogs on the beach as I spotted them.

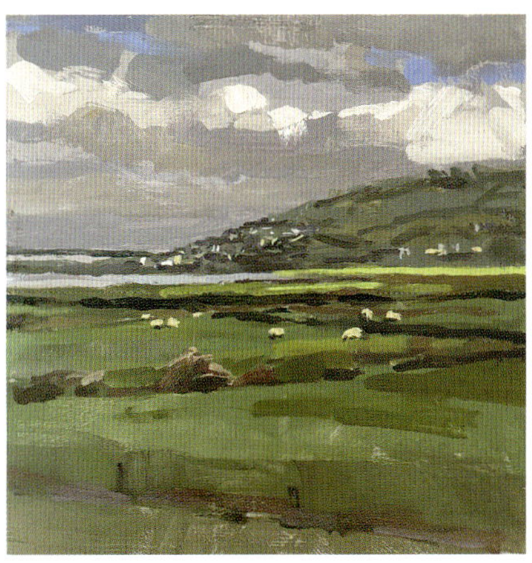

Number six 1.45–2.50pm

I needed a rest from the wind so I came halfway down the pebble ridge looking inland. The clouds were beautiful and there were gaps of blue sky. I enjoyed the change of view to fields and sheep.

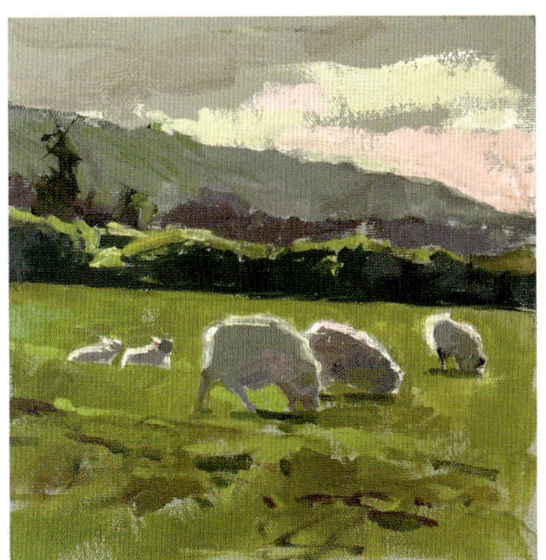

Number eight 5.15–6.00pm

I decided to head back towards Appledore and spotted these sheep and lambs in a field by the side of the road. The contre-jour light was wonderful, and this was an exhilarating one.

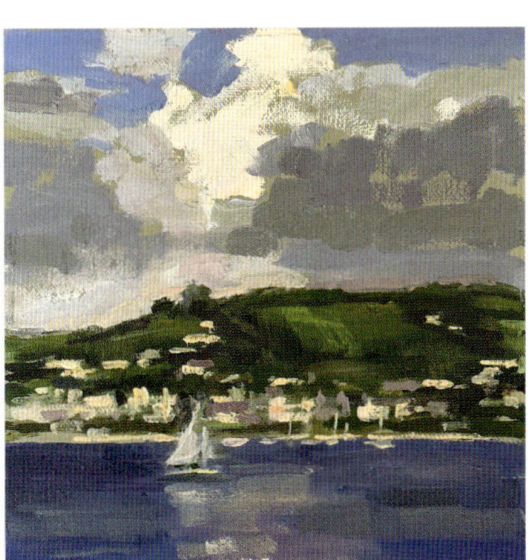

Number nine 7.45–8.45pm

After a good meal I decided it would be best to paint the last two where I started the day, from the bus shelter. The golden evening light seemed to heighten the colours – the sea in particular now appeared a deep, dark, intense blue. The houses in the distance were now warmly lit by the setting sun.

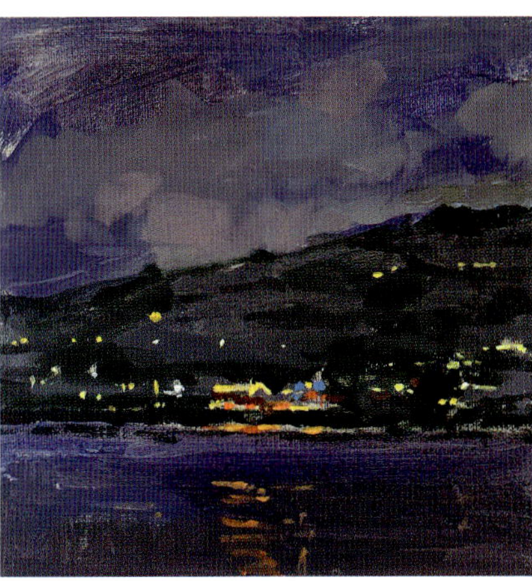

Number ten 9.15–10.00pm

Finally, the last one at the end of a long day. A nocturne looking across the estuary, towards the lights of Instow village.

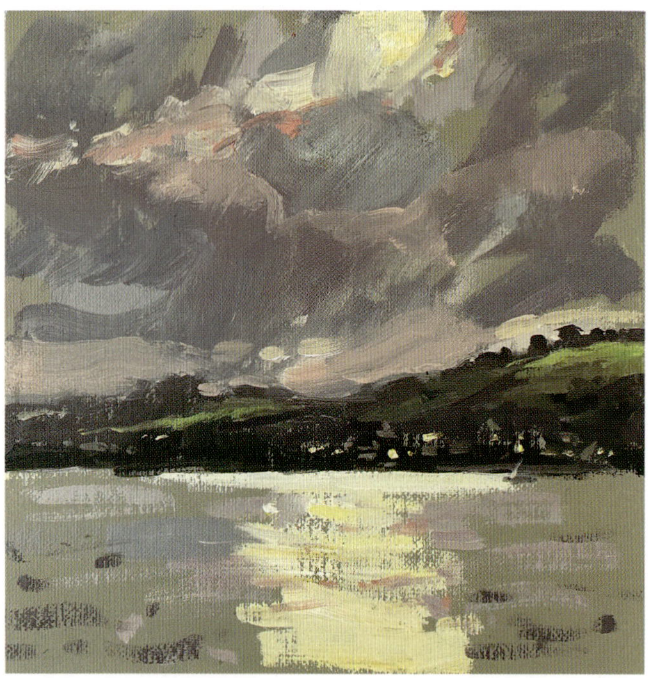

Lessons from the day

I feel as though I learnt a lot in undertaking painting ten pictures in a day. Even after finishing the first painting, I was aware that I probably wouldn't have chosen to paint from this viewpoint if I hadn't been keen not to waste time walking around. This painting – which I was really pleased with – wouldn't have existed.

A funny thing happens when you get into the flow of painting after painting: you become aware of subjects everywhere. It's like your eyes have been opened to the possibilities. I find it helpful to stay in the same spot and just change your viewpoint, or to paint the same scene as the light changes throughout the day.

For my project day I painted in only three places so as not to waste much time packing up and moving around. It was really interesting to start and end the day in the same place. A bus shelter in Devon became my plein air studio for the day, as the weather changed from sunshine to heavy rain and back again.

The first and the last paintings of the day. It was significant to begin and end in the same place, looking across the water from Appledore to Instow. The change of light – from the early morning sunlight bouncing off the water to the dark nocturne, with the artificial lights in the buildings taking precedence – gives these two paintings of the same spot a completely different atmosphere.

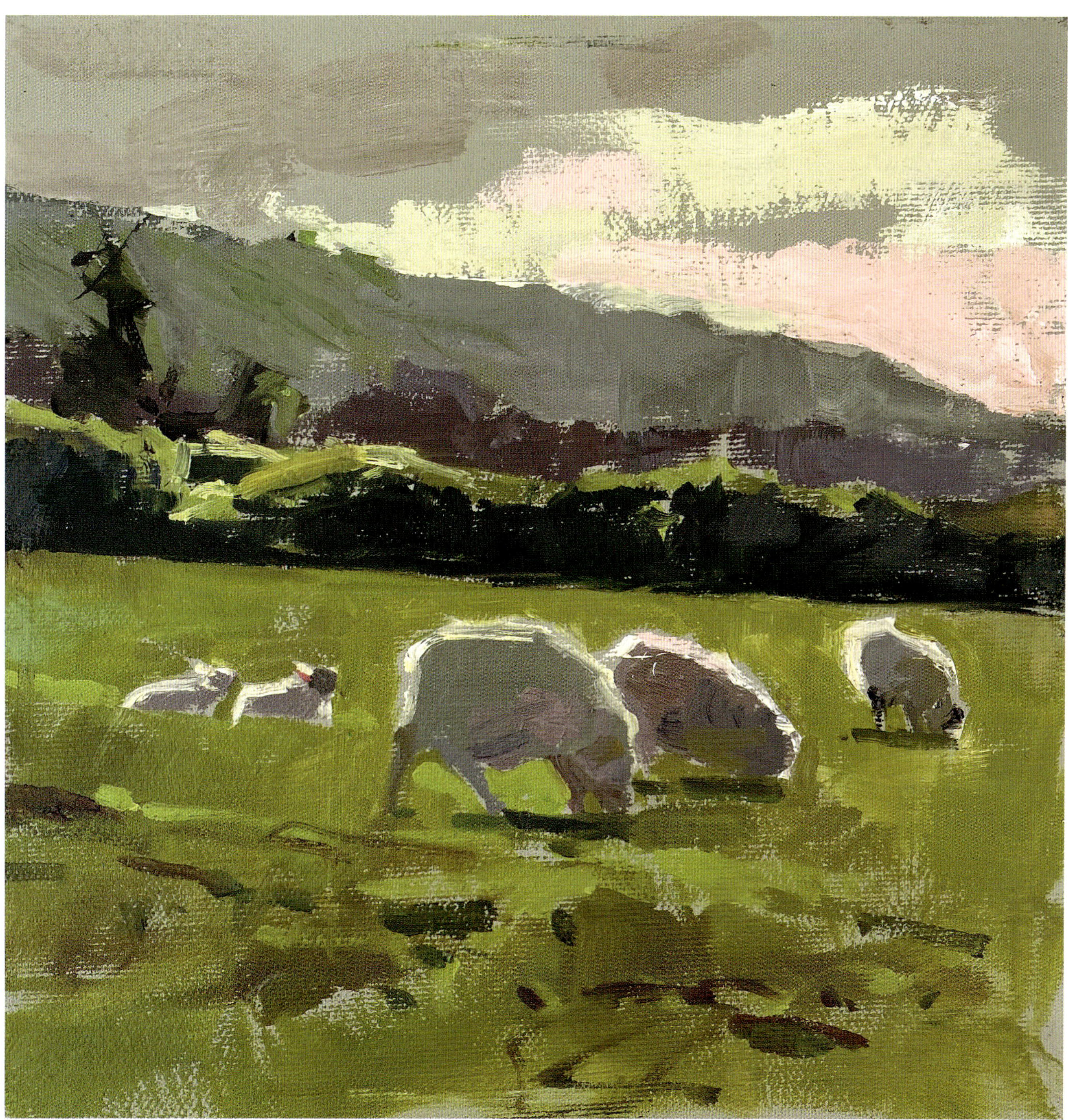

Number Eight
20 x 20cm (8 x 8in)

If I had to pick a favourite from the day this would be it, so much fun to paint. I'm very glad I started with the sheep and painted the rest around them, as they soon moved further away.

Slowing down: painting over multiple sessions

We've spoken a lot about the importance of working quickly en plein air to meet the challenges of the moving sun and the constantly changing subject. This can be very frustrating to deal with, especially if you're not a fast painter and would prefer a slower pace of working. Perhaps you're still getting to grips with colour mixing or are new to using oil paints and this is hindering your ability to get the painting down quickly enough. One way around this is to work on the same painting over multiple sessions.

I don't do a lot of this myself but on those rare occasions I have really enjoyed coming back to the motif with a half-painting already on the canvas. It's such a relaxing feeling to arrive refreshed and raring to go with the groundwork already in place.

Fishing Cottage, Lympstone
30.5 x 30.5cm (12 x 12in)

This was painted over two afternoon sessions in a key window of time when the sun was hitting the front of the cottage, but the shadows cast by the buildings opposite hadn't yet started creeping up onto the cottage and boat shed.

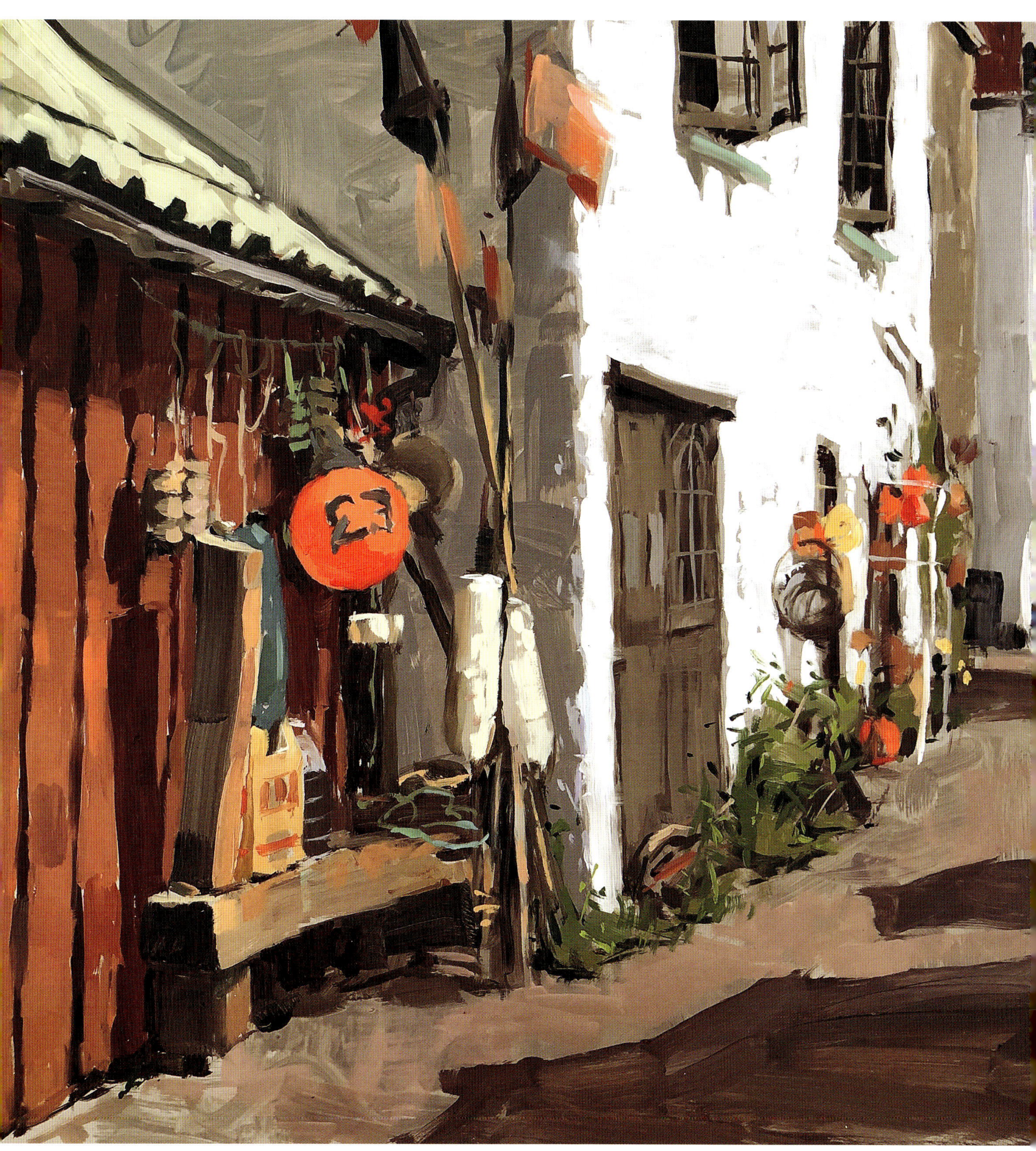

Why take the multiple session approach?

There are a number of advantages to working on a piece over a number of painting sessions:

- It gives you an opportunity to work on a larger piece that you would not usually be able to complete in a single two- or three-hour session.

- You can experiment with building up an oil painting using layers of paint, glazing or scumbling while still being able to work from life.

- It gives you a chance to tackle something more ambitious than you normally would, such as an outdoor portrait or busy street scene.

- You prefer a slower pace or more methodical approach, perhaps breaking up three painting sessions into first drawing, then a value underpainting and finally colour.

- When painting an architectural subject and you wish to include lots of figures, you will find it much easier to work in layers, allowing the surface to dry between each. You might tackle the structures first, for example, and use subsequent sessions for placing figures within the composition.

- Having time with the painting away from the subject in between painting sessions allows you critical thinking time and an opportunity to spot drawing errors.

- Like me, you may aim to have every colour and value shape nailed during the first session, and use a follow-up stint for refining and checking what you have and adding a few details.

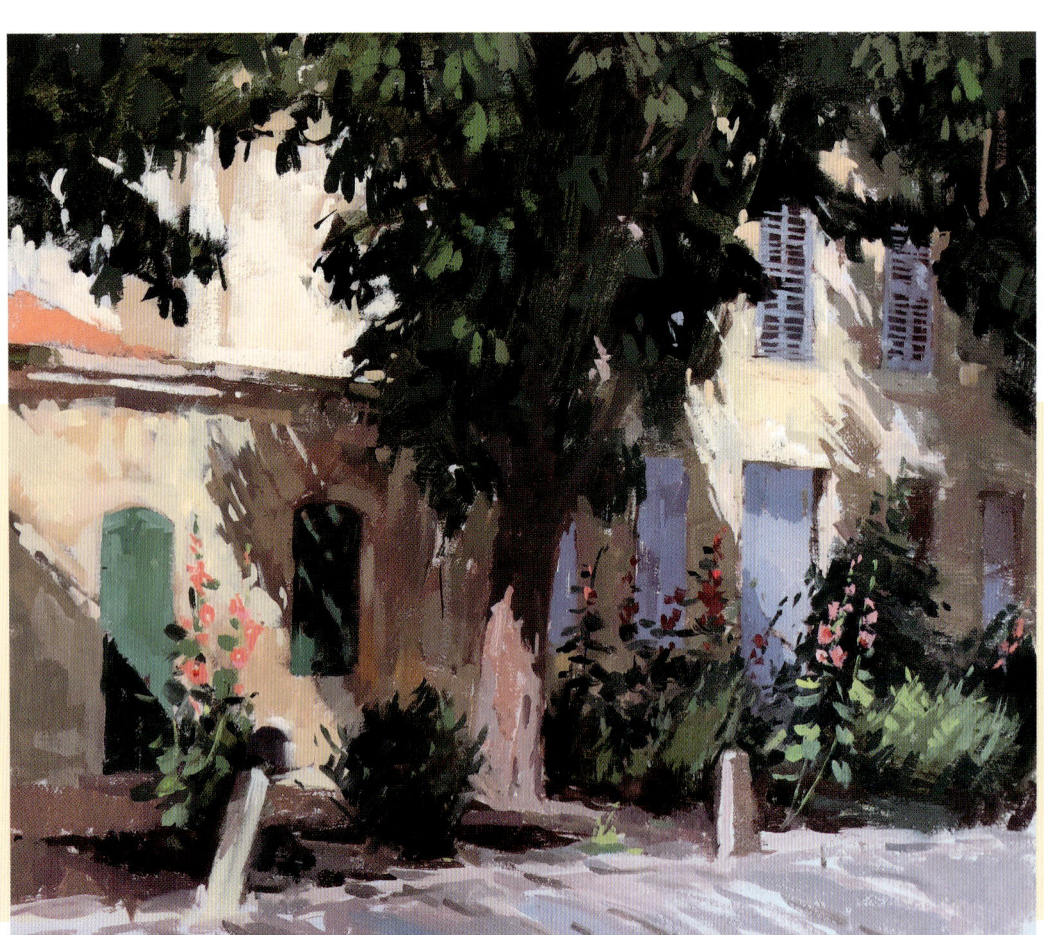

Horse Chestnut Shadows at Saint-Martin-de-Ré
40.5 x 30.5cm (16 x 12in)

During a painting trip to Île de Ré, this one was painted over two sessions to ensure the cast shadows from the horse chestnut trees were in the same place.

Snow-Covered Path at the Allotments

We don't get many days of snow where I live, but on this occasion the snow came with a quite violent storm they named 'the Beast from the East'. Blizzards, strong winds and bitter cold made painting conditions difficult. I struggled with this one for as long as I could but eventually had to admit defeat.

I thought that I might finish it in the studio at some point but never got around to touching it. Two years later, on another snowy day, I had the chance to take it back. Funnily enough, apart from the snow having drifted in from a different direction, the scene hadn't changed at all in the intervening years. The cold and wind weren't as extreme this time, so I had a much more enjoyable time working on it again.

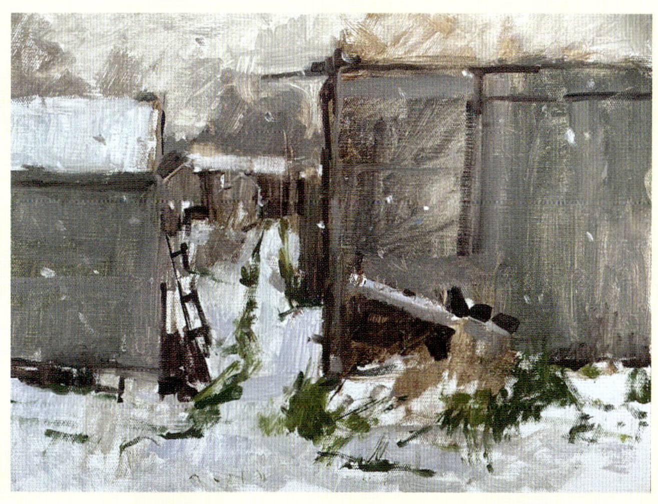

After the first session.

The finished painting – completed two years later.

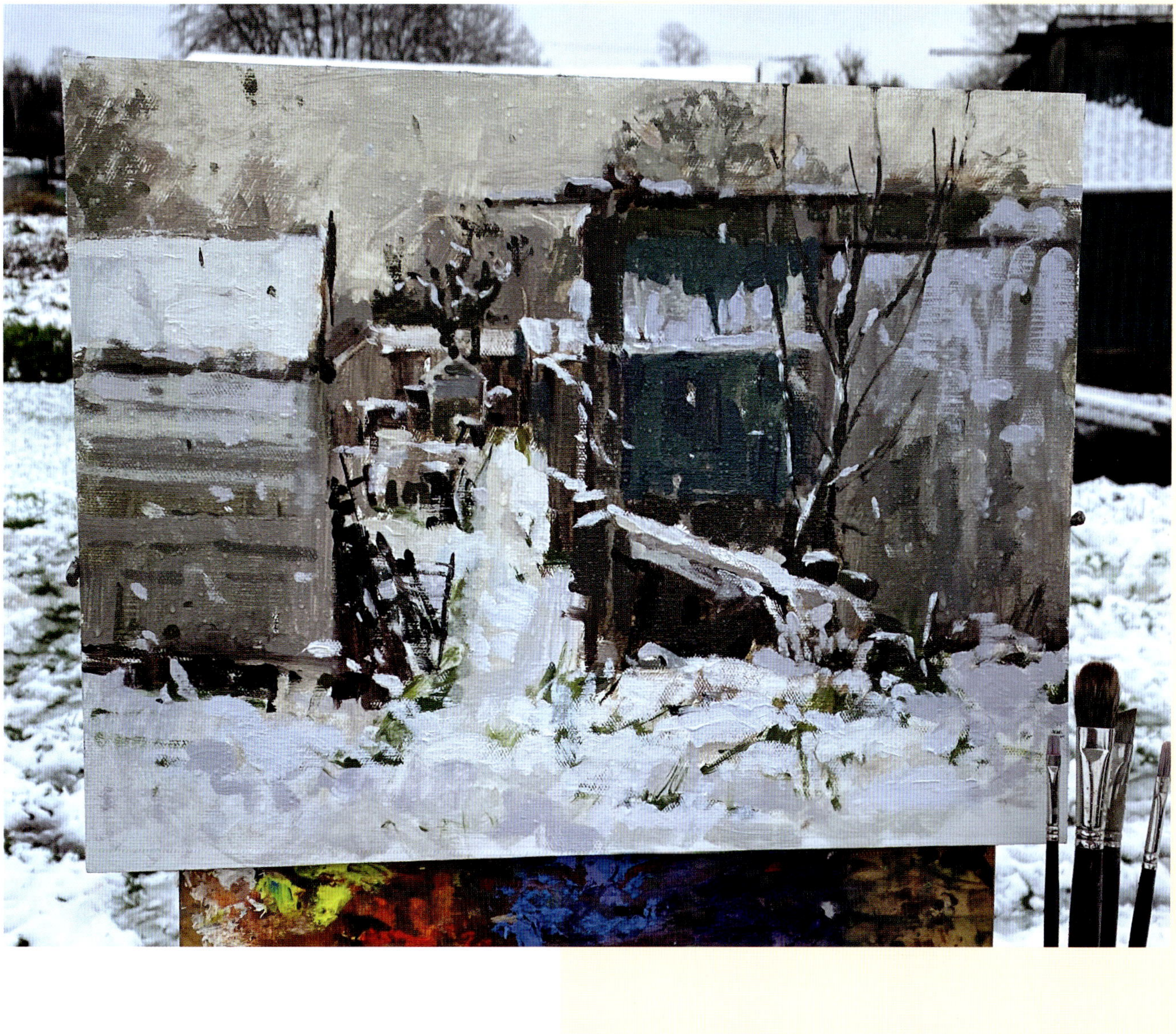

What to do between sessions

Here are a couple of ideas you might want to try in between painting sessions on a piece:

- You can scrape back the surface with a palette knife or use a crumpled-up paper towel to break up edges and shapes. This can create really interesting marks and give variety to your edges. Any strong edges can easily be reintroduced at your next session.

- Try looking at the painting in a mirror to help spot drawing mistakes – the new point of view will quickly highlight anything that has become familiar.

- You may choose to blot the painting when back in the studio. This will make it an easier surface to work on when it's dry, without any ridges of paint. Take a clean piece of newsprint paper, lightly press it down over the whole surface of the painting and then lift it off carefully. It removes excess paint and oil but you still see where everything is, like a slightly ghostly version. It has a pleasing effect of softening what you have, giving a uniform and workable surface. This method is often known as 'tonking' after Henry Tonks, a former professor of fine art at the Slade School of Art.

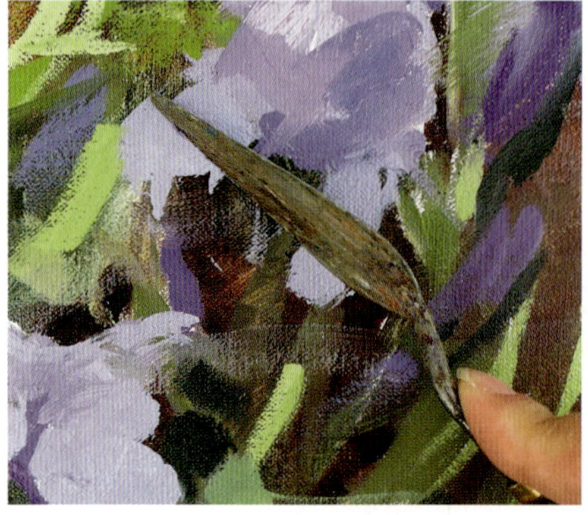

Scraping back by drawing the edge of a palette knife over the surface.

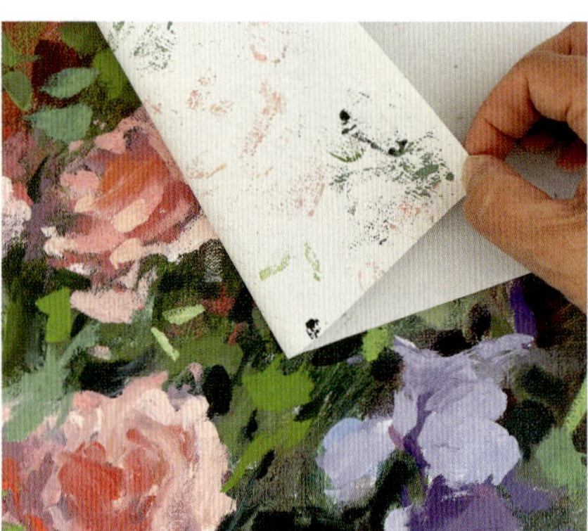

Tonking softens the surface while removing excess paint and oil.

Tip and ideas

Here are a few things to think about if you're going to try multiple sessions on the same painting:

Consistency Aim for the same time of day and weather conditions each time. You want the subject and conditions to be as similar as they can be for each painting session. Choose your times of working accordingly.

Dedicate a session to drawing and notes Knowing that you'll have the opportunity to return, you can take more time and care getting the drawing right. You might notice you could do with a particular colour for this painting that you don't usually carry – magenta for pink flowers, for example – and an early drawing session allows you to make a note to bring it with you next time.

Pause for thought After the first session you should spend time looking at the painting in the studio and considering where you'd like to take it. Ask yourself if there are any changes you need to make to the drawing or any parts of the subject that you need to pay better attention to when you're next on site.

Don't leave it too long Minimize the time gap in between visits to help avoid big changes – and be prepared to return to a scene to find it changed in ways you hadn't expected. (This can be a change for the better, of course!)

Keep the best parts Be careful not to lose all the fresh direct marks you made previously with subsequent overworking. Remember the areas that you decided needed more attention when you had a critical look in the studio. Work on these, leaving well alone the parts which are already satisfactory.

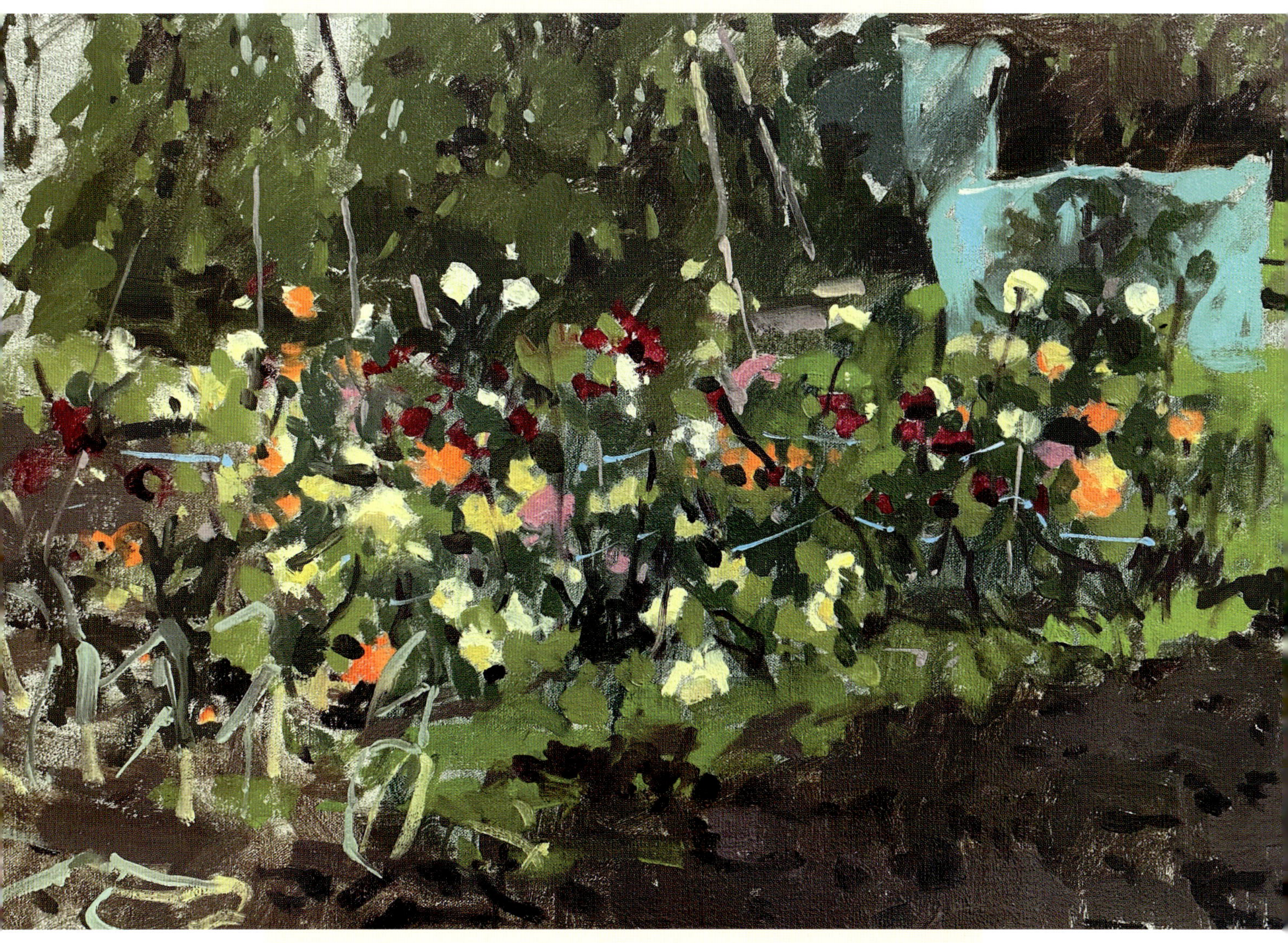

Dahlias at the Allotments
51 x 25.5cm (20 x 10in)

I started this larger painting on canvas with the intention of painting it over two sessions. I got a lot accomplished in the first session, but was really pleased that I had planned to return to the location. I made a note to look more particularly at certain areas in the background, and some leeks which I spotted growing in the foreground.

Looking forward to the second session already, I decided it was going to be really enjoyable to take my time finishing off the painting. Six days later I had my chance and I walked over to the spot with my equipment and painting – but it wasn't to be. Both the beans climbing in the background and all of the dahlias had been pulled up, leaving bare soil. Almost nothing remained of my subject. Taking multiple sessions to finish a painting doesn't always work out the way you'd hoped!

The Crab Hut

The weather forecast at Wells-next-the-Sea, in Norfolk, UK, looked set fair for the weekend, so after painting a few smaller studies of the beach huts, I felt confident enough to start this larger canvas.

Day one

I remember feeling really relaxed in the early stages of this one. Sometimes if you're warm and enjoying yourself you can get lulled into a false sense of security! I started with an outline sketch in a neutral grey to see how much I would take of the subject and how my composition would be arranged.

The sun was coming and going behind clouds throughout the afternoon, but it was that punchy contrast when the sun was out that I was after. The striped windbreak, lit by the sun, was an eyecatching element that I wanted to make the 'main event' of my painting. As a focal point, it provides a strong tonal and colour contrast with the shadowy area underneath the beach huts.

I felt it would be important to have a few figures populate the scene, so I sketched those in as they came into view. I tried a standing figure near the huts and also a lady sitting in a deckchair with her dog.

Fairly soon after starting, I made sure I had a tonal wash in place on all the shadow areas. This would serve to remind me which parts had been in the light. With this in place, I started on those light value colour shapes. There was a lot of colour mixing involved, with each hut having its own particular colour identity – I find their individuality a great part of their charm.

By the end of the first day, I had most of the colour shapes, both light and dark, in place. A satisfying end to a good day's painting.

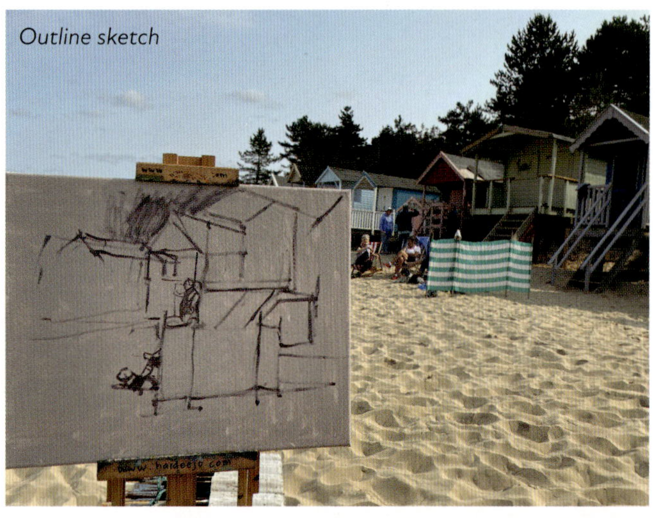

Outline sketch

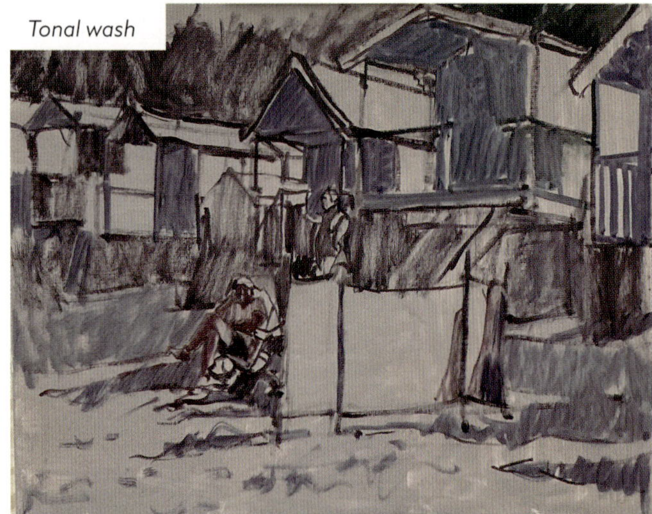

Tonal wash

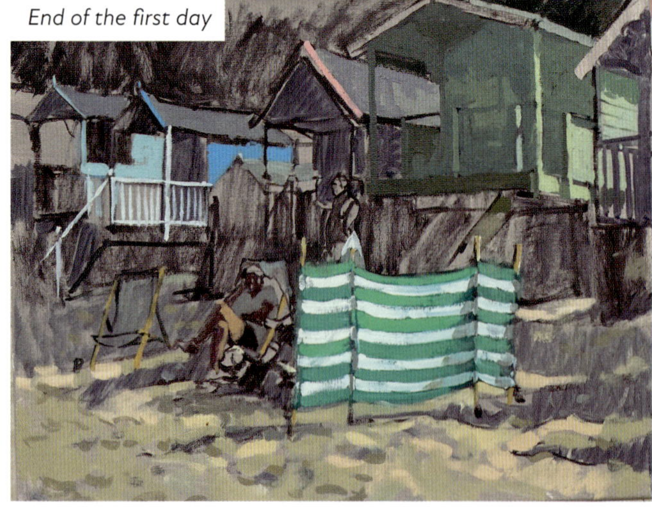

End of the first day

Day two

The next day thankfully brought the same weather conditions, so I headed down at the same time of day for another session to make some alterations and refinements.

I changed the central figure because I wasn't particularly happy with the previous one and preferred the direction this lady was facing. The shadowy figure in the background was removed, because I felt I just didn't have enough of a memory to get it finished. I added an extra dog on the other side of the windbreak, then turned to continue working on the more distant huts, which I ran out of time to finish on the first session. Because I was able to see them again at the optimal time, I could also confirm the shadows on the beach and huts. To finish, I put in the detail of the painted crab on the green hut.

The finished painting
51 x 40.5cm (20 x 16in)

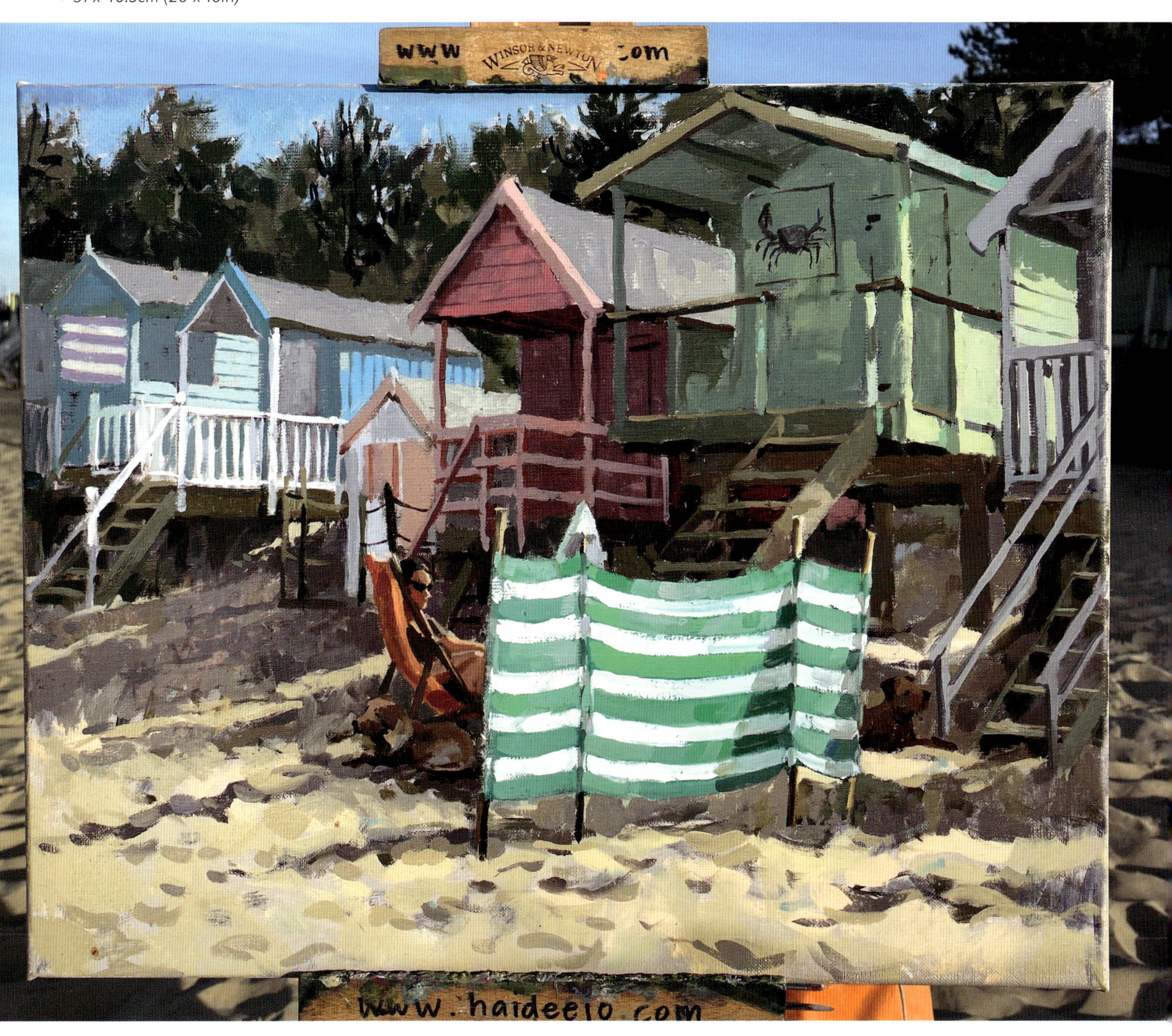

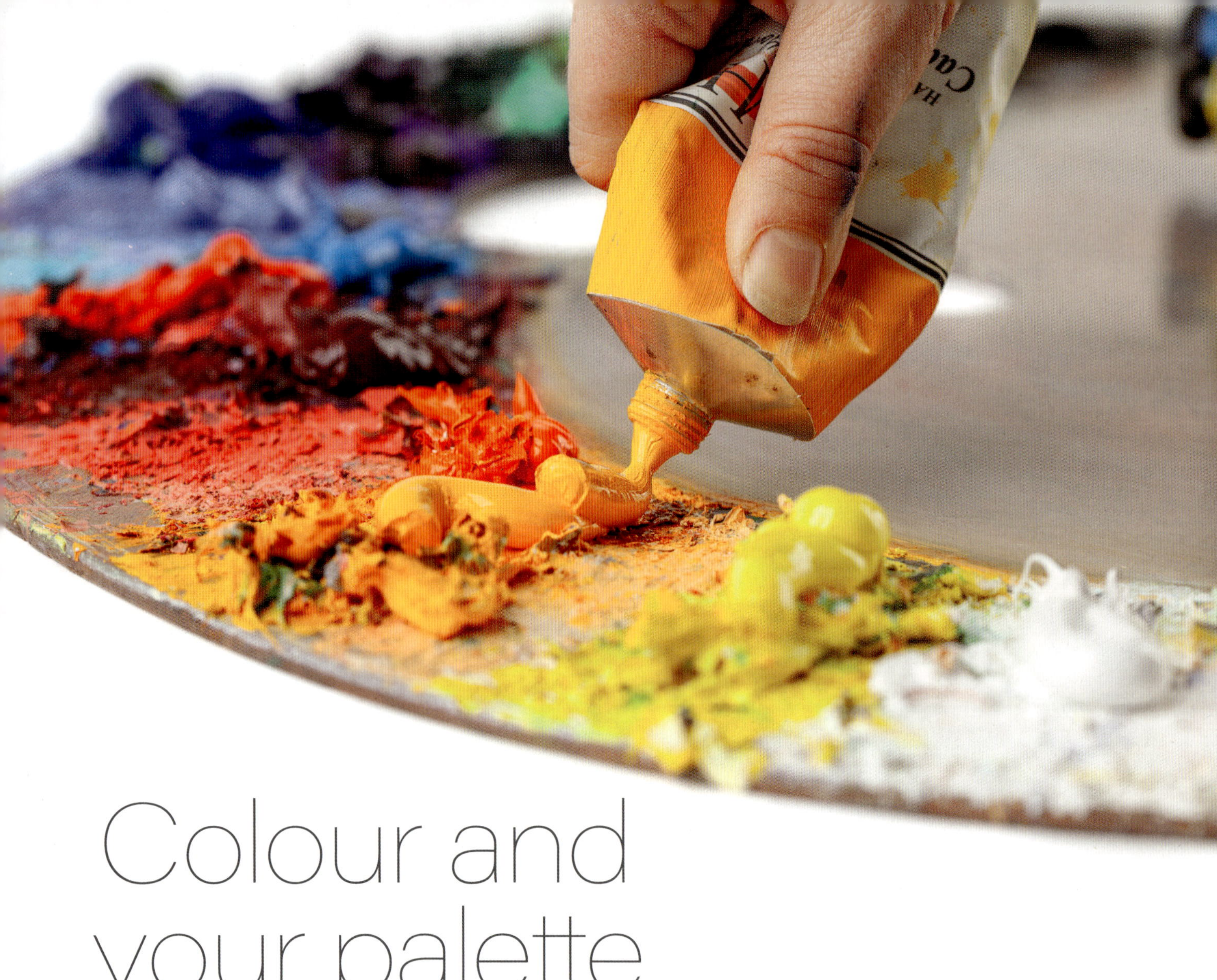

Colour and your palette

In my studio I have four large baskets full of oil colours, sorted into whites and yellows; pinks, oranges and reds; blues, greens and violets; and earth colours and blacks. Some of the colours in my baskets are old friends that I cannot do without, such as ultramarine blue and alizarin crimson. I have used and replaced tubes of these paints many times over.

Colour is such a source of joy to me that I often experiment with new paints. Like buying new brushes, collecting paints becomes a bit of a hobby. I will try out new colours a few times in the studio. Some become a new part of my broader palette, while others languish at the bottom of the basket for evermore. Occasionally, I'll buy a new colour simply because I like the look of it, I like the name of it (cinnabar green or Persian rose being a couple), or another artist mentions they can't do without it.

It is in my studio that experimentation with these new colours mainly takes place. When I am out and about en plein air I need my familiar, tried-and-tested palette with me.

Although buying and trying different tube colours is a lot of fun, we do need to understand the basics of colour mixing to be able to get the best out of any colours that we choose.

My standard palette is detailed on page 20; but using a small, limited palette is a good way to find out what you can do without the complexity of too many options.

Which colours might you choose to add to your palette?

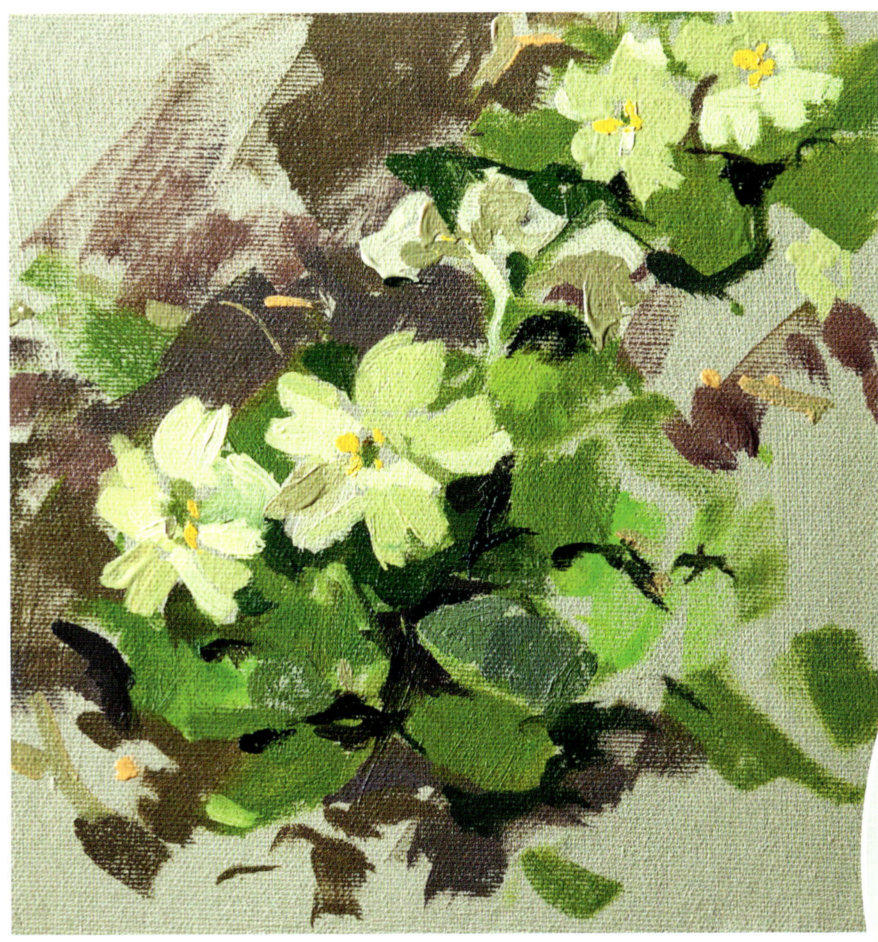

20.5 x 20.5cm (8 x 8in)

Painted with three primary colours plus titanium white. Look at the variety of subtle colour mixes that is possible with just three colours.

> ❛As a matter of fact, an artist has to deal with only three basic colours: red, blue, yellow (all the rest are combinations of these fundamental colours). Everyone knows this, but few pay attention to the fact. Thus, the first step for the artist is to learn to see these primary colours and to distinguish them separately one from the other. ❜
>
> Nicolai Fechin, 1881–1955

Primary palette

Practise first in the studio with a limited palette consisting of just the primary colours and see how far you can go with three tubes of paint alone, plus titanium white. In this case I have chosen bright yellow lake, permanent rose and ultramarine, but you can use the three closest colours that you have.

Experiment with mixing the secondary and tertiary colours from these three primaries. What kinds of orange, violet and green can you make? Tint them with white and dull or desaturate them using the complementary colour. For example, mix a green then add increasing small amounts of red until you get to brown. Mix a violet with the red and blue, then add yellow and white and see how many beautiful greys you can make.

Any time you are painting en plein air and you get into a muddle about the colour you are mixing, think of the three primaries. Ask yourself, should I add more red, yellow or blue to this mix to get closer to the colour that I am after?

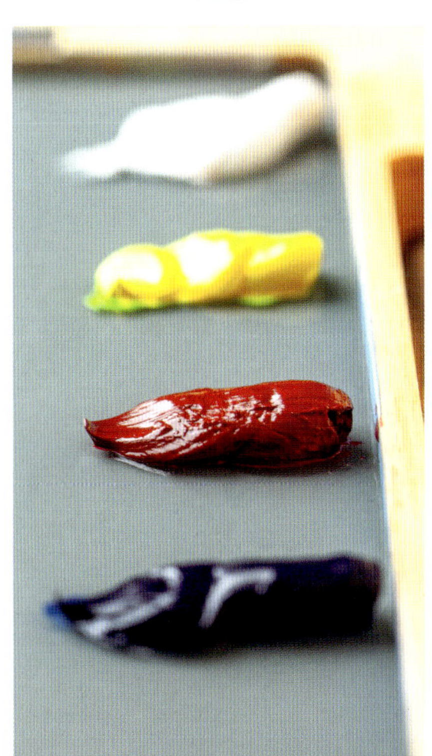

Monochrome palette

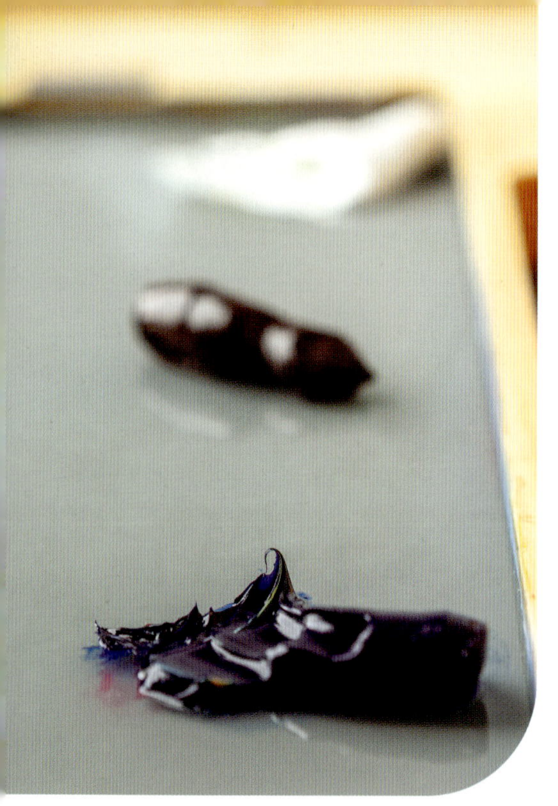

By reducing or stripping out the consideration of hue from your painting, you can better concentrate on values and key. Mix a very dark grey using transparent red oxide and ultramarine blue, and then add increasing quantities of titanium white to create a whole range of values from light to dark. You can vary the colour temperature of these grey mixes by adding more red oxide for warmth or more blue to cool down the colour. If you don't have these two particular colours you can use any similar pair, such as burnt umber or burnt sienna and cobalt blue.

As well as being a great learning exercise in recognizing and using tonal values, I think these monochrome studies are rather beautiful in their own right. They can also be used for a tonal value underpainting (see page 74) if you return to the subject at the right time of day for the light – you can also, of course, work further on them in the studio instead.

If you do decide to apply colour on top, you can match the value of the colour to the value you already have in place in your underpainting. Try just a spot of colour then squint your eyes. If the colour disappears, you know you have the right value. If your spot of colour leaps out because it is too light or too dark, you need to adjust it.

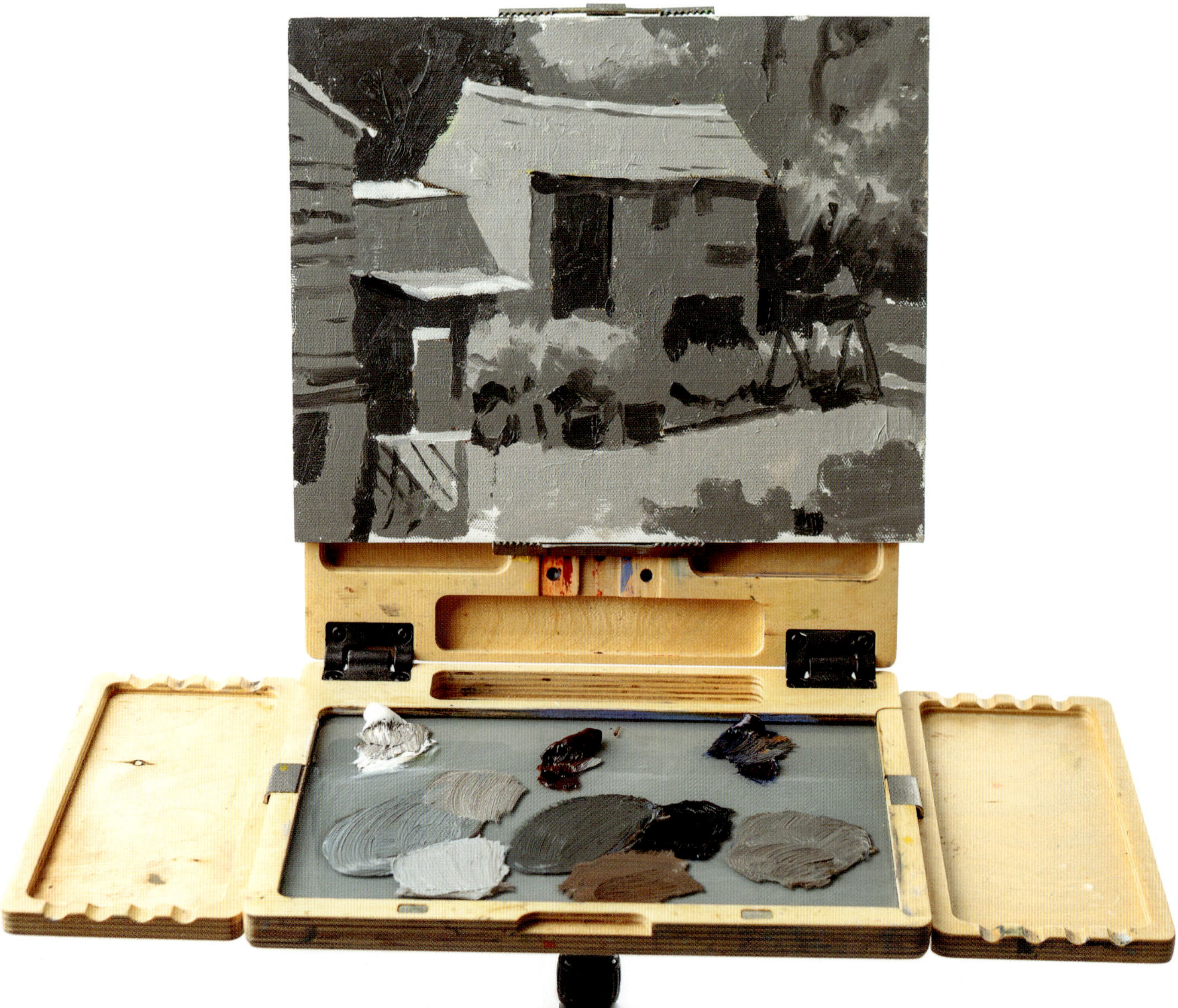

Extended primary palette

In practice it would be extremely difficult to find three perfect primary colours from which you could mix every secondary colour in a clean and saturated hue. Most artists therefore adopt an expanded version of the limited primary palette. This palette includes a warm and a cool version of each of the primary colours, plus white. In this example of an extended primary palette I have used bright yellow lake (a cool yellow), cadmium yellow deep (a warm yellow), cadmium red light (a warm red), alizarin crimson (a cool red), phthalo blue & zinc white (a green blue) and ultramarine (a violet blue). Titanium white is included, too.

   With the palette described here, you would choose the cadmium red light and cadmium yellow deep to mix an orange; the bright yellow lake and phthalo blue & zinc white to mix a clean green; and the alizarin crimson together with ultramarine to mix a violet. It is this small but versatile palette that I use as the basis for most of the demonstrations in the book, together with occasional additional colours that are noted.

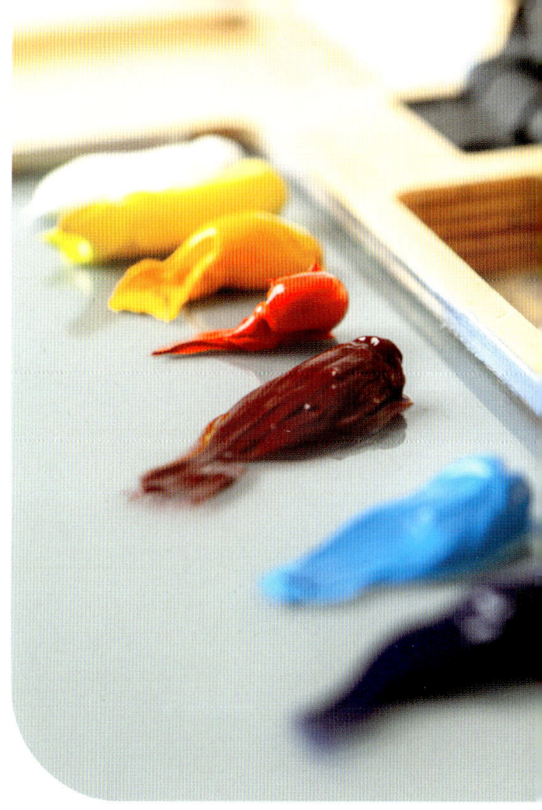

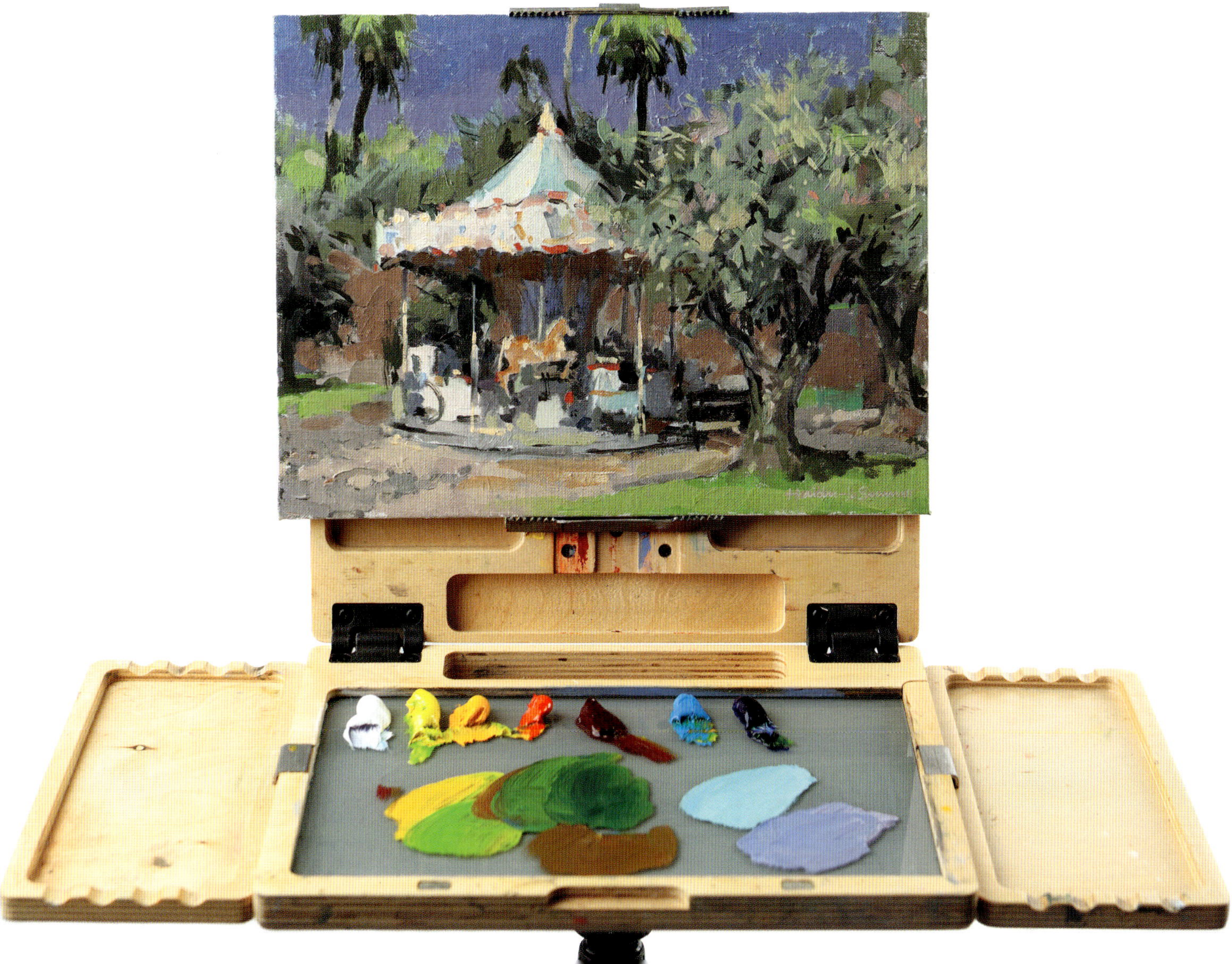

Underpaintings

We mostly think of plein air paintings as being completed in one session (alla prima, to use the traditional term), without too much layering of paint. This helps to avoid any muddiness, particularly when dark colours mix into lights. As you will have seen throughout this book, my usual aim is to place the right colour for a shape first time, working onto a plain canvas that has previously been prepared with a neutral grey hue (see page 25). However, there are other ways of working and, with a little prior thought and planning, it is certainly possible to use layers of colour while painting en plein air.

Tonal underpaintings

In *The Crab Hut*, on pages 68–69, I created an underpainting of dark washes, using oil colour thinned down with low-odour solvent. This monochrome beginning helped me to establish the composition, shapes and tonal values, in turn giving me a framework on which to later build up colour.

Vibrant underpaintings

Another approach – that used here – is to create an underpainting in a complementary colour to the image. Gaps are left in the surface so hints of the underpainting can be seen through it. By utilizing different colour notes of the same value beside each other, the colours seem to vibrate. It's an effect that cannot be achieved in the same way by using mixed colours, and is often used in impressionist painting.

After painting *Cypress Trees and Roses*, I wanted to explore a little colour vibration, just to see what difference a vibrant underpainting in complementary red would make to the greens of the finished painting.

You could use oil colours for an underpainting like this if you worked in two sessions with drying time in between, used fast-drying alkyd oils, or added a fast-drying medium to your standard oil paints. For convenience and to avoid any unwanted mixing between complementary colours, I used acrylic paints for this vibrant underpainting, and then oils for the top layer of colours.

Please note that it is fine to paint with oils on top of dried acrylic paints, but never the other way round because of the way oils need to dry over time.

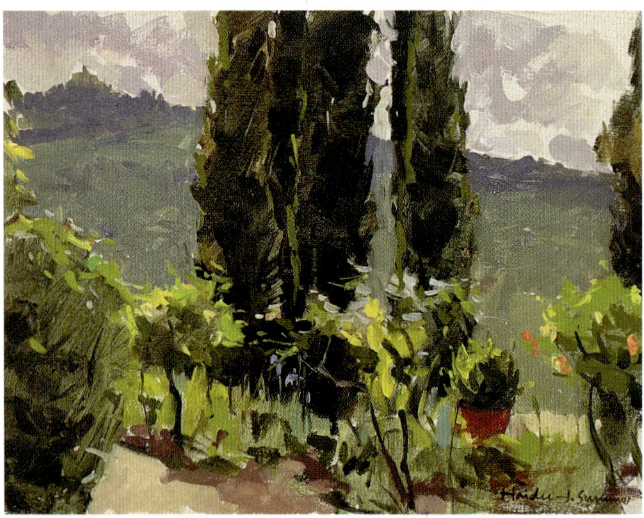

Cypress Trees and Roses
30.5 x 23cm (12 x 9in)

I chose this alla prima plein air painting from Italy as my inspiration for this example. Because the painting consists mostly of greens I decided to use red, the complementary colour to green, for my underpainting.

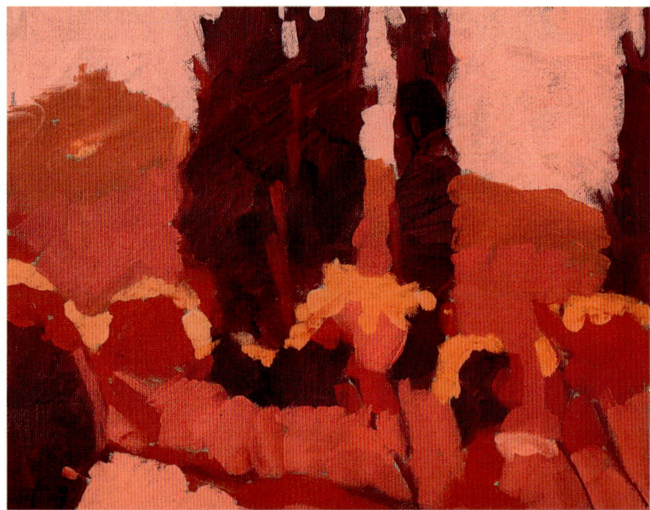

The complementary underpainting
One way to do this would have been to paint my whole board with one tone of warm red, but in this case I decided to paint all of the main value shapes in red tones. I did this using acrylics for their fast drying properties. I then had a map of the tonal value shapes, which I left for a short while to dry.

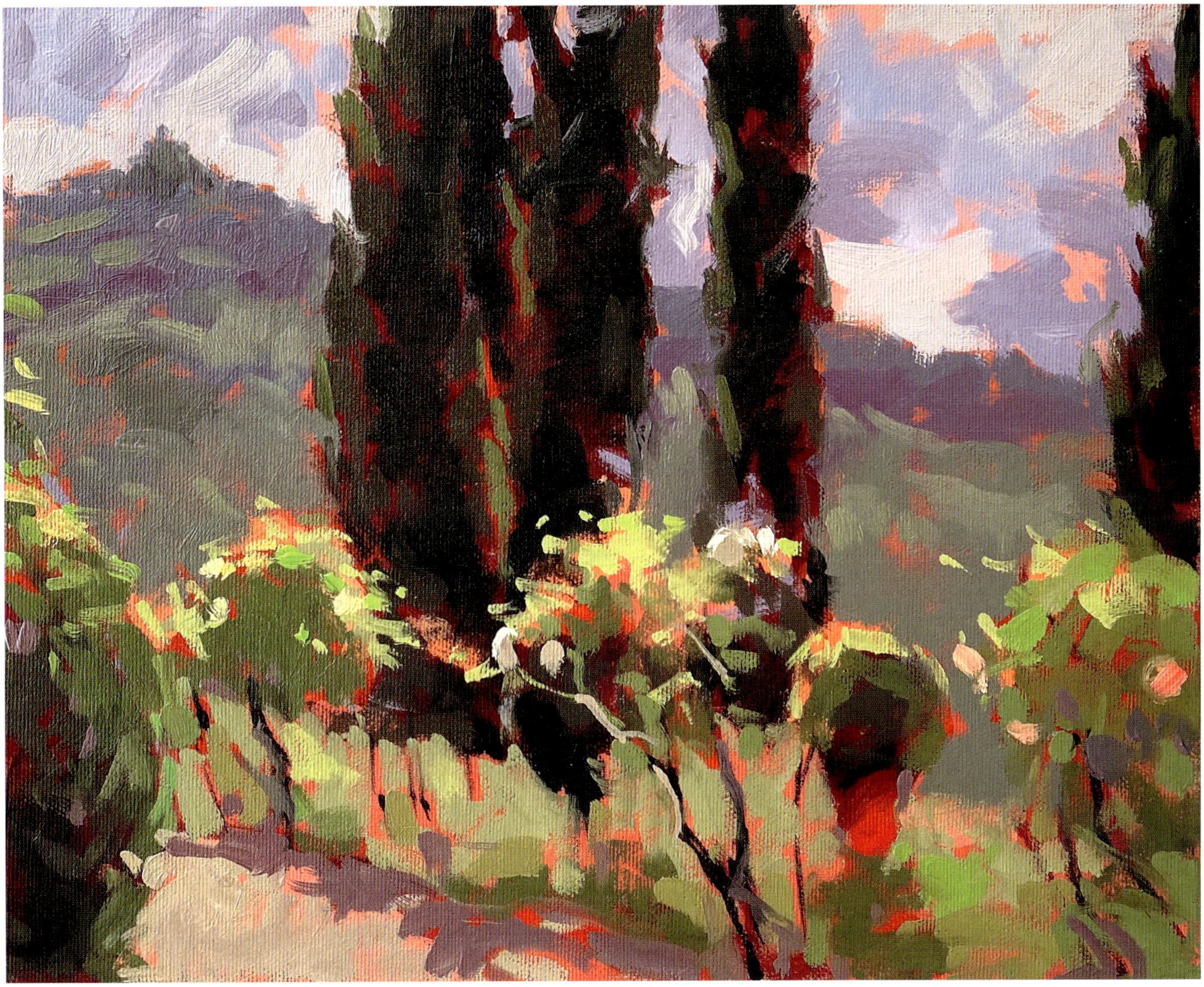

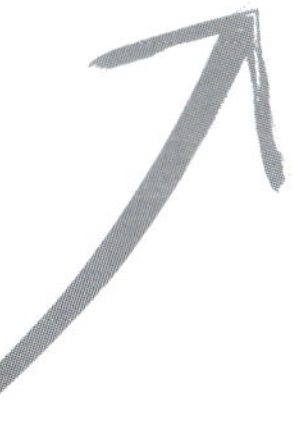

Cypress Trees and Roses with Red Underpainting
30.5 x 25.5cm (12 x 10in)

I used oil paints then to finish the painting with the colours of the landscape, taking inspiration from my original plein air painting. If you want to try this method for yourself, it's important to leave lots of gaps where the underpainting colours can show through, and not to cover it all up – which is easily done!

I think the effect is very lively, and here I particularly enjoy the pinks showing through in the sky and the dark reds in the cypress trees.

'A green and pleasant land'

Capturing greens in the landscape

When it comes to mixing colours, I often hear other artists saying that they don't like painting subjects which feature a lot of green hues as they struggle to mix the 'right' green. How to mix greens is also a question I'm frequently asked when demonstrating. To me it seems to be quite a handicap to love painting landscapes but not to love the colour green – especially if you live in a verdant region – so I've put some thoughts together here that I hope will be of assistance. If you're going to paint landscapes, greens will be hard to escape so you'd best have a plan of action for tackling them.

I think one of the reasons artists might struggle with capturing greens in the landscape is an overreliance on ready-mixed greens from tubes: you might find that all your greens are looking the same, and also somewhat unnatural. If this is the case, I suggest you get into the habit of mixing your own greens from primary colours before you experiment with the tube colour greens. I painted for at least fifteen years without any ready-mixed greens on my palette whatsoever, and I still usually leave these behind in the studio.

> ‘ They'll sell you thousands of greens. Veronese green and emerald green and cadmium green and any sort of green you like; but that particular green, never. ’
>
> **Pablo Picasso, 1881–1973**

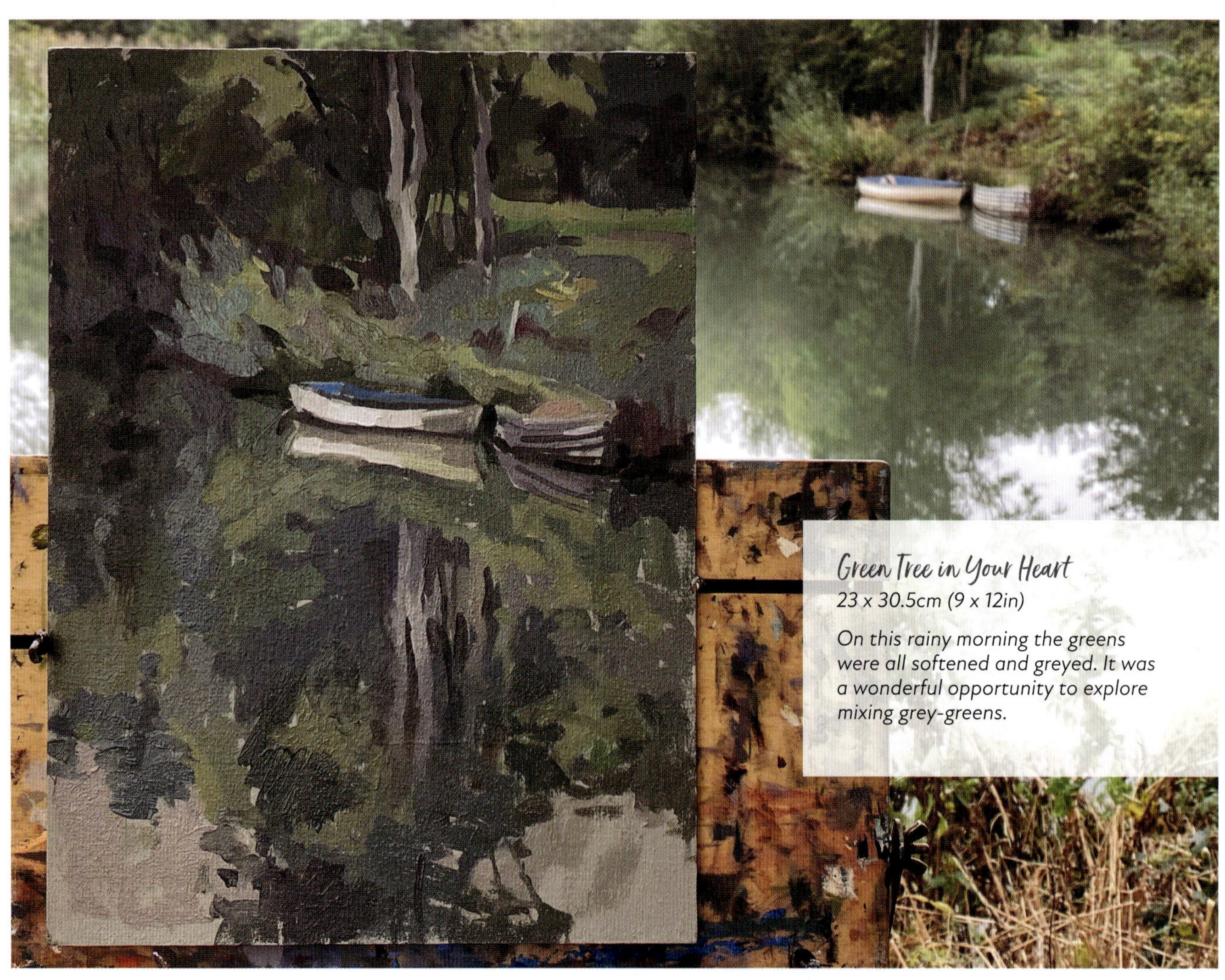

Green Tree in Your Heart
23 x 30.5cm (9 x 12in)

On this rainy morning the greens were all softened and greyed. It was a wonderful opportunity to explore mixing grey-greens.

Mixing your own greens

Some of the available green paint colours are extremely vibrant and quite unlike what we are seeing before us in nature. If you first learn to mix your own greens and then later introduce green tube colours, you will be better able to modify them to get what you need.

This exercise will stand you in good stead when you're out in the field. Pick up a range of green home décor paint colour swatches from a DIY store so that you can practise your colour mixing and matching skills in the studio, away from all the other complexities involved in producing a full painting. Do be patient while doing this exercise, and don't be satisfied until you can paint a dot of your colour mix onto the coloured swatch and it matches exactly.

Mixing greens

In both example mixes below, a yellow is combined with a blue. The top row shows the pure colours at either end, with different proportions in between. In the centre is an even mix of both consituent colours, producing a mid-green mix in each case.

In the second rows, the same vibrant green mix in each case is created on the left. Increasing amounts of cadmium red light are added to the mix as you work along the row to the right. As the complementary colour to green, the increasing amounts of cadmium red light added gradually desaturate the hue, producing a beautiful range of greens and browns from just five paints.

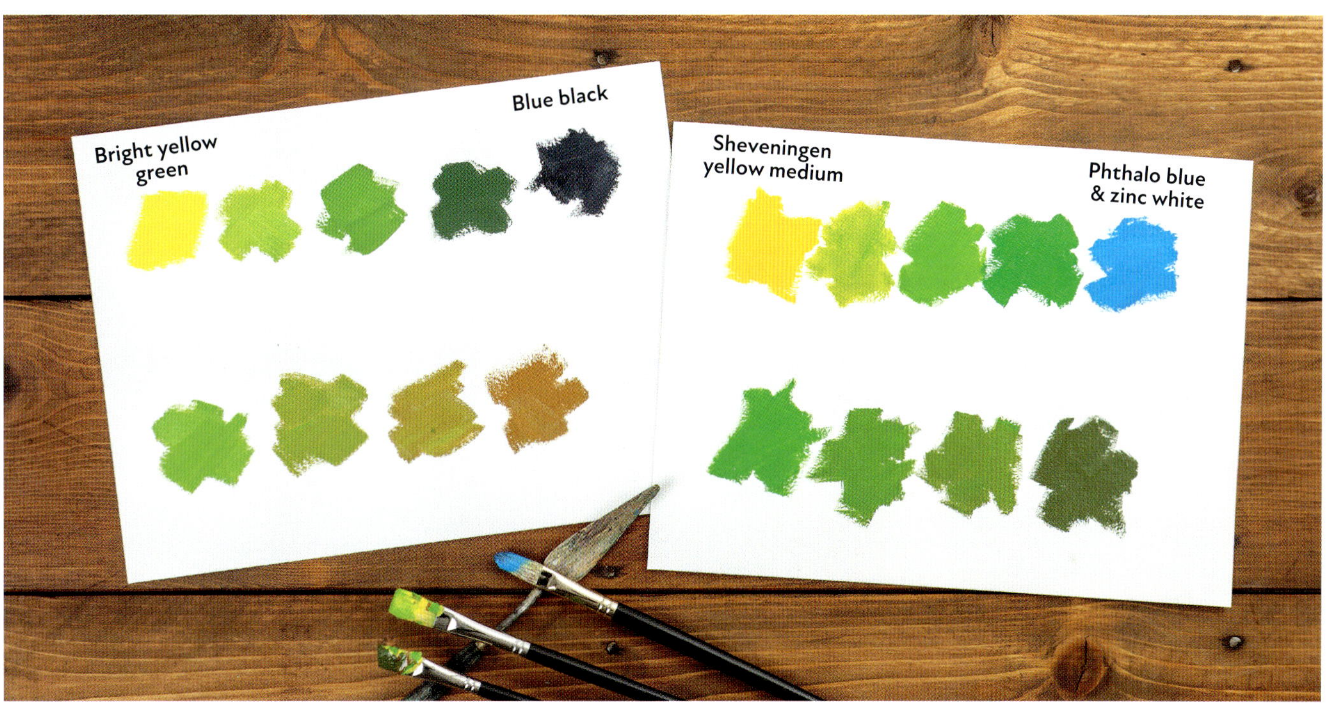

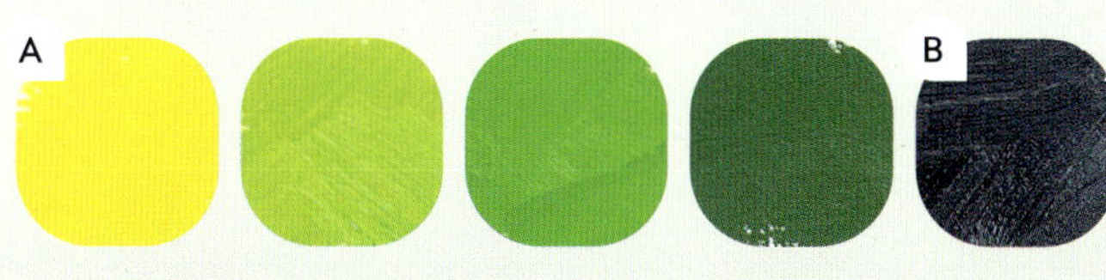

Vibrant mixes

Combinations of bright yellow-green (A) and blue-black (B). Using just two colours helps to ensure bright, vibrant results.

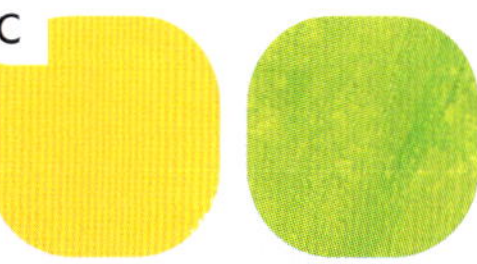

Desaturating

Here, combinations of Schveningen yellow medium (C) and phthalo blue & zinc white (D) have been used. The mid-green mix (E) is then used as the basis for the desaturated greens.

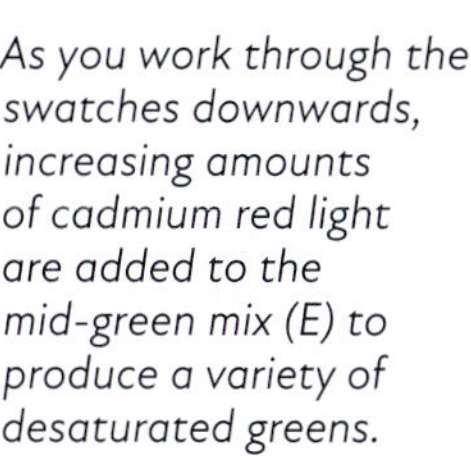

As you work through the swatches downwards, increasing amounts of cadmium red light are added to the mid-green mix (E) to produce a variety of desaturated greens.

Qualities of colour

When mixing any colour, the key things to identify are its hue, value and chroma. This is how I assess the varieties of green (or indeed any other colour) that I'm seeing within my subject. In turn, this helps me to work out how to mix the colour that I need:

Hue What colour bias has the green – that is, does it tend towards yellow or blue?

Tonal value How light or dark is it compared to other colour shapes around it? How does it compare to the lightest light and the darkest dark within the subject?

Saturation Is the colour vivid and saturated, or greyed-down/neutralized?

Get into the habit of thinking through a description of the colours in these terms before you start to mix anything on the palette.

In practice it works like this: for a dull, dark green I might combine ultramarine, a dark and red-biased blue, with cadmium yellow deep, a red-biased yellow. For an olive green, I might start with a cadmium yellow or yellow ochre, and add blue-black. For a punchy, high-chroma sunlit green I might choose a cadmium lemon yellow (light value, green-biased yellow) and a cerulean or phthalo blue (green-biased blue). I might even add a little white to lighten the value – although not so much that the green mix loses its colour identity or the warmth from the yellow.

After mixing a green you will likely need to modify or neutralize it: when we are looking at a landscape through the particles and water in the atmosphere, the effect can be to greatly reduce the chroma in the greens. The surrounding colours and the colour of the light also have parts to play, which is why the same green foliage can appear to be quite different in different circumstances. There are no easy formulas: observation is key.

Fortunately there are many ways to knock back greens that are too high in chroma – try cadmium red, permanent rose, alizarin crimson, transparent red oxide, yellow ochre, burnt sienna, raw umber, magenta or pale rose blush for starters. If your greens are looking too garish, spend a day in the studio on colour mixing, practising how to mix vivid greens and then how to dial down their saturation. I often add cadmium red to neutralize a green mix, but it's a powerful colour so you need to add it to your green mix in tiny increments to avoid making brown or red.

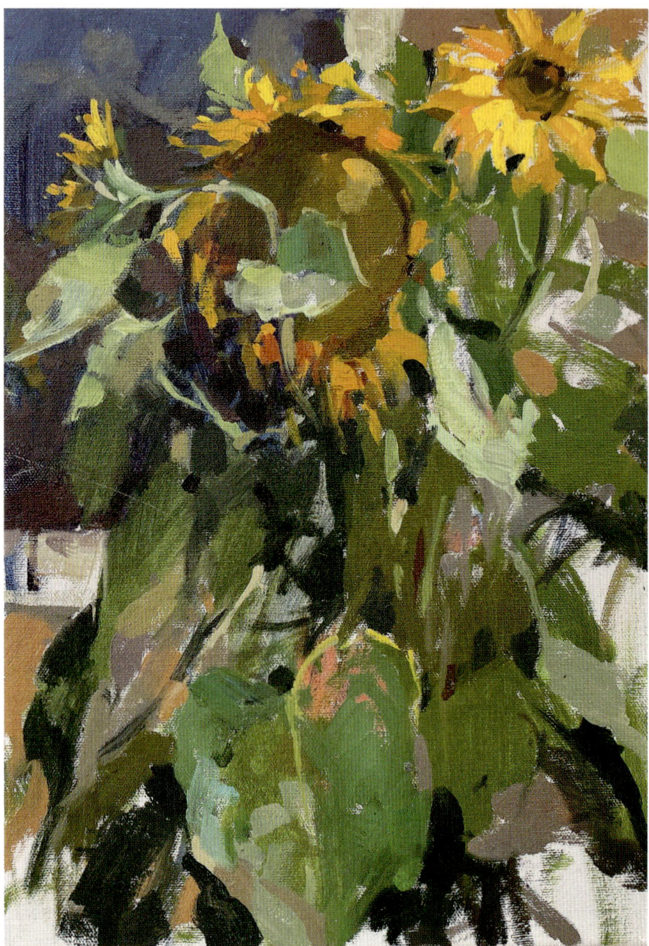

Giant Sunflower on a Hot July Day
25.5 x 35.5cm (10 x 14in)

In this close-up painting of a sunflower I relished discovering a whole gamut of values, hues and chroma within the greens. The effect of strong sunlight is enhanced by contrasting the greens with patches of pink and terracotta.

There are no easy formulas or recipes to capture the variety of greens you will see, but happily there are also many ways to arrive at any given colour.

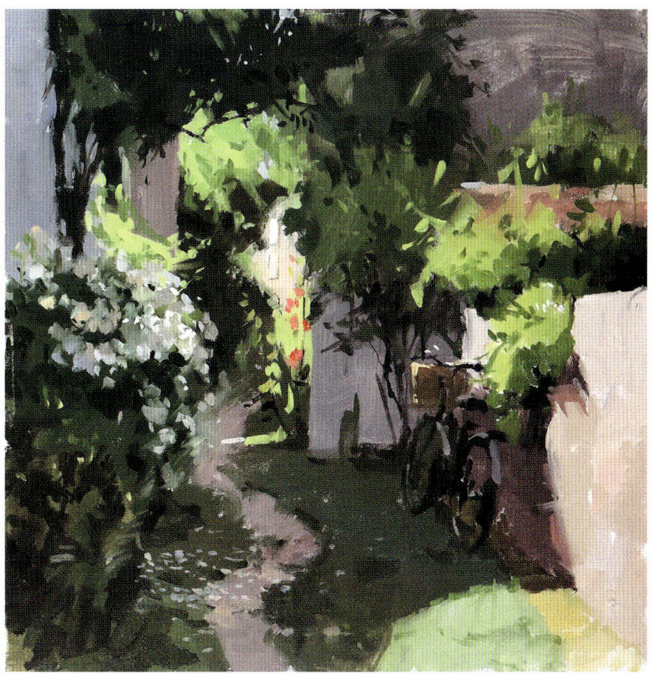

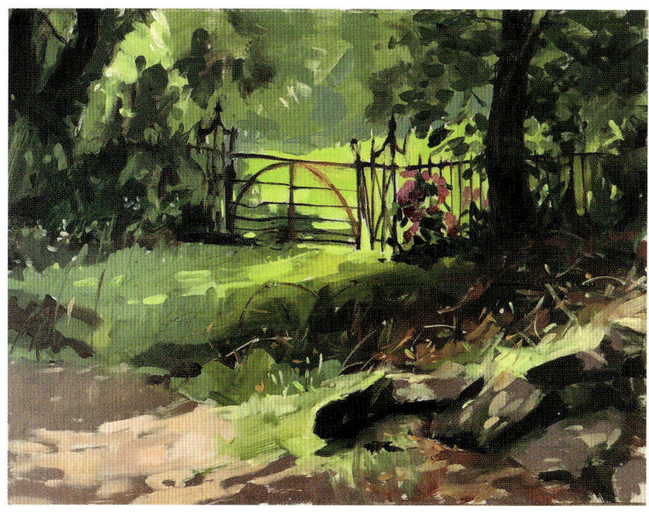

Fragrant Pathway, Île de Ré
30.5 x 30.5cm (12 x 12in)

A whole range of warm and cool greens can be seen on a sunny day, as this painting amply demonstrates.

Iron Gate at Wortley Hall
30.5 x 23cm (12 x 9in)

The high-chroma yellow-greens in this painting direct the viewer to the focal point of the gate, and I've reserved the punchiest green for the gate area to draw maximum attention here. This is enhanced further by the colour contrast with the pink rhododendron flowers. Secondly, there is a diagonal shaft of light coming across the foreground which reveals the interesting rock shapes and gives us an easy entry into the painting.

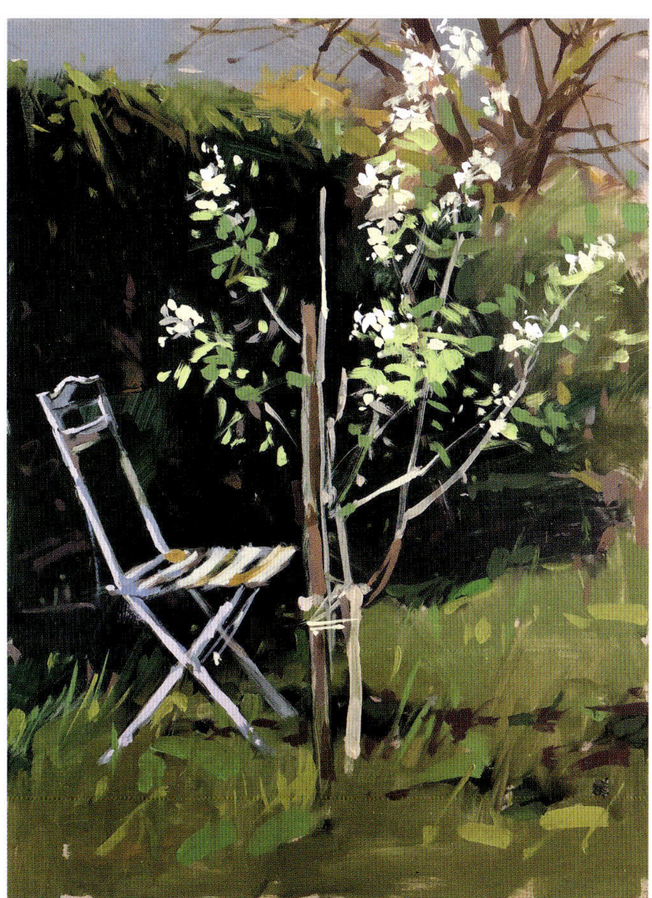

Pear Tree and Little Blue Chair
23 x 30.5cm (9 x 12in)

A very simple but effective idea: a sunlit tree standing out against the dark hedge behind.

Fog and Ruby Chard

This little study, painted in my garden, builds on what we've learned about the blocking-in approach and mixing a range of muted greens. It also shows how I approach persepctive and atmosphere in foggy conditions. It was a fun little project on a chilly winter morning.

Working from home, of course, means that there's no need to bring 'just-in-case' equipment like your phone or seasonal clothes: just pop back inside if you need them!

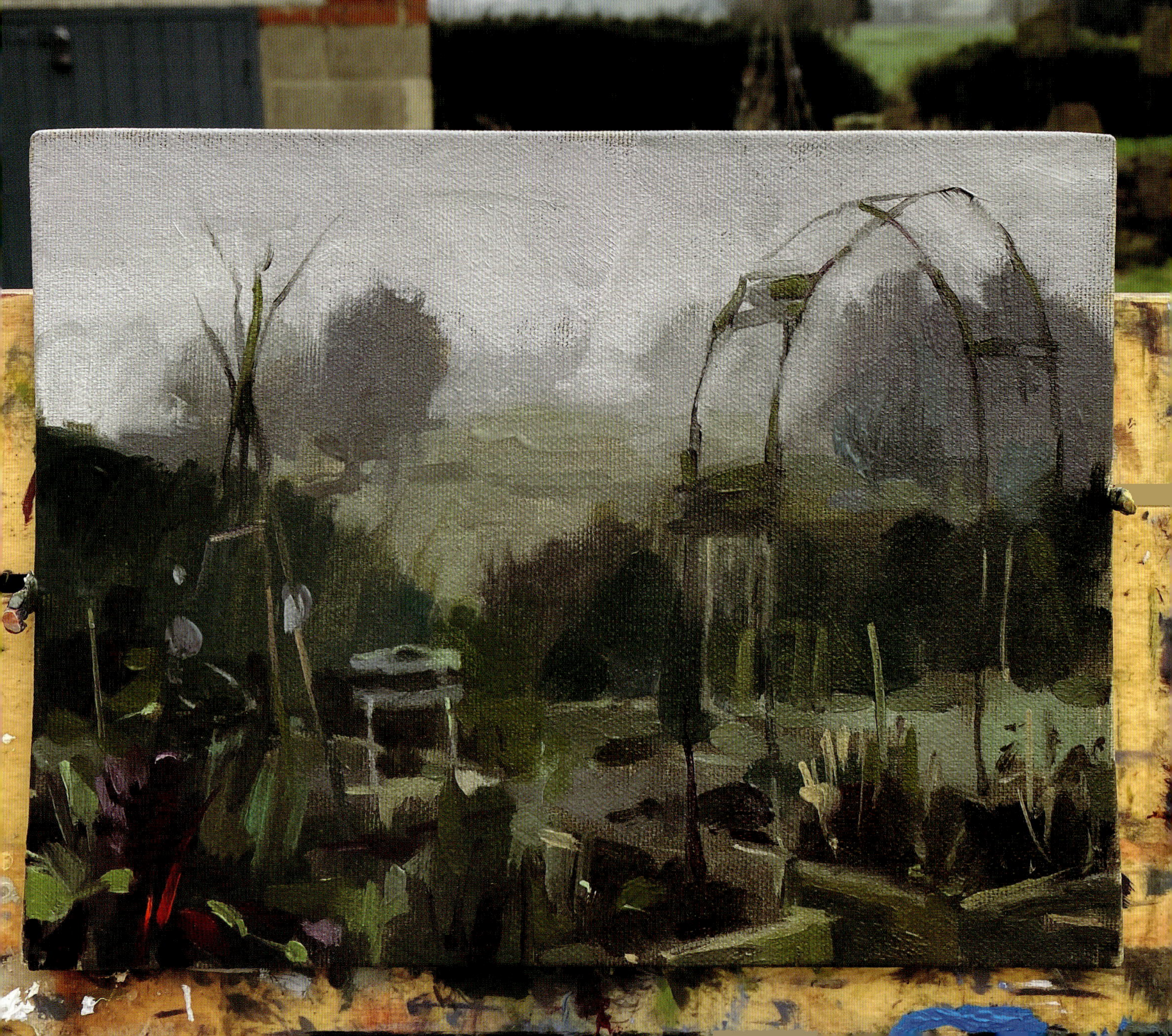

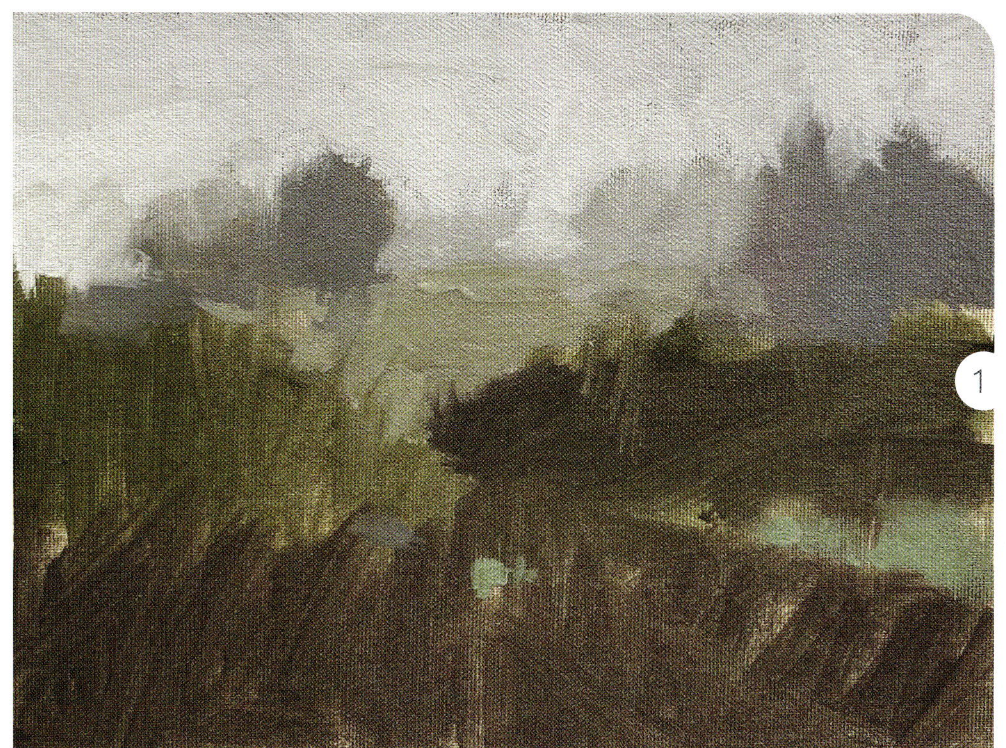

Large shapes: blocking-in

I started with a green-brown mix, thinned down with low-odour solvent, applied for the foreground garden area and hedge. I felt it was going to be incredibly important to get across the softening effect of the fog on the landscape, and the particular tonal value relationships. Although I usually try to hold off using white for as long as I can into the painting process, in this case I needed to use it to get that soft grey sky and the distant trees.

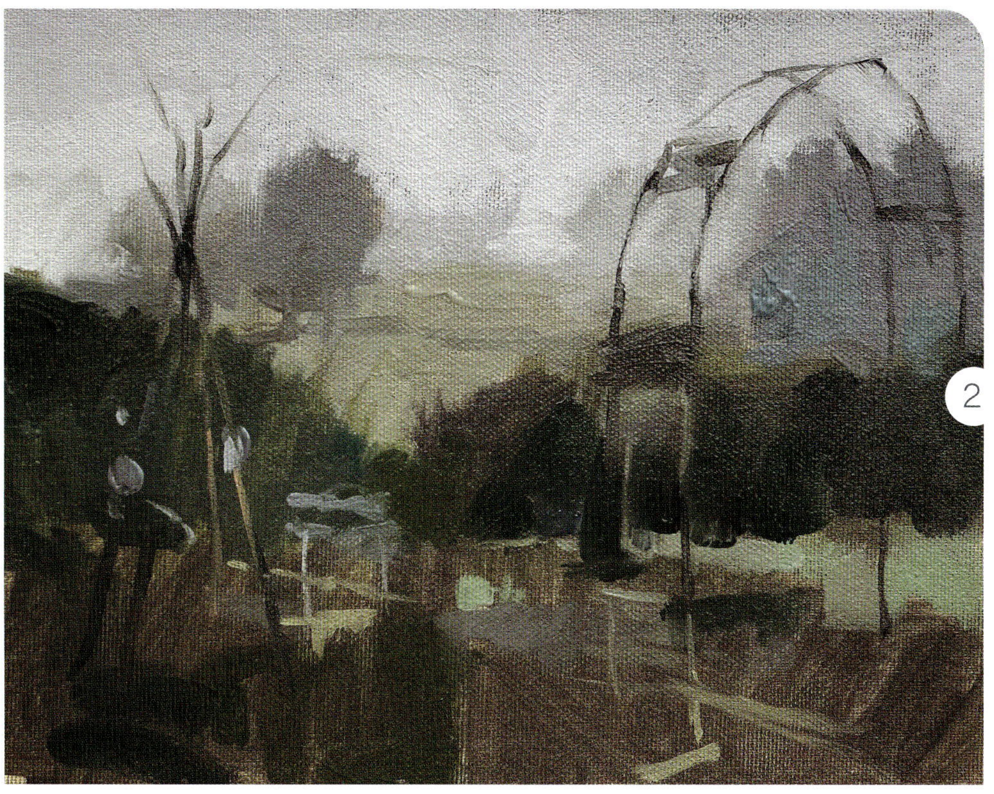

Smaller shapes

When I was satisfied with the distant landscape, I worked further into the foreground and hedge, introducing the smaller shapes of the willow arch and wigwam canes. I find it is possible to paint a darker colour over wet paint of a light value, but in order to do so, you need to keep dipping back into the darker colour on your palette and using the lightest pressure when you apply it.

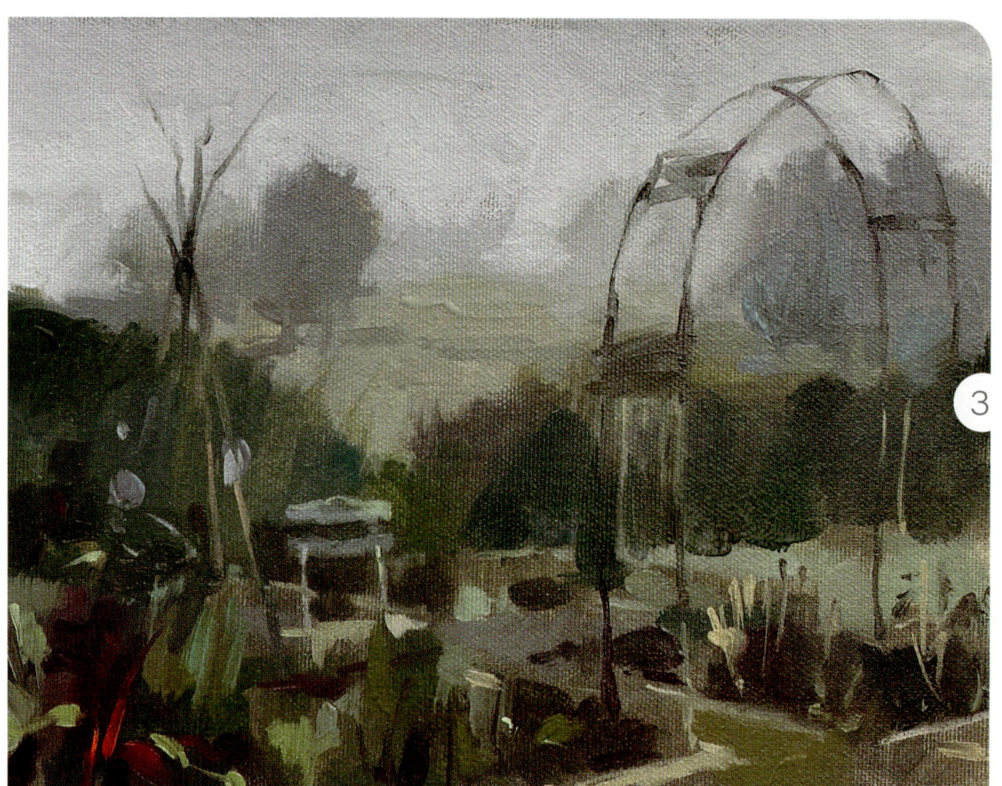

Colours and details

From here it was a case of suggesting the leaves and stems of plants, along with some detail in the chair. The ruby chard in the lower left provided a useful contrasting colour; I painted it with a dark red for the foliage and a lighter higher chroma red for the stems. (You could use transparent red oxide and cadmium red light for these.) A light value line picked out the top edge of the wooden planks which make up the sides of the vegetable beds.

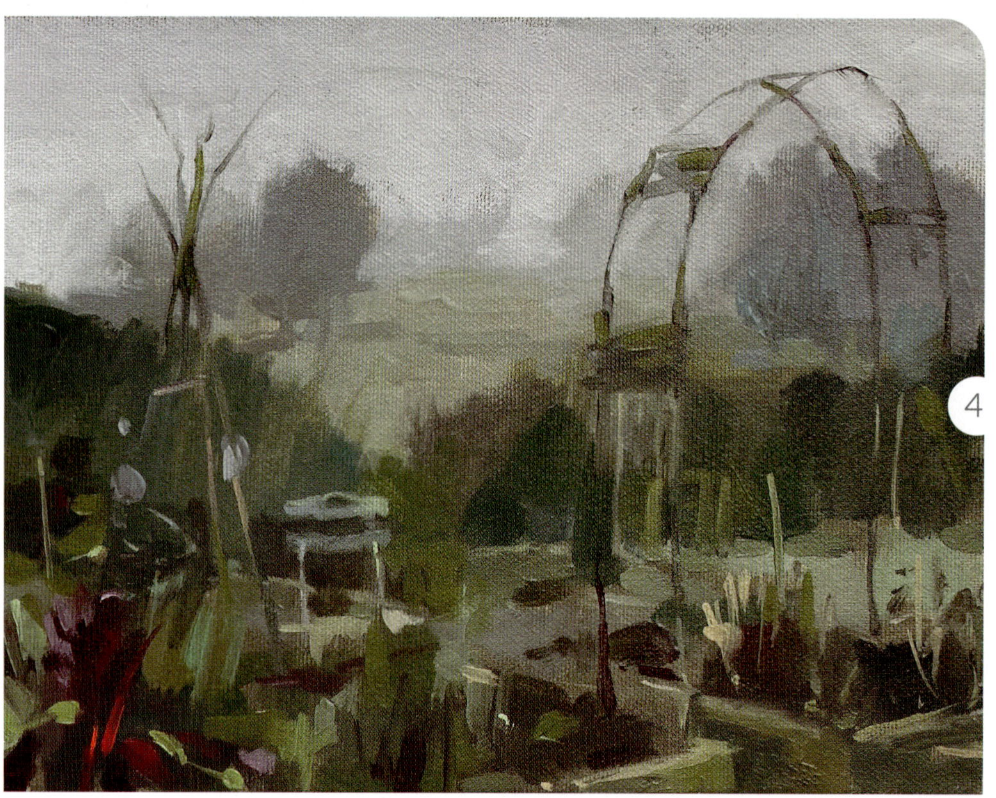

Highlights

For the final highlights, I used a small round brush and a light value mix – the precise hue is far less important than the value – to put in a few verticals. These suggest the garden canes and reconfirm parts of the chair.

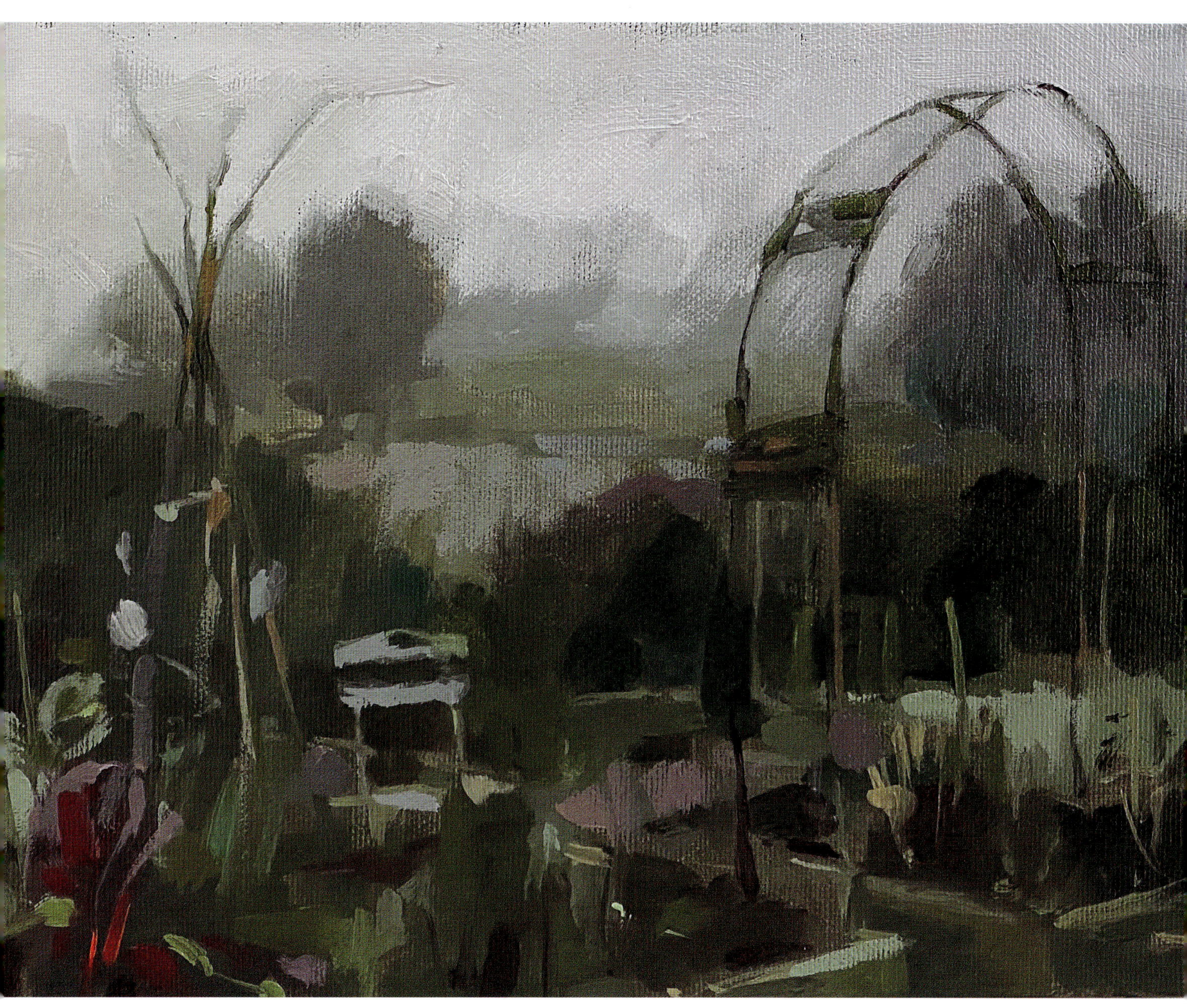

The finished painting
25.5 x 20.5cm (10 x 8in)

Design and impact: composing and realizing your artwork

' The artist must never forget
that he is dealing with the entire canvas, and not with any one
section of it. Regardless of what he sets out to paint, the problem
remains one and the same. With his own creative originality, he
must fill in his canvas and make of it an organic whole. '

Nicolai Fechin, 1881–1955

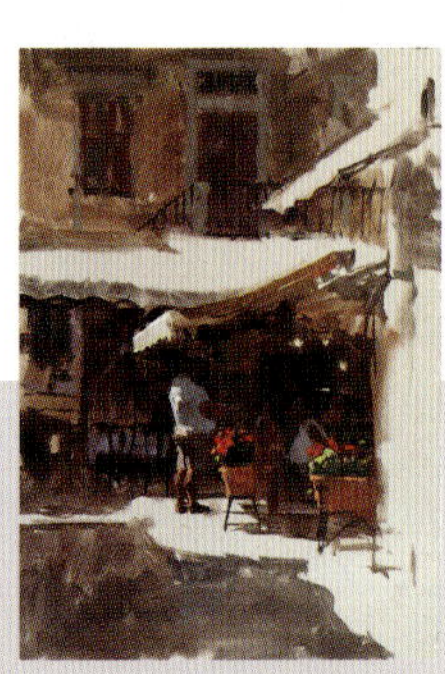

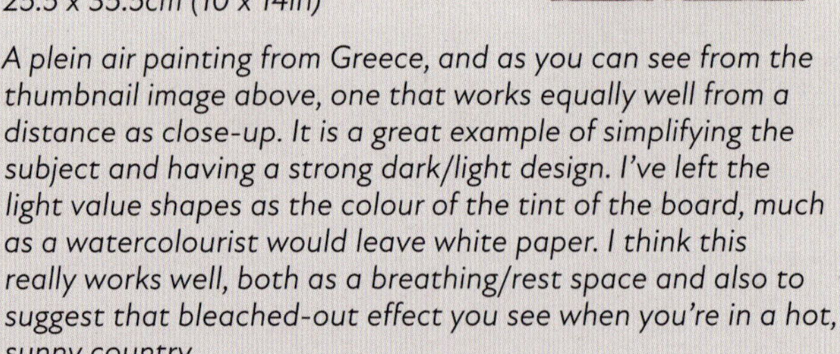

Whatever the subject, its components are abstract shapes, value and colour; and so we need to consider our painting subjects in this way from the outset. The key to successful composition is being aware of and arranging these shapes within the boundaries of your picture surface to create a compelling design and communicate an idea.

It's always worth spending some time planning the painting before you start applying paint; even with just a few thumbnail sketches to test out the composition. The composition or design is the backbone of the painting. It doesn't matter how beautifully you mix the colours or put the paint on, if the composition is weak to start with, the painting will not be able to achieve a strong impact.

Have you ever seen a painting in a gallery pull and intrigue you from across the room? That's the power of good design. We can assess our own work by looking at photographs of our paintings on a screen reduced down to a small thumbnail size; it's a very similar effect. Which ones still 'read' as a compelling image when scaled down in this way?

Above and opposite:
Awnings and Geraniums, Symi
25.5 x 35.5cm (10 x 14in)

A plein air painting from Greece, and as you can see from the thumbnail image above, one that works equally well from a distance as close-up. It is a great example of simplifying the subject and having a strong dark/light design. I've left the light value shapes as the colour of the tint of the board, much as a watercolourist would leave white paper. I think this really works well, both as a breathing/rest space and also to suggest that bleached-out effect you see when you're in a hot, sunny country.

The diagonal lines created by the awnings and the shadow on the floor both point towards the focal point of the figure. The strong horizontal and vertical lines serve as an anchor to pin everything down and contain it within the picture plane. There's very little detail in this painting, but the red spots of the geraniums and the few highlights and dark accents suggest so much of the activity within the subject.

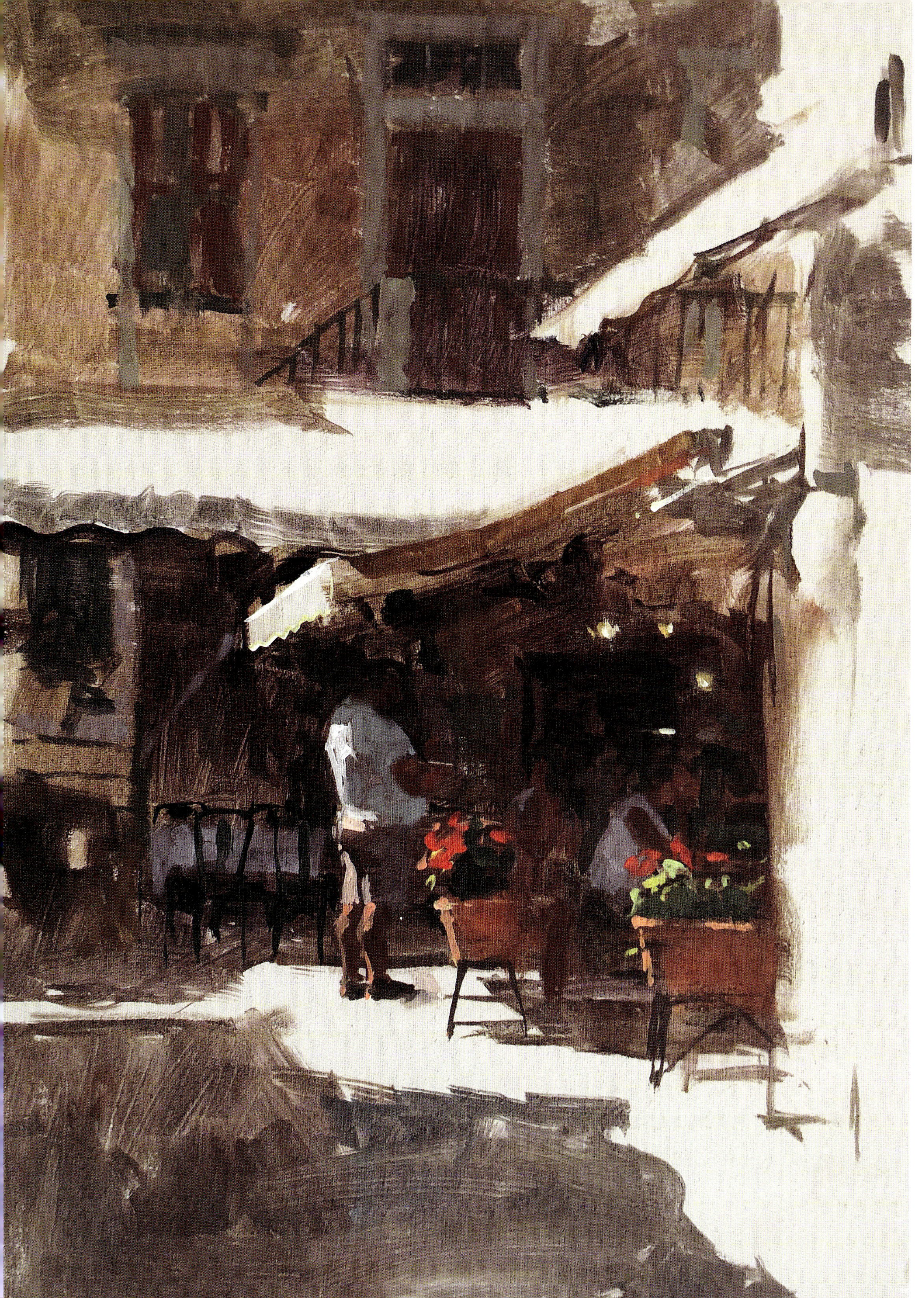

Creating work with impact

How do you create work which has this impact? First you need an idea of what you want to say in the painting. What is it about in particular – an effect of light, colour, shapes or an emotion?

Next you need to consider and use the whole picture space. Don't place your subject arbitrarily and start painting if there are unresolved parts of your subject that you don't know how you'll tackle. If there is a large background area in the scene that you don't like, don't know how to deal with and won't enhance your painting, don't start painting and just hope that when you get to that part the solution will become clear. Crop it out right from the beginning, and hone in on the area which interests you.

I've seen many a student struggle because they have taken on too much of the scene instead of just the part they actually wanted to paint. If you're looking at a building and the element that excites you is the doorway and flowers growing over the porch, fill your canvas with the doorway and porch. There's no need to include the roof, chimney and all the upstairs windows.

With the use of space decided, plan your values. Squint to simplify what is going on and see if the subject has good potential value-wise. Can you reduce what you're looking at to a compelling two or three value design, as shown below?

Thumbnail sketches in two or three values help you to see if the painting can have a strong design. As you look at your subject, try to see the shapes in relation to the rectangle or square that you will be working with. A viewfinder is a very good tool to help with this. Train yourself to see in value masses rather than looking at the individual objects.

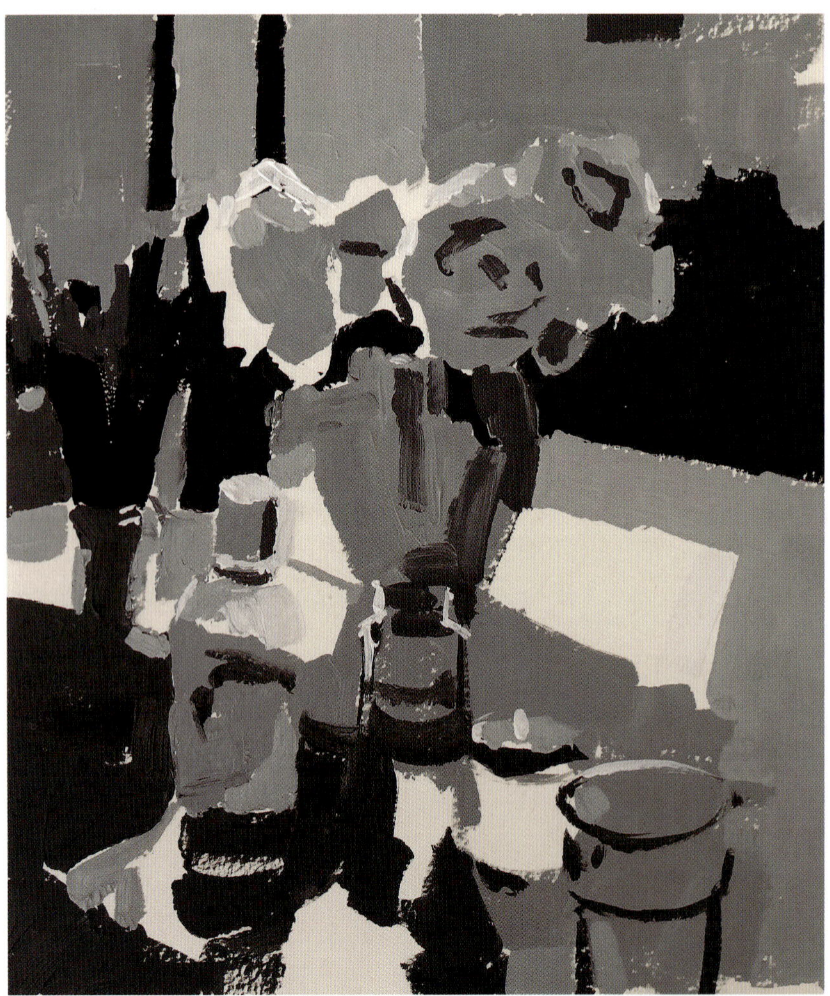

Studio still life, value study
A painted study in three tonal values breaks the subject down into its simplified structure of abstract shapes.

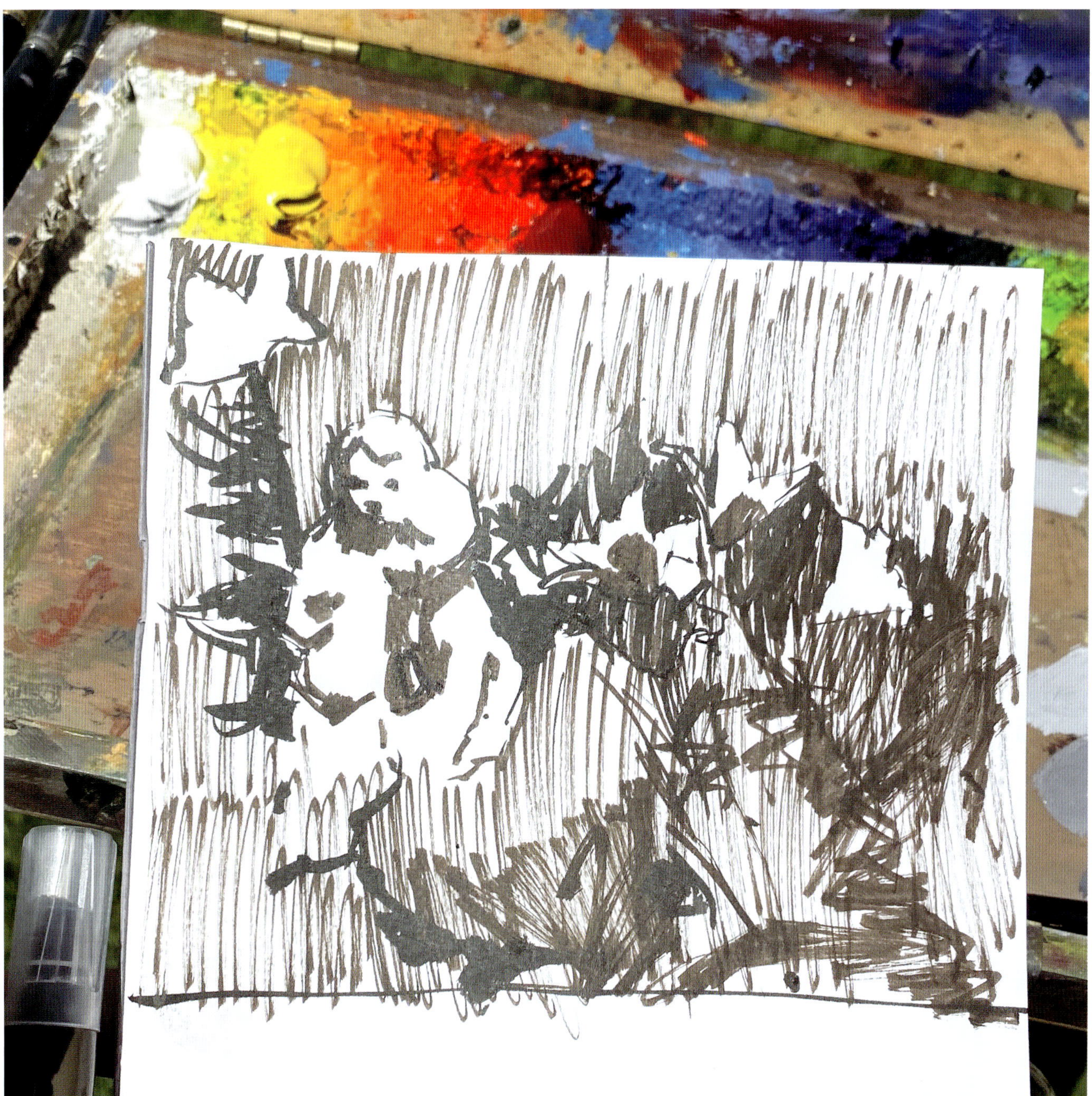

↑ Planning sketch

It's a very good idea to make a quick planning sketch when thinking about your composition and value shapes, to see whether your plan will work. You can make as many of these as you like and pick the most effective composition. When making planning sketches, ensure that the proportions of your sketch are the same as your painting surface.

The importance of contrast

This painting, *Narrowboat Garden*, illustrates the important role contrasts – in terms of both colour and value – have to play in guiding the eye in a painting and creating a compelling design.

You can use emphasis to direct the eye. There are five areas of peak contrast in this painting. Your eye moves between these focal points. In these places there are the strongest value contrasts which I've accentuated with hard edges.

Supporting these areas of contrast – and just as important as them – are the passages containing subtle contrasts and soft edges. If everyone is shouting, no one is heard.

A Tonal contrast The light narrowboat tiller bar stands out strongly against the dark.

B Tonal and colour contrast The eyecatching highlight of pink on the bow, set against the darkest area of blue, helps to bring that part of the boat forwards.

C Tonal and colour contrast The orange light here complements the blue surrounding it, drawing the eye.

D Tonal contrast This short line, where the side of the boat meets the trees behind (towards the front of the boat), helps to bring the front of the boat closer. I've deliberately darkened the area of trees above it and lightened the edge slightly, to accentuate the light hitting this part of the boat.

E Tonal contrast I've chosen to make this bucket, with a tree growing in it, slightly lighter than the others to accentuate the strong dark edge of the soil within. Note also that none of the white buckets are painted in exactly the same way, creating a sense of distance and rhythm rather than flat repetition.

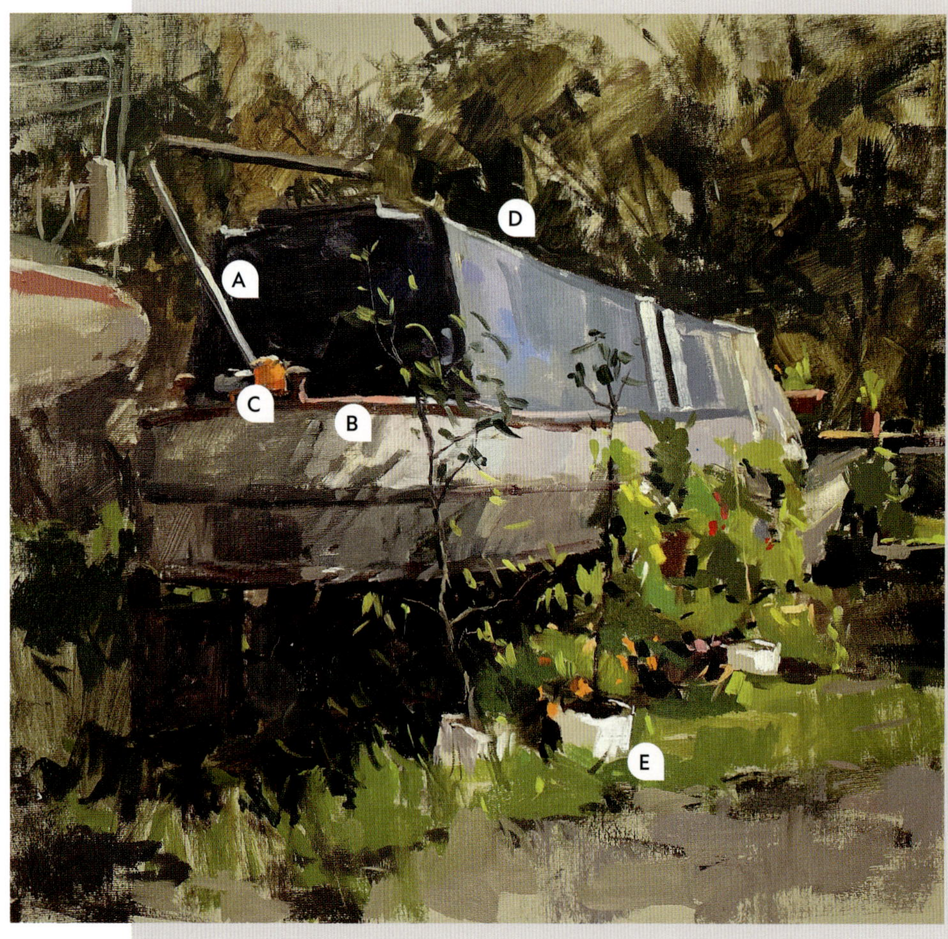

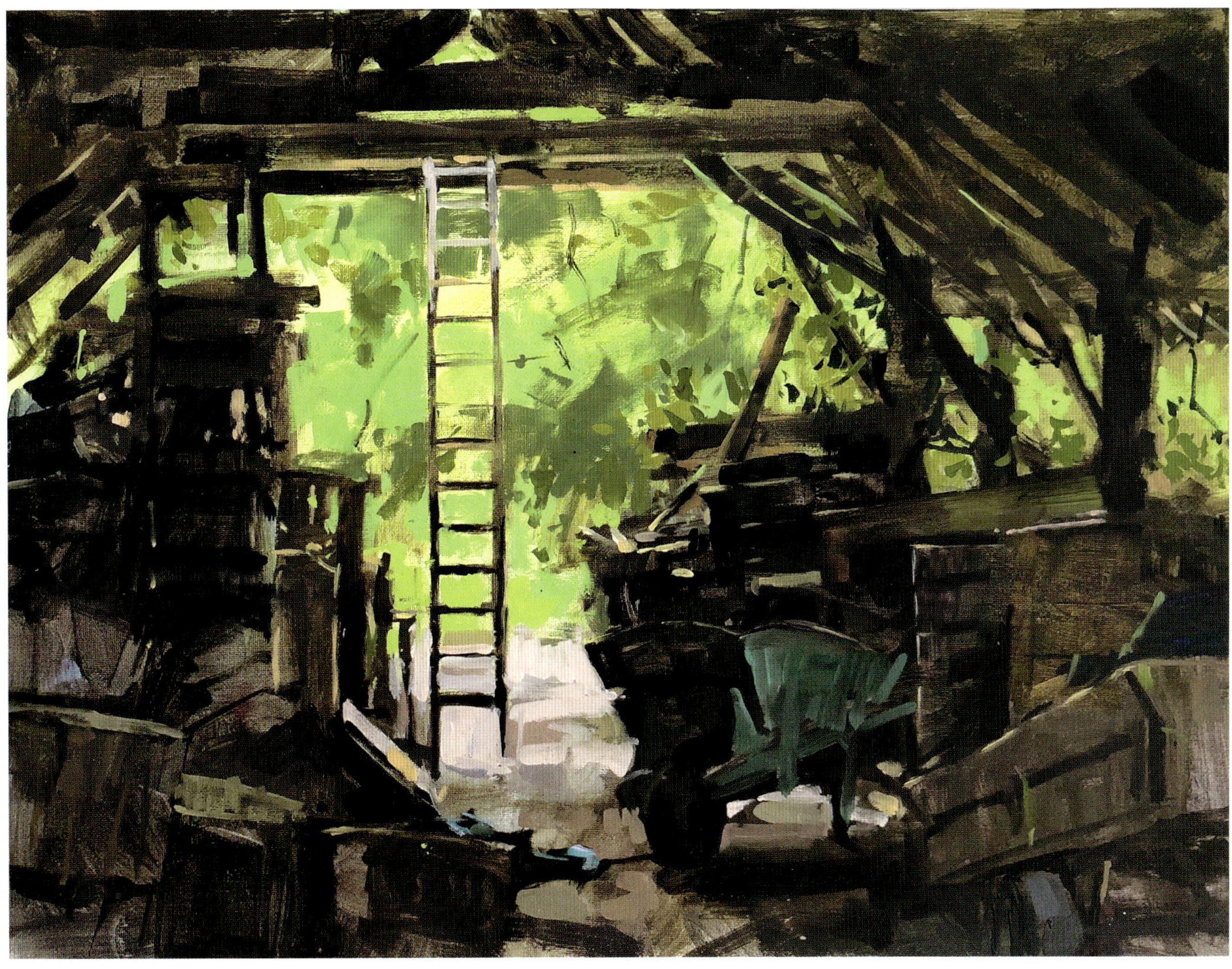

View-through compositions

This is a good example of a 'view-through' composition. I was attracted to the interesting abstract shapes formed by the gaps of green light seen through the structure of the old barn, and the strong colour and value contrast of the inside versus the outside. I was careful to bring some of those greens down into parts of the dark interior so that the two areas were integrated in colour while being very separate in value.

I chose to lighten the value of the ladder in the painting from how I was actually seeing it because I didn't want it to act as a barrier to the viewer and stop them being able to 'travel' outside to the open space beyond.

The information is all there for the taking when painting en plein air, but it's up to the artist to use that information to serve the painting, placing emphasis in relevant areas and de-emphasising others. Avoid placing the strongest value or colour contrasts close to the edges of your picture surface, or you risk sending the viewer out of your painting.

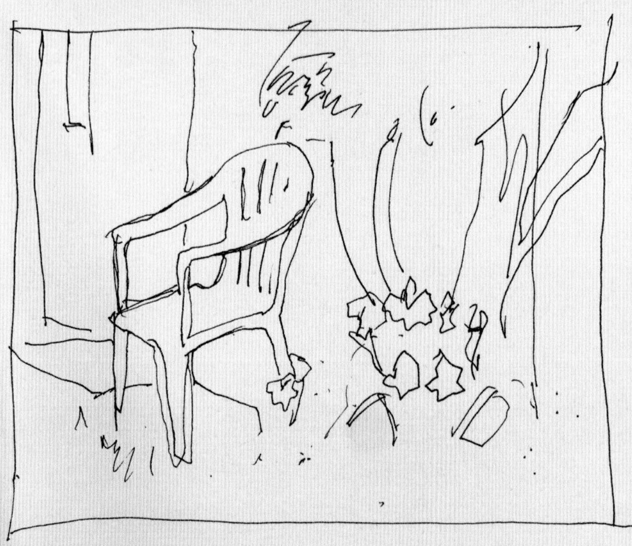

Line drawing
This drawing shows me some shape and line but so much is left vague or unknown, such as the direction of the light.

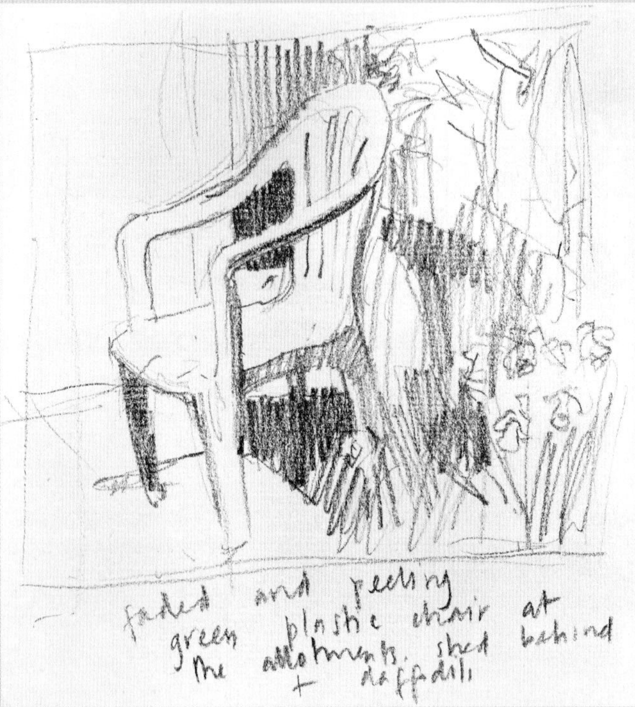

Value drawing
As it includes information on both shape and value, this is a better sketch to use as reference for painting than the line drawing above.

Composing with drawings

It's not always practical to take your full painting kit and oils everywhere you go, but a small sketchbook and a pencil is much more manageable to slip into a pocket. It's therefore possible to make drawings from life and then use those as a springboard for creating paintings in the studio. While not strictly painting en plein air, sketching outdoors requires many of the same skills – and producing sketches that are to prove useful requires a little thought and preparation.

If you are sketching outdoors with the intention of painting from your reference back in the studio, get as much relevant information as you can. A simple line drawing, such as the example at the top left, won't give you enough material to go on, and nor will a sketch of separate parts of a subject. You need a full composition.

Making a tonal value study, such as the example below left, will give you all that you need to know in terms of shape and value for your painting. Since we usually sketch in monochrome, a sketch that includes written notes about colour, such as the example opposite, is better still to support your painting. I also sometimes record sounds, smells, general impressions or feelings conveyed at the time to act as an aide-mémoire back in the studio.

Photographic reference

You can, of course, take supporting photographs too, but photographs will often not represent colours the way you remember them. They can bleach out the details in both light and dark value areas, and notoriously make anything in shadow look black. More to the point, photographs can't be selective and emphasise the parts of the subject that interest you. The camera will not discriminate and will present all the components of the scene it is pointed towards with equal significance. The ability to make decisions and emphasise areas is where our sketches can prove to be a lot more useful as references from which to paint.

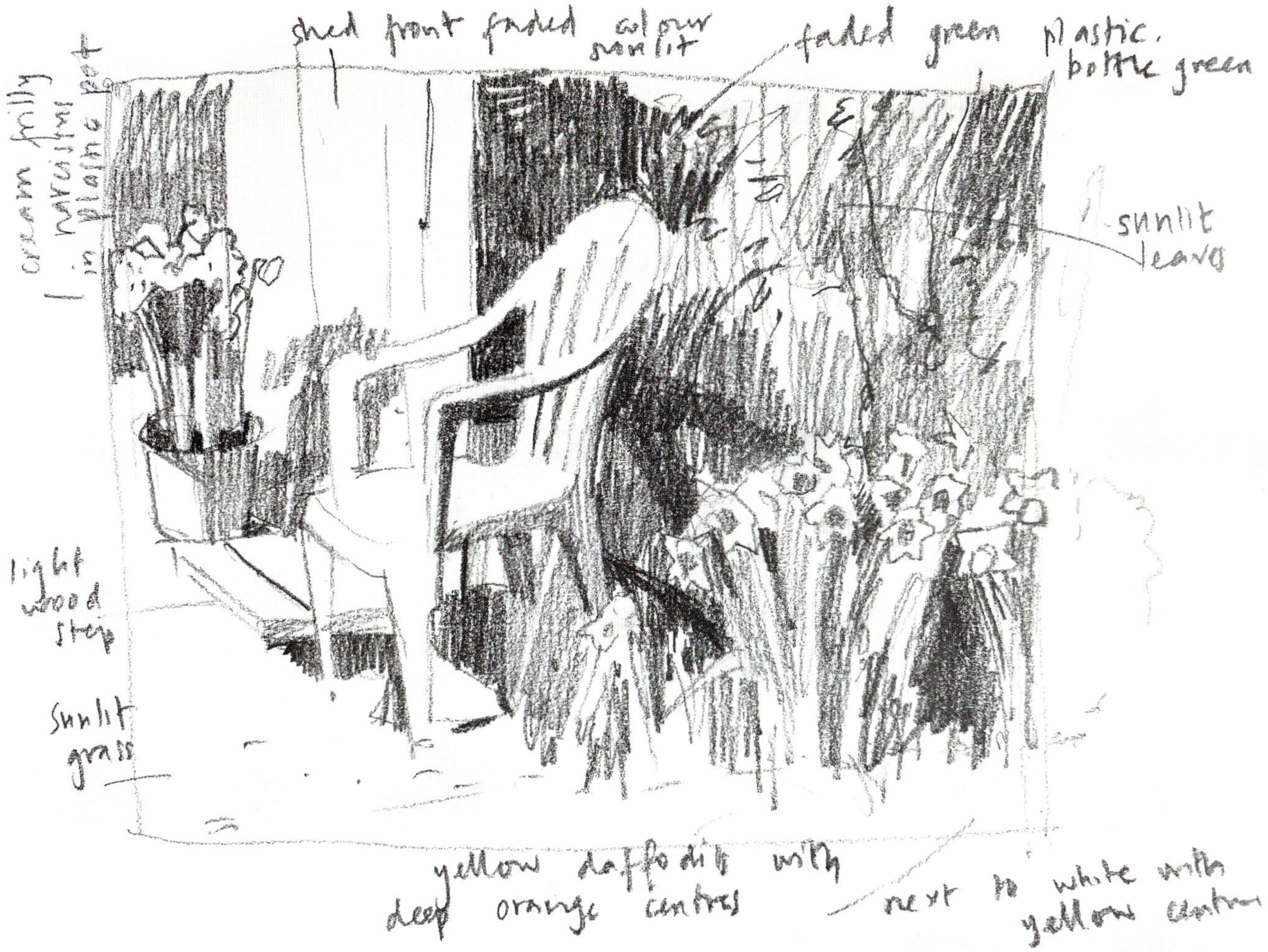

cream frilly narcissus in plastic pot

shed front faded colour sunlit

faded green plastic. bottle green

sunlit leaves

light wood step

sunlit grass

yellow daffodils with deep orange centres

next to white with yellow centres

Information drawing
Of the three sketches shown on these pages, this is the best to paint from. It is a complete composition and contains all I need to know about the value shapes, together with supporting written notes about colour.

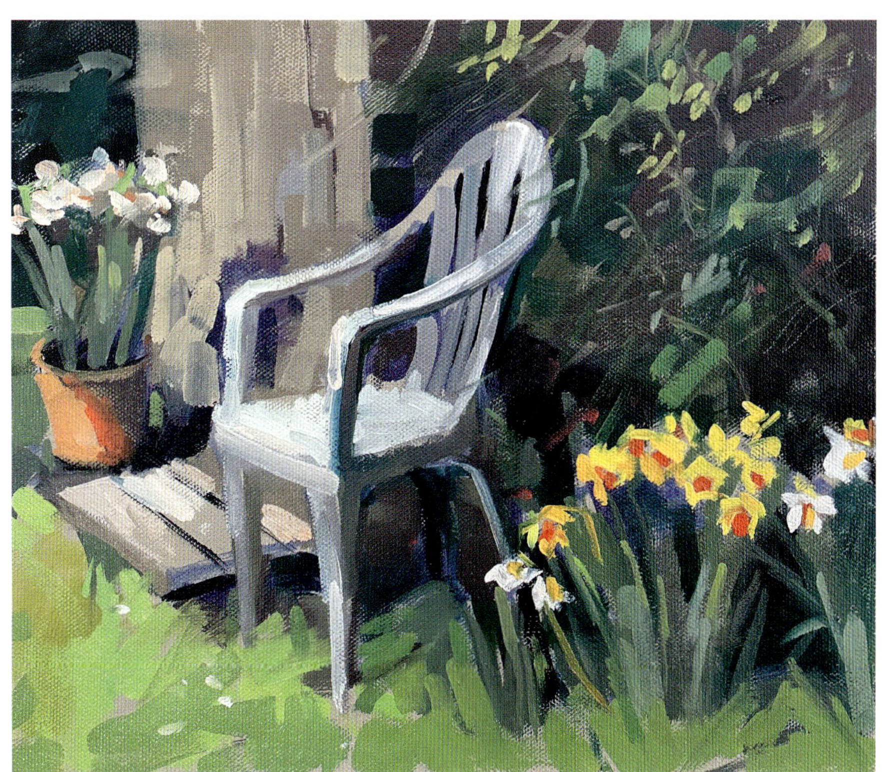

Plastic Chair and Daffodils at the Allotments
30.5 x 25.5cm (12 x 10in)

I painted this using only the third sketch (above) as reference. I really enjoy working from a good drawing with the right sort of information. I feel more free to make departures from the drawing than when I am working with the real subject in front of me.

Expressive brushwork

Good brushwork is deliberate brushwork. Loose and painterly brushstrokes are not the result of a careless or carefree approach to painting, far from it. They are the natural side effect of a deliberate and considered approach to placing colours and values. Conversely, too much smudging and blending of brushmarks – until they disappear in a blurry haze – is usually a result of the artist's indecision and worry, and an attempt to fix problems by overworking. The painterly approach is to make deliberate brushmarks that show your individuality, like handwriting.

It's impossible to talk about brushwork without talking about edges, where two adjacent areas of colour meet. In any painting, ideally you are looking for edge variety. If the whole thing is painted with hard edges, the effect can be that everything in the painting is competing for our attention, and the result looks stiff and unnatural. If all the edges in the painting are soft, we struggle to focus our attention anywhere. As in a piece of music, we need both loud and quiet passages.

Take guidance about edges from the subject. If you can't see a clear distinction between two adjacent 'spots' of colour when you half close your eyes – don't paint one. Your brain will love to interfere and tell you there should be an edge or separation between objects, but learn to trust your eyes instead. Use sharp clear edges and strong value contrast where you want to direct the viewer's eye to a focal point; and leave well alone edges that soften or disappear entirely when you squint.

Brushwork and detail

The level of detail and finish that you aspire to is a personal choice and it would be a boring world if we all responded the same way. My own taste is that I like paintings to look as though they have been painted: I like to appreciate the picture surface and abstract marks upon it every bit as much as the illusion of depth created within the painting. What interests me is that people perceive a level of detail in my paintings that isn't really there. I love them to get right up close to the surface and see the abstract marks, dots and patches which had led them to believe that they could see, for example, a whole village on a mountainside.

I think of each painting as needing a balance between descriptive shape and suggestion. You can still convey a strong idea and hang on to that idea if your taste is for exquisite detail, but consider rendering some parts of the painting in a more suggestive manner so that you can actively direct where your viewer focusses their attention. Standing back often to look at your work makes it easier to assess the overall vitality of the work and not to risk losing that by trying to perfect insignificant little areas of detail that aren't adding any real value. Knowing when to stop is hard, but think of your painting as a collaboration with the future viewer and try to leave a little something for them to work on.

> ' Remember that a painting – before being a battle horse, a nude woman or an anecdote of some sort – is essentially a flat surface covered with colours, put together in a certain order. '
>
> Maurice Denis, 1870–1943

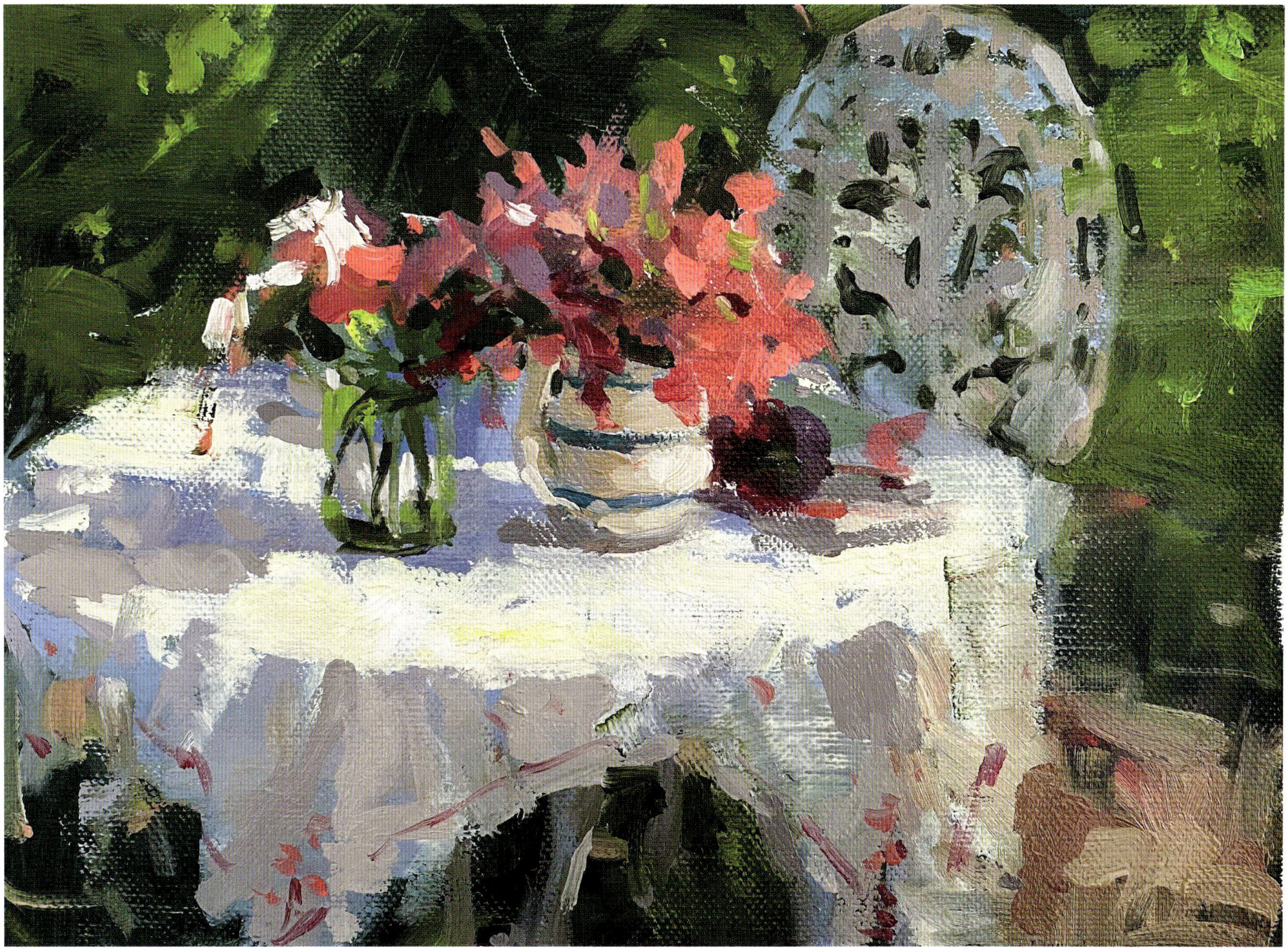

Garden Table
28 x 20.5cm (11 x 8in)

Everything in this small painting was treated to lively and expressive brushwork. Along with the value and colour shapes which underpin the composition the brushwork further helps it to pack a punch.

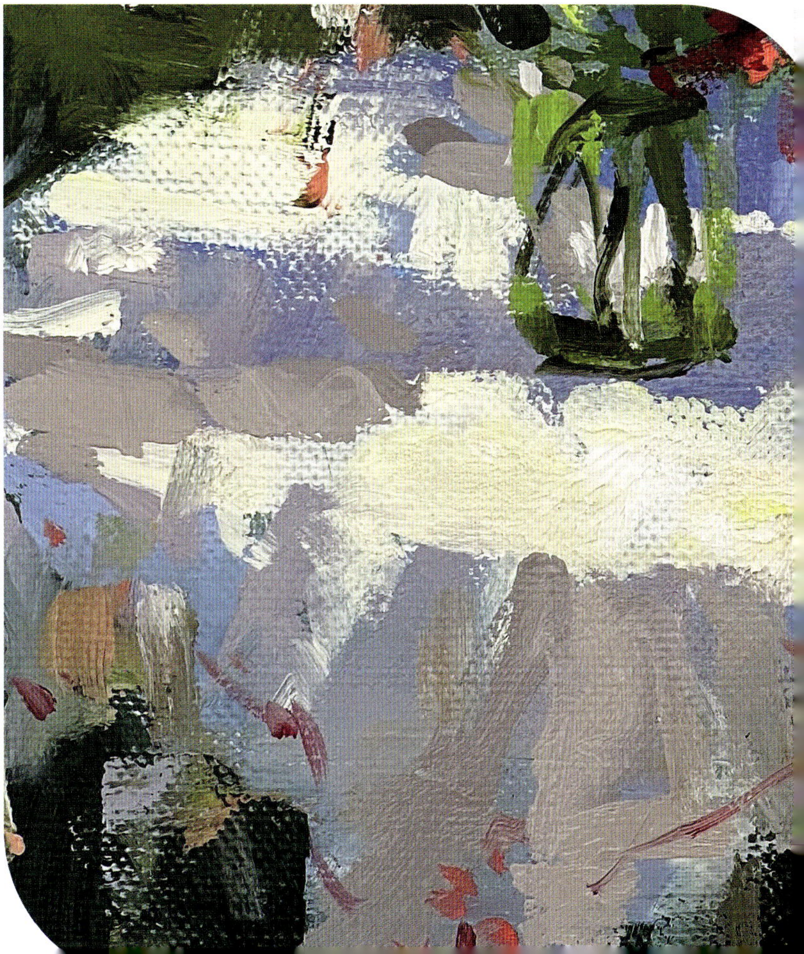

During the painting of the tablecloth the colour hasn't been fully mixed on the palette, so the streaks of broken colour in both the light and shadow families enliven this area.

As well as obvious brushmarks and thick impasto areas, there are smudged and broken edges and scratched-out parts, lending a stimulating variety to the picture surface.

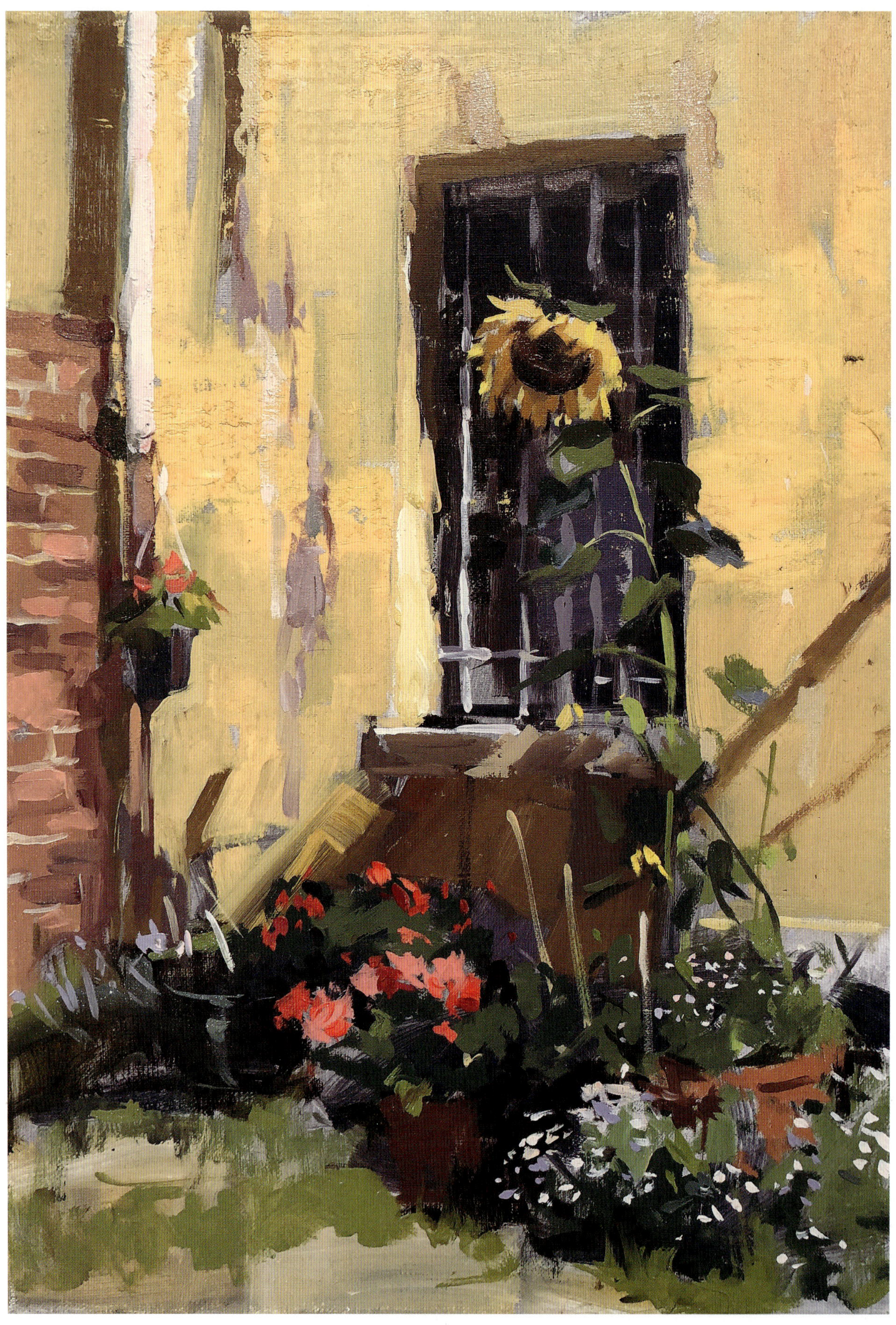

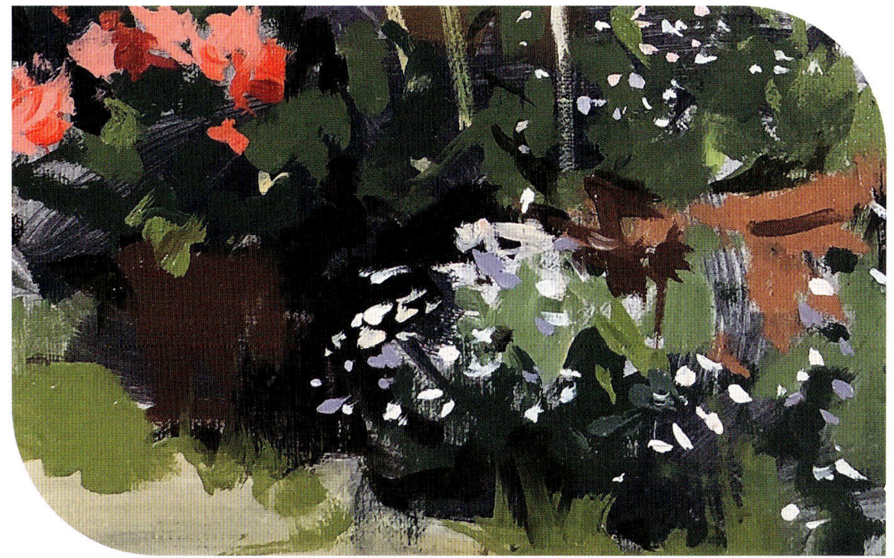

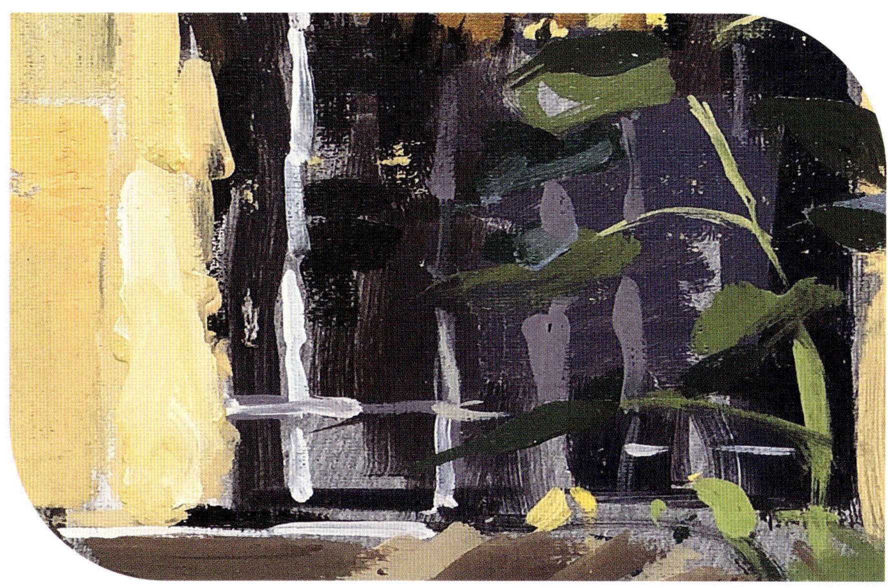

Yellow Wall, Sunflower
25.5 x 35.5cm (10 x 14in)

Think of your brushwork as enlivening the picture surface. A flat, painted wall in front of you doesn't have to be rendered in your painting with flat and boring brushwork. Look at how this yellow wall in the painting has a lively application of paint, with thinner and thicker passages, changes in direction of the brushmarks, and colour subtleties.

I wanted to suggest old and peeling paintwork, so brushwork in this painting was particularly important, but you never want to tackle a flat area of colour in your painting as if you were painting a wall in your house.

When I'm painting foliage I often apply my brushmarks in the general direction of growth. As always, simplicity is key to my approach. The plants/flowers in the foreground appear to be detailed, but when you look up close (see above left) you'll notice that I've loosely painted two values of green and then two values for the flower colours which sit on top of the greens, painted in short jabs and spots.

Straight lines in a painting don't have to be too straight. In the detail above right, notice how I've painted the bars at the window in playful broken and wavering lines which enhances the joyful feeling of basking in the warm sunshine.

Free-Range Hens at Low Bradfield

Looking for a subject on a hot, cloudy summer's day I spotted this farm and asked for permission to come into the farmyard to paint. The chicken hut and barns behind were an appealing subject, although sadly it didn't look likely that they would be lit by direct sunlight at that time.

This influenced my composition. I decided to make the hens the main focal point of the painting, as a result of which I chose to place my board vertically, using a portrait format. That way I could include all the farm buildings in the top half of my panel, while still leaving plenty of room in the bottom half for the foreground and hens. I would try to lead the eye towards the farm buildings using the hens. The perspective was quite interesting because I was looking uphill towards the buildings, and I couldn't see any part of the barn roof from my viewpoint.

▶ You will need

SURFACE
28 x 33cm (11 x 13in) muslin panel, prepared with a warm grey tone

COLOURS
An extended primary palette (see page 73) with the addition of raw sienna, raw umber, transparent red oxide and blue-black

BRUSHES
A range of filberts and flats in sizes from 6mm (¼in) to 20mm (¾in)

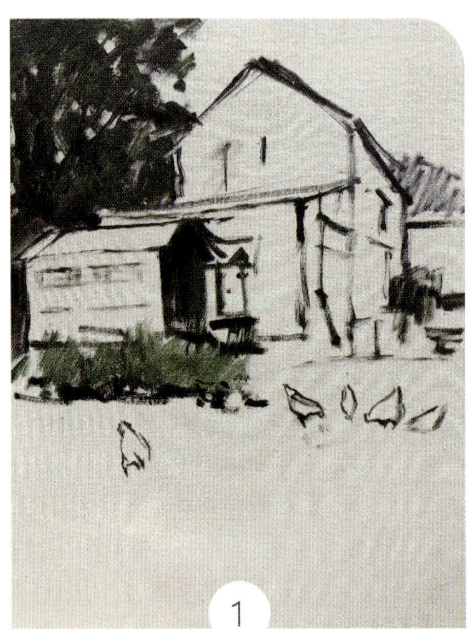

1

To start, I mixed a dark blue-green from ultramarine blue with cadmium yellow thinned with a little solvent. With this I marked in a rough outline of the buildings and scrubbed in the dark area of trees on the left-hand side. I used a 12mm (½in) filbert to draw in some of the shapes of the more distant hens, taking care to check their size in relation to the buildings.

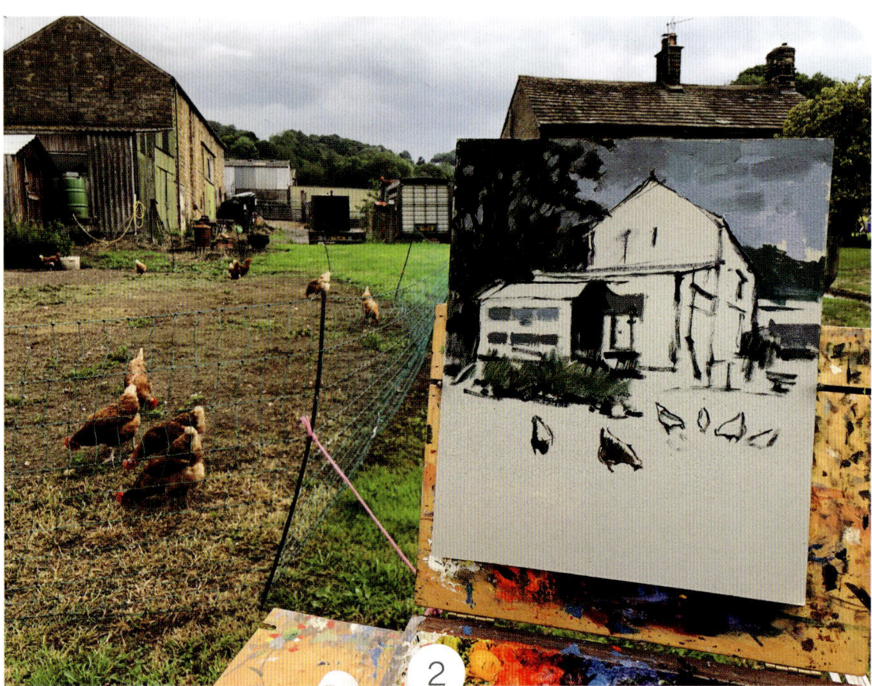

2

With the structure in place I started blocking in the sky colour, using a mix of ultramarine, crimson, raw umber and white. For the buildings I used mixes of raw sienna, ultramarine, raw umber and white. I blocked in a mid-value green for the shrubs near the hen hut and the patches of grass.

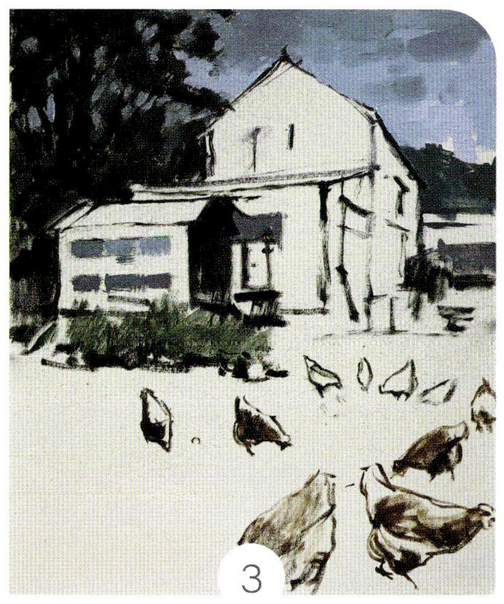

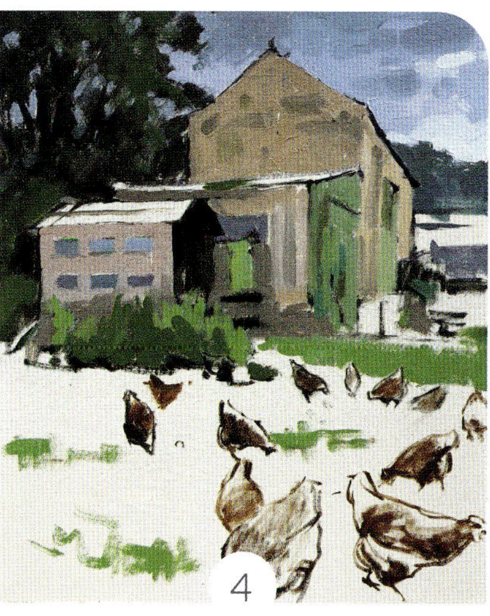

Tip

If you need to check or finish the drawing of a single hen, keep an eye out for another in a similar position.

When working with wildlife it's good to remain flexible. When a couple of hens came closer, I stopped and quickly drew them in using the paint remaining on the palette.

I continued to build up the colours of the hens and the warm mid-toned earth around them.

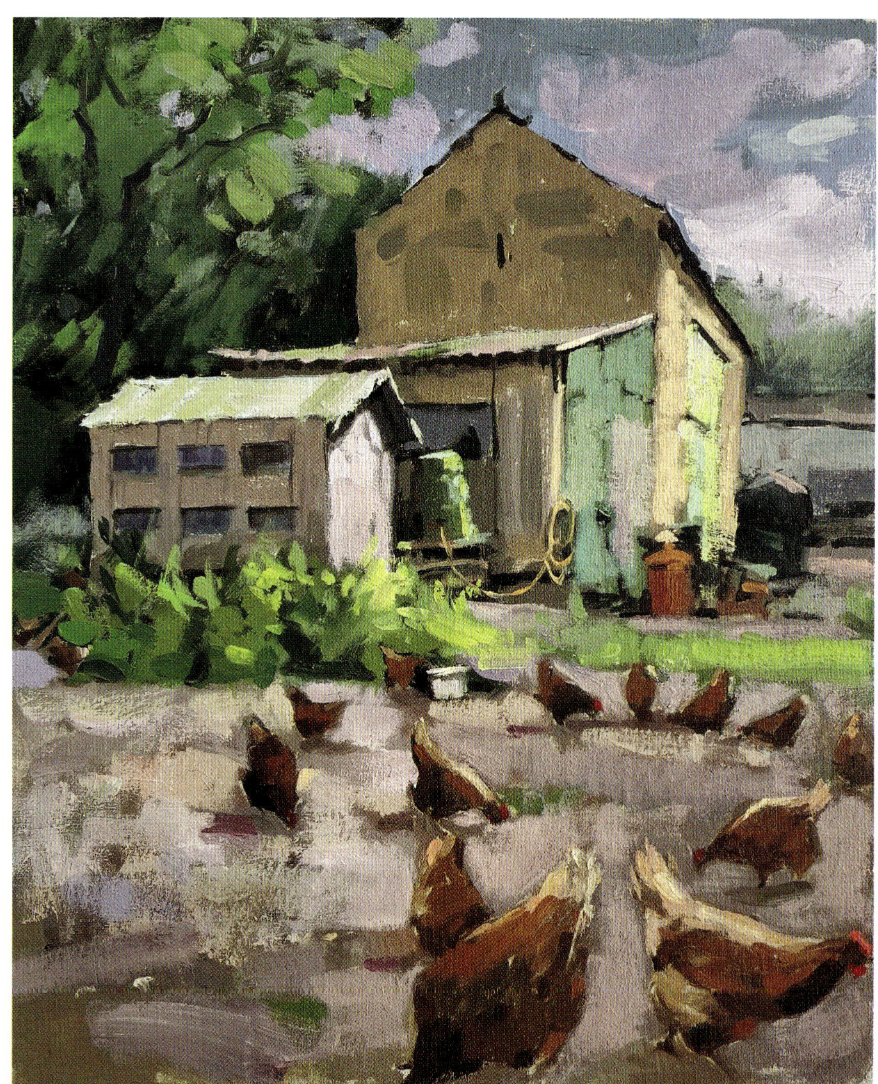

The finished painting
28 x 33cm (11 x 13in)

Once back in the studio I decided that the overall effect was quite dark and gloomy, so I lightened the fronts of the buildings and foliage as if the sun had broken through the clouds.

Suggesting distance in the landscape

In representational painting one of the things we try to communicate is a sense of space and depth. Artists through the centuries have used some great devices for fooling the eye into thinking that the flat picture surface is three-dimensional.

This is a quick guide to the common methods of suggesting distance. They're not hard and fast rules, and you don't need to use them all in every painting. Think of them as extra devices in your tool kit that you can draw on when necessary, and if you have a painting that lacks depth maybe you can check it against these ideas and consider what you could have done differently.

Size, scale and overlapping objects Objects appear to get smaller in size at a constant rate as they get further away from us. In the case of repeating objects, such as fenceposts, the gaps between them also decrease. Recognizable objects in a painting, such as cars or people, give us clues as to scale and distance. Overlapping objects makes it easy for the viewer to judge space in a painting.

Atmospheric or aerial perspective When we are looking through veils of atmosphere, water droplets and other particles in the air affect the colours that we can see in the far distance. The colours of objects further away from us become more neutralized and move towards the blue-grey. How we use this as a device in painting is to remember that warm colours and details advance, while cool purples and blues and soft transitions recede.

Edges and contrast Strong contrasts draw the eye and jump forwards; that's either tonal value or colour contrast. Use both colour and value contrasts together for maximum impact and keep those to where the focal point is; usually in the foreground or middle distance. In a landscape which encompasses great depth, avoid strong colour or value contrasts in the far distance. Similarly, reserve texture, detail and hard edges for those parts of the scene that are closer to you. For the distant parts, employ soft edges and close colours and most often you'll need to keep values at the lighter end of the value scale.

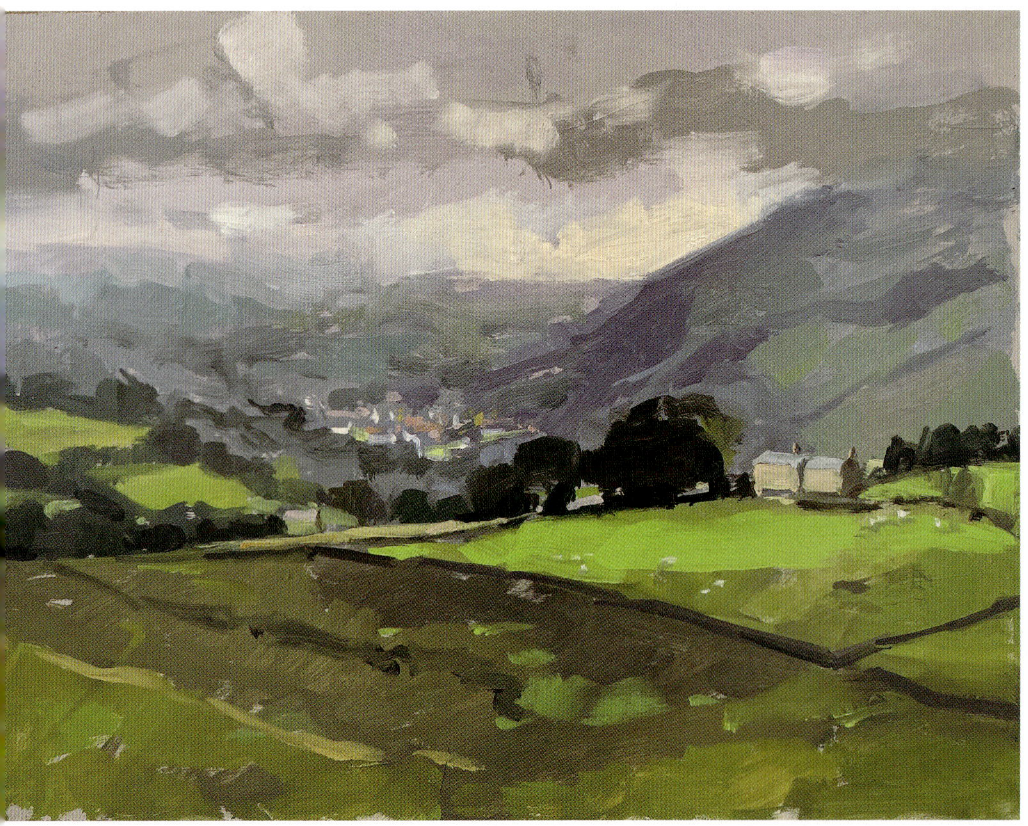

Garsdale, Yorkshire Dales
30.5 x 23cm (12 x 9in)

Notice on this one that the hills become bluer and lighter in value towards the distance. The strongest value contrast and most saturated colour green is in the middle distance, because that's where my focal point is in this painting: on the group of farm buildings. The lines of the stone walls also act to lead the eye into the painting and towards the focal point.

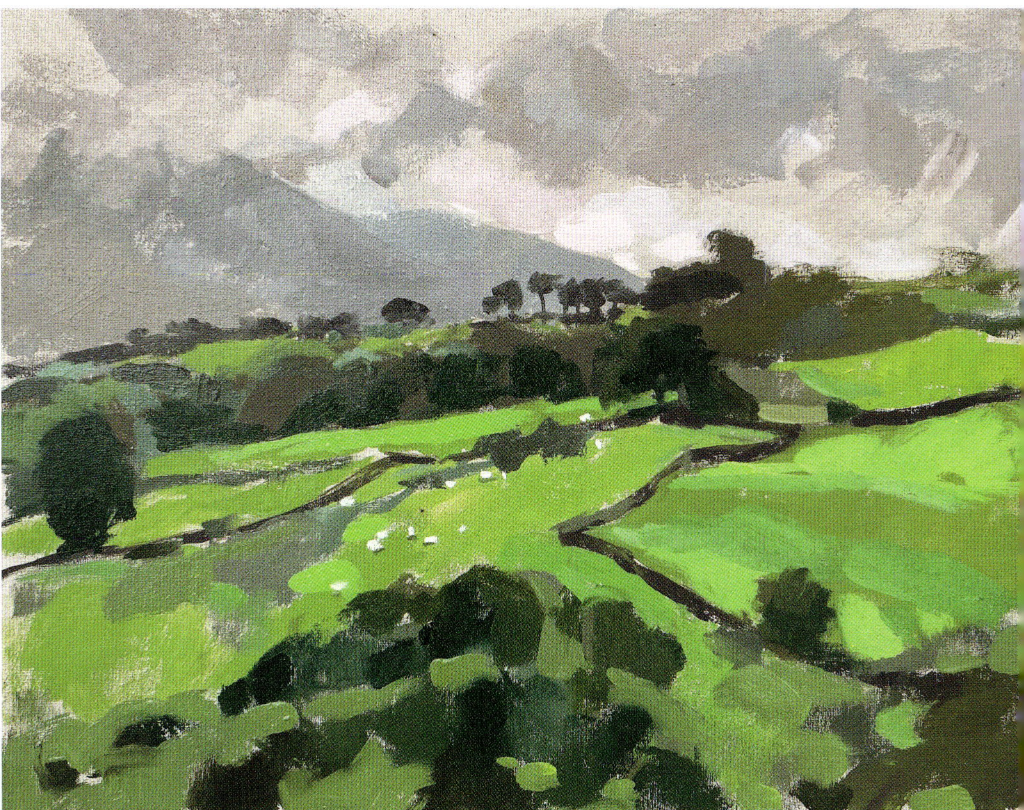

Rain Approaching, Yorkshire Dales
30.5 x 23cm (12 x 9in)

Again, here the dry stone walls make useful lines leading us in to the painting. The atmospheric perspective causes the distant hills to appear lighter and bluer in colour, and because of the rain I had a great opportunity here to let those hills disappear into the clouds and sky.

Linear perspective Not as frightening as it sounds, it's a good idea to learn the basics of one-, two- and even three-point perspective. One-point perspective is relevant when you are facing a subject directly: for example, imagine you are standing in the middle of a road, looking along it into the distance. The parallel lines of the edges of the road appear to converge in the distance at a vanishing point on the horizon (our eye level) line. In two-point perspective we are looking at objects, such as buildings, from the corner, in which case there are two vanishing points and two sets of orthogonal lines appearing to converge together. Three-point perspective is only needed in extreme circumstances, such as when looking up at a tall skyscraper or looking down from a great height. These methods are useful for predicting how things will appear to look on the picture plane, or for checking the accuracy of your drawing. With that said, I also believe you can do just as well without relying on the theory, if you work hard to practise good observation and paint just what you see.

Tip

Perspective applies to the sky too, not just the land. Try making your closest clouds larger and let them contain more value and colour contrast than more distant clouds.

> ❝ Perspective is to painting what the bridle is to the horse, the rudder to a ship. There are three aspects to perspective. The first has to do with how the size of objects seems to diminish according to distance: the second, the manner in which colours change the farther away they are from the eye; the third defines how objects ought to be finished less carefully the farther away they are. ❞
>
> Leonardo da Vinci, 1452–1519

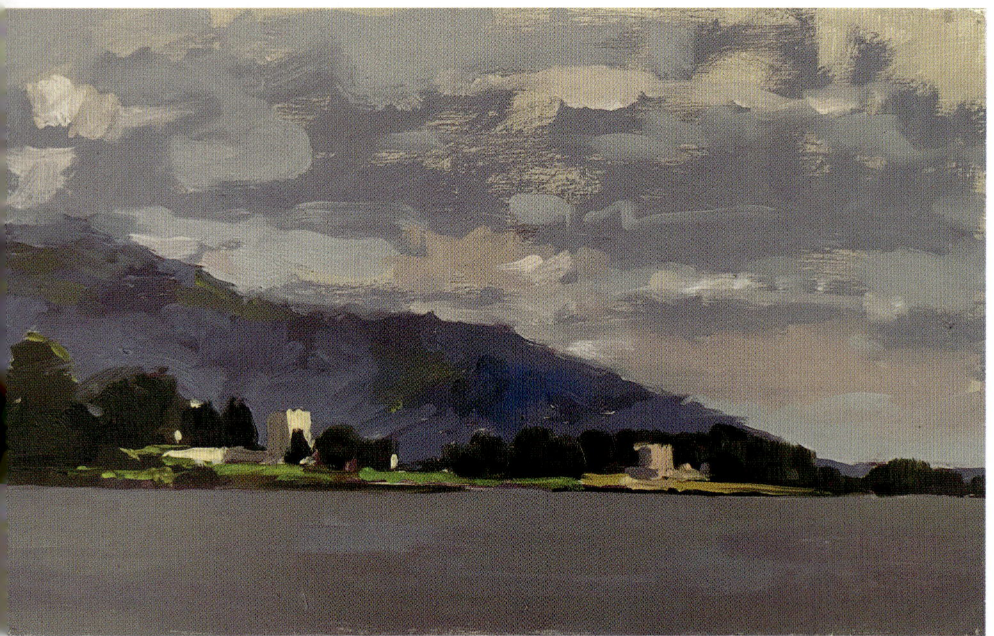

A Glimpse of Sun, Loch Leven
25.5 x 15cm (10 x 6in)

The foreground of this one is a body of water without much going on, so the focal point and the strongest contrasts here are actually in the middle distance. Notice that I have placed different emphasis on the buildings, so that they don't compete for your attention. The church on the left has the lightest lights and slightly more saturated colour, drawing the eye more than the muted, softer building on the right.

When you're standing in a place like this you can see the effects of atmospheric perspective clearly. On the highest part of the mountain I have softened the edge by letting the clouds travel right into it. The clouds that are closest to us have stronger value contrasts than the more distant cloud shapes.

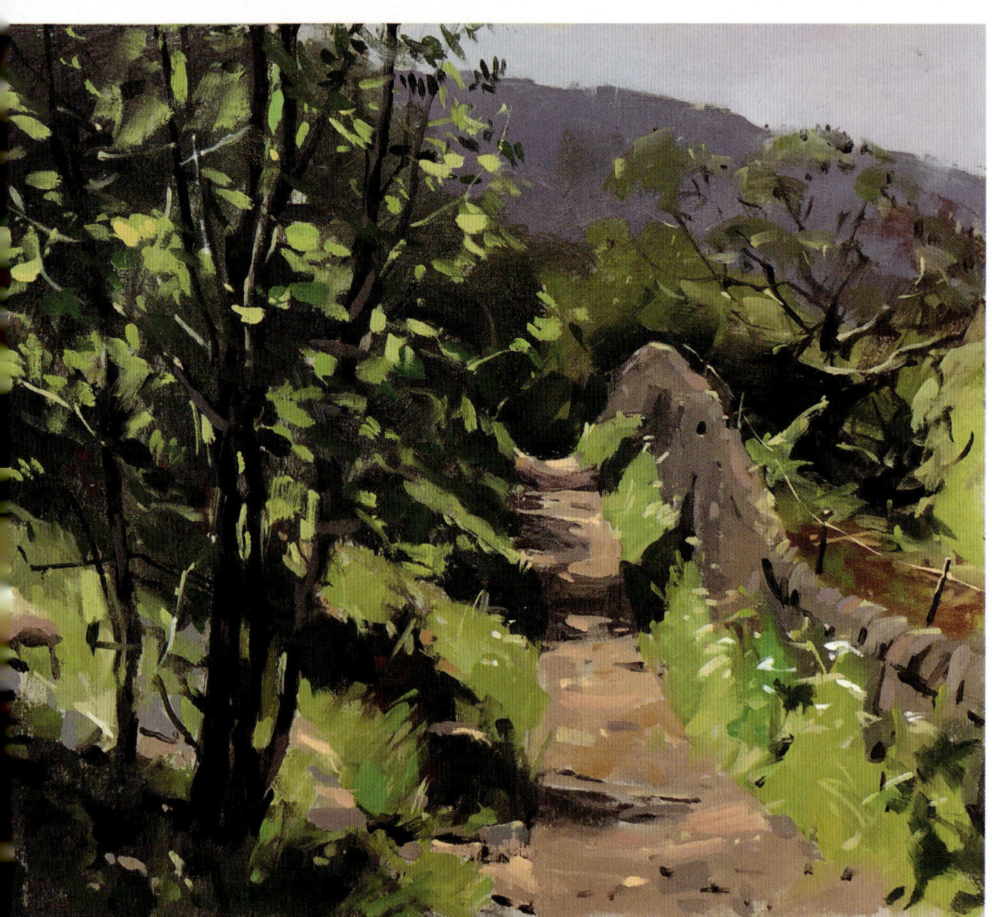

Footpath at Crowden on a Hot Day
33 x 28cm (13 x 11in)

You can see here the effect of linear perspective as the path narrows the further away it gets from us, and the posts above the wall get smaller and thinner as they recede. There is so much blue in the hill behind that we can understand it is a fair distance away. The flowers in the grass verge are white, but I've only let the closest flowers be really white, the farther ones are a slightly darker tone.

Using a viewfinder

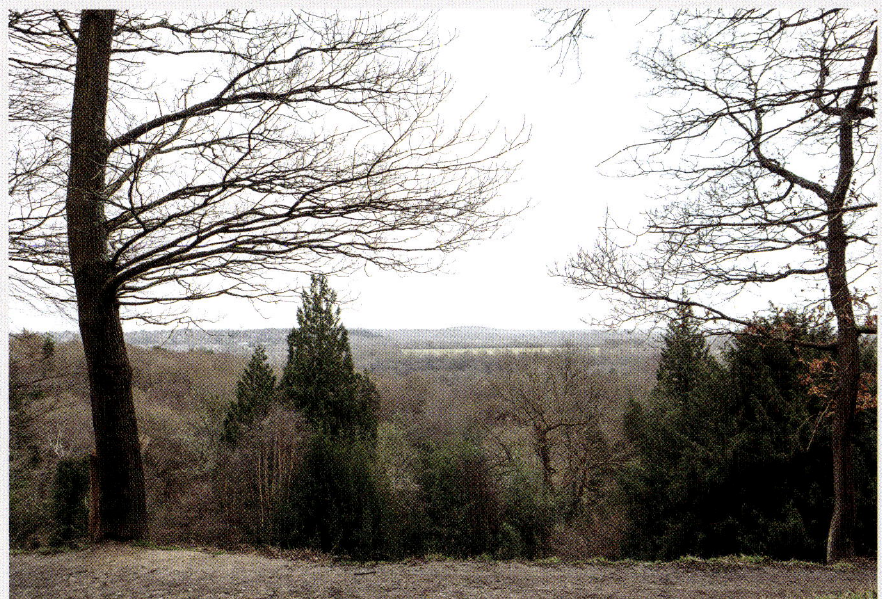

What's our way into this scene? How can we find the best composition? A viewfinder can help us simplify what's in front of us, and visualize our options more easily.

Using a simple viewfinder can help a lot with seeing a potential composition for a painting. A couple of sturdy pieces of cardboard cut into L shapes will do the trick. Hold them up as shown below, overlapping to create a small, adjustable window you look through, as shown in the detail.

Make sure that the shape of the aperture that you are looking through has the same proportions as your painting surface. Then you can use the viewfinder frame to note where objects in your composition will reach the edges of your panel or canvas.

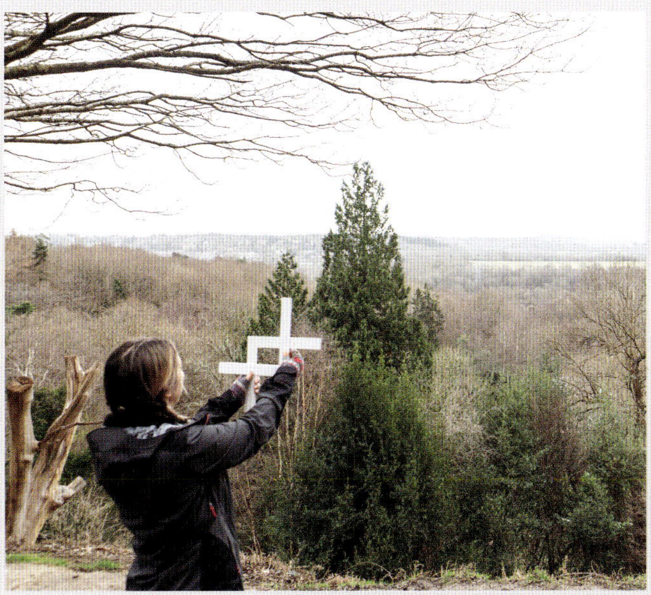

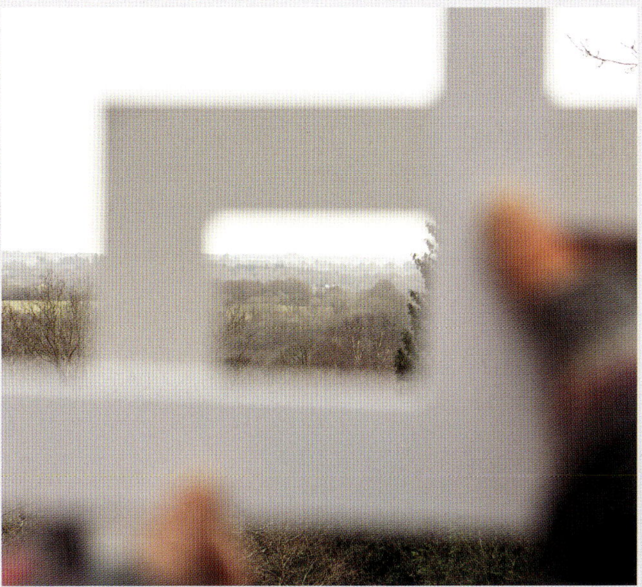

MIDGROUND HILLS The fields and trees are suggested with a variety of greens, although the greens are less saturated here than in the foreground, and tend more towards blue-greens.

HILLTOP TOWN The town is lit by the sun, suggested by a few blocks and horizontal dashes of colour. I've avoided using details or strong darks here because it would visually jump forwards and not sit back into the middle-distance hills.

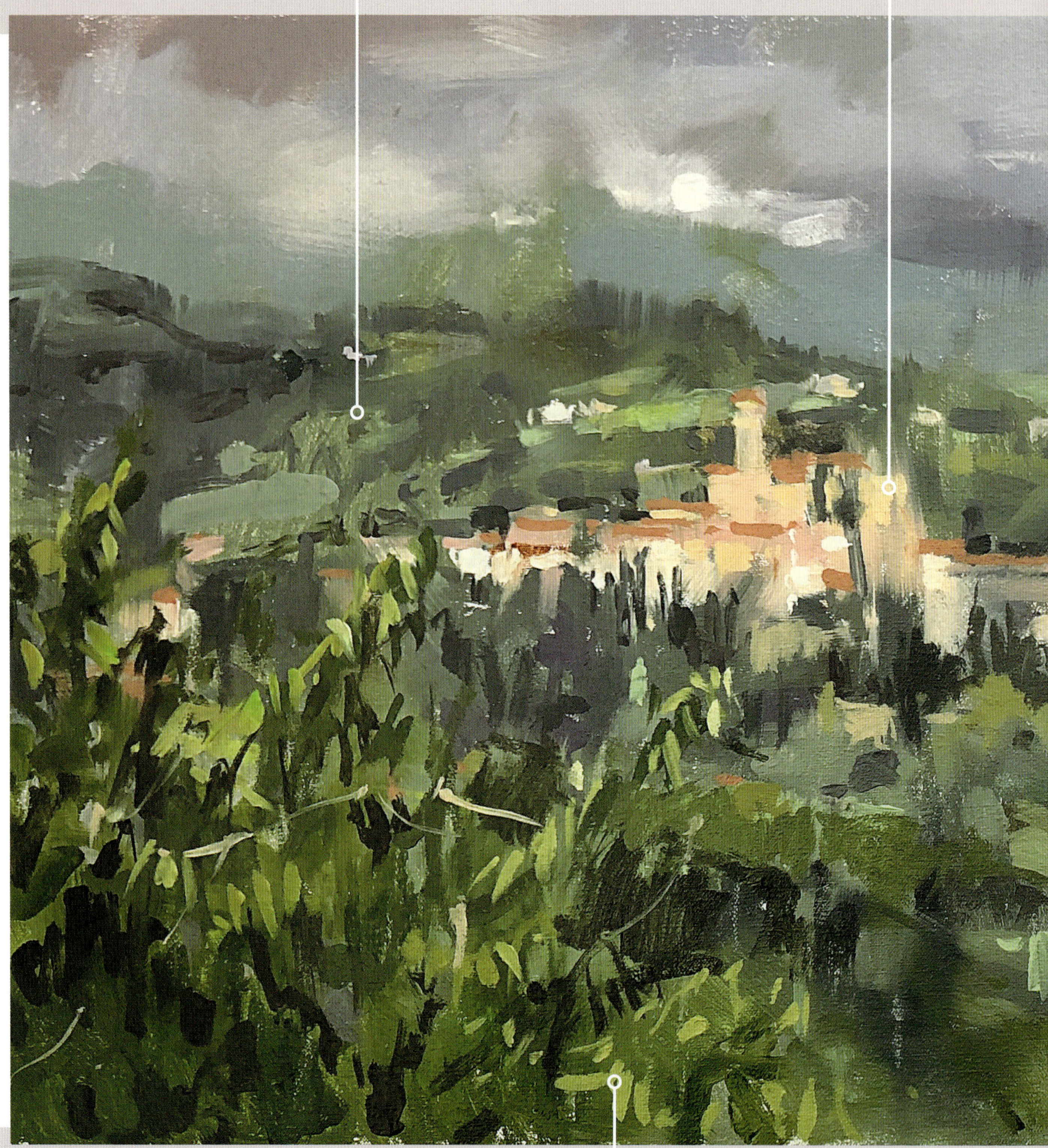

Low Cloud in the Valley, Lippiano
61 x 30.5cm (24 x 12in)

FOREGROUND SHRUBS The foreground shrubs are painted with detail and strong tonal value contrast.

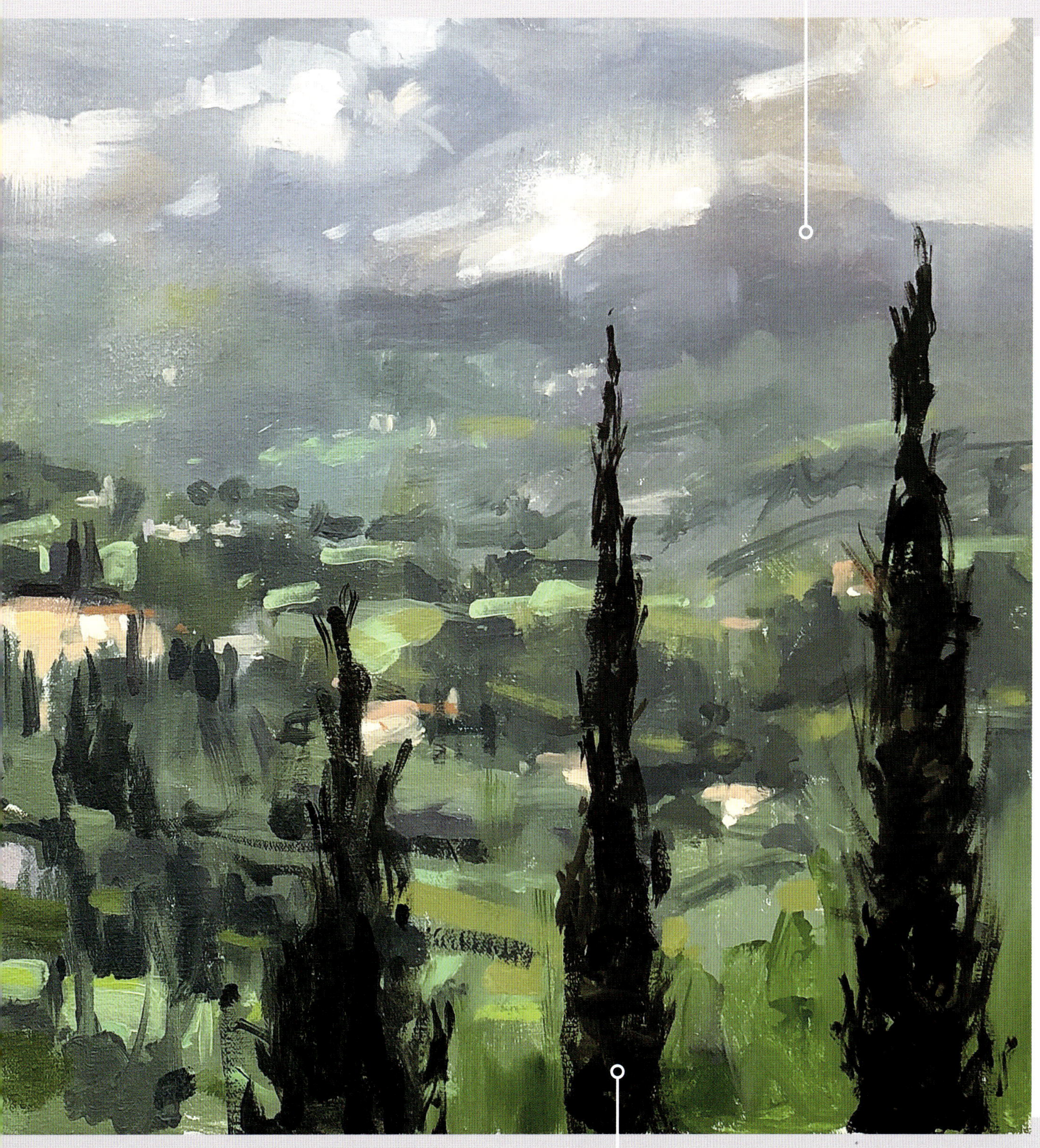

DISTANT MOUNTAINS Here there is less colour, less contrast, and colours tend towards blue. The hill tops merge and soften into the clouds, with no hard edges in this part of the painting.

CYPRESS TREES The cypress trees are in the foreground and contain the darkest darks in the painting.

Sight–size painting

Sight–size painting aims to portray the subject at the exact size you see it, by sticking to one viewpoint and using a measuring technique. Working sight–size can be very useful if you struggle to see relationships between various points in your subject, or to judge distances or angles. You might choose to use it for greater accuracy if you paint challenging scenes that rely on precise drawing to succeed.

I tend to judge drawing by eye, but I occasionally use the sight–size method if I want to take in a large breadth of subject matter and be quite precise about it. Sometimes, if I notice that what I want to place in the painting happens to be around sight–size, then I might take a few quick measurements of nearby buildings, boats or similar, just to place the first drawing marks to get me started.

I would recommend that you start by practising sight–size drawing using a soft pencil and cartridge paper. Use anything that you can see around you as a subject with which to practise: furniture in your home or workplace, for example. Accurate results depend completely on using the correct technique, so it's worth putting in lots of practice.

The sight–size method

When painting sight–size, you will need to place your panel both up high at your eye level and beside the chosen view of the subject. You should be able to stand in one position and easily see both subject and panel with minimal eye movement.

Close one eye, hold up your paintbrush vertically at arm's length, and measure a distance within two points on your subject using the space between the top of the brush and where you place your thumb. Next, lift your arm down and transfer this measurement directly to your surface. Make short marks registering where points are; you can flesh these out later.

Start with one accurate measurement between two points and then gradually build outwards from there. Measure not only the obvious parts of the scene, for example the height and width of a door, but also the distances in between points of interest, or the negative spaces.

You can use a paintbrush for taking the measurements, or anything long and thin, such as a pencil or knitting needle.

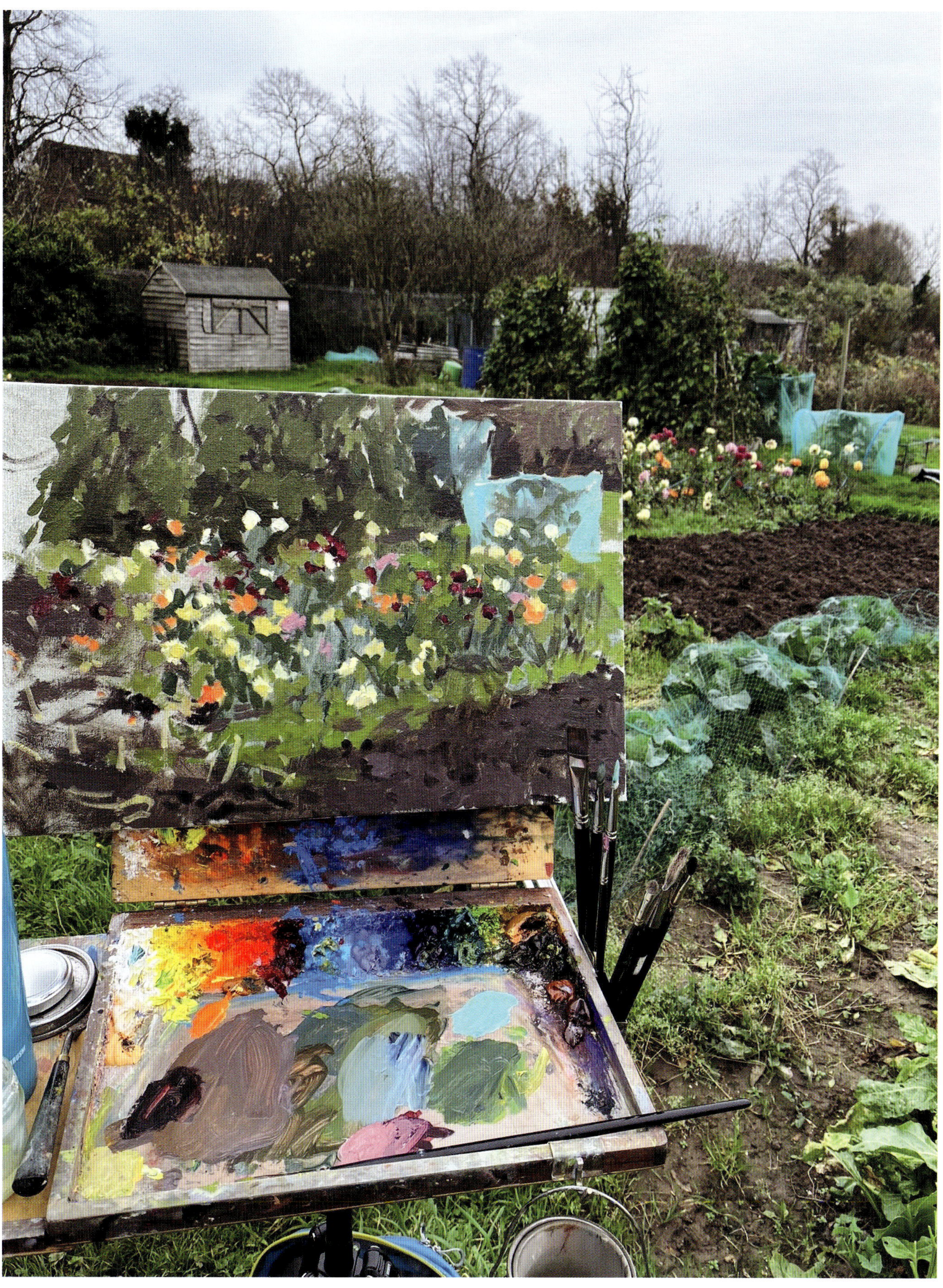

Waterfall

In this example of sight–size painting, I started with a thin wash of varied greens to get an idea of colour down before starting to draw shapes. I wanted to ensure that the parts of the water flow that I found most interesting were included, so spending time finding the right vantage point and getting properly set up was the key to success here.

SURFACE

33 x 35.5cm (13 x 14in) muslin panel, prepared with a warm grey tone

COLOURS

An extended primary palette (see page 73) with the addition of green gold, blue black, raw umber and raw sienna

BRUSHES

A range of filberts and flats in sizes from 6mm (¼in) to 20mm (¾in), plus good quality hog bristle brushes

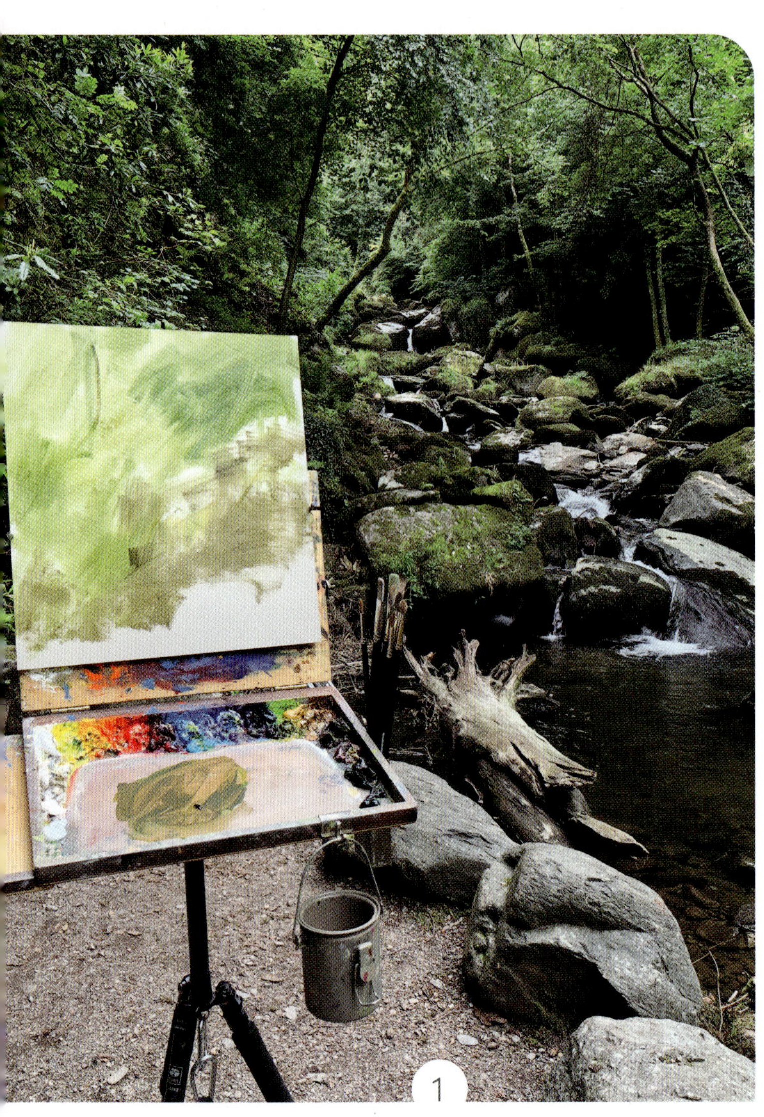

At first I washed on green gold, raw umber and raw sienna thinned with low-odour solvent to get started with the green colour palette straight away.

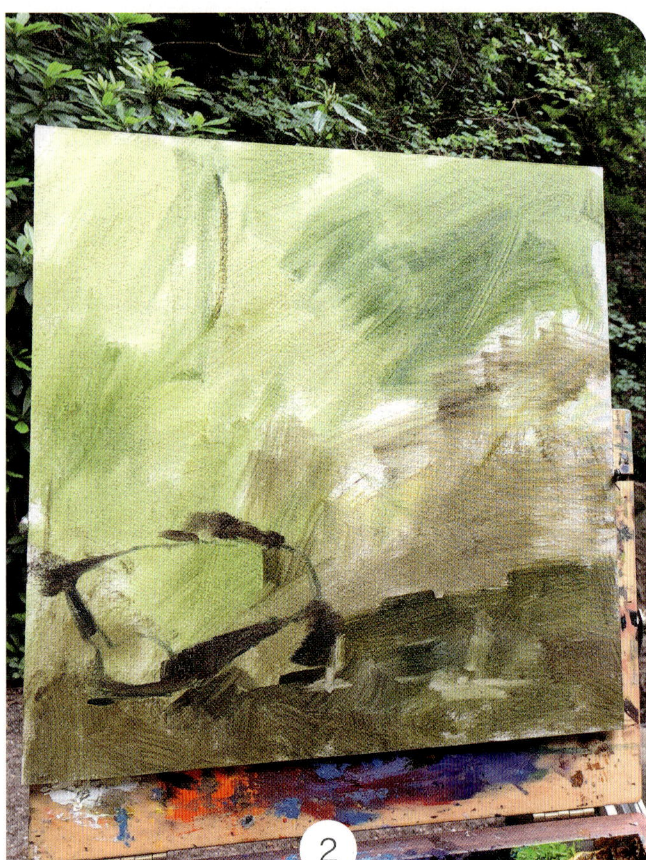

Using a brush I took height and width measurements of the largest closer rock and placed that in the lower left-hand quarter. I sketched in the outline of the rock with thinned raw umber at the size I was actually seeing it from my vantage point. With this in place, I then applied a slightly darker muddy green for the water below the rock.

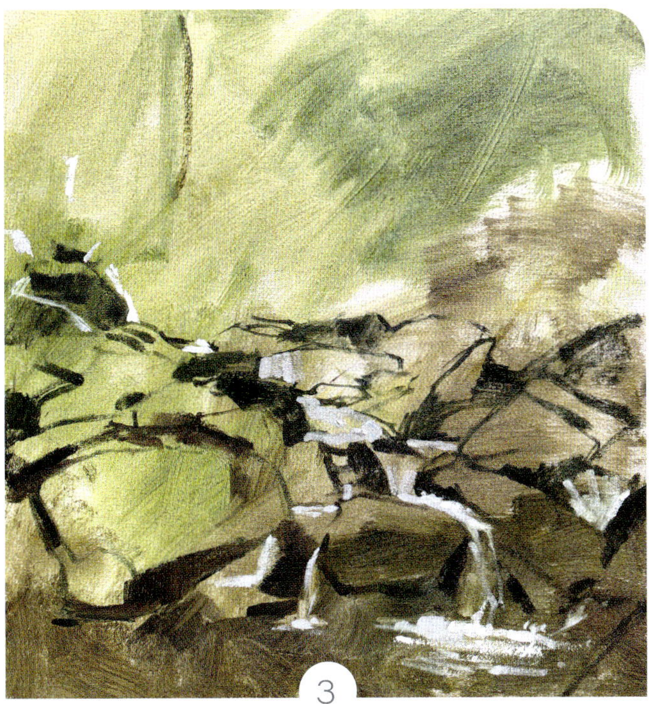

3

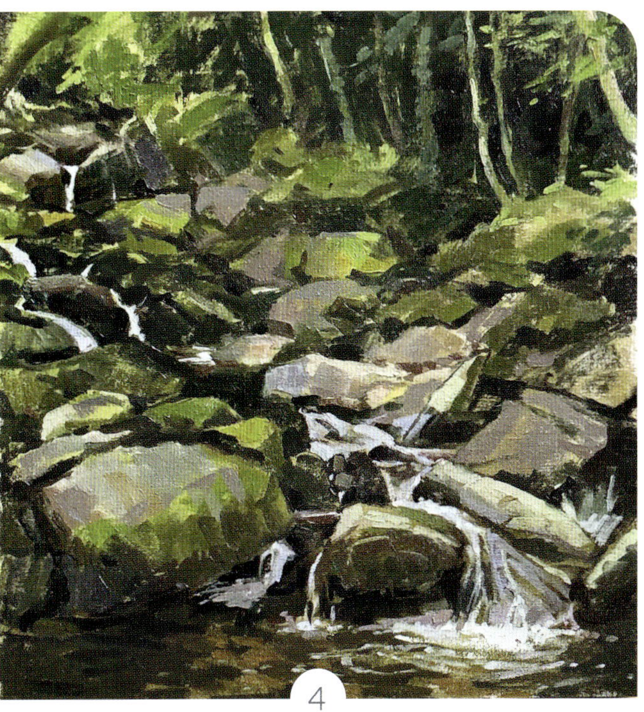

4

With the first rock in place I worked outwards from it, measuring and positioning the other large rocks, and checking their relative heights as I went along by holding the brush horizontally. I also started introducing the flowing water in a very light grey.

I stopped measuring after all the main rocks were in and painted the rest by eye, including the trees on the far side of the river.

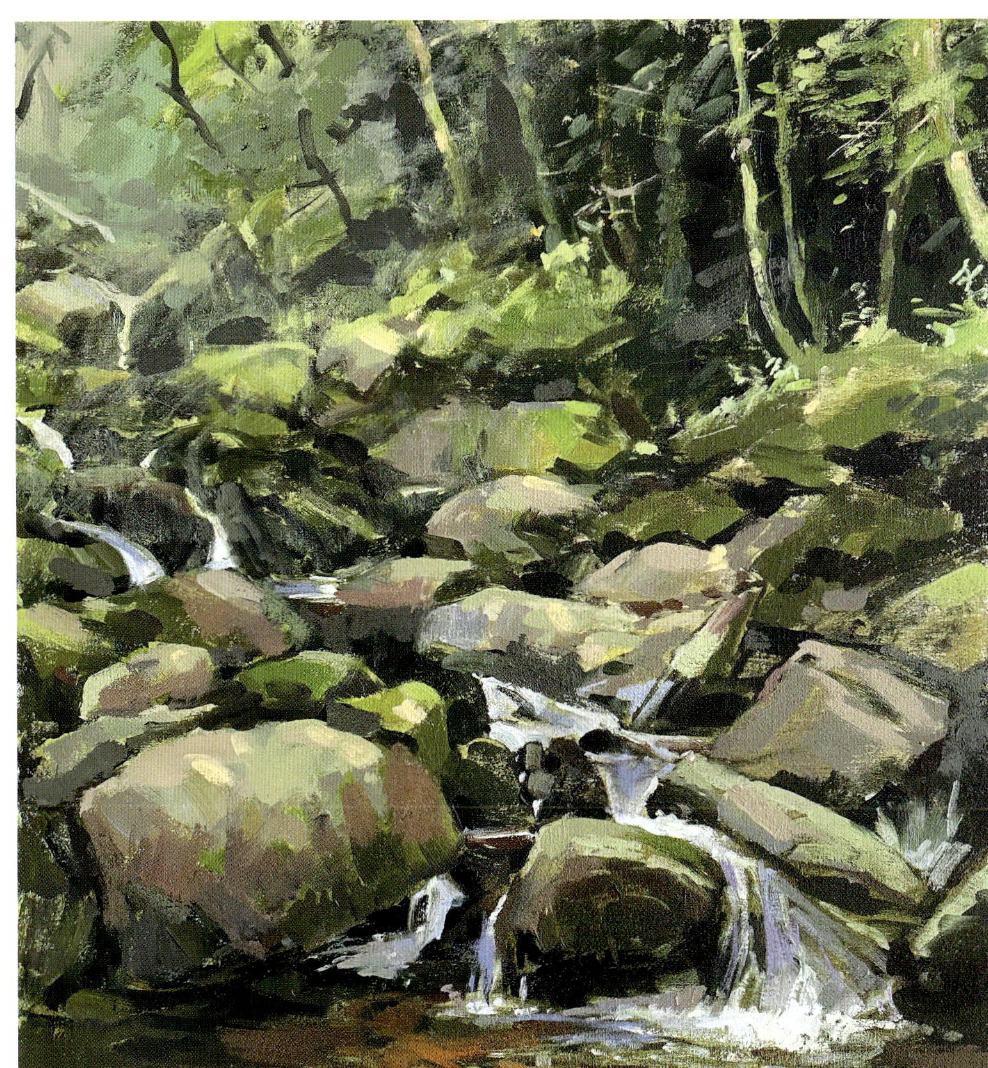

The finished painting
35.5 x 33cm (14 x 13in)

Glen Lyn Gorge, Lynmouth
in Devon.

Still life en plein air

For a change of pace from landscapes, why not try looking for a still life outdoors, or setting up your own at home? There's an endless choice of suitable subject matter, and a still life can be as simple as a small group of objects arranged on a table.

The fumes from working with oil paints dissipate in the open air and it's also a great way to further practise plein air painting without having to travel further than your own garden.

As noted earlier, painting at home has many obvious advantages for still life: anything that you might choose to paint indoors can be carried outside instead on a dry day, you needn't worry about forgetting any supplies – and refreshments are readily available!

Finding the right space

If possible, position yourself where you can see both the still-life subject and your painting on the easel at the same time, and have room behind you to step back. Stepping back away from the painting allows you to see how it's working as a whole while simultaneously comparing it with the subject. I find this simple technique extremely helpful.

Having enough room to step back will also encourage you to hold the brush loosely and use your whole arm to paint with, rather than moving from the wrist. This helps to achieve a more spontaneous and painterly finish in the finished painting.

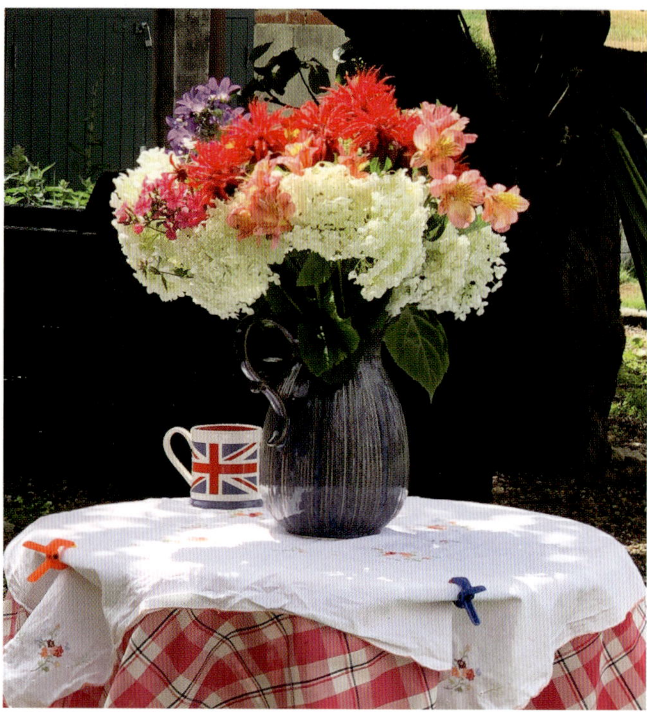

A simple still life, set up in my garden at home. The mug adds interest, echoes the colours in the jug and flowers, and helps to bridge the gap in height between the table and blooms.

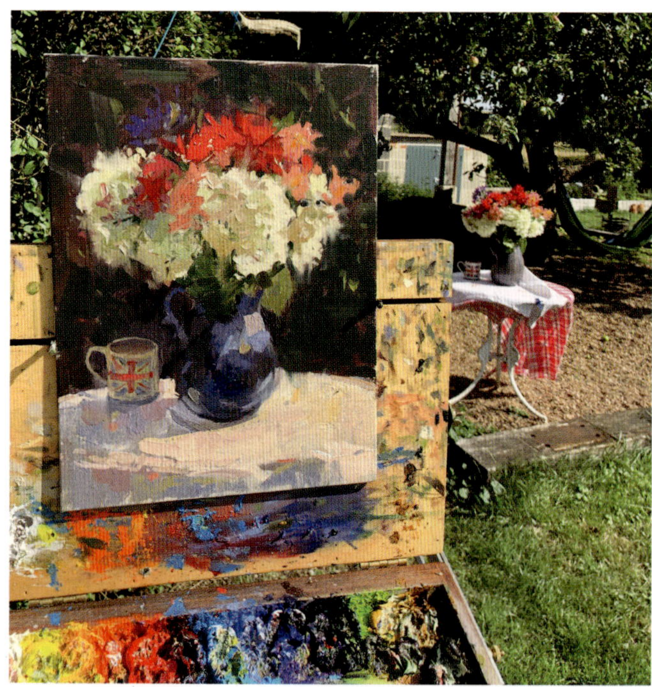

This picture shows my viewpoint – I can take in both the still-life subject and the painting on the easel in one glance.

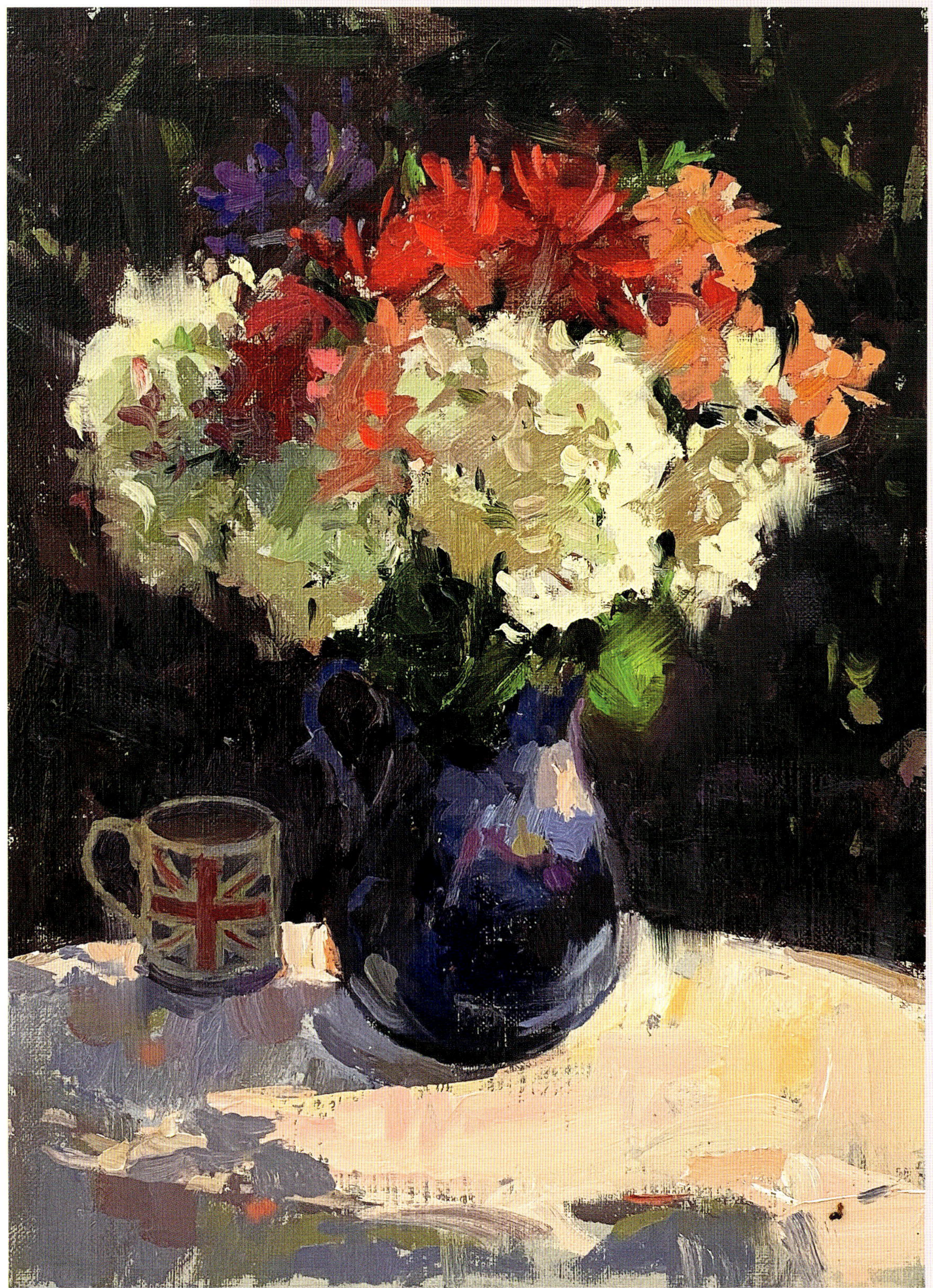

Garden Flowers in Blue Jug
23 x 30.5cm (9 x 12in)

I was pleased with how I managed to capture the quality of the light on these large blooms in a still life set up in the garden. There is so much to think about, even in a deceptively simple arrangement like this.

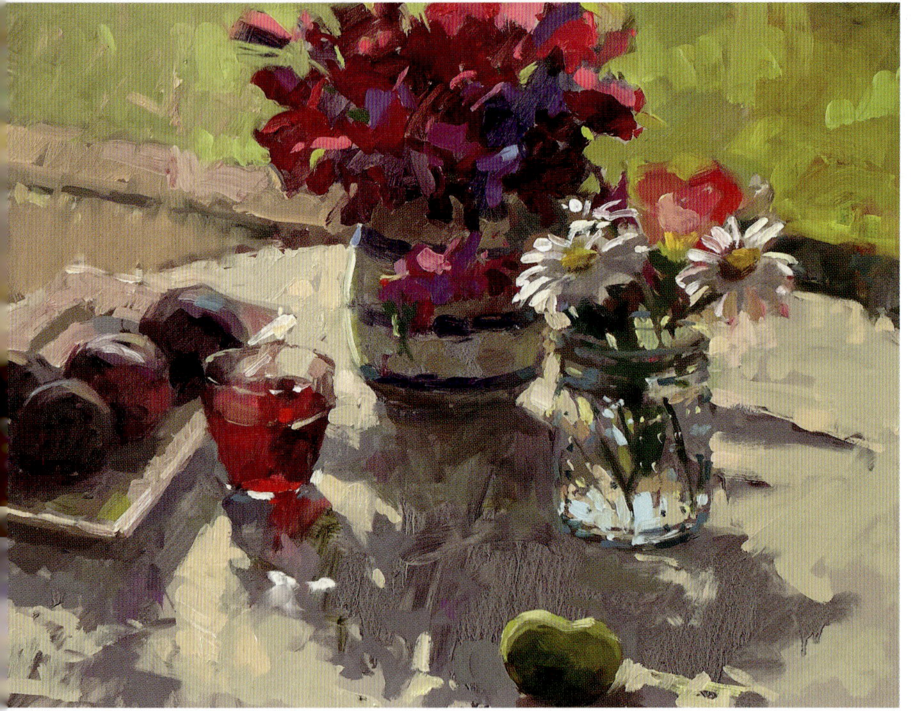

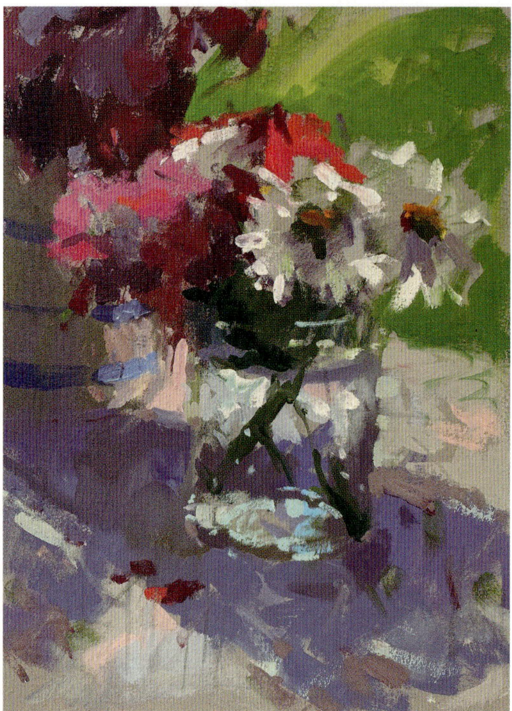

Making choices: setting up a still life

Whether you are setting up your own still life, or keeping an eye out for one you find while out and about, look for elements that have different sizes or heights. If you are setting it up yourself, move the elements around until you start to see an arrangement that excites you.

Aim for asymmetry: you don't want to have an even number of objects lined up in a row. Change your position to look at the set-up from different viewpoints – not forgetting higher and lower. Moving a group of objects onto a low table or a wall can open up different possibilities. Try placing your still life in direct sunlight, dappled light or in full shadow before making your decision.

Once you are happy with your arrangement and position, start by making some quick sketches to explore the options for composition. Look for a path through the painting that the eye can follow, using the way objects are connected and overlap, and also the space between objects.

Consider choosing part of the still life to be a focal point and allowing other parts to have softer edges, less contrast and more mystery. For example, in a bouquet of flowers you may pick out one or two large flower heads and experiment with having the others (or the more distant flowers) in soft focus. The examples above show two different approaches to the same floral still life.

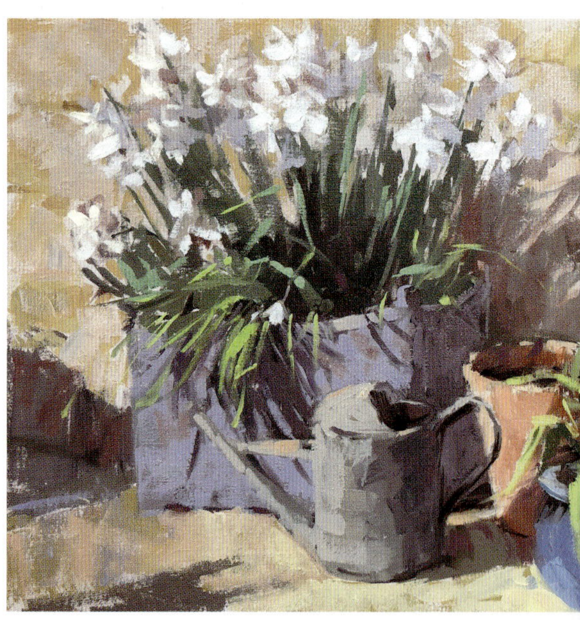

White Daffodils in Planter
28 x 25.5cm (11 x 10in)

An unarranged still life, consisting of these lovely white daffodils in a planter with a watering can and a few other pots. I particularly liked the shadows cast by the flowers in the morning sunlight.

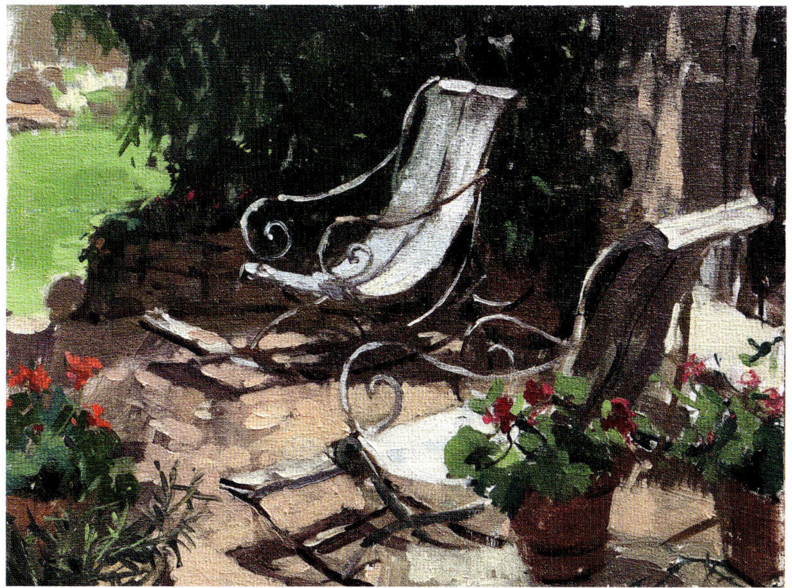

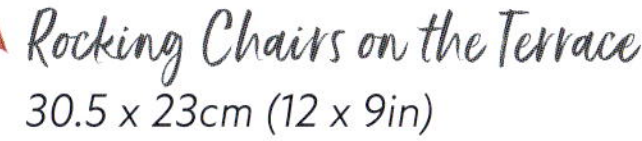

Rocking Chairs on the Terrace
30.5 x 23cm (12 x 9in)

A still life doesn't have to mean small objects. I loved the shapes of these rocking chairs with their curled arms, which I spotted on an Italian terrace.

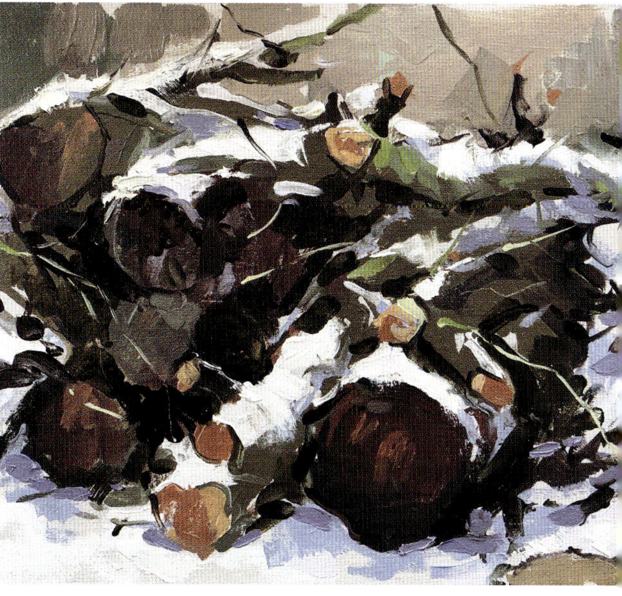

Woodpile in Snow
25.5 x 20.5cm (10 x 8in)

A fascinating challenge of light and dark shapes. I love the abstract properties of this little painting and the colour palette.

Memory and still life

The exercises on improving your visual memory (see pages 52–55) also work well with a still life, rather than a photograph. You can try this in the studio by setting up a simple still life with three to five objects, or heading out into the great outdoors to find a suitable site.

- Position your easel facing away from the still life, so that you are positioned in between the objects and your easel.
- Set a timer for five minutes and spend the five minutes carefully observing the still life, notice how the shapes and angles relate to each other.
- Turn towards your canvas with your back to the still life arrangement, painting from memory for the next five minutes.
- Take it in turns for as long as you wish until you want to call the study finished: five minutes observing and then five minutes painting each time.

Lilies and Cherubs
30.5 x 25.5cm (12 x 10in)

I like to hone in on small details in the garden to make a painting about. This little statuette of a pair of cherubs hiding in a flower border is a perfect example.

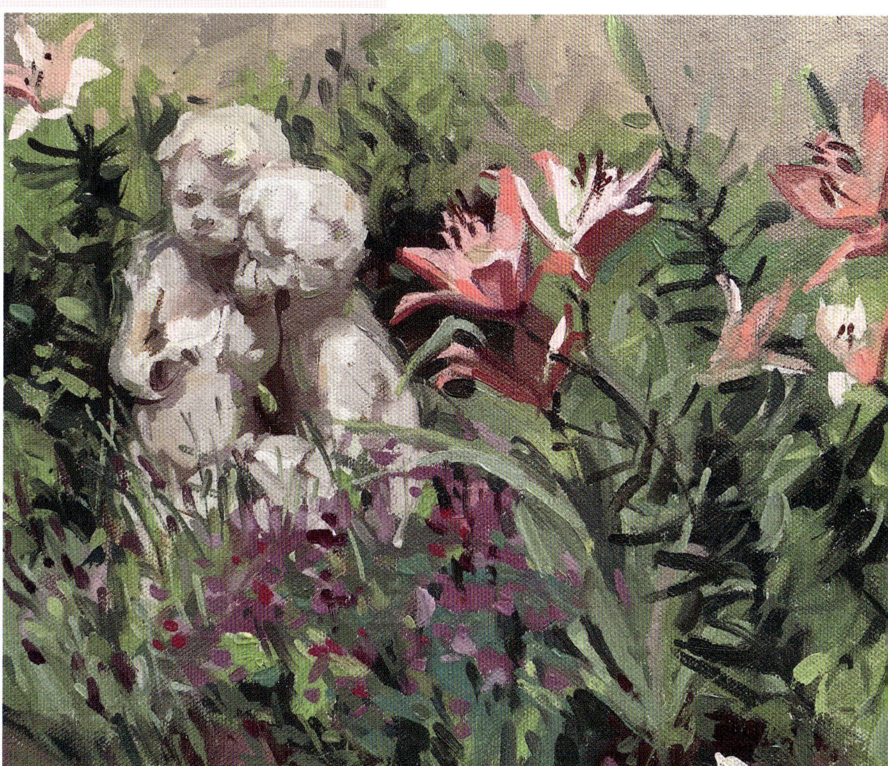

Found still life

Setting up your own still life is all well and good, but I'm always on the lookout for a good found still life. Happening upon objects in their environment can give a cohesive and natural feel to your still-life painting.

Great places to find ready-made still-life subjects are boatyards and harbours, gardens and antique markets. Be open-minded about what makes a suitable subject, and get used to choosing a painting subject based on shapes, light and pictorial elements, rather than what the objects themselves are used for.

I am drawn to those areas of clutter that often appear beside sheds or greenhouses. What appeals to me is the fascinating array of shapes which a pile of objects can make together – I love to figure them out and how they relate to each other while painting, like a puzzle.

You don't have to spend time composing or rearranging the scene, you just make use of what's already there. I find it so exciting because I wouldn't have been able to imagine those shapes without seeing them, and I certainly wouldn't have come up with them in a still-life arrangement of my own making.

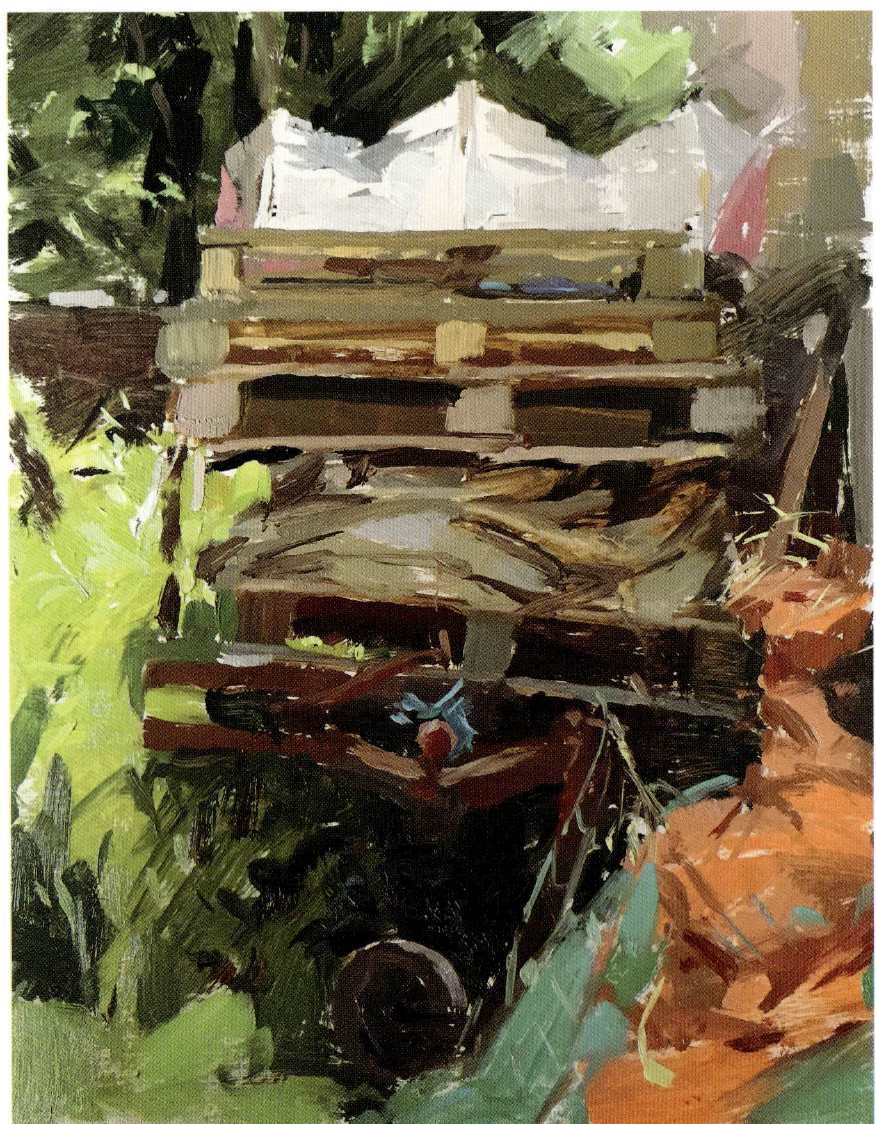

Boatyard Clutter
15 x 20.5cm (6 x 8in)

This was a workshop demonstration about how to simplify a complicated scene. The result is a painting about interesting shapes and light. I don't know what all the objects are and it doesn't matter at all; proving that it's not what you paint but how you paint it that's important.

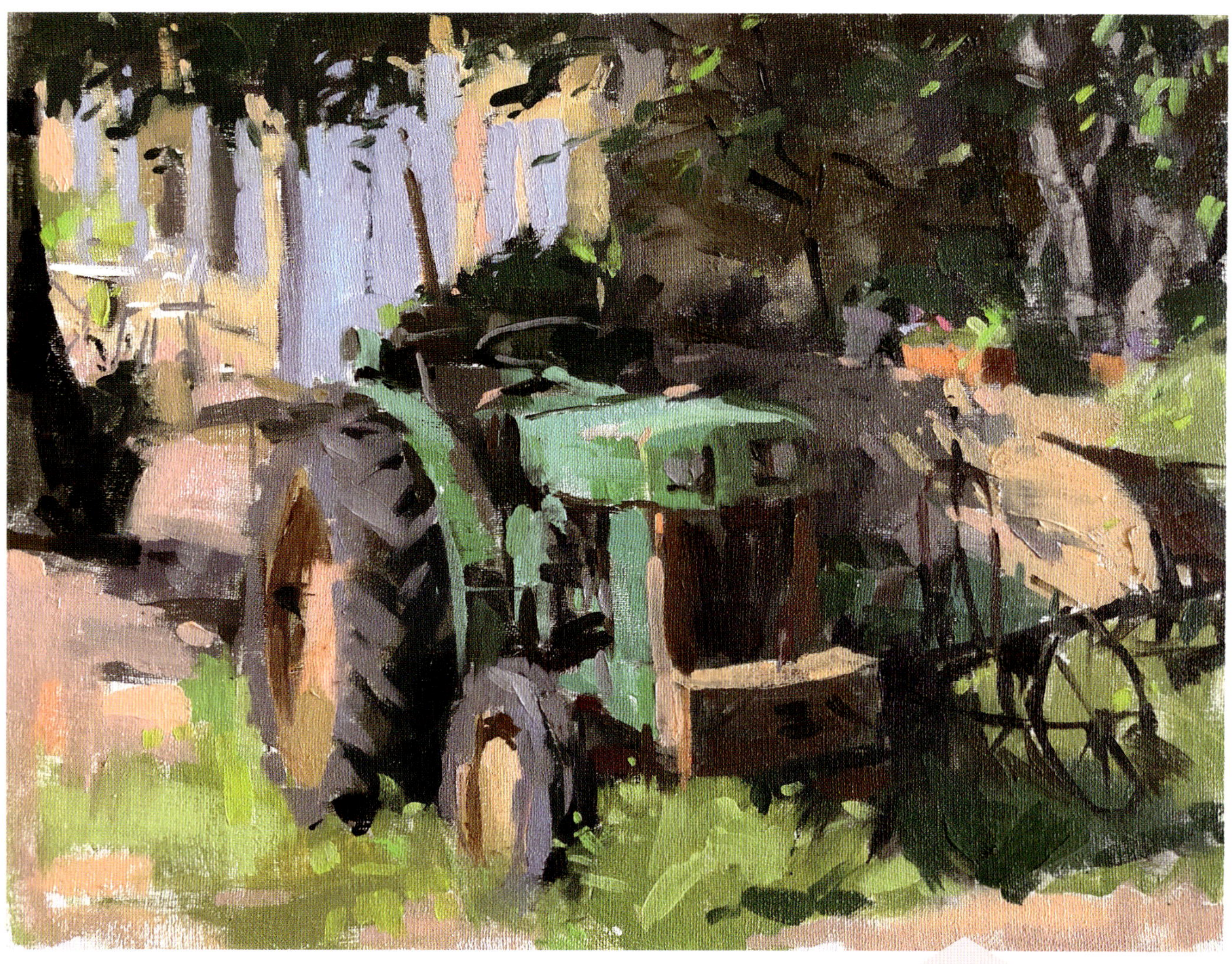

▲ *Old Tractor at Le Somail*
30.5 x 23cm (12 x 9in)

I was delighted to see this old tractor basking in the warm sunshine in France. It obviously hadn't been moved in quite some time, and made the perfect found still life.

Changing your perspective

When working on a found still life, it's a good idea to turn away from the subject from time to time and regard the painting on its own. Viewing it in reverse in a mirror or, in a pinch, reflected in your phone screen, can help you to spot any major drawing problems.

Consider where the painting currently stands, and ask yourself what is the biggest difference you could make to move from where it is to where you'd like it to be when finished.

Go on from there to ask yourself what else the painting needs to improve it. Keep in mind the initial inspiration behind it, or the feeling you are trying to convey.

Log Pile

Having scouted out this area of recently cleared woodland, I spotted this log pile – a great found still life, full of abstract shapes and an interesting variety of hue and value. The church in the distance provided another focal point and further depth to the subject. This seemed a good spot to practise using a soft, muted palette to suit the overcast weather and the lack of any strong colour in the stripped-back woodland.

You will need

SURFACE
30 x 20cm (11¾ x 8in) linen panel, prepared with a warm grey tone

COLOURS
An extended primary palette with the addition of green gold, raw sienna, transparent red oxide, Indian yellow and blue black

BRUSHES
A range of synthetic flats and filberts in sizes from 6mm (¼in) to 20mm (¾in), plus a couple of small synthetic or sable round brushes

When working with a found still life, it's particularly important to spend time deciding on the viewpoint you want in your painting, and getting properly set up.

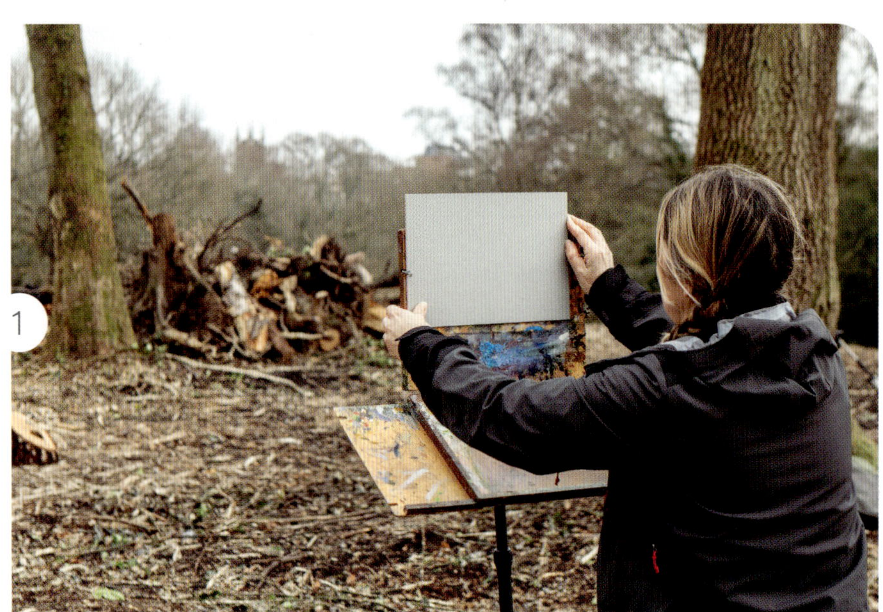

To find my way into the painting I loosely established the main shapes: the log pile, church tower and trees using a dark mix of ultramarine and transparent red oxide, thinned down with turps.

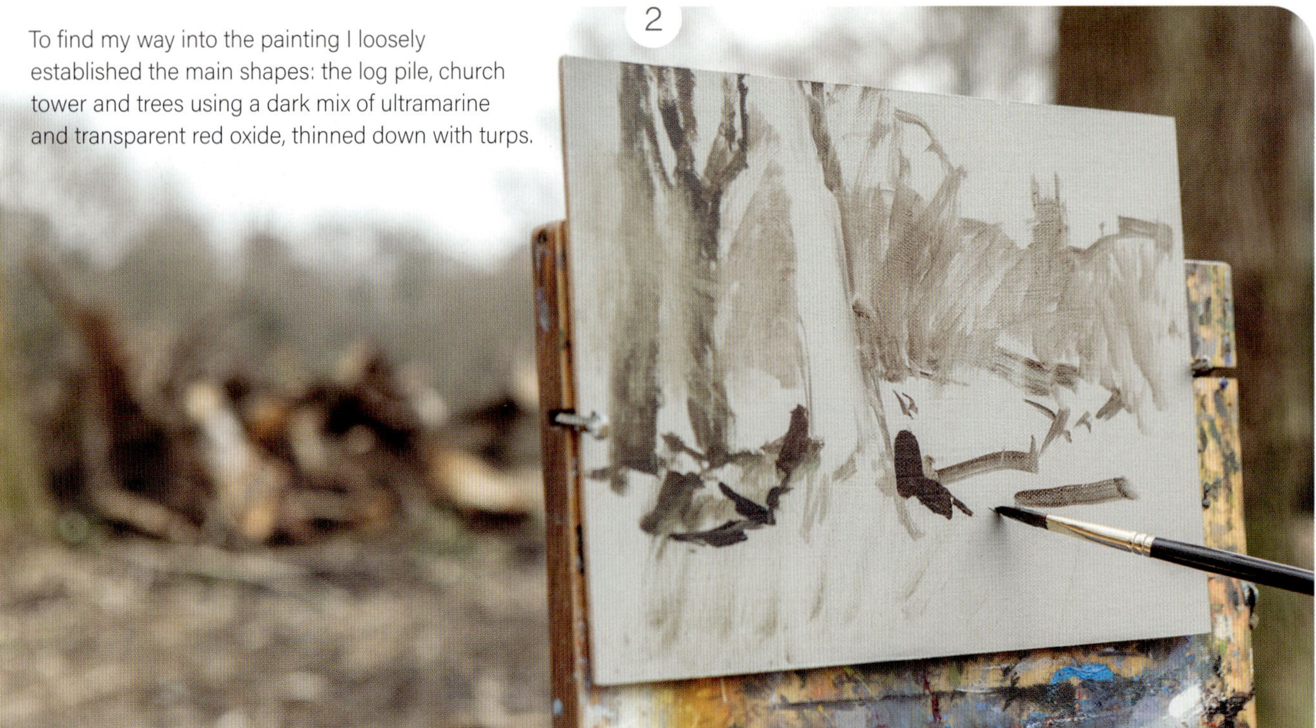

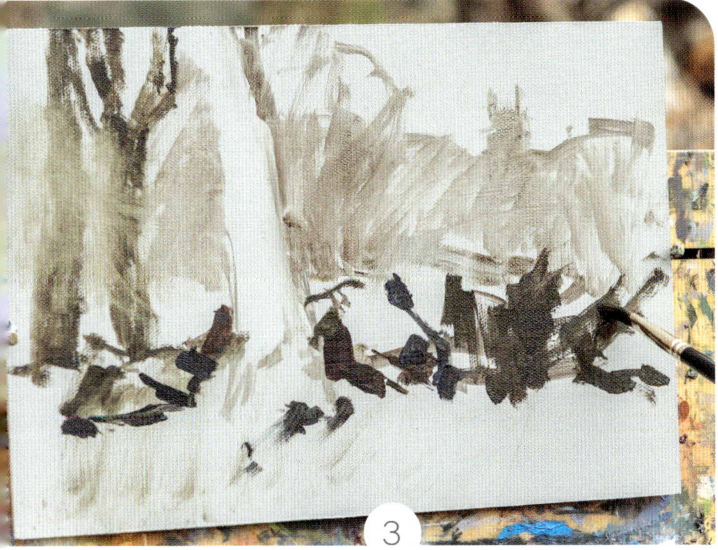

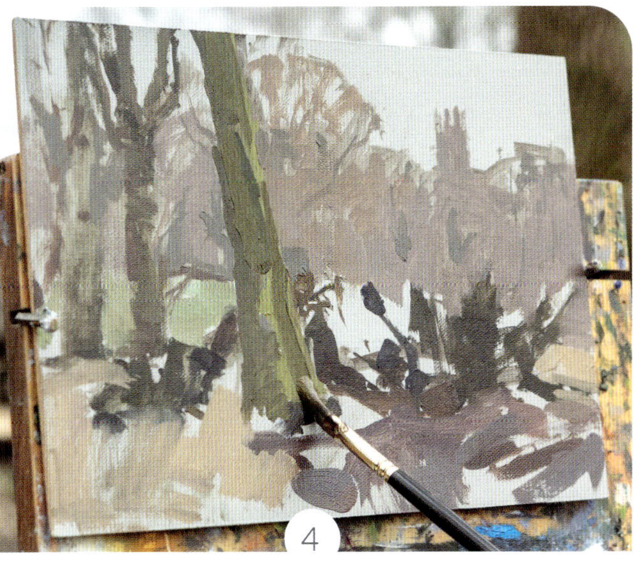

As I worked, I added more of the same paints (ultramarine and transparent red oxide) to the mix to strengthen it. The stronger tone helps to break the painting into two planes as it develops: a fainter one for the distance, with the focus on the church; and a bolder one for the foreground, with the log pile as the key focus.

I introduced Indian yellow into the mix for the foreground tree, to give it a golden glow and a more saturated hue.

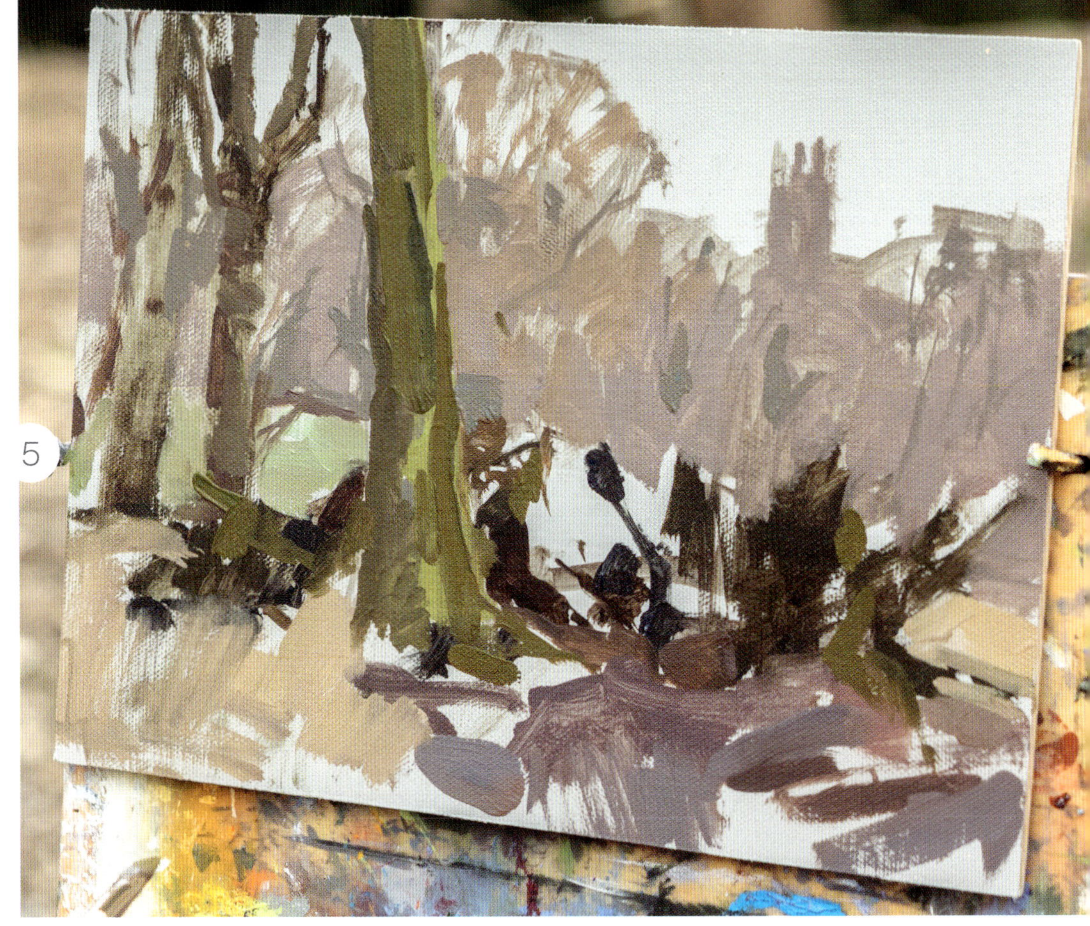

With the main shapes and colours all now in place, I stepped back to assess. I made a mental note to ensure the darkest darks and stronger colours were kept only in the foreground plane as I continued to build up the painting.

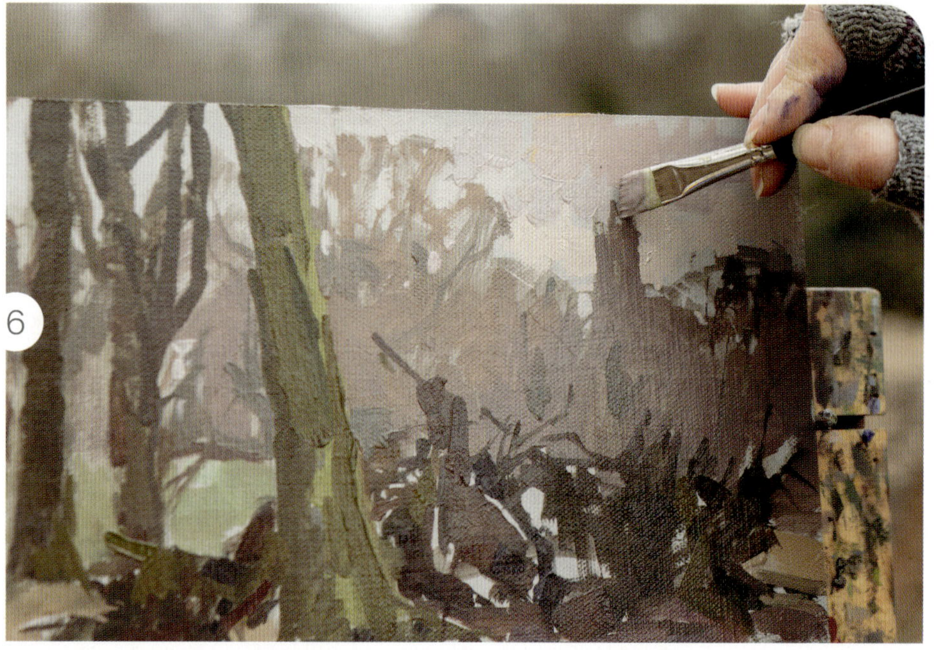

Up until this point I hadn't painted the sky. This was because its colour and value were going to be close to the colour already tinting the board. Now, however, I wanted to cut into and around the church and tree shapes, so I mixed up a suitable light grey for the sky and used a flat brush with a crisp edge to apply it.

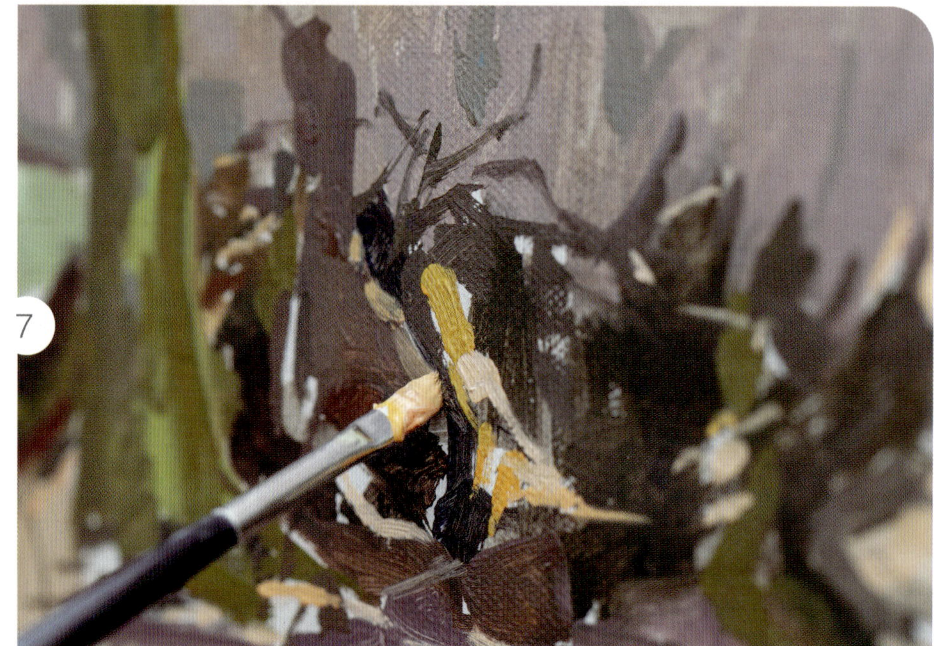

I switched to smaller 6mm (¼in) filbert brushes to build up both light and dark details within the log pile itself, and to add some small branches sticking out here and there, overlapping the background.

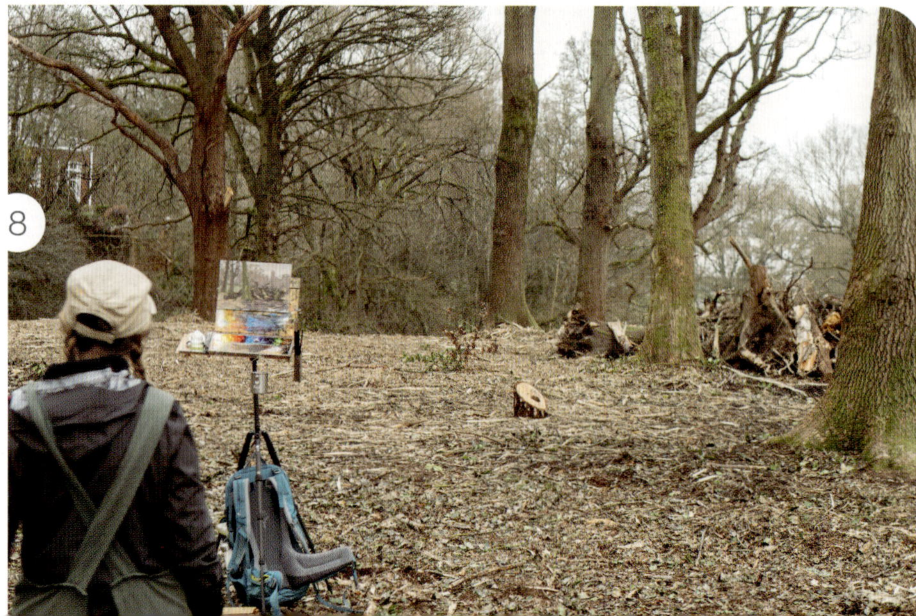

With all the elements of the painting now in place, it was time to step back and assess the painting together with the scene, before making any final adjustments.

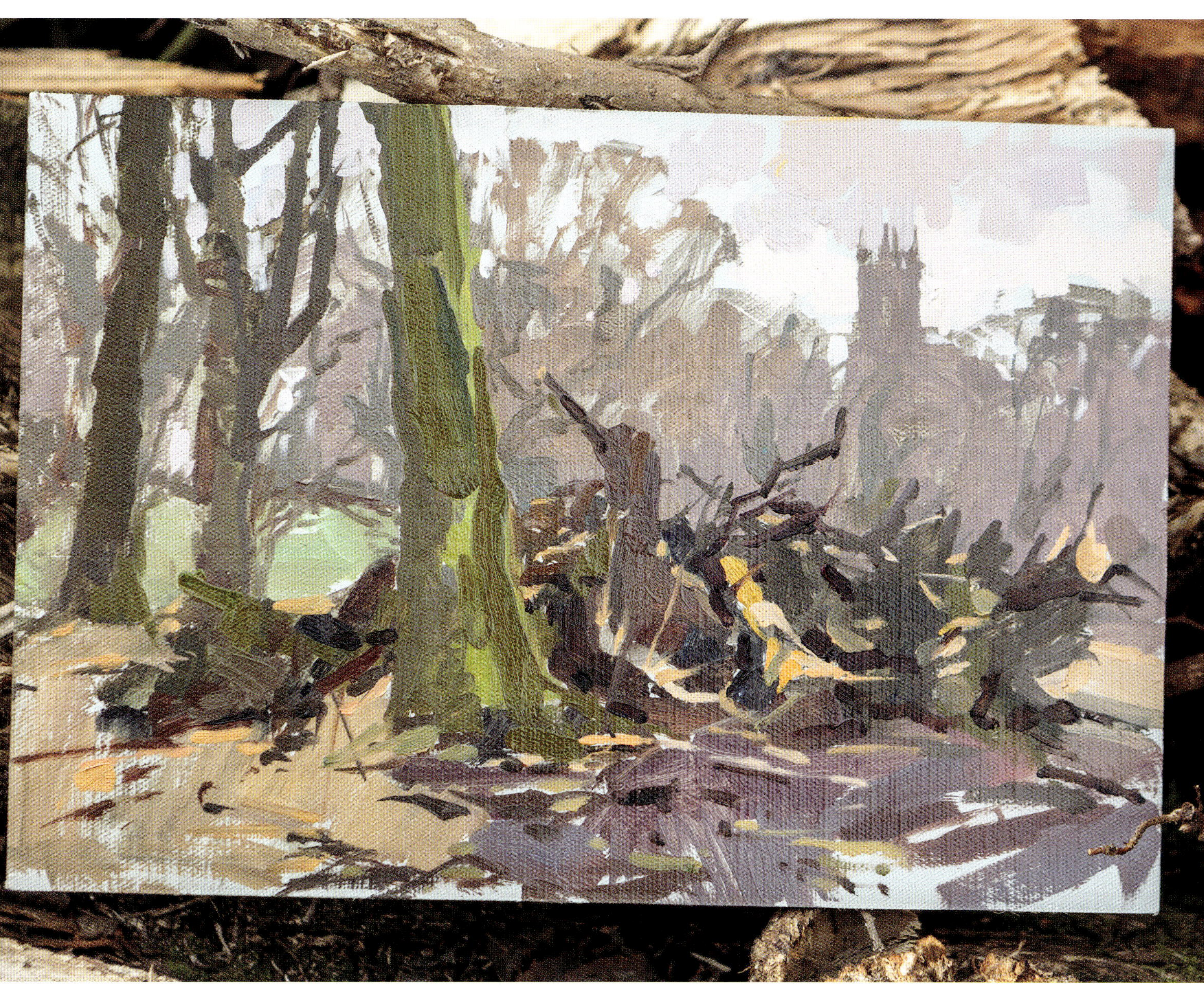

The finished painting
30 x 20cm (11¾ x 8in)

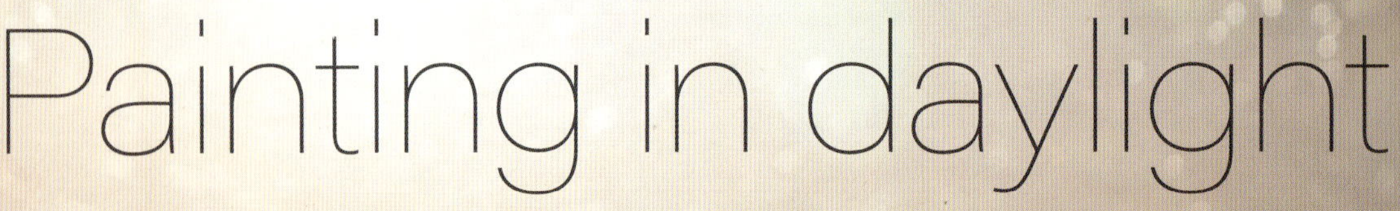

Painting in daylight

Light – and particularly daylight – is at the heart of all my work. What I love most is the chance to portray sunlight in my paintings, so it's a treat for me to paint on sunny days. Working in strong sunlight and dealing with shadows, however, doesn't come without difficulties, so I wanted to offer you some advice in this chapter. We also look at ideas and tips for painting other effects of light, such as the opportunities offered by a low sun in the early or late hours, and how you can approach the absence of daylight offered by painting at night.

Whatever effect of light you are painting, strive to make every mark count. For me, fresh, direct brushmarks, and a simple, economical approach are the best way to capture the poetry of the fleeting effects of light.

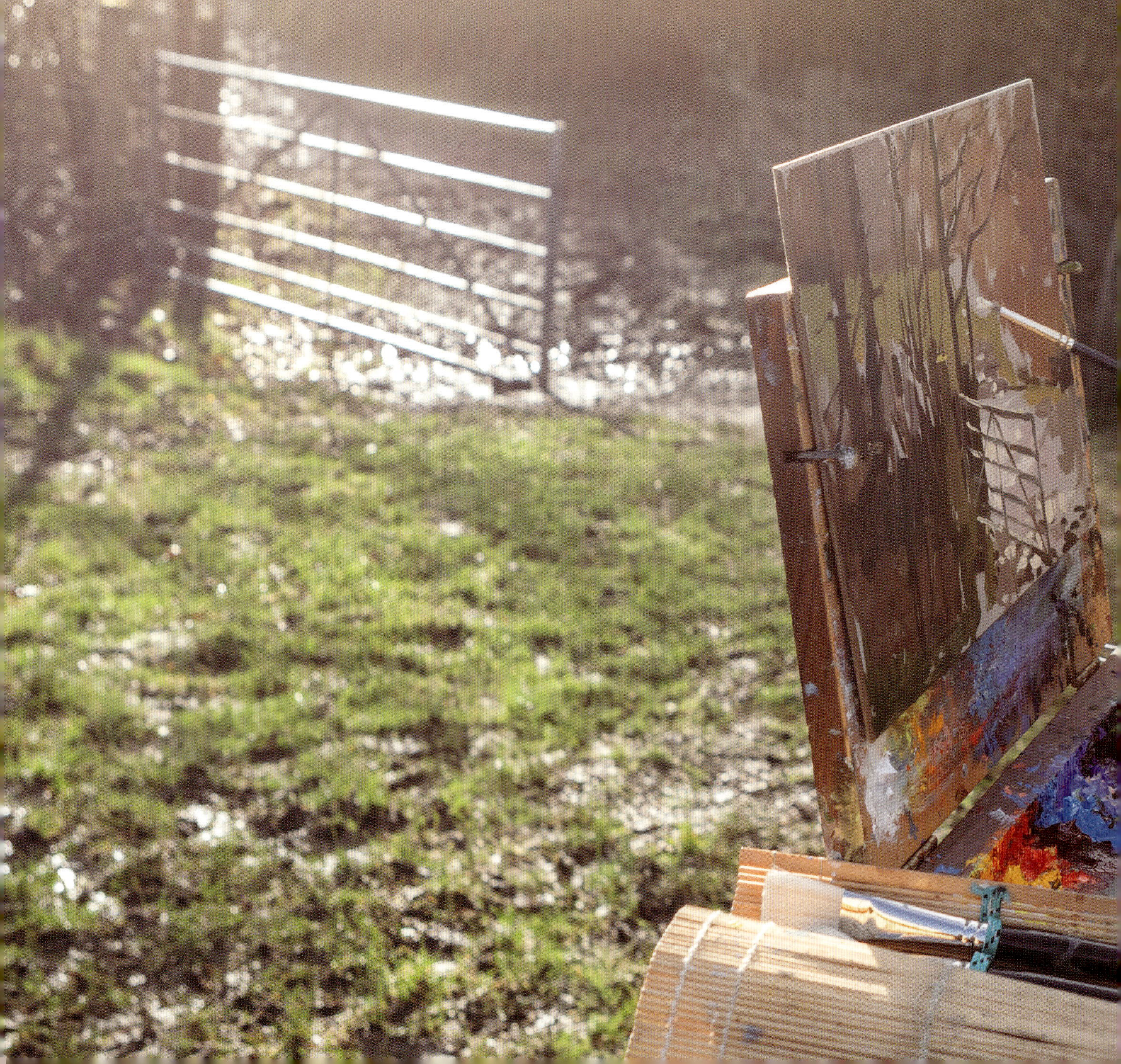

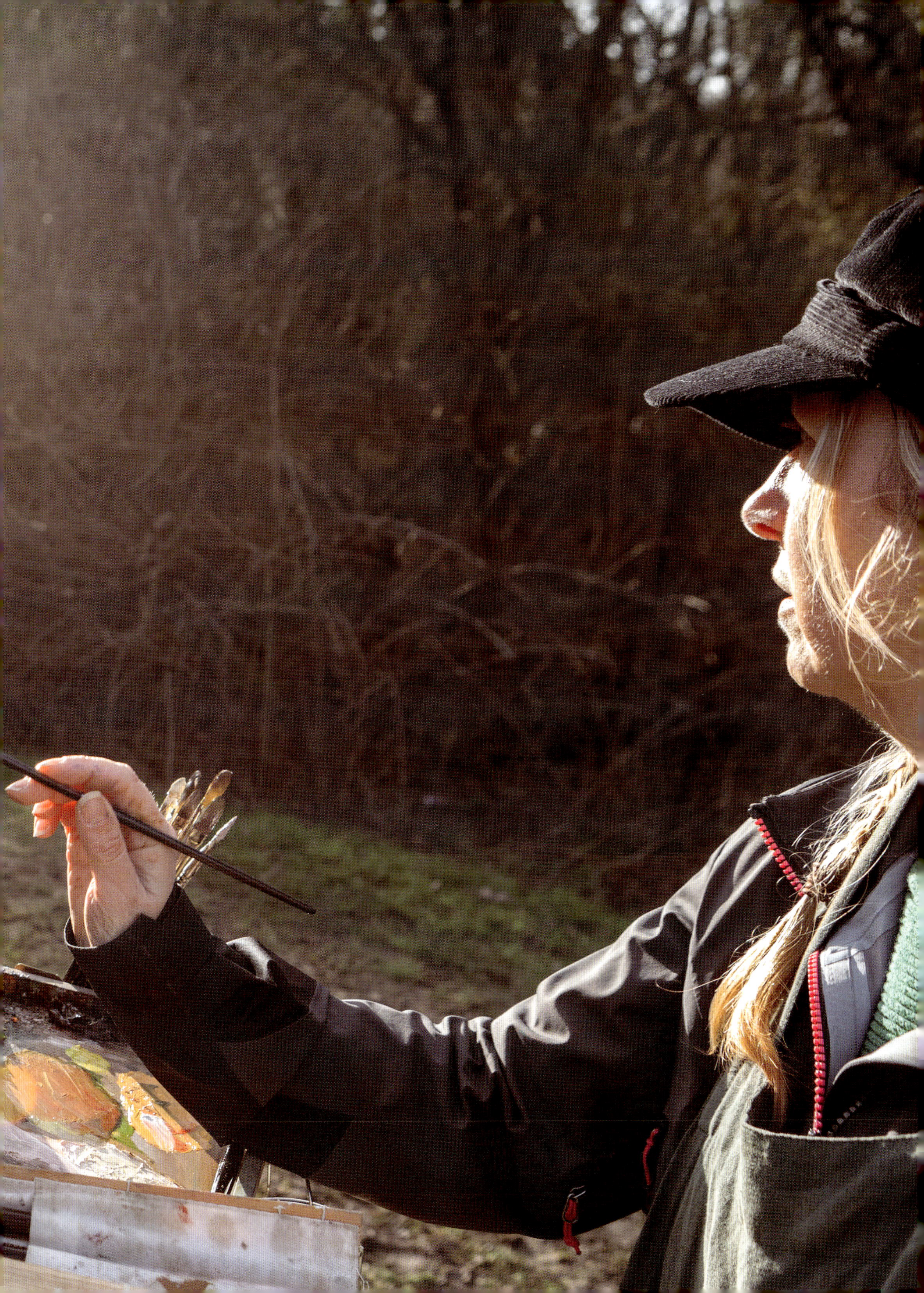

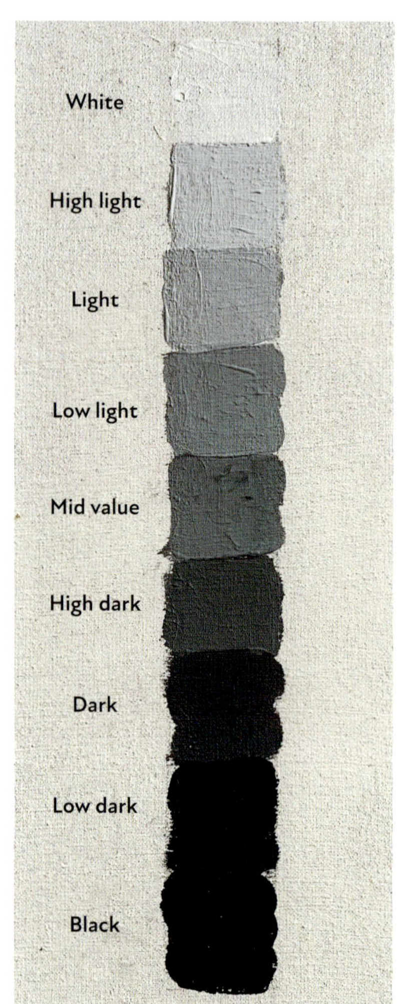

Tonal value scale, from pure white at the top to pure black at the bottom. Hold it up to compare it with the area you're painting, and it will help you to identify the tone you need to mix.

Setting up in sunlight

As noted on page 50, it's important to anticipate the movement of the sun, so when setting up, identify where it is and in which direction it will move during your painting session. This will give you an idea of the ways your scene will change. You could use a compass or an app on your phone to tell you in which direction the sun will be moving. Anticipating other potential changes can also be very helpful. After laying in the groundwork we can choose to focus our work on those parts likely to change the soonest. I use a neutral colour mix to get all my shadow shapes blocked-in early on before they change.

There is a real danger of ending up with a dreadfully dark painting if you paint with the sun directly lighting your painting surface. In these circustances, it's easy not to realise what's happened until later, when you view the painting indoors – and it can be so disappointing. Try to keep an even and indirect light on both your painting surface and palette. This can usually be achieved simply by turning your easel slightly, or at worst you may need a parasol or sunshade. Another way to help with this is to make yourself a tonal value scale (see left) on a strip of paper or cardboard and take that out with you to check your values as you're painting.

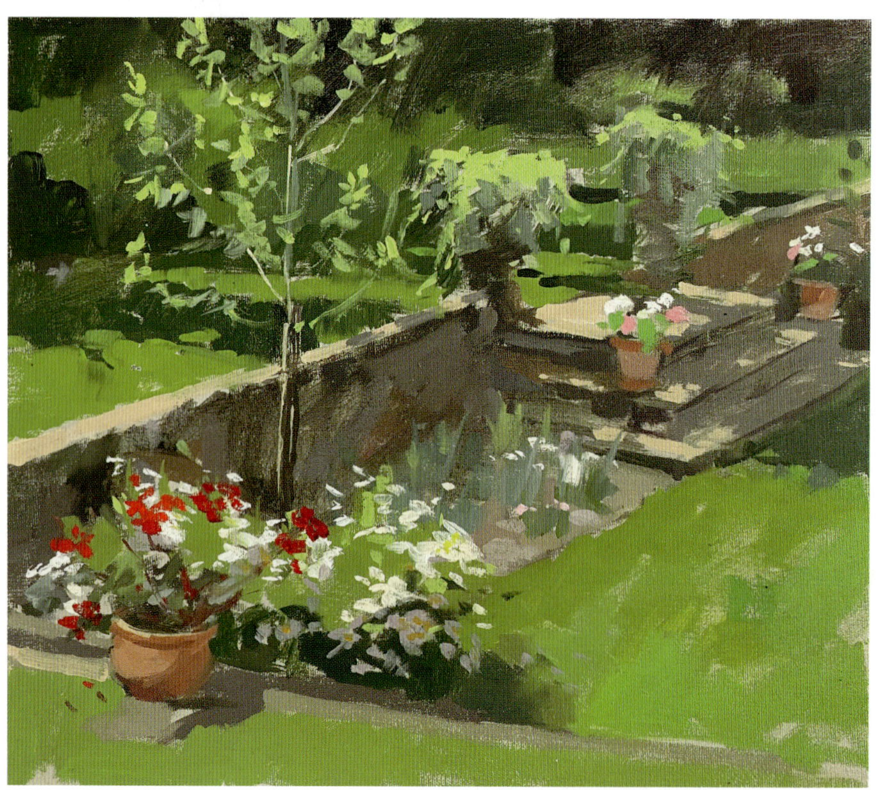

Steps at Russell House
33 x 28cm (13 x 11in)

As is so often the case, here it's not the objects themselves that provide my inspiration, but rather how the light travels across them. I'm repeatedly attracted to steps because of the interesting things that happen when they are touched by the light. In this case, it was the dappled sunlight seen through the tree shadows.

There are so many wonderful instances of light against dark, and dark against light in this painting. The strong diagonals and verticals also serve to lead your eye through the composition.

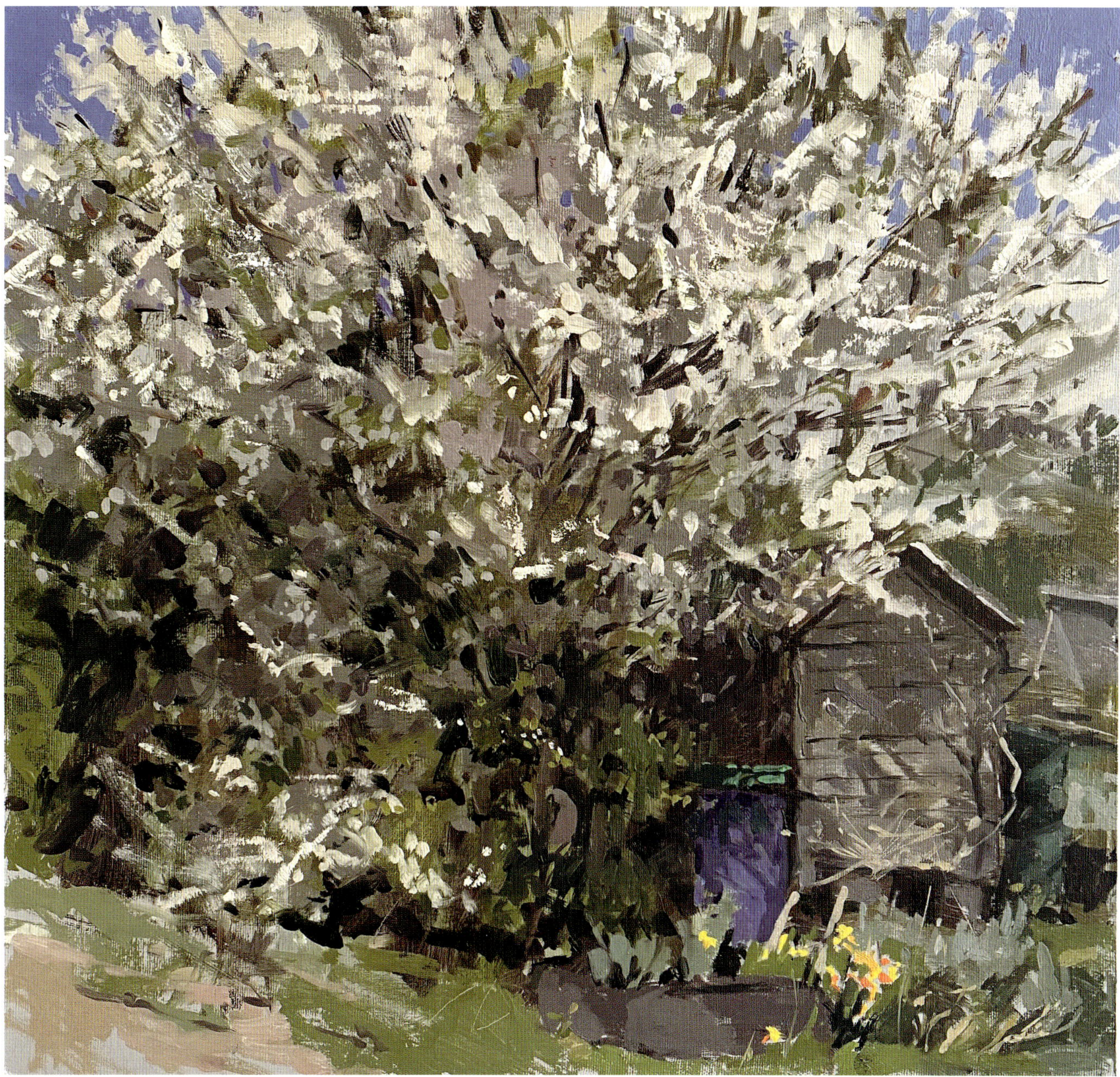

Damson Tree at the Allotments

38 x 35.5cm (15 x 14in)

The impact of this tree in blossom was so impressive I wanted to really fill the canvas with it, getting the shed in almost solely to show the large scale of the tree.

I started by painting the darker branches and blocked in a range of warm greys to represent the deeper blossoms. These greys make a backdrop to the sunlit white and cream flowers, which I applied on top with thick paint and a variety of marks, including stippling with a splayed brush, using just the tips of the bristles.

The deep blue sky, even though it only makes up small parts of the painting, also tells us that this was a beautifully sunny day.

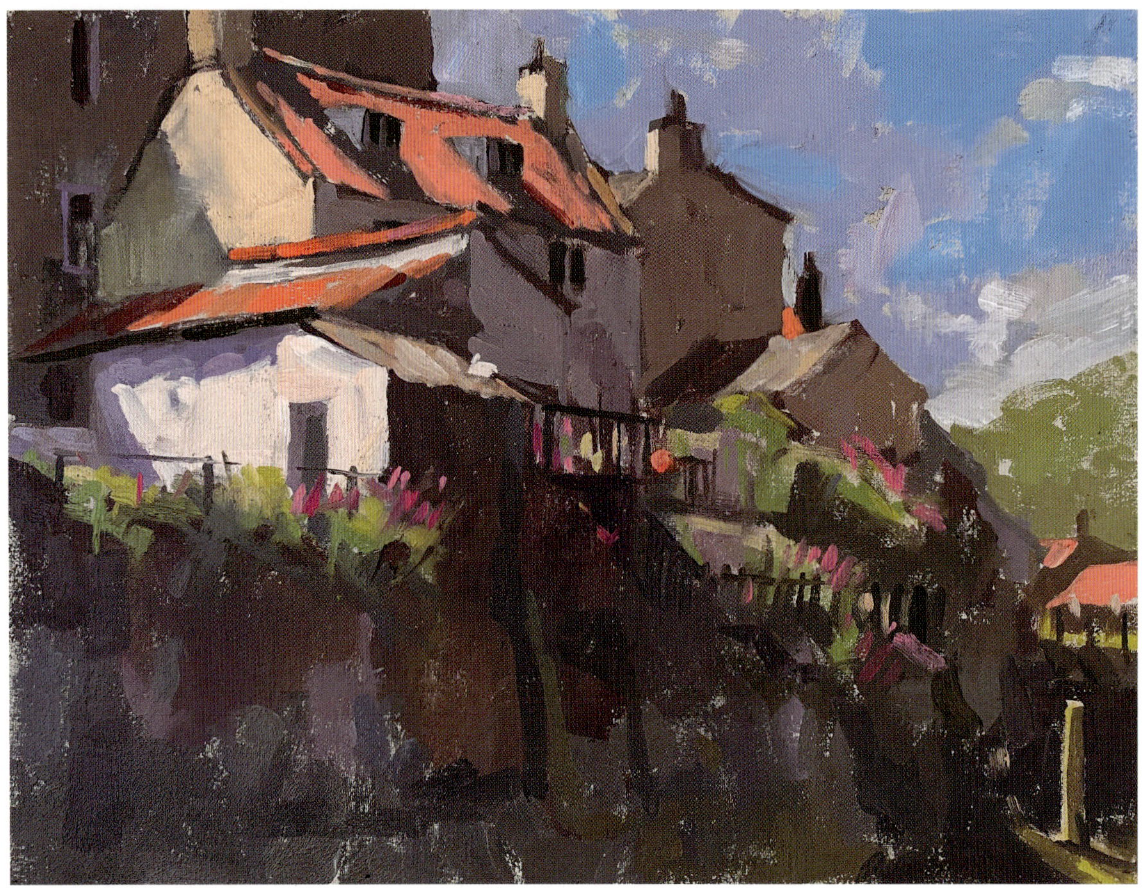

Cottages by the Beck
30.5 x 23cm (12 x 9in)

This painting shows the use of a full range of values to show the effect of sunlight, from the darks of the stone walls in shadow to the sunlit walls and rooftops. I've kept the strongest value contrast for the edge where the whitewashed wall in the sun meets the dark wall and this brings that particular building forwards and the other buildings stay behind.

There is a variety of muted colour within the darks which all share the same value, and I have used more saturated colour in the sunlit parts such as the rooftops and blue sky.

Reflected light

Beside direct light – that which comes straight from the sun (or other light source) – you also need to be aware of indirect light; which is reflected from nearby objects. The main thing to remember when you see reflected light is to keep it subordinate to the main light source in your painting. Tonally it will always be a few shades darker than anything being directly lit by the sun, so don't let it mislead you.

If you stare too long into a shadow area you will start to see more and more tonal variation there. Take a broader view and keep comparing across the whole subject, asking yourself how warm or cool, light or dark is this area as compared to that area.

Sunlight and shadows

The colour of a cast shadow (where an object blocks the direct light) depends on the local colour of the surface it's falling on, the colour of the light source, and any reflected light which is bouncing in from nearby surfaces or the blue sky. Shadow edges may be hard or soft, and often soften as they move further away from the object casting the shadow. Observe the shape of the shadow carefully and don't assume anything; and treat the shape of light spots within a dappled shadow likewise.

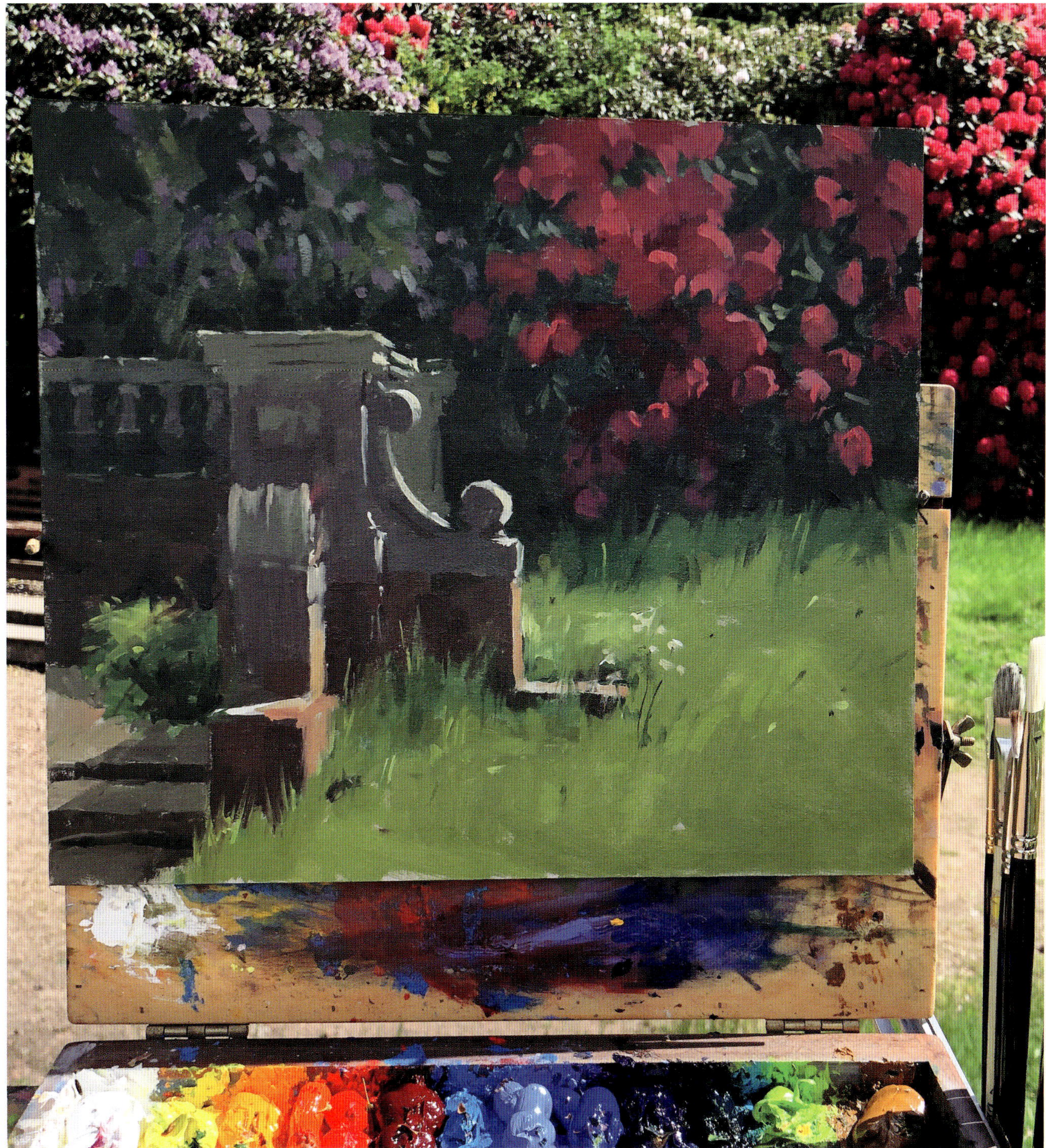

Romantic Corner, Wortley Hall
33 x 28cm (13 x 11in)

This painting is two-thirds in shadow and the other third is mostly the long sunlit grass in the foreground. It is the effect of the sunlight that lifts this painting out of the ordinary.

I positioned myself where I could see the sun striking the side of the interesting architectural feature in the garden, picking out its lovely curves against the dark greens of the rhododendron bushes behind.

Pink Cherry Blossom Against the Sky

I painted this on a beautiful sunny day, when the sky looked a deep, dark and delicious blue against the vibrant pink blossom. I decided to compose the painting focussing on a smaller section of the tree to really make a powerful statement about those cheerful rounded pink blooms against the deep blue sky. I wanted to make them large and to almost fill the canvas with them.

To start with I used a canvas panel which had already been oil primed with a mid-value warm grey tint. I decided that the darker parts of blossom would be darker than my primer colour, the sunlit parts would be lighter in value and some of the pinks in-between would be a medium value, matching my primer value. It was extremely useful to remember this plan as I worked.

You will need

SURFACE

28 x 33cm (11 x 13in) muslin panel, prepared with a warm grey tone

COLOURS

An extended primary palette with the addition of kings blue deep, magenta, permanent rose, transparent red oxide and raw umber

BRUSHES

A range of filberts and flats in sizes from 6mm (¼in) to 20mm (¾in), plus a few small round sables

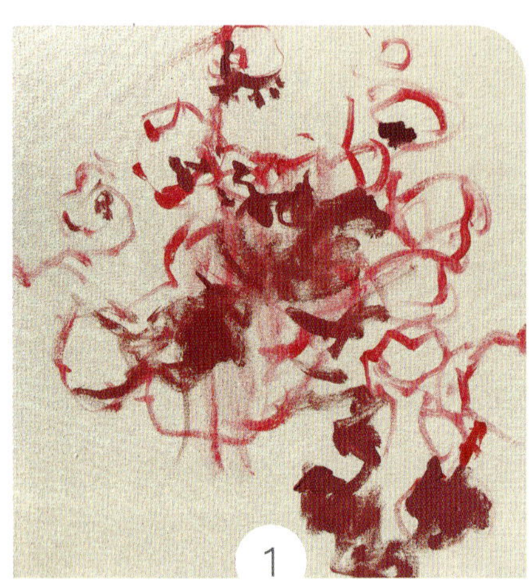

1

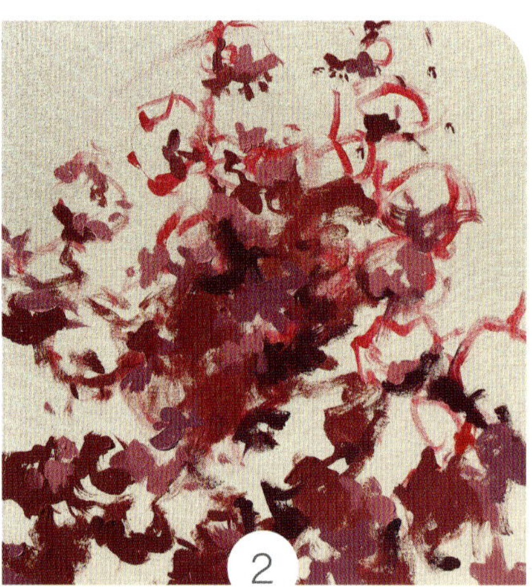

2

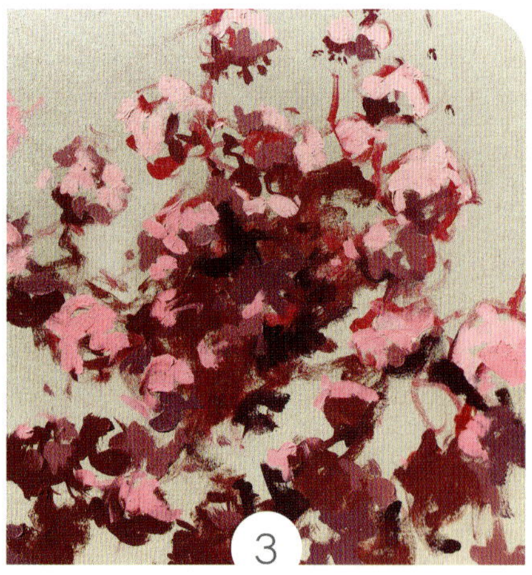

3

Blossom on a tree is one of the most enticing subjects in spring but it can be very difficult to know where to start. The abundance of delicate petals, branches and unfurling leaves can be a dizzying prospect to paint. The secret, again, is to take a broad view of the shapes and masses, ignoring the small details completely. I began using a very saturated mid-value pink – just magenta and alizarin crimson – to make a loose drawing to place the main groups of blossom.

I mixed a couple of darker pinks for the shadow areas and started massing those in. I had to half-close my eyes to get an idea of what that overall dark value mass looked like. I began to vary these pinks, making them cooler or warmer in places to avoid a flat effect.

I next moved to the light value pinks: the parts receiving direct sunlight. Although you generally need plenty of white to make a light value colour, be careful you don't end up with something chalky and bleached of colour. It's favourable sometimes to add more colour even if the value becomes a shade darker. In this case I still wanted a saturated pink even in the lightest parts of the blossom so plenty of colour (permanent rose and magenta) was mixed in with the white.

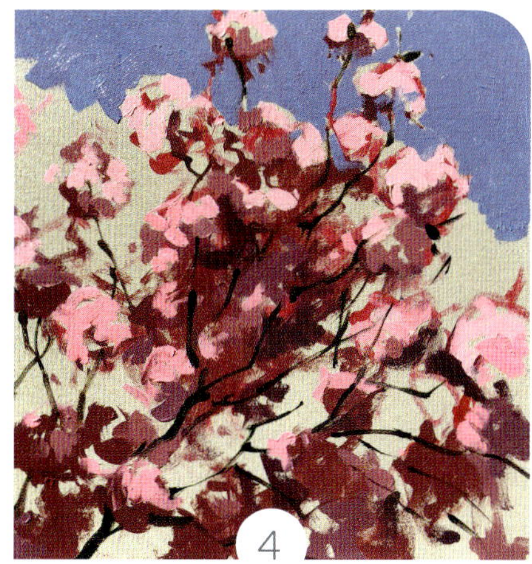

4

I used a small round brush and a warm reddish dark to put in twiggy branches connecting the clumps of flowers. Next I began to paint the deep blue sky around the shapes of the flowering branches. To keep the colour clean when painting sky around other shapes, I first paint the clear dry areas away from any other colour, and when that is all done, I start to paint the edges where the sky colour meets the pinks.

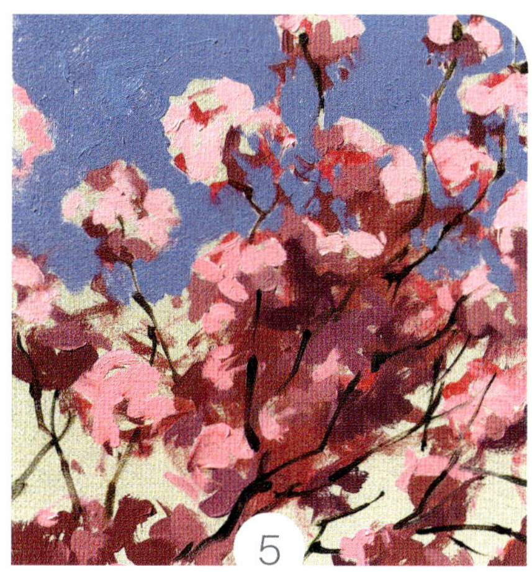

5

To finish, I added some medium value pinks on some of the blossoms, to serve as a bridge between the light and shadow colours and make them look more rounded in shape. Finally, I picked out a few sunlit branches using a very light value greenish-brown.

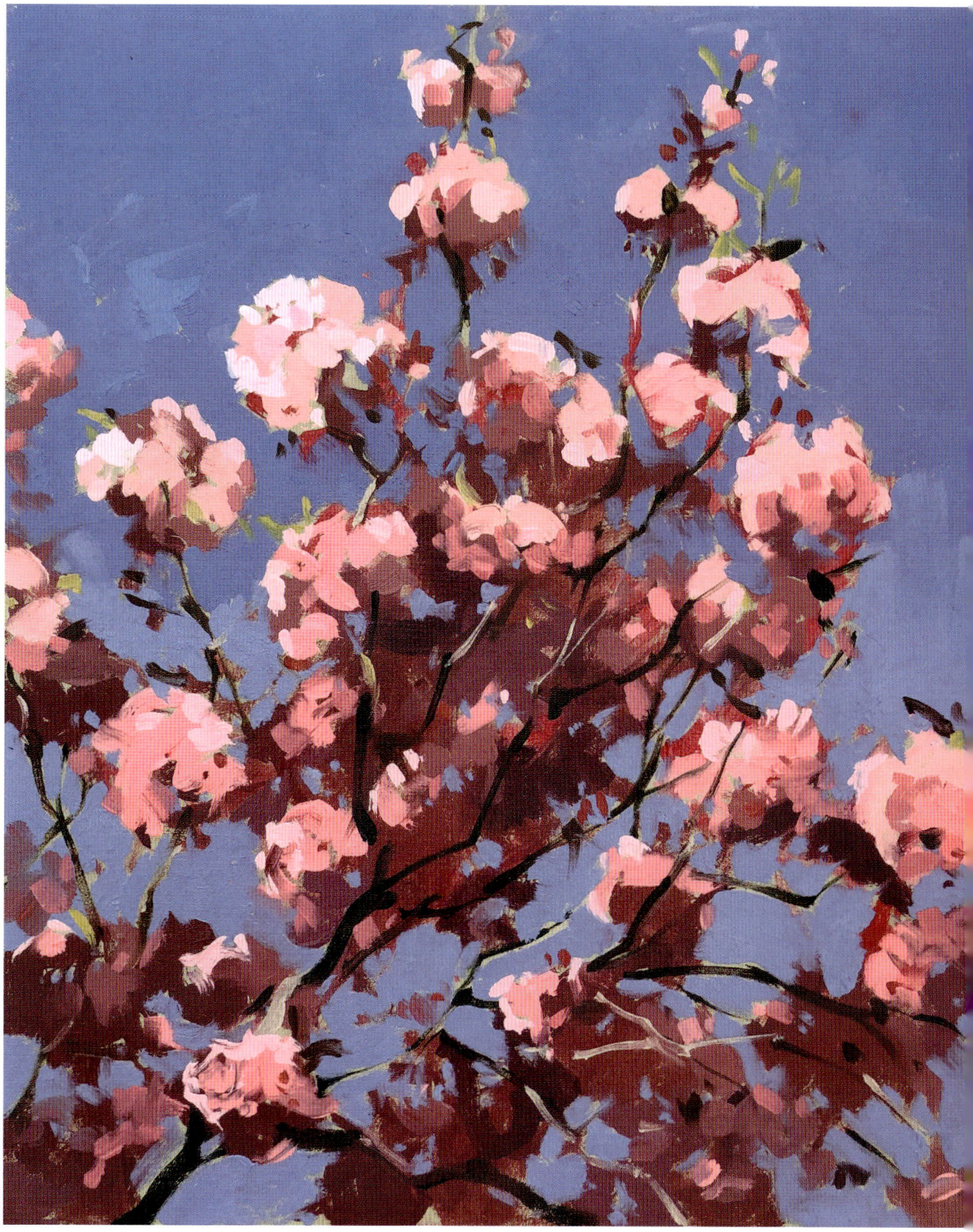

The finished painting
28 x 33cm (11 x 13in)

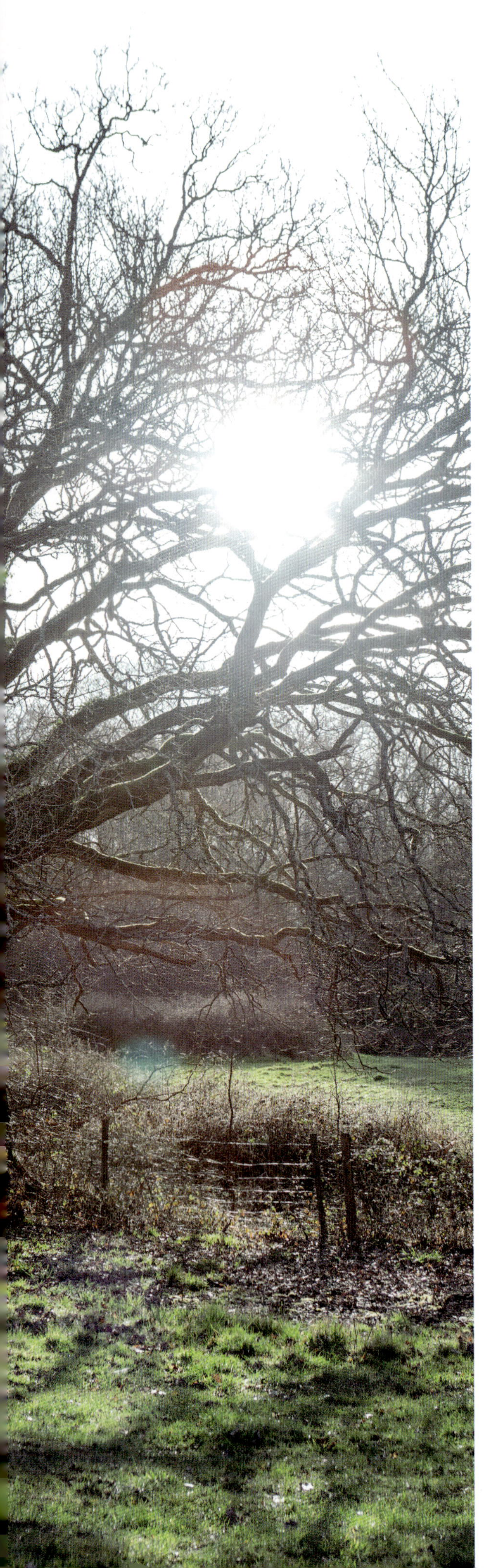

Painting contre-jour

Contre-jour means 'against the day', and in painting terms it describes the situation of the artist looking towards the sun. This dramatic lighting effect turns forms into flattened silhouettes, simplifies and combines shapes and hides small details. Long shadows can stretch out towards you on the ground, depending on how high the sun is in the sky. This means that even the most mundane group of objects or buildings can become a rich source of inspiration when viewed in this way.

The contre-jour approach lends itself well to a more abstract, more suggestive way of painting. I find it exciting that our brains can understand so much about the shadowy subject matter of a contre-jour painting, when all it has to work with are the small clues provided by the intense highlights that hit the tops of surfaces and provide haloes of light around figures.

Dark shadowy areas group together and can be enchanting. They become full of intrigue for the viewer, as you can't quite tell where one object finishes and another starts. Within these shadow areas, colours are subdued, and I have fun with letting a variety of dark hues bleed into each other. I don't want to show any separation between 'things', instead allowing them to become one dark mass together; the subtle differences of hue being held together by the same value.

Opportunities

Although colours generally appear more muted in a contre-jour scene, occasionally you'll find within your subject the magical effect of a spot of brilliant saturated colour as the sun shines through a translucent manmade object such as a colourful plastic bucket or fishing net. The same spellbinding effect can be seen when there is a person with red or brightly coloured hair between you and the sun.

The intense highlights you will see when painting contre-jour have a harder edge when they are hitting a solid hard surface, and become softer-edged when lighting a moving or multi-faceted object such as cascading hair or running water. It's worth smudging those brushmarks with your finger or a soft brush to show the difference.

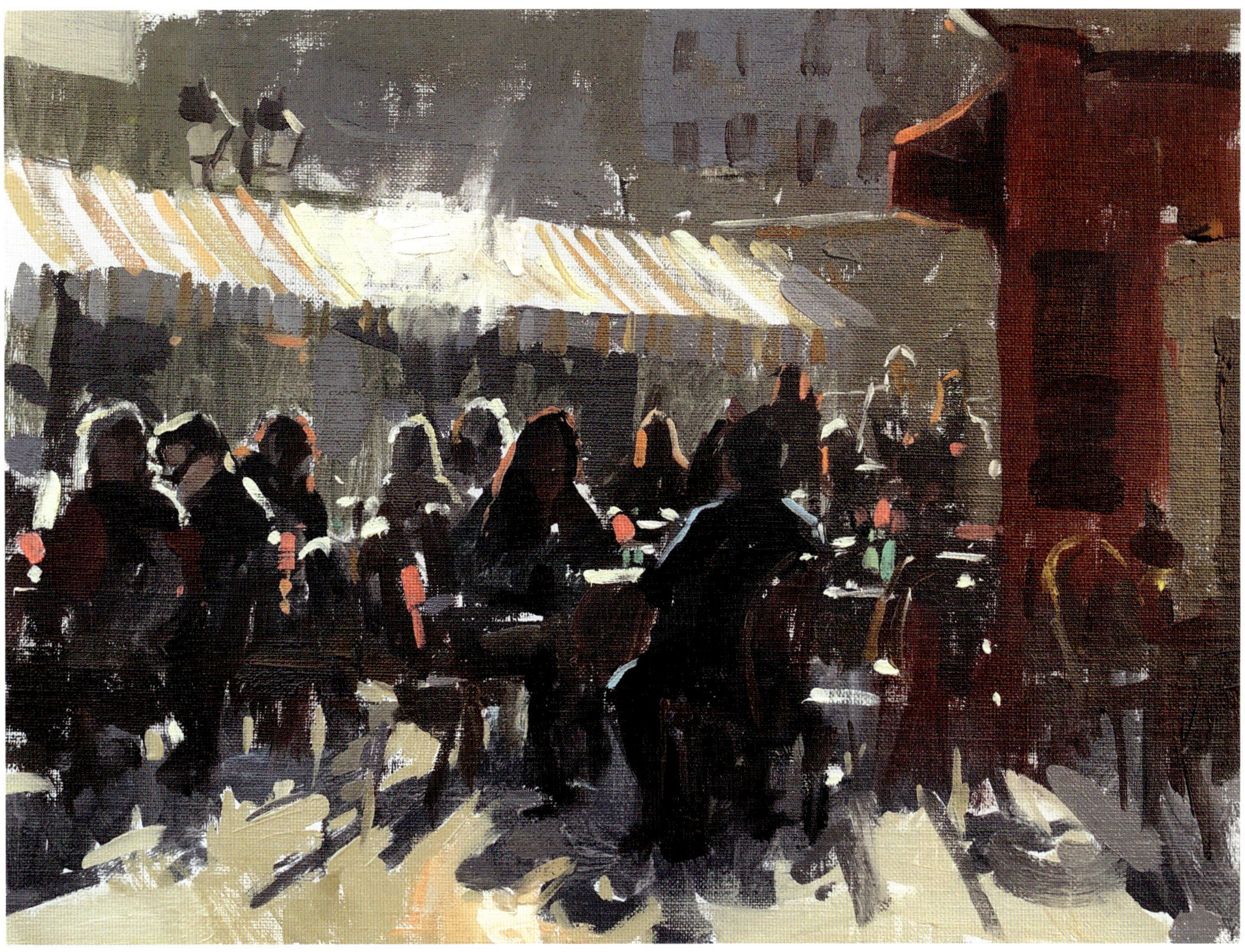

Challenges

There are practical difficulties of looking towards the light, and it's not comfortable for everyone. You'll need a wide-brimmed hat or umbrella to protect your eyes; sometimes I even wear both sunglasses and a hat if the sun is low.

Before you start painting, consider how much light there is on your surface and palette by turning your easel to different angles. It is easy to miss how dark your colours are when your painting surface is against the light and, as when painting with the sun shining directly on your surface (see page 120), you can have an unpleasant surprise when you view the painting inside later on.

Aperitifs at the Flower Market, Nice
30.5 x 23cm (12 x 9in)

This really was a fleeting impression, painted late in the day as the sun was going down and the café was about to close. Another low-key subject, I knew that I had to block in the darks with a large brush straight away – there was no time for drawing. A race against the clock like this can often lead to a painting with great vitality and freshness, and I'm happy with the light and atmosphere that I managed to capture here in a single fleeting hour.

Creating a glow

For painting contre-jour, it's a good idea to work on a mid-toned surface to start with so that you can quickly start to see the tonal parameters you are working between. Ensure that the darks are dark enough to let the highlights stand out brightly against them, whilst keeping a colour identity within those dark shadows.

Mix a little colour into your white for the highlights, again keeping a colour identity. This might be a little Indian yellow or cadmium lemon, or it may need to be tinted according to the local colour of the object being lit, but do try to avoid using just titanium white alone. It can look too cold and chalky and lack the necessary vibrancy to suggest real light.

A very strong light highlight against a very dark dark can have quite a lifeless look to it: a slight lightening of value around the strong highlight can do a much better job of replicating a bright glow. This can be achieved with a judicious smudge of a highlight into a dark with a finger (or a soft brush) here and there, or by removing some colour from the closest dark before painting on the highlight. The idea is to get something of a subtle halo or echo of that brightest highlight. Think of it as letting the light seep into the dark somewhat.

This principle is shown in the fountain detail below. Note that the dark background is lightened and smudged before its edge meets the highlight of the top of the fountain.

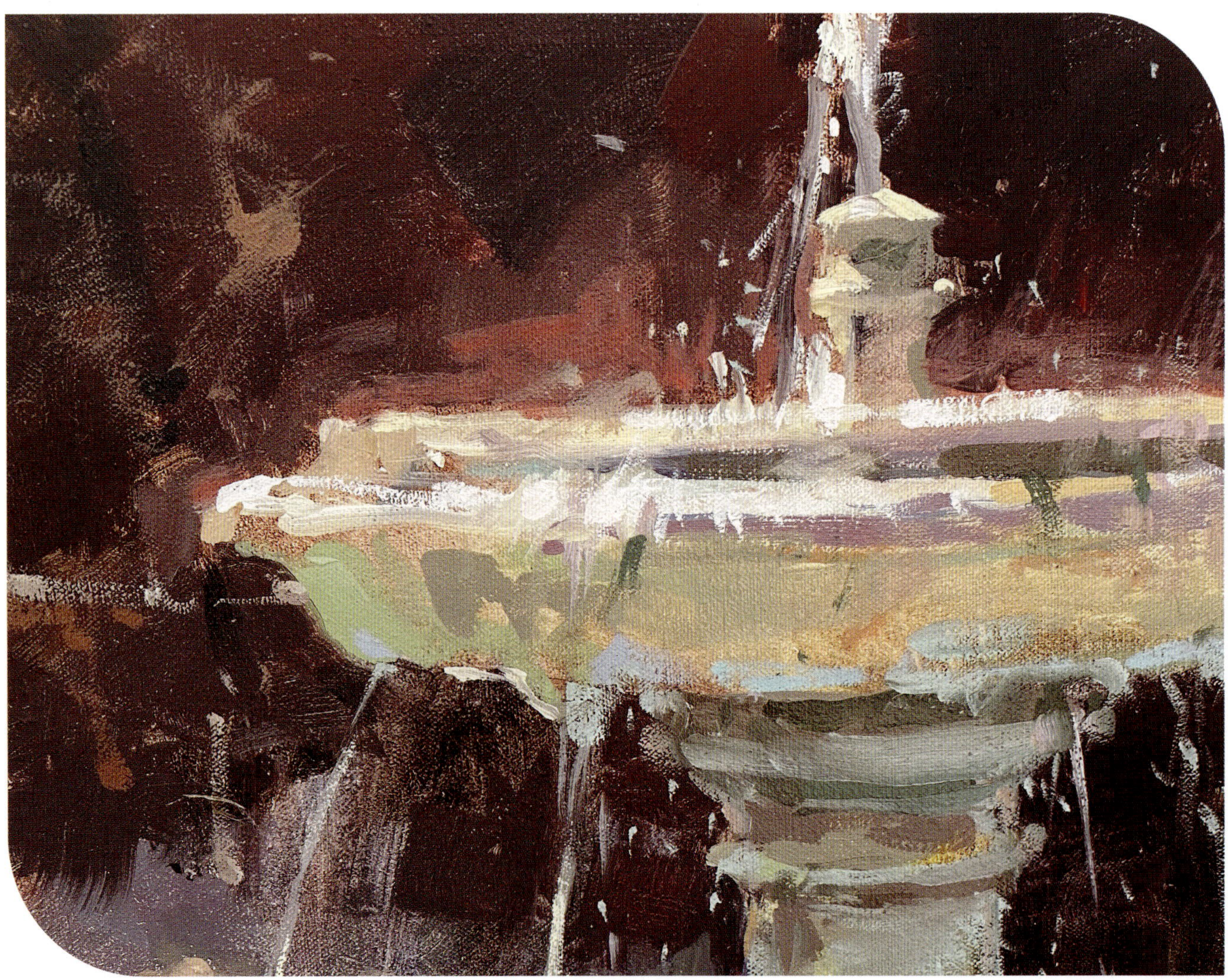

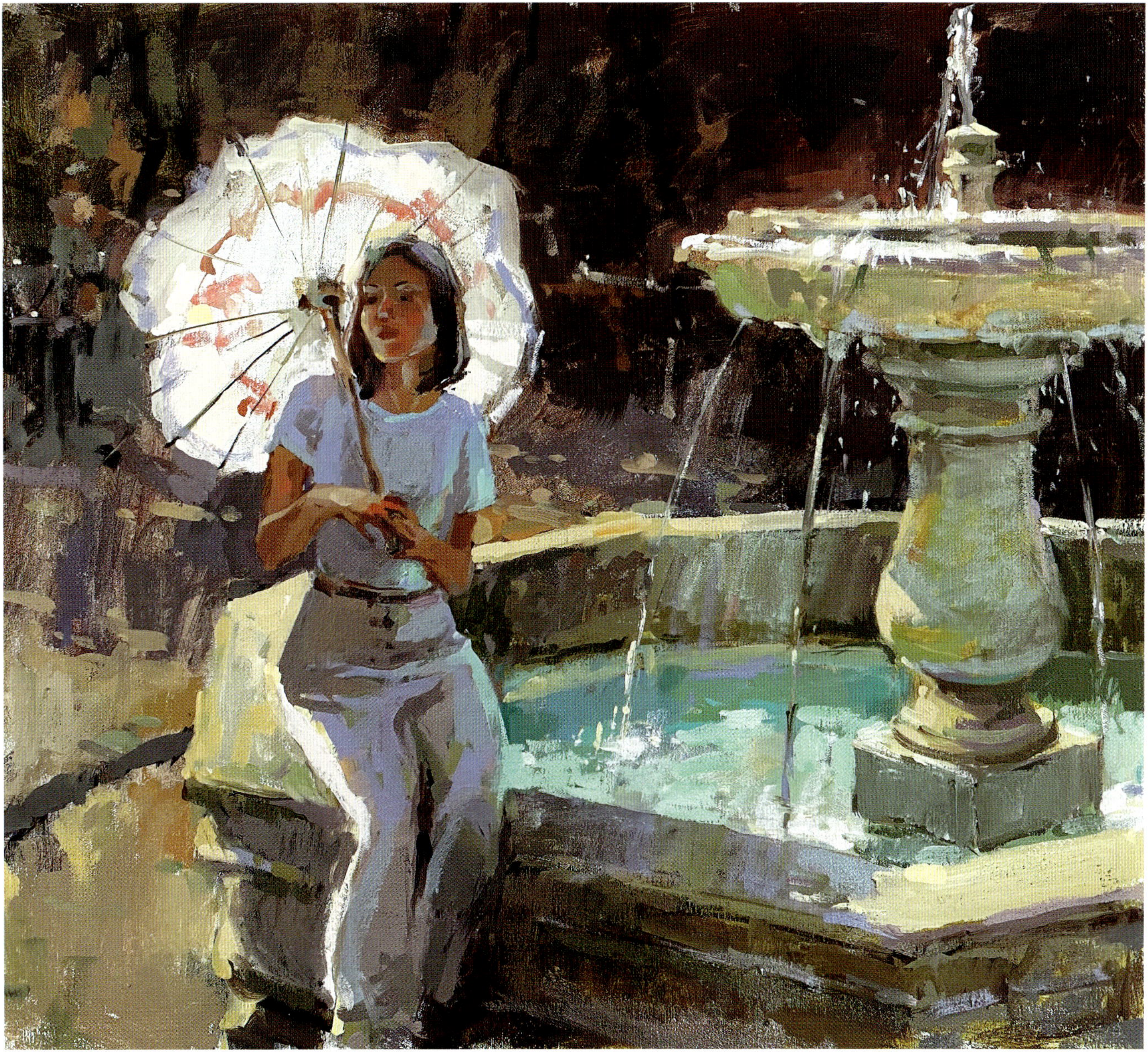

Margarita by the Fountain, Seville
45.5 x 40.5cm (18 x 16in)

On a painting trip to Seville with friends, we were fortunate to be able to arrange two hours with a lovely young model. I wanted her to be contre-jour so that the light would glow through the paper parasol; and the fountain made a beautiful setting for this idea.

There was a lot of reflected light to deal with, bouncing off the water and the hot stone, so it wasn't straightforward by any means. The trick with reflected light is making sure the value of the colour still sits within the shadow family, and doesn't become anywhere near as light in value as those places which are being lit directly by the sun.

It was a large and quite tricky painting to grapple with in the time allowed, and I had to tweak parts of it back in the studio later.

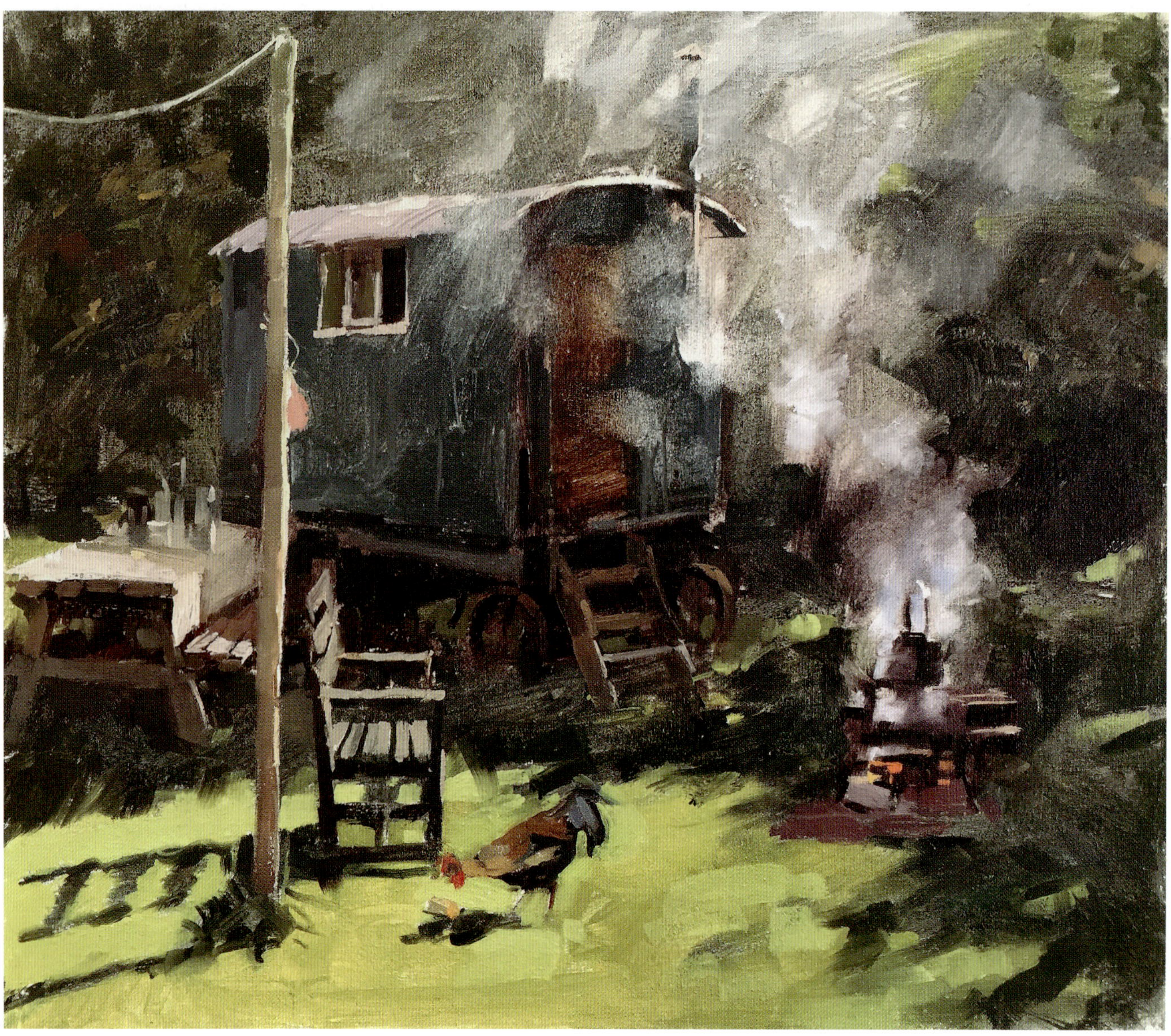

Shepherd's Hut and Smoke

35.5 x 30.5cm (14 x 12in)

As you can see from the direction of the shadows, I wasn't looking directly towards the sun with this one. Nevertheless, the effect was still very much a contre-jour one, with the light coming through the smoke being the effect that drew me to this subject.

The darks of the shepherd's hut and the trees behind it soften and merge into each other, letting the lit steel roof reveal to us the size and shape of its structure.

Most of the smoke that you can see isn't applied paint, but rather where I've removed dark paint with a rag dipped into solvent.

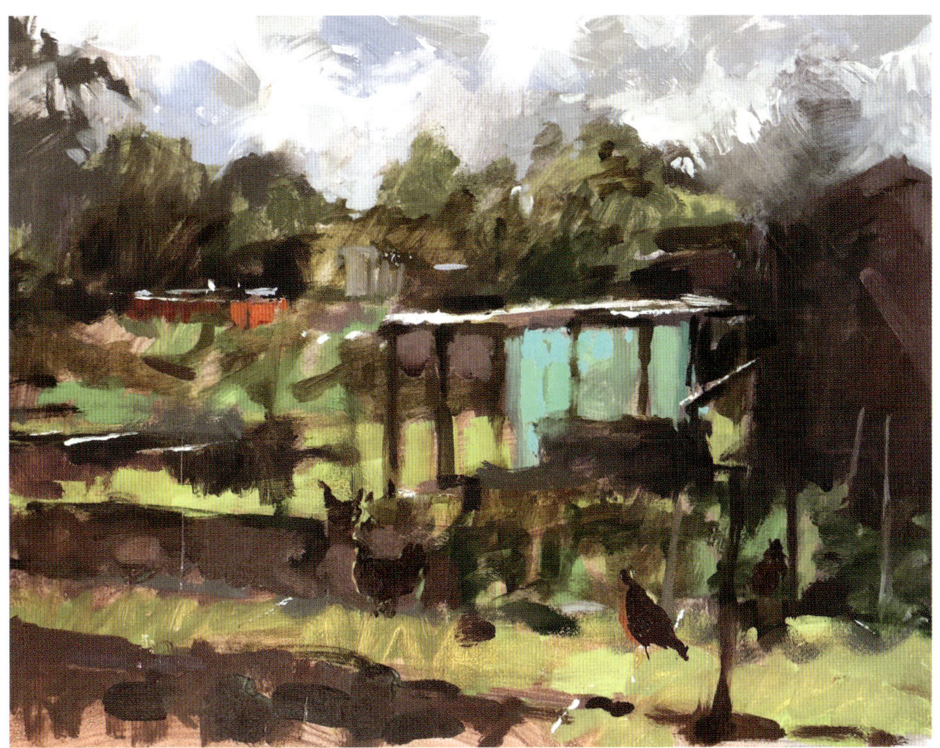

Green Netting at Holt Allotments
30.5 x 23cm (12 x 9in)

This one was a lively and rapid study, all about the light coming through that translucent green netting. However seemingly humble the subject, the simplest light effect can be reason enough for me to make a painting.

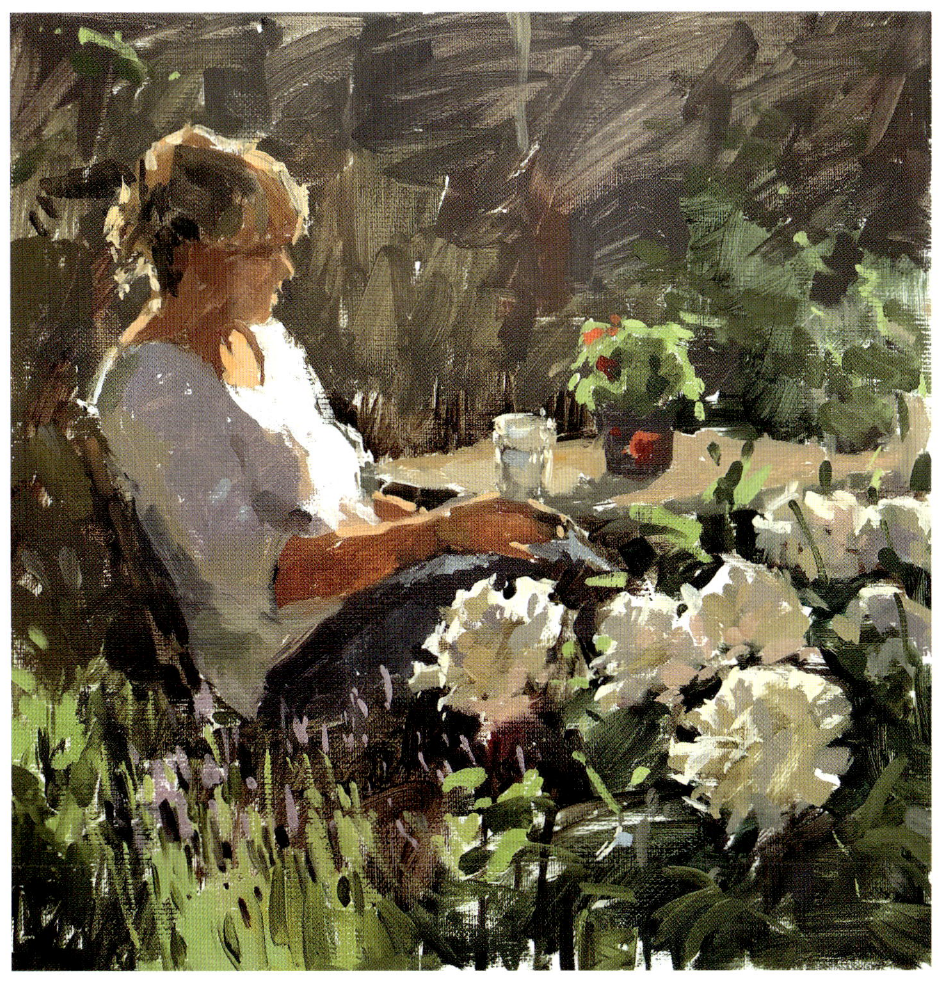

A Week of Peonies
30.5 x 30.5cm (12 x 12in)

I set out with the intention of painting a study of the peonies, but when I saw my friend sitting down at the table beyond I had a different idea. I loved the effect of the rim lighting around her head and shoulders, echoing the halo of light which appeared around each of the large white flowers.

In the foreground area of foliage, not too much work was required – just a dark background green wash to start with, then some light value green brushmarks to represent leaves struck by the light.

Beyond the Gate

After a rainy afternoon, it was a treat when the skies cleared and there was an opportunity to paint a quick contre-jour study. I knew the sun wouldn't hold for long so I didn't waste any time searching for a subject and set to work painting this nearby gate. I wanted to capture the dazzling light on the wet mud and the transparency of the leaves plus the sparkling touches of light on the wet branches and foliage.

It's worth noting that I started with a panel which was already tinted with a warm grey. This is really helpful when you're going to be painting a dazzling light effect. The light values, applied later on, will really stand out when seen against this mid-tone.

You will need

SURFACE
30.5 x 23cm (12 x 9in) panel, prepared with a light warm grey tone

COLOURS
An extended primary palette (see page 73) plus cadmium green light, raw sienna, transparent red oxide and raw umber

BRUSHES
A range of filberts and flats in sizes from 6mm (¼in) to 20mm (¾in)

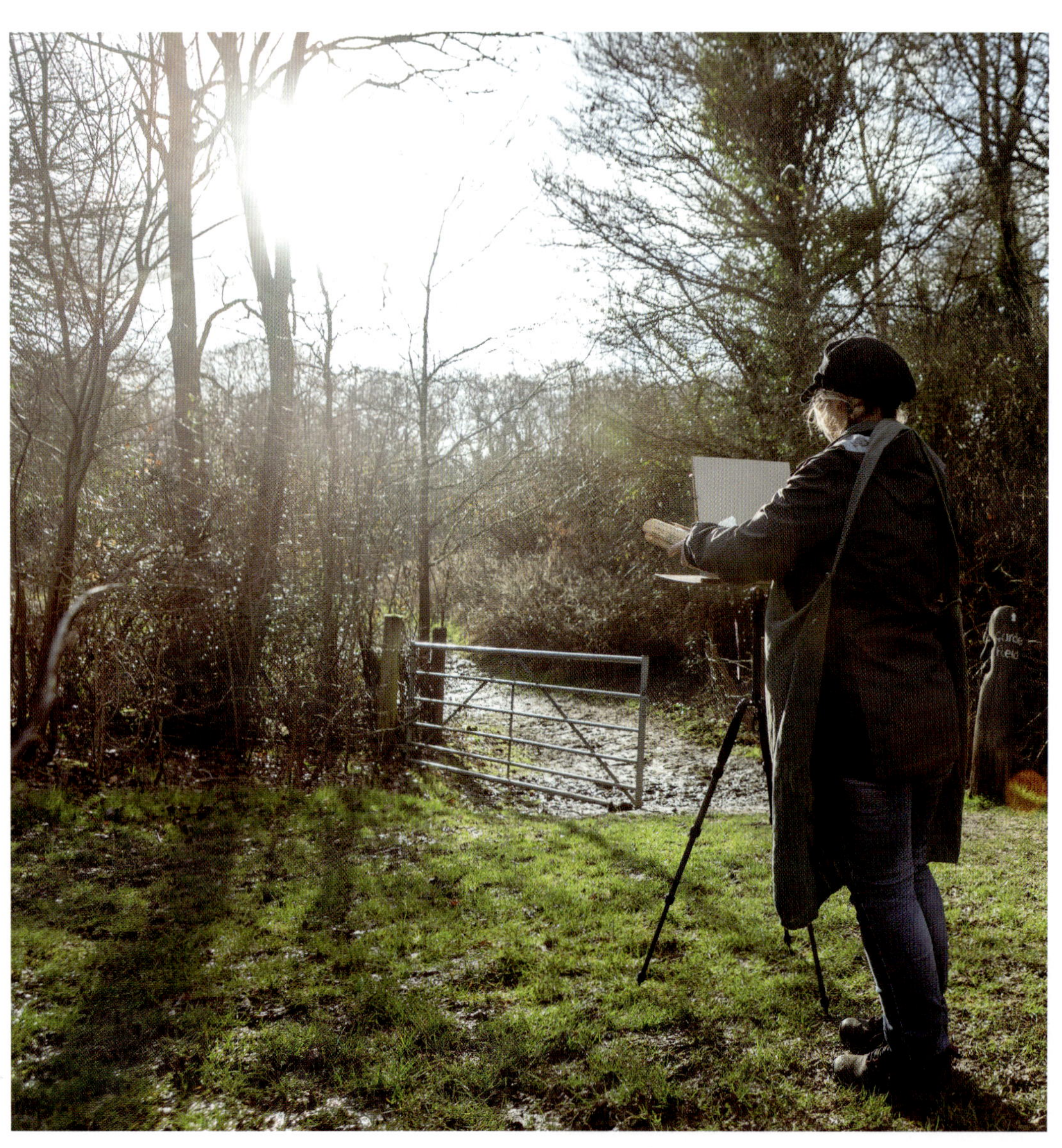

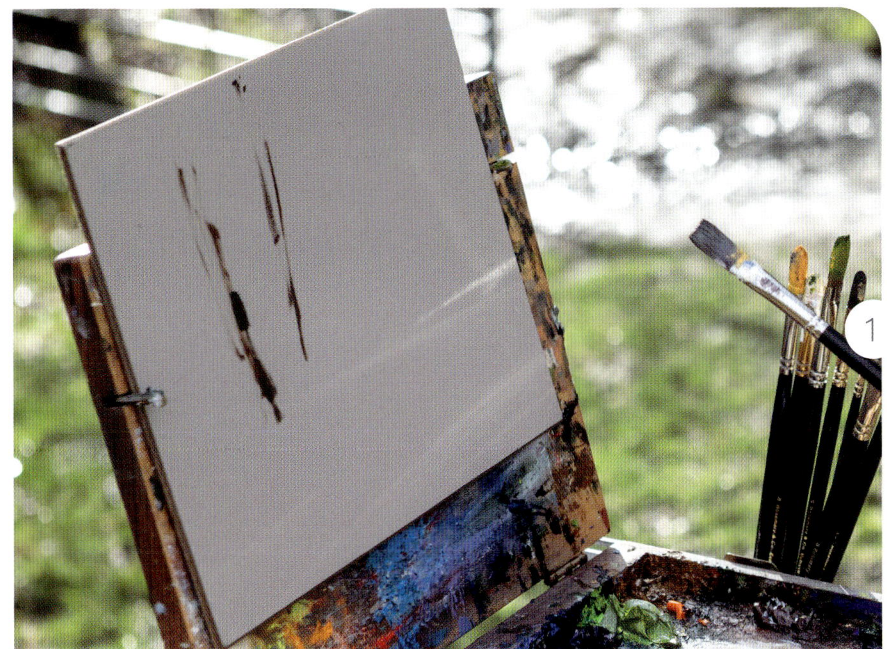

I used a flat brush and raw umber to begin sketching out some structure in the composition, using raw umber to start to mark in the trees, and leaving enough space on the right-hand side of the panel to fit in the gate.

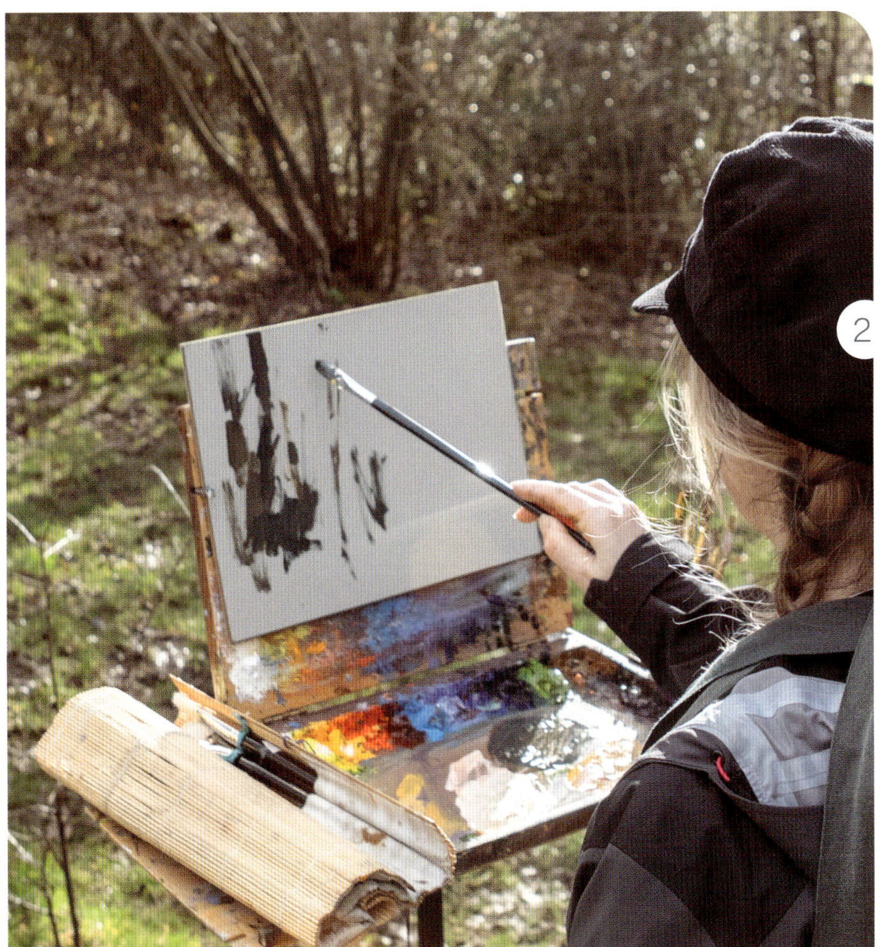

Mixing raw umber, ultramarine blue, crimson and transparent red oxide together made a range of colourful darks which I used to block in the trees along with the dark foliage and branches below.

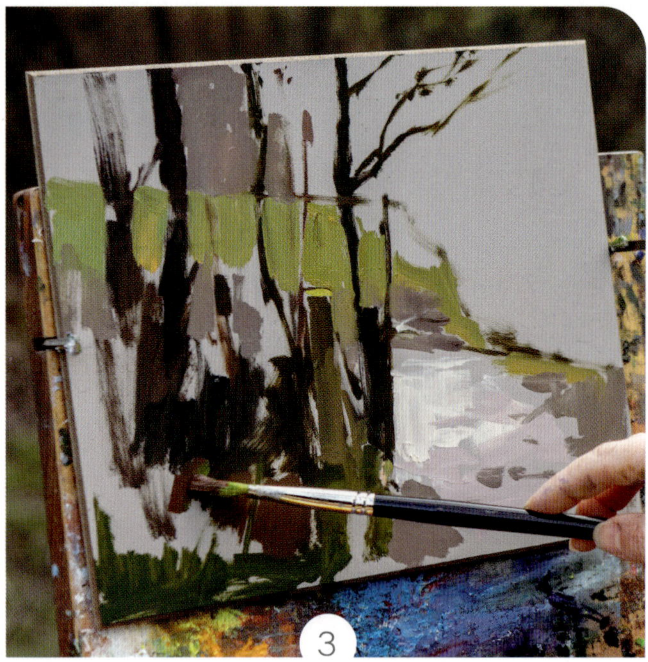

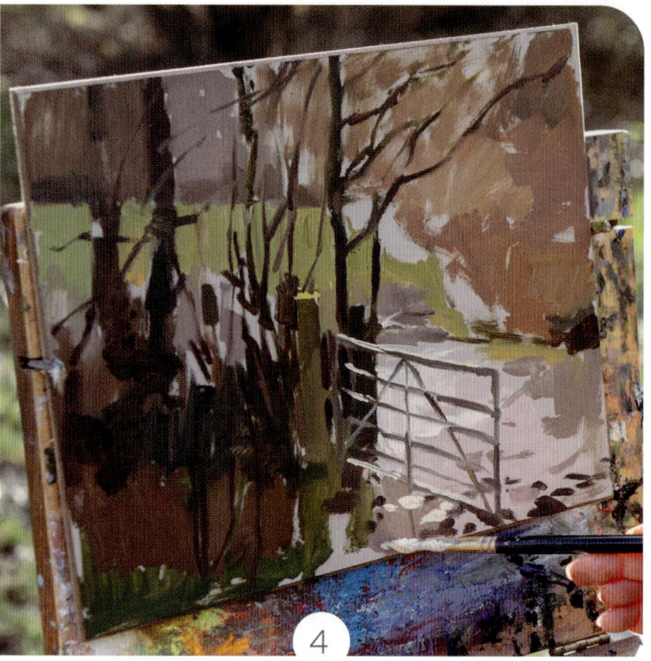

3 With the dark area in place, I mixed mid-value colours to block in the landscape beyond the gate, and darker browns and greens for the foreground below the trees. I also wanted to check how the wet mud might look against them, so I applied a very light value to the area by the side of the fence post at this point.

4 I painted in the structure of the gate, being careful not to make it too dark, as that can kill the effect of looking towards very bright light. In addition, I knew I would probably smudge, lift out or lighten parts of the gate as I continued. I also started on the warm autumn colours of the background trees at this point.

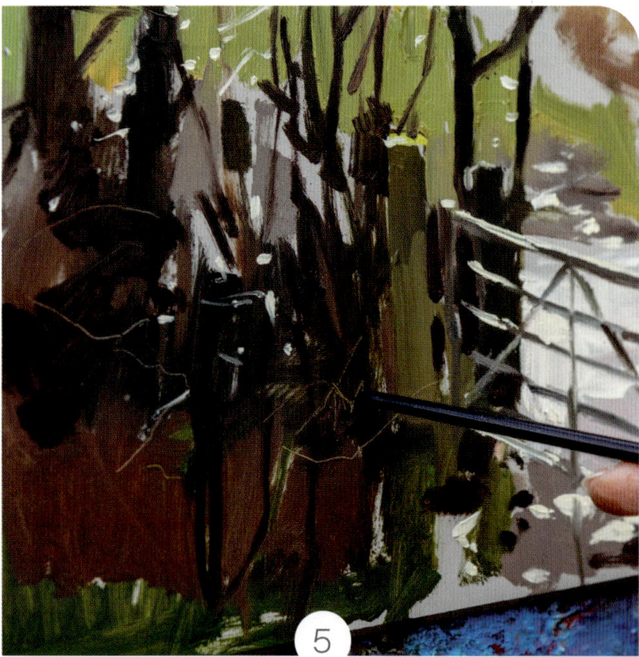

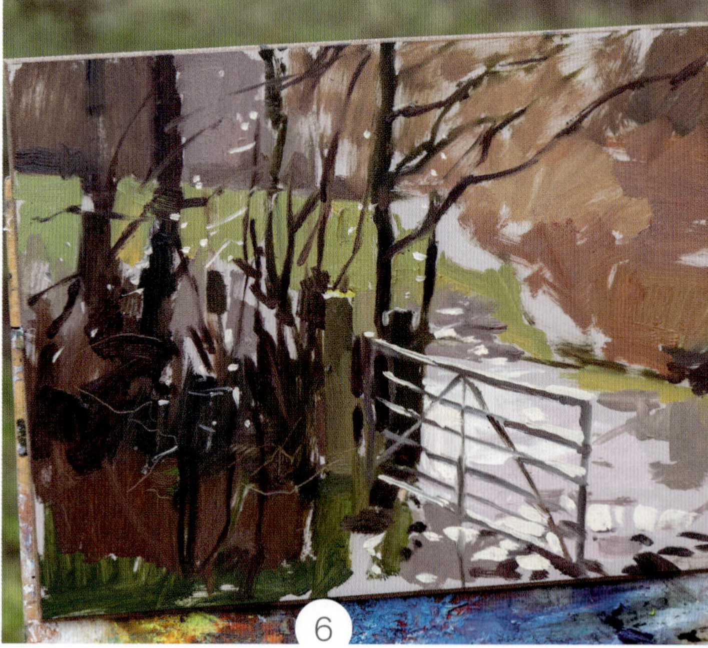

5 With a small 6mm (¼in) filbert brush, I started to paint on the little highlights which sparkled on the wet branches and foliage. I also used the other end of the brush to scratch out some thinner twigs in the undergrowth.

6 At this stage everything was blocked in; but the sun had disappeared behind clouds, so I paused. I decided I needed to warm up the light value of the sunlit mud and that it would be beneficial to warm up the gate and gate post too with the addition of red and orange.

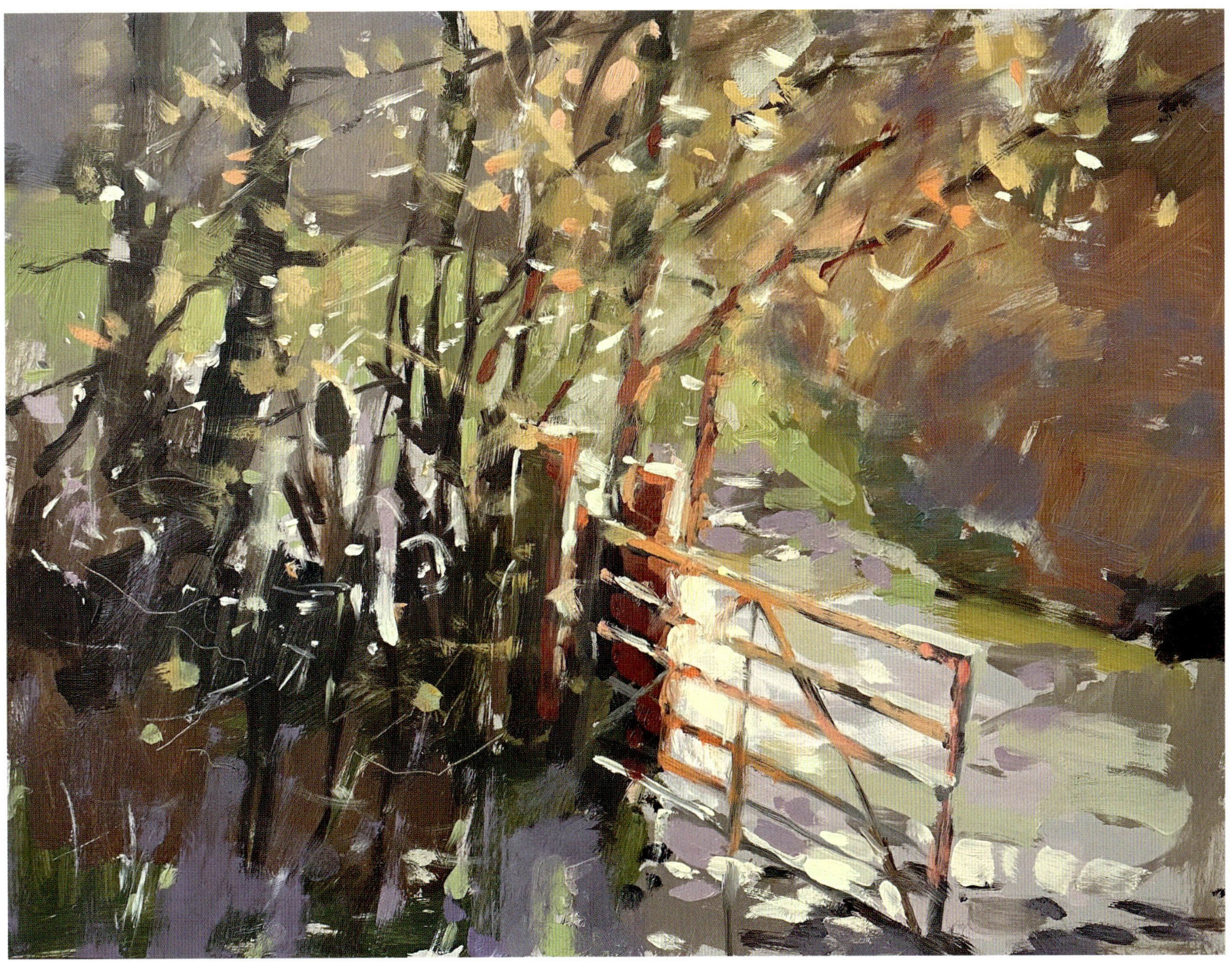

The finished painting
30.5 x 23cm (12 x 9in)

The final touches were the dabs of light value yellows and oranges to represent sunlit autumn leaves. I allowed some parts of the metal gate to disappear into the shiny mud, which heightened the effect of looking into blinding light.

Nocturnes

It's quite fun to have a go at painting nocturnes – that is, paintings of evening or night scenes – particularly if you've travelled to a beautiful destination on a painting trip and you want to make the most of every minute. You can take a bit more time over nocturnes because you haven't got the ever-moving sun to cope with. Urban subjects in particular take on a whole new persona in the hours of darkness, and it can be interesting to paint a subject such as a restaurant in both the daytime and at night and observe the differences.

Consider getting your drawing stage in while there's still daylight. When it becomes dark you can then move onto colour with a framework of shapes already in place. Plan ahead for how you will light both your palette and painting surface so that you'll be able to see what you're doing. You can often make use of streetlamps or the light coming from shop windows and restaurants, but be mindful of the colour cast and try to avoid lights that are too warm, too cool or simply strongly-coloured. If you find you enjoy painting nocturnes, you can buy specialist lights to clip on to your equipment with their own rechargeable battery packs. Alternatively, you could use clip-on book lights or a head torch.

When you're painting at night it can be really hard to see your colours properly, and when you later see the painting in daylight, the colours can come as quite a surprise! It is good practice to always place your colours in the same order on your palette, and doing so will certainly stand you in good stead with nocturnes, as it will allow you to work intuitively, relying on your experience and familiarity with where particular paints always sit in your palette.

Identify what the main light sources will be within the subject, then decide which you want to include in the painting and where to best place them in your composition. I suggest leaving gaps where you want those brightest lights to be while you paint in all the surrounding dark colours. It's true that you need dark in order to show light, but a splodge of white paint next to a black area won't necessarily read to the viewer as a light source within the painting. Instead, try painting a halo effect (see 'Creating a glow' on page 128) around your brightest lights, using a darker value than the actual light source but lighter in value than the dark sky. It's a good idea to soften and blend the halo into the dark surrounding it, as hard edges here can also kill that believable effect of light. In terms of the colour spectrum, the halo will move away from the colour of the light source with a prismatic shift. What this means is that if the light source is yellow, the colours in the halo will travel from orange through red to violet, depending on how much of the scattered light you can see in the atmosphere. Bear in mind that we only have pigments to paint with while trying to describe the effects of light, so it's all about finding out what we can do within the limitations that we have.

I started painting this in the evening while it was still light because I anticipated that the lighting within the shop would become stronger as it became darker outside – with the result that the painting would be all about that contrast of the warm, bright, artificial light inside the shop with the cool, dark, exterior.

I particularly enjoyed how the light spilled out from the doorway and onto the pavement; and how the light reflected off the shiny paintwork above the doorway. The shop was full to the brim of pottery artefacts; had I concerned myself with drawing each one, I would have been there for days. Instead, I kept squinting to help me pick out larger shapes amongst all the details and kept the treatment of the shop interior loose and fluid.

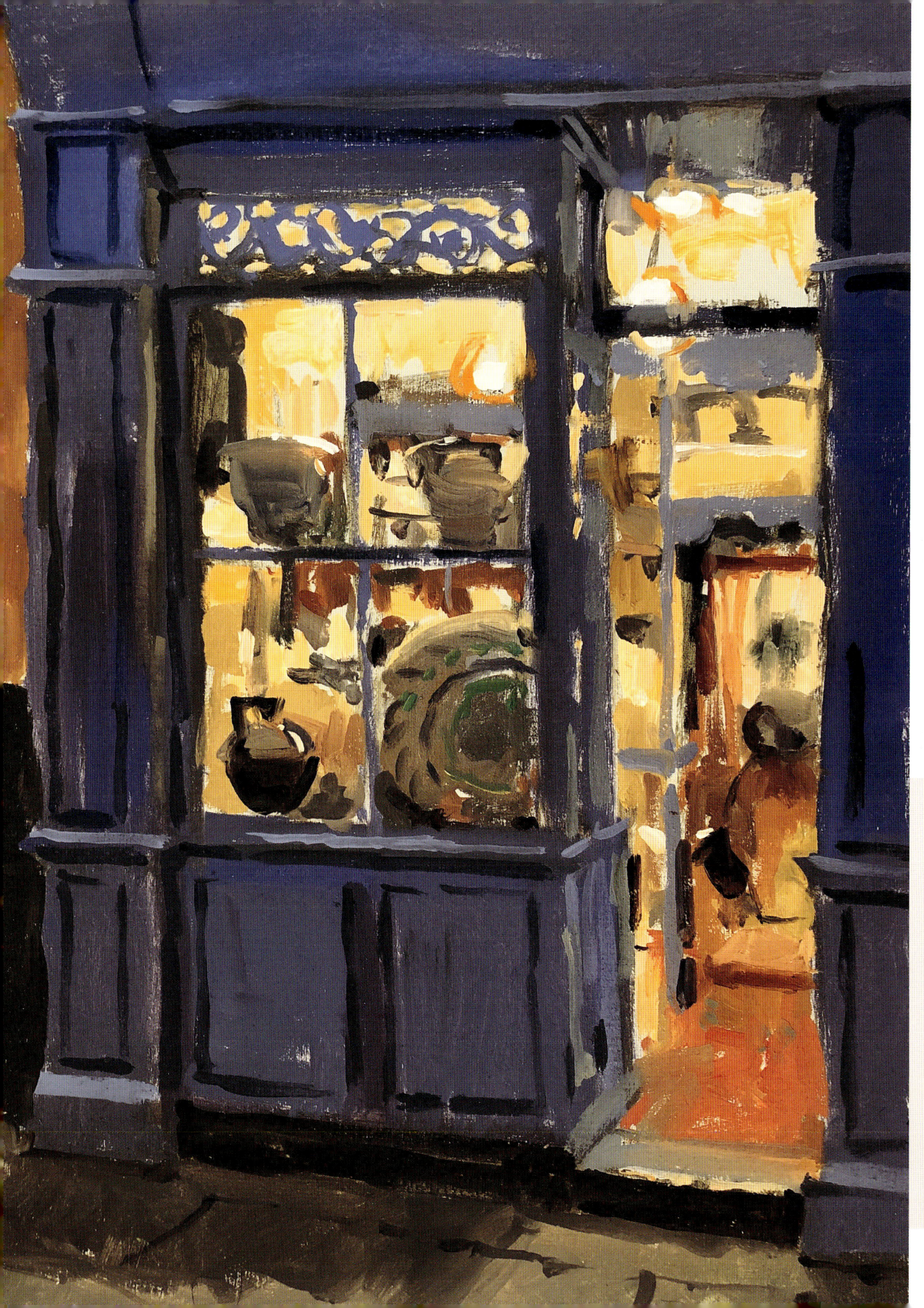

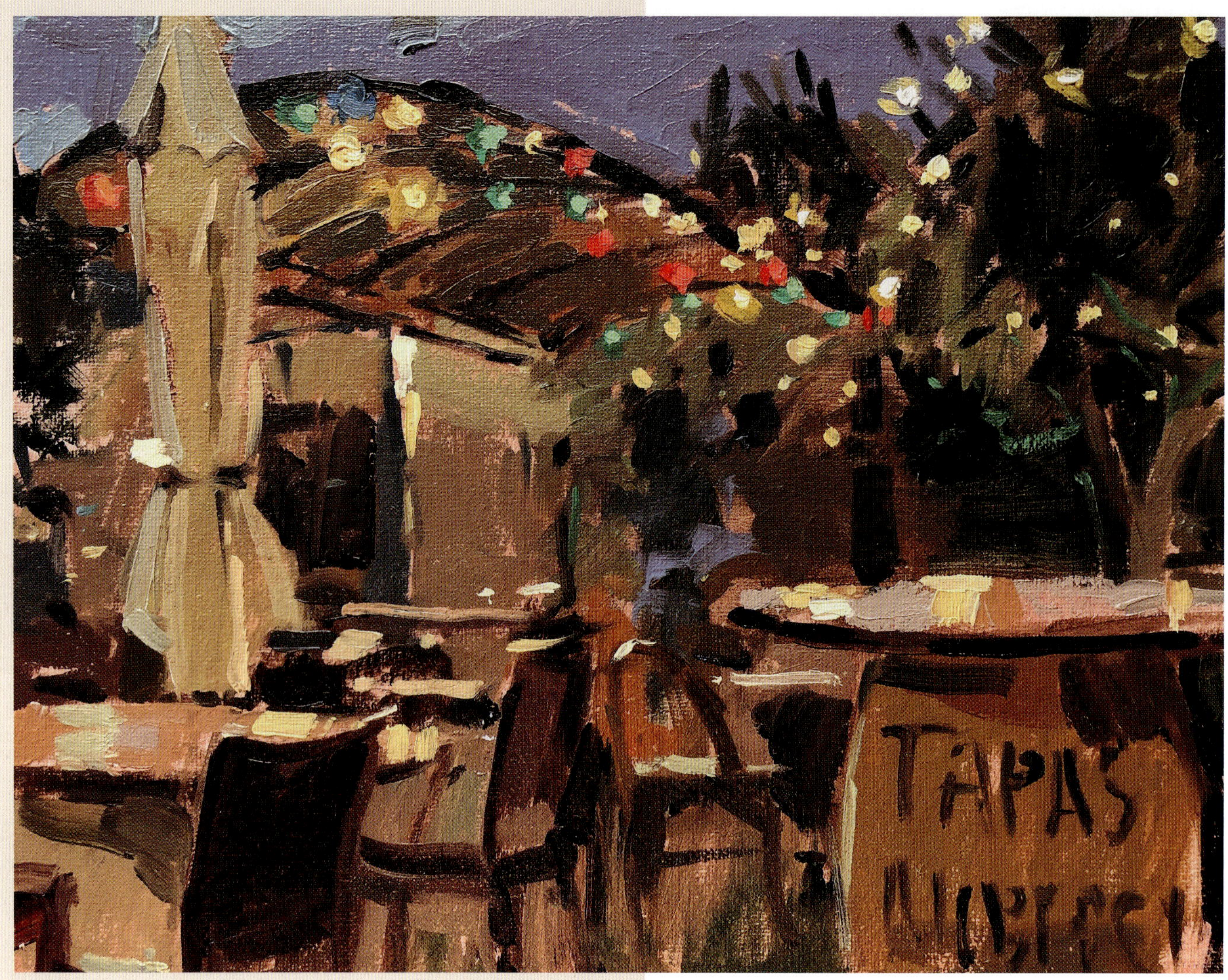

Tapas at Le Somail
25.5 x 20.5cm (10 x 8in)

I painted this nocturne in France without any plan of attack, and using a very poor headlamp that was getting dimmer and dimmer as time went on. In the end I had to use my phone torch to be able to see my painting and palette!

I don't think the composition is up to much but it's quite a lively and fun little painting, and I enjoyed putting on the multicoloured lights. It's a shame that the restaurant didn't have any clients seated outside that evening, as figures would have added scale and interest.

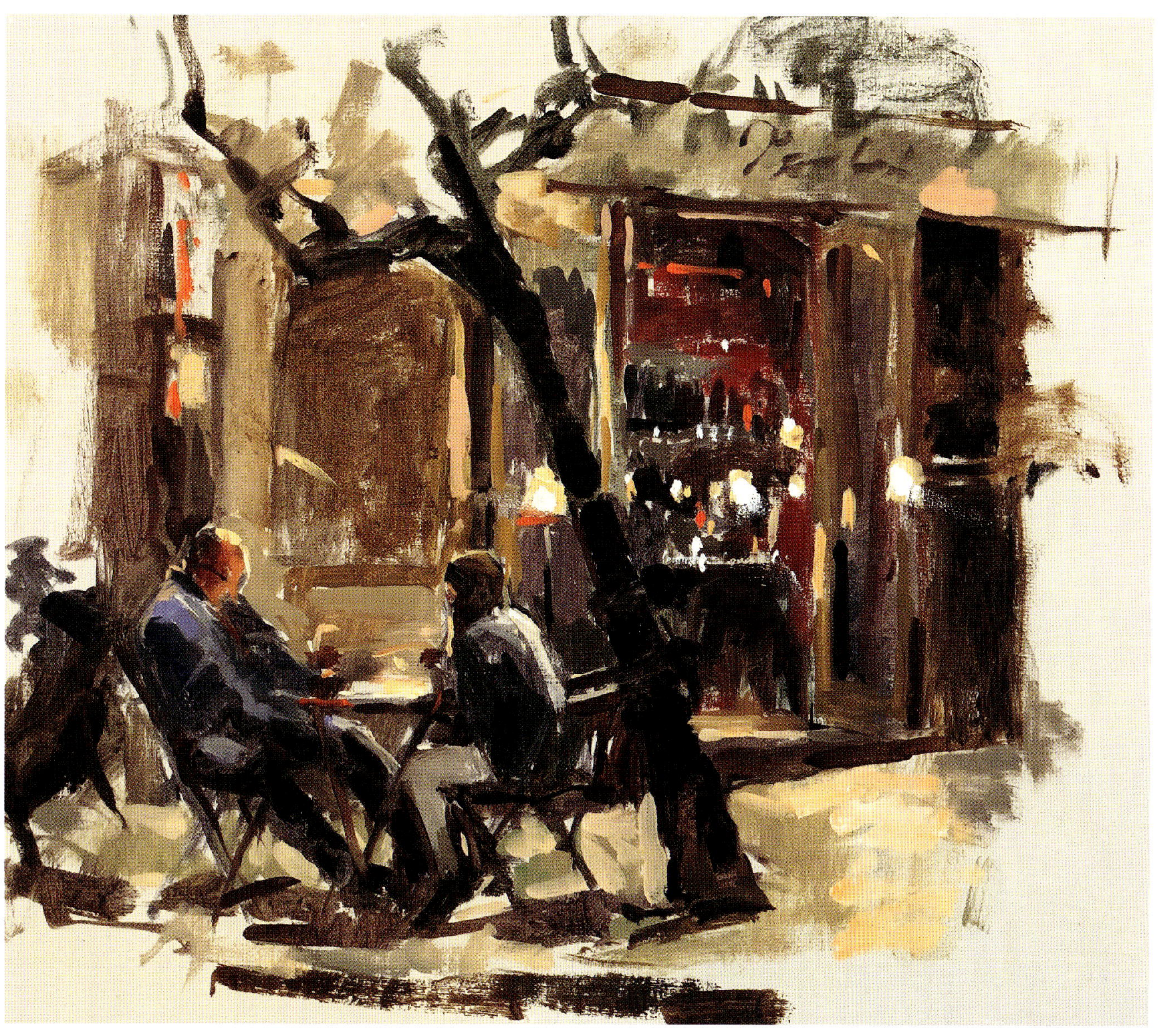

Tapas for Two
30.5 x 23cm (12 x 9in)

I was tired after a busy day of painting when I spotted this bar while sitting at another table across the road. I was attracted to all those lamps within the interior, which looked warm and dark and mysterious. I also enjoyed the light hitting the top of the table and the man's bald head. In order to show the highlight on his head I had to block in the darks behind him quickly. You can see from the brushmarks how rapidly this block-in of the darks was executed.

After I'd painted the seated figures and those lamps I felt tired and I lost interest, but looking at it afterwards I rather liked the sketchy, unfinished look and think it works well as a vignette.

Working with the weather

In a book of plein air painting it would be remiss of me to not discuss the effects of weather patterns beyond clear sunshine. The weather has enormous significance for artists like us, who choose to paint outside. Using common sense and being prepared with the necessary equipment will set you off on the right path, and while the experience of getting out there and actually doing it in different weather conditions will surely be the best teacher, in this chapter I share some advice to save you from a certain amount of trial and error. I also want to take the opportunity to extol the virtues of painting outside throughout the year in various weather conditions, and encourage you to think of plein air painting as more than just a summer activity.

Inevitably, outdoor painters have to prepare for the weather as much as it's possible to do so. Where I live in the UK, we experience a range of weather conditions from wet and windy, snow and hail, storms, fog, overcast skies, chills, warmth, and brightness – and it can change many times in a day. Ours is a temperate climate, so temperature-wise I don't have anything too severe to deal with, and plein air painters in the UK are unlikely to have to tackle any extreme weather scenarios (or worry about deadly insects, snakes or wild animals, for that matter). Indeed, although we may wish for more sunshine, we are a fortunate lot! Of course, you may have a quite different scenario to deal with, so while I speak from a British standpoint, much of the information in this chapter applies universally.

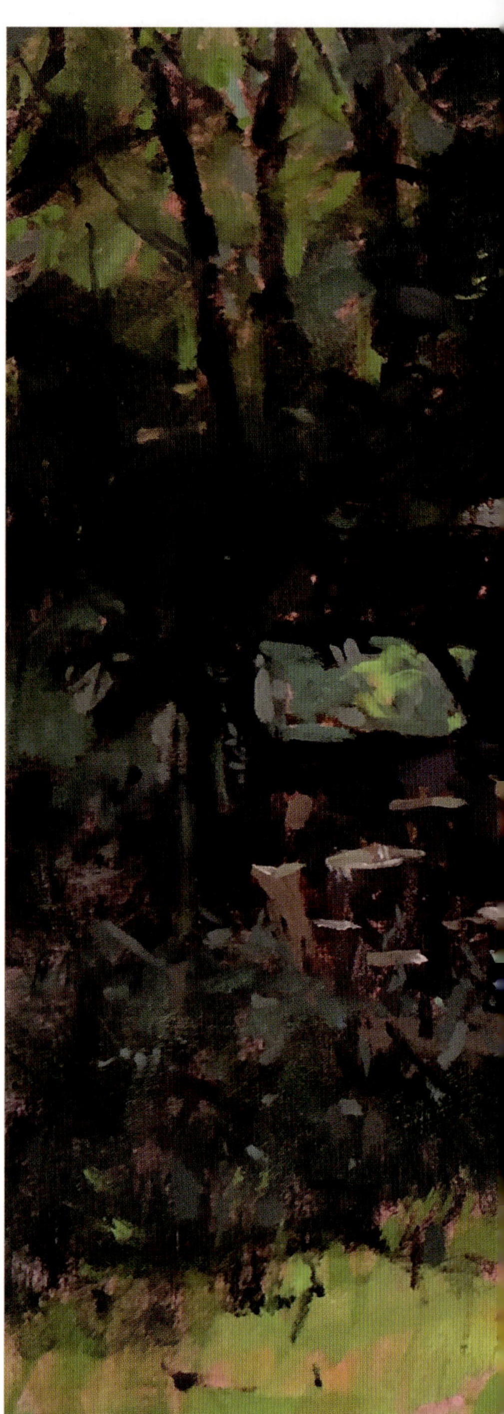

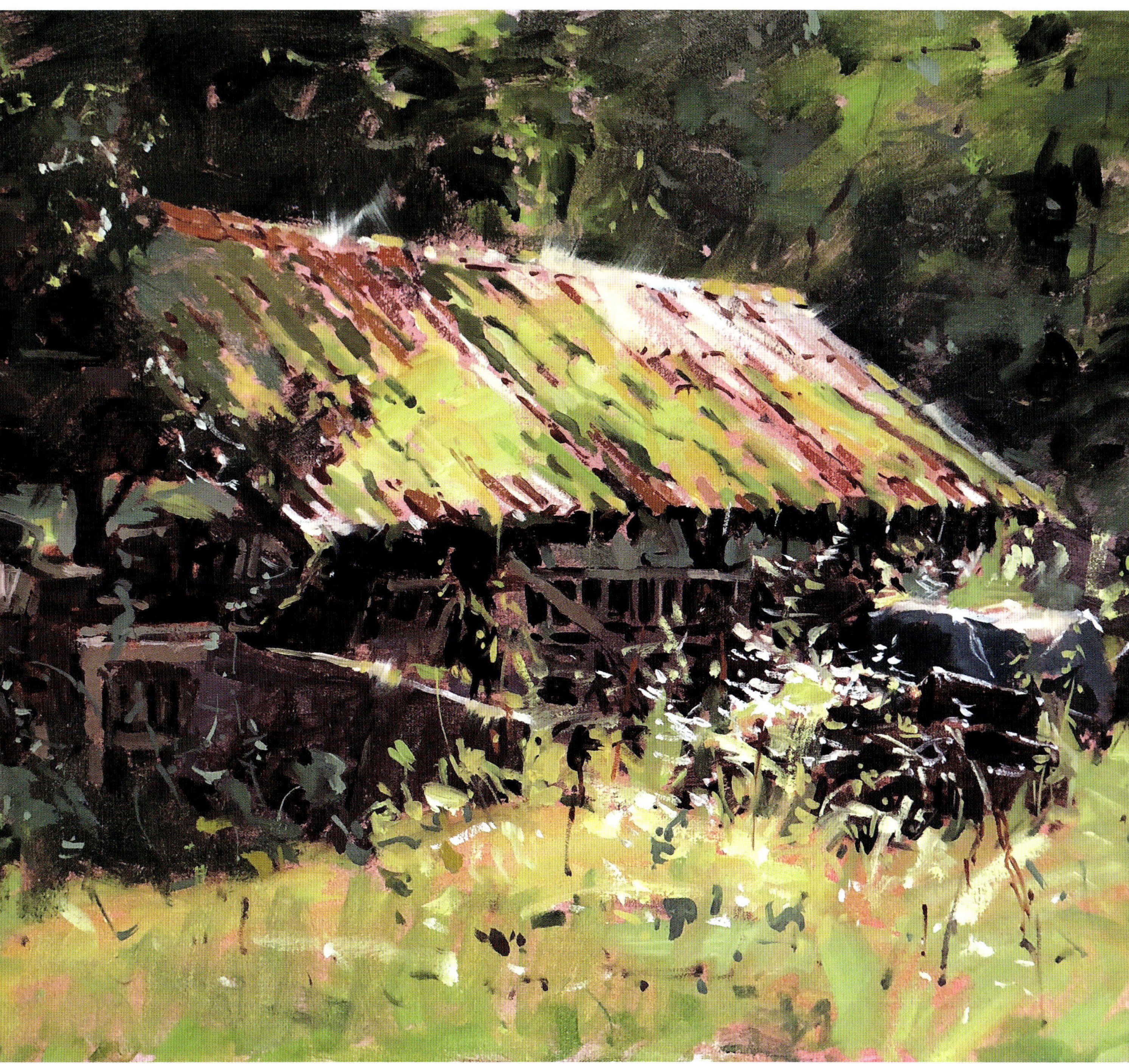

Out Behind the Old Woodshed
61 x 38cm (24 x 15in)

Here's an example of a painting where changeable weather conditions worked in my favour. It was painted in Ludham, Norfolk, on a September day which changed from full sun to heavy downpours and back to sun again many times. This gave me a dazzling scene of light bouncing off the wet terracotta roof tiles, the foliage and the equipment in front of the barn. It's exhilarating trying to capture such a sparkling effect.

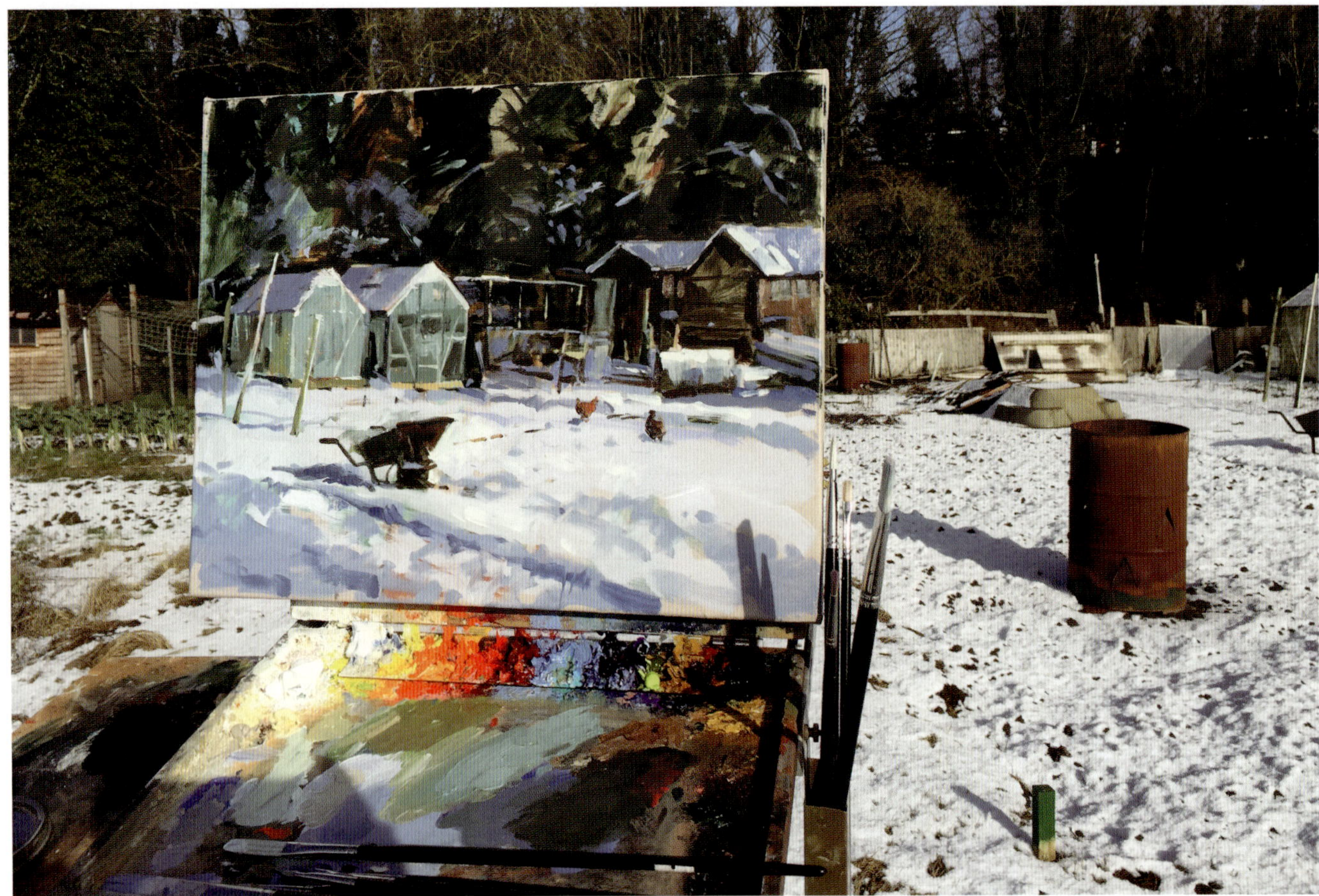

Preparation

I've often come across artists who think that painting outside is an activity only suitable for a warm and sunny day, but I urge you not to wait for what you consider to be the ideal conditions. You could spend the best part of the year holding out for the 'perfect' day, and even a bright and promising morning can quickly cloud over and become something altogether different. If you are a fair-weather painter the disappointment brought on by a change in weather can adversely affect your mood, particularly after waiting for so long and with such high hopes. It's far better to plan regular outings and be willing to take whatever the weather throws at you.

Tackling the weather is all about being prepared. The aim is to be as physically comfortable as possible on site so that once you get to work on the painting you can focus all your attention there. Be organized for the season and the likely weather you'll experience. In winter, additions to my kit are fingerless gloves, a woolly hat, lip balm, earmuffs and a hot drink in a flask. In summer these are replaced with a sun hat or cap, sunglasses, sunscreen and a water bottle.

All year round I keep certain extras in my car in case they are needed – wellington boots, umbrellas for rain or sun, a warm fleece top, waterproof jacket and waterproof overtrousers which I can pop on in very wet or muddy circumstances. You may have your own key essentials which are relevant to where you live, such as insect repellent/citronella spray or binoculars. Warm and sturdy walking boots with a good grip are essential for me as I need to be comfortable walking and standing for hours at a time. I do believe, as Alfred Wainwright said, that 'there's no such thing as bad weather, only unsuitable clothing'.

Fair weather and sunshine

If you're just getting started with plein air painting there is much to be said for choosing an overcast day when the subject before you may remain relatively unchanged for hours. On a sunny day you will have to deal with shadows which are constantly moving, and after two hours you will be looking at a completely different subject to the one you started with.

I speak elsewhere in the book about ways to deal with those shadows (see pages 44–45), but it's worth a word of caution here to remind you not to try to chase the light. If the day is sunny but with clouds coming and going, don't try to change your painting each time the scene changes, as you'll likely end up with something overworked and incoherent. Stick to a simple message regarding how the light affects your subject, which will often be your first impression of the scene.

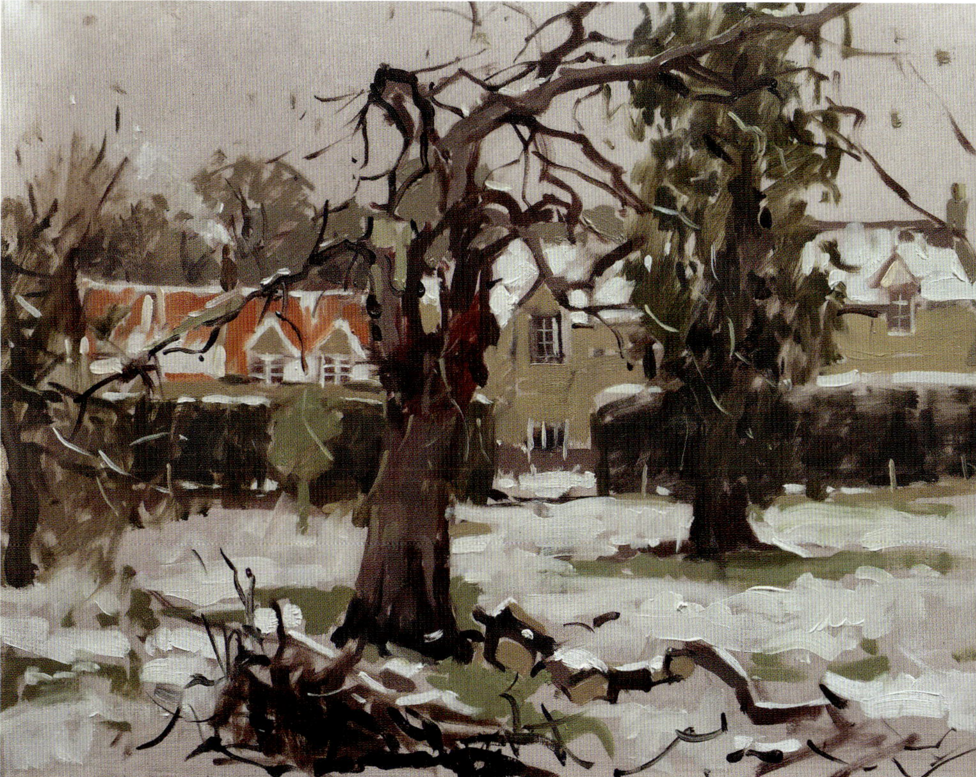

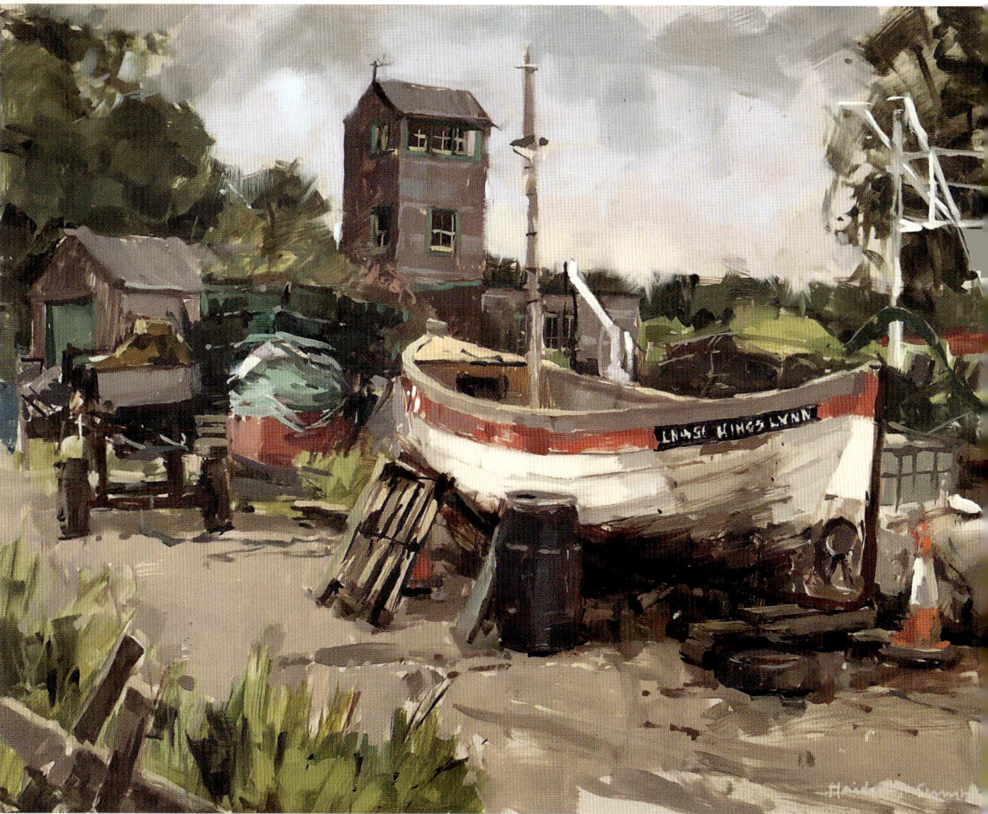

Top:

Snowfall at Leadenham
40.5 x 30.5cm (16 x 12in)

Right:

The Lookout, Brancaster Staithe
35.5 x 28cm (14 x 11in)

Both of these pieces were painted in Norfolk, on dreary overcast days. Although there are no cast shadows in these conditions, there are still lights and darks to be found, along with plenty of colour. Although I'm not much of a sky painter, I do really enjoy trying to find the subtle colour changes of the grey clouds.

Rain

Something we do get a lot of here in the UK is rain, but rain needn't stop play for us hardy plein air painters. The softening effects of rain (or high moisture content in the air) on the landscape, or the tantalizing reflections on city streets and pavements can make the extra efforts required to paint in the rain extremely worthwhile.

When painting in rain, I try my best to keep the rainwater away from my palette and the painting. Although some painters don't seem to mind, I find the emulsifying combination of oil and water on the palette very frustrating to have to work with. Water on the surface of the canvas or panel can cause adhesion problems for the paint, too, particularly on an acrylic primer base. Nobody wants to see their painting disappearing before their eyes!

Tips for painting in the rain

There are many types of clip-on umbrellas available, and you may find one that works with your easel set-up. However, a lightweight pochade and tripod system can easily become unbalanced by the extra weight of a clip-on umbrella, so when I am caught in a sudden rain shower while painting, I usually hold an umbrella in my left, non-painting, hand while continuing to work.

Rain is, sadly, often accompanied by wind, which makes using an umbrella a fairly hopeless activity, although one with wind vents incorporated will fare better. If facing both rain and wind, or if I am painting on a stubbornly rainy day, my preferred approach is to find some sort of roof or overhang to take shelter under for the duration of the painting session. A large tree often does the trick.

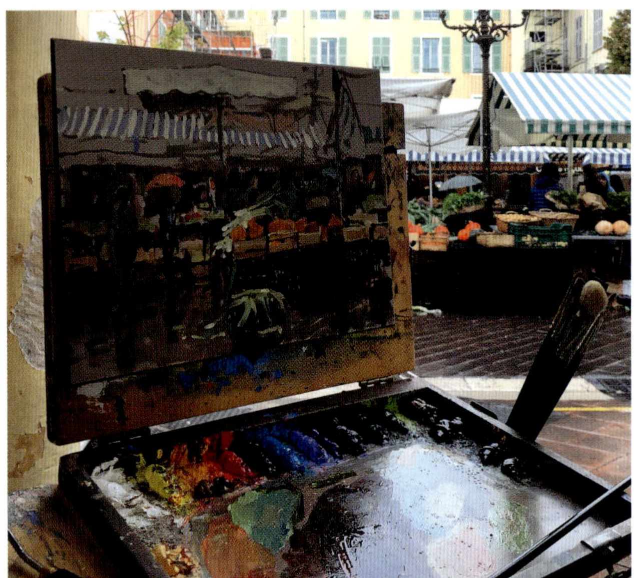

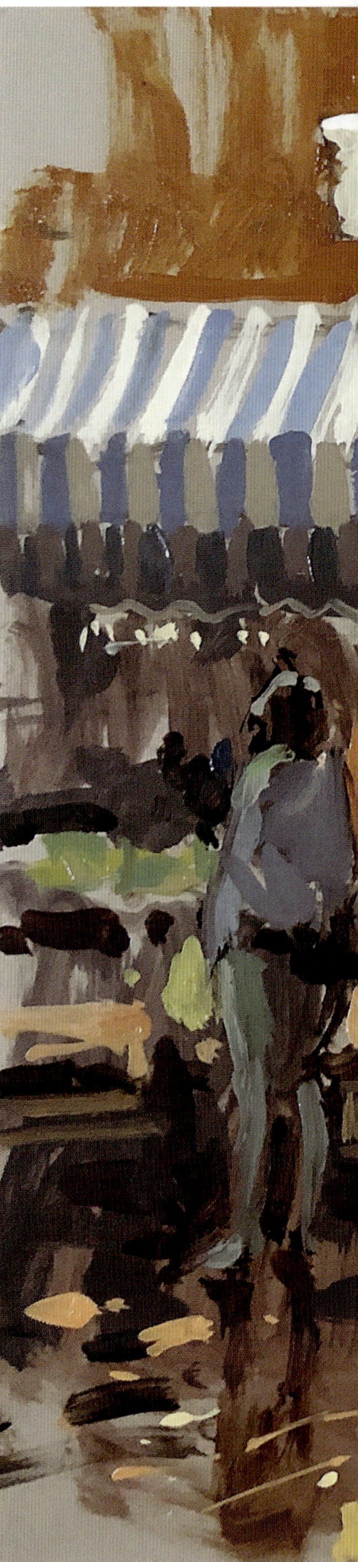

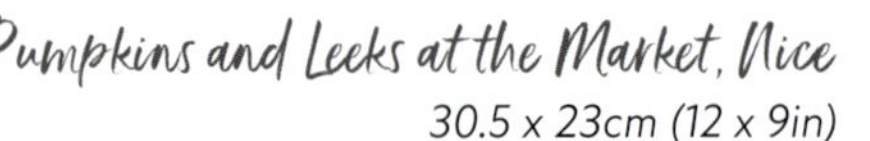

Pumpkins and Leeks at the Market, Nice
30.5 x 23cm (12 x 9in)

While in Nice for a short painting trip the weather was disappointing, but I wanted to go home with some paintings regardless. On this particular day the rain didn't pause all morning, so I found an archway to stand underneath to paint and then selected my viewpoint from there. Every now and then the incessant rain would change from a steady fall to a hearty downpour which caused so much splash-back from the pavement that I had to open my umbrella and hold it out directly in front of my easel.

Such circumstances are challenging and I sometimes find myself asking, 'Why am I doing this?', but the resulting artwork, along with the feeling of pride invoked by overcoming difficulties, always makes the painting session seem most worthwhile after all.

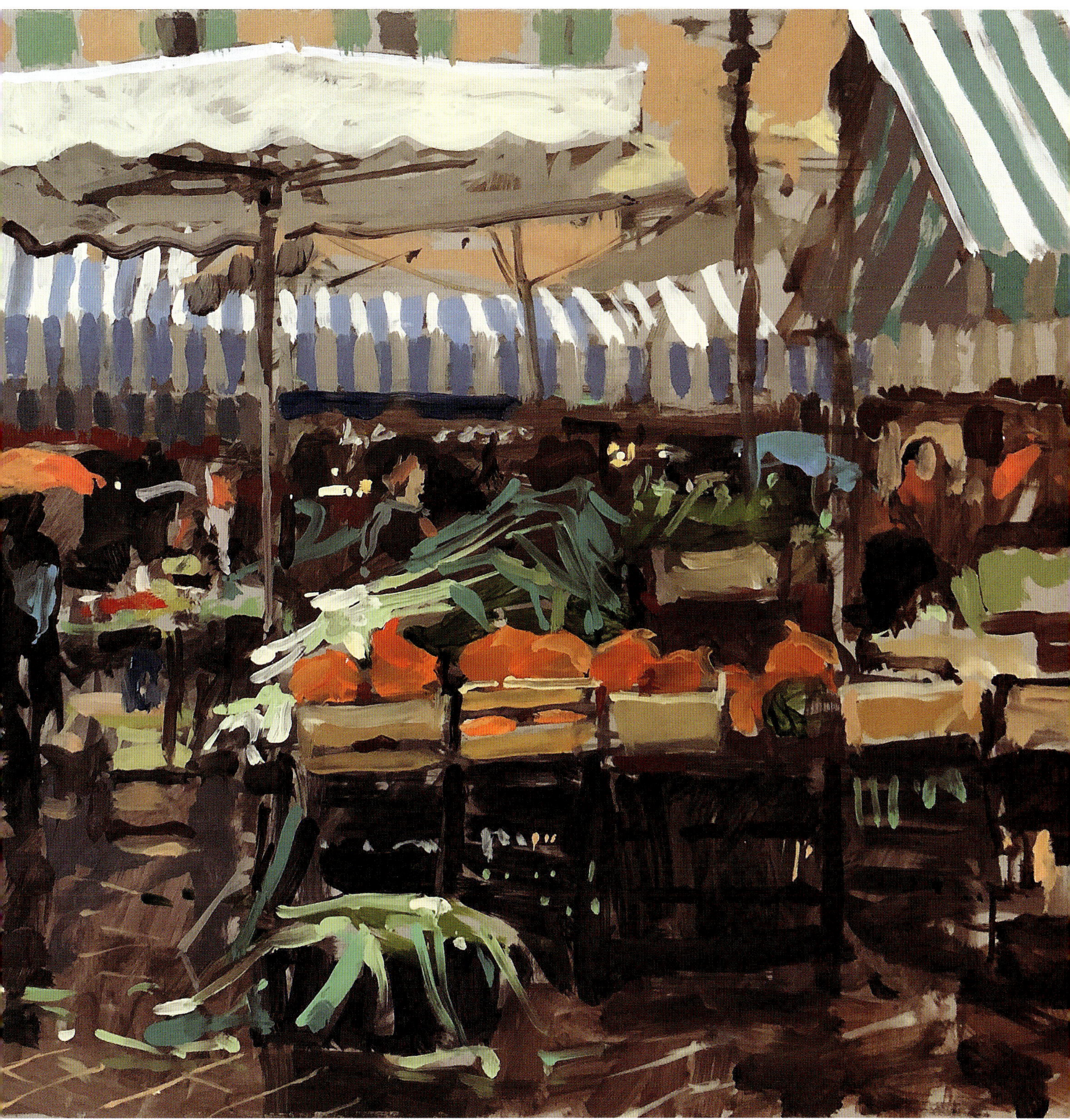

Wind

Strong winds can make a painting session really feel like a battle. My first choice would be to choose a more sheltered position, if that's an option. My next priority is to make my painting set-up as stable as possible, as I dread the whole lot crashing to the ground, possibly causing damage to the kit as well as the loss of all the solvent.

Tips for painting in the wind

When it comes to choosing your tripod for painting, it's a difficult choice between getting a heavier, more stable one, or a lightweight one that's easier to carry but risks being blown about. If you use a French box easel you can weigh down the base with rocks if you can find some nearby – although these solid wooden easels already cope a lot better with wind than a pochade and tripod set-up.

If you are painting in strong winds with a lighter easel, try increasing the angle of the tripod legs so that the footprint is wider and hang your bag on the ring underneath the central column using a carabiner clip. You can add extra weight to the bag using bottles of water or heavy stones if there are some nearby.

Even having taken all those measures, I still won't leave my tripod unattended in those conditions, as a sudden strong gust can displace even a sturdy set-up.

As a final word of advice, while it can seem frustrating in strong winds to try make a small, particular mark or a straight line, as your arm and brush are being constantly shaken, try to look upon this 'wind wobble' as a happy side effect of a blustery day. After all, we don't want our paintings to be too neat and precise!

> **'** In a world that's always shouting, try a whisper. **'**
>
> **Tony Merrick ROI, 1948–2018**

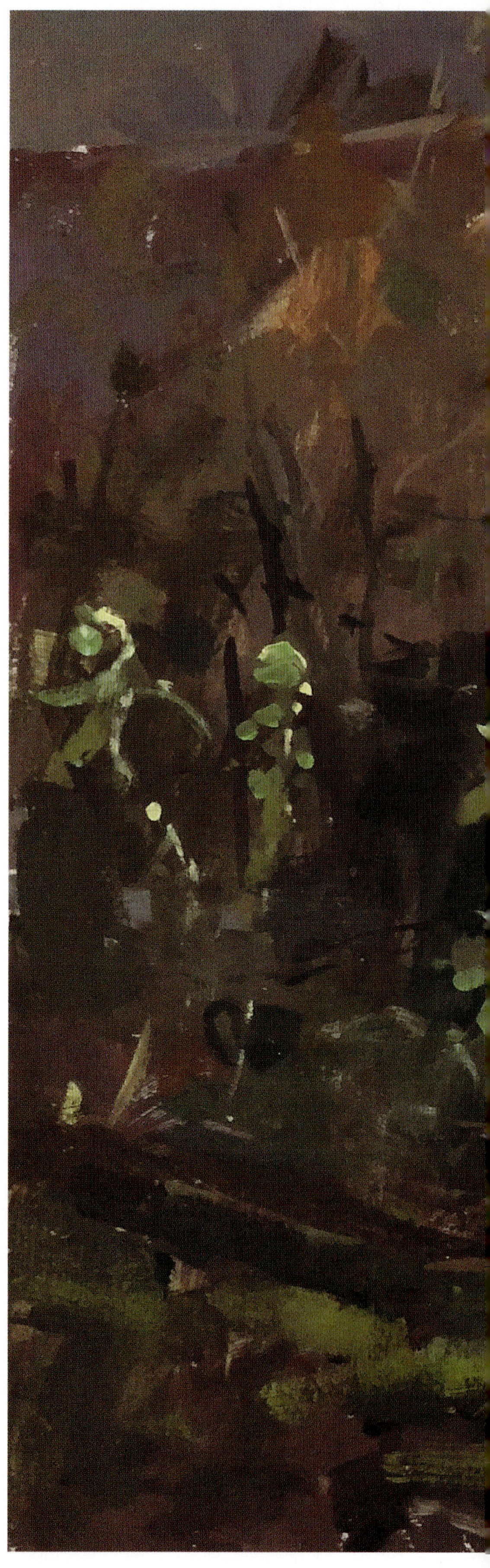

Greenhouse Greys
35.5 x 28cm (14 x 11in)

This was painted in early January, with powerful gusts of wind and a strong likelihood of rain. I embraced all the subtle colours to be found in a landscape on such a day, and was further buoyed by listening to the radio on my phone, and a couple of nice conversations with allotmenteers during the session.

I love the quiet painting that resulted from this session. It reminds me of advice that the artist Tony Merrick ROI once gave to me, 'In a world that's always shouting, try a whisper'.

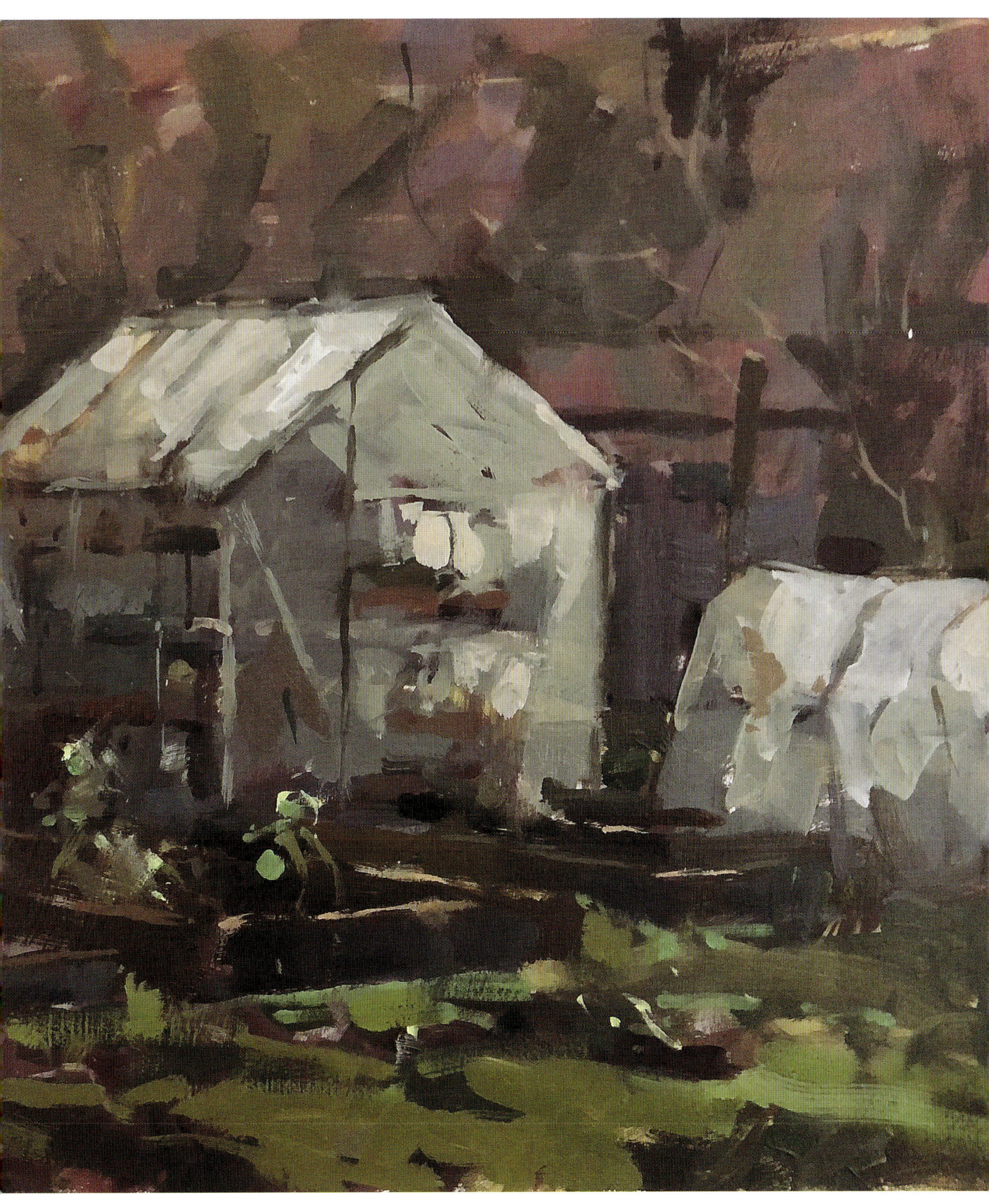

Snow

Snow is my favourite weather effect for painting in. Doubtless the scarcity of snow days in Lincolnshire, UK, where I live, heightens my enjoyment of it. Snow has a transformative effect on the landscape, making the familiar unexpected and new. It's such a delicious surprise to get out there and see what the arrival of snow has brought to your local surroundings.

Because the roads are not so good in snow and because I want to make the most of it and not waste lots of time driving, I tend to stay local and head for the nearby allotments.

Working on site as much as possible provides me with so much stimulus and food for thought. My time with the snow on the ground is limited, and speed is of the essence if I'm going to make the most of the opportunity. Oil paints are ideal for working in wintry conditions because they are not affected by the kinds of temperatures we have in the UK. The freezing point of linseed oil is around -20°C (-4°F), which makes them a safer bet than watercolours or acrylics.

I fully embrace the new challenges of painting a snowy subject: the reflected light in the shadows when the sun is shining, or chasing the close values that appear when the sky is overcast. Subtle colour mixing is the order of the day, as snow certainly can't be described within the painting as just pure white. Searching for the colour bias among all the subtle greys keeps me on my toes. Don't be fooled into thinking that snow is all about the cool colours. Depending on the light conditions you may see warm pinks and oranges, and greenish greys as well as blues and purples.

A snowy subject can have a full range of value contrast on a bright clear day, or a narrow band of tonal values when there is a dull overcast sky, blizzard or fog. I used to be disappointed if the sun wasn't shining as I was longing for those crisp shadows on the snow, but no longer – when there is a narrow range of tonal values I have more reason to explore subtle changes in colour temperature.

The real lesson here is that it's definitely worth going out to paint when you think the weather conditions are less than ideal. Thinking about it as an exercise or process rather than having great expectations about the end result may help with overcoming procrastination and just getting out there, whatever the weather.

Tips for painting in the snow

Snow falling on the palette during the painting session can be a real nuisance, but an umbrella that clips on to the easel will help. For comfort, you might like to keep your feet off snowy and icy ground by standing on a piece of polystyrene or cardboard.

It makes sense to work quickly on small panels. I try to stick to an hour at most and I set a timer on my phone to remind me. Making small drawn sketches and taking notes are useful for studio work later, as are photographs. I recommend that you take a walk around in between paintings to warm up and get the blood flowing. That's a good time for spotting the next subject and taking reference notes.

As with mixing greens, try to forget all about formulas: there really is no substitute for careful observation. Make comparisons constantly across the whole subject to judge value and colour. Ask yourself is this area lighter or darker, warmer or cooler, than that?

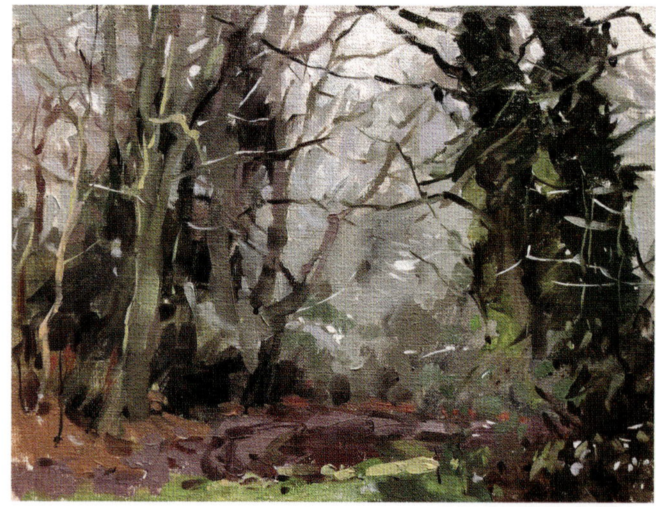

Frosty Trees at Great Monk Wood
30.5 x 23cm (12 x 9in)

I painted this one from the relative comfort of the front seat of my car, on an extremely cold and foggy day in February.

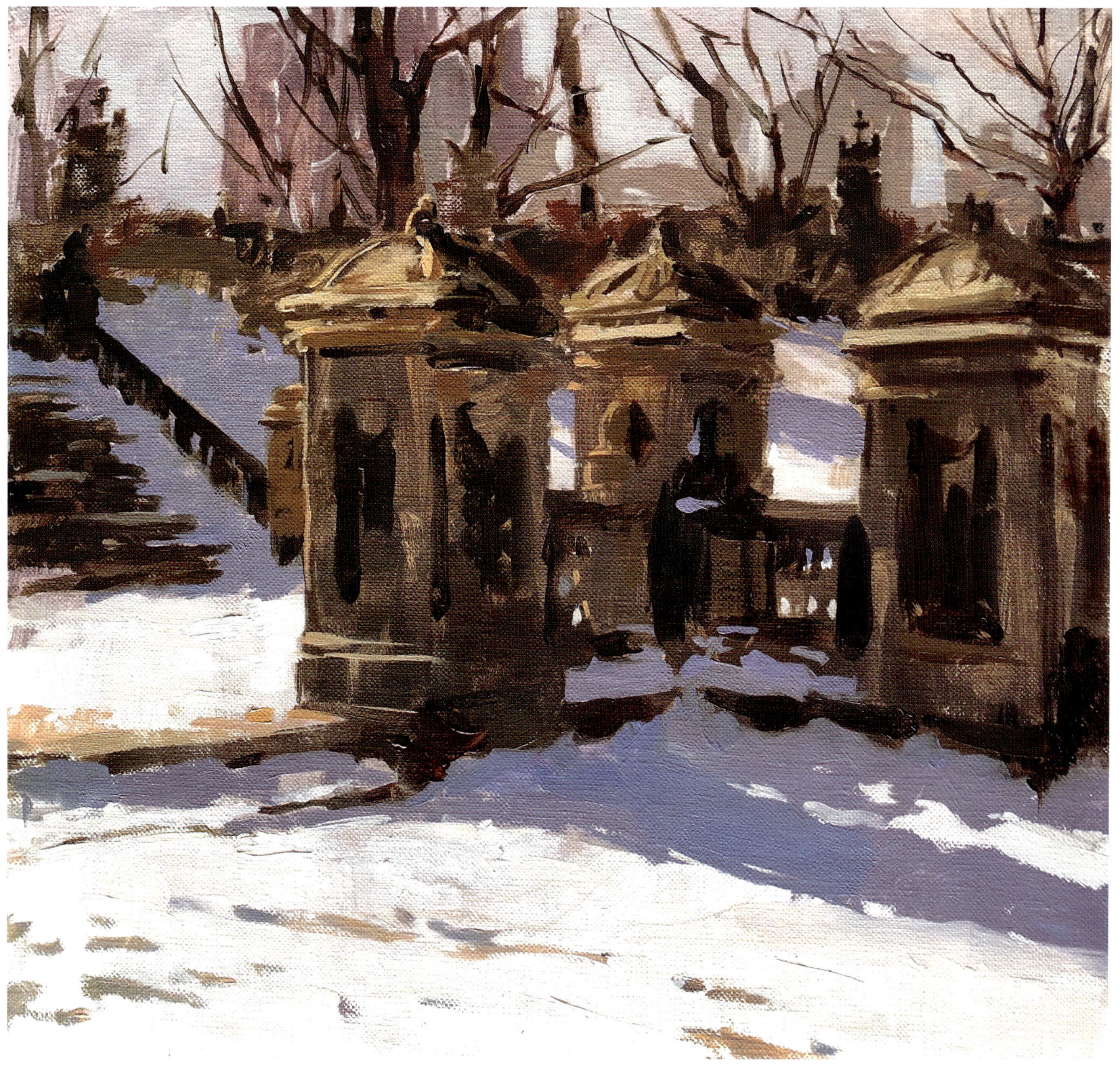

I was so delighted to find snow when we arrived in New York, I just had to make the most of it. During this trip I painted in my coldest conditions yet out in the Hudson Valley – a shiveringly cold -15°C (5°F).

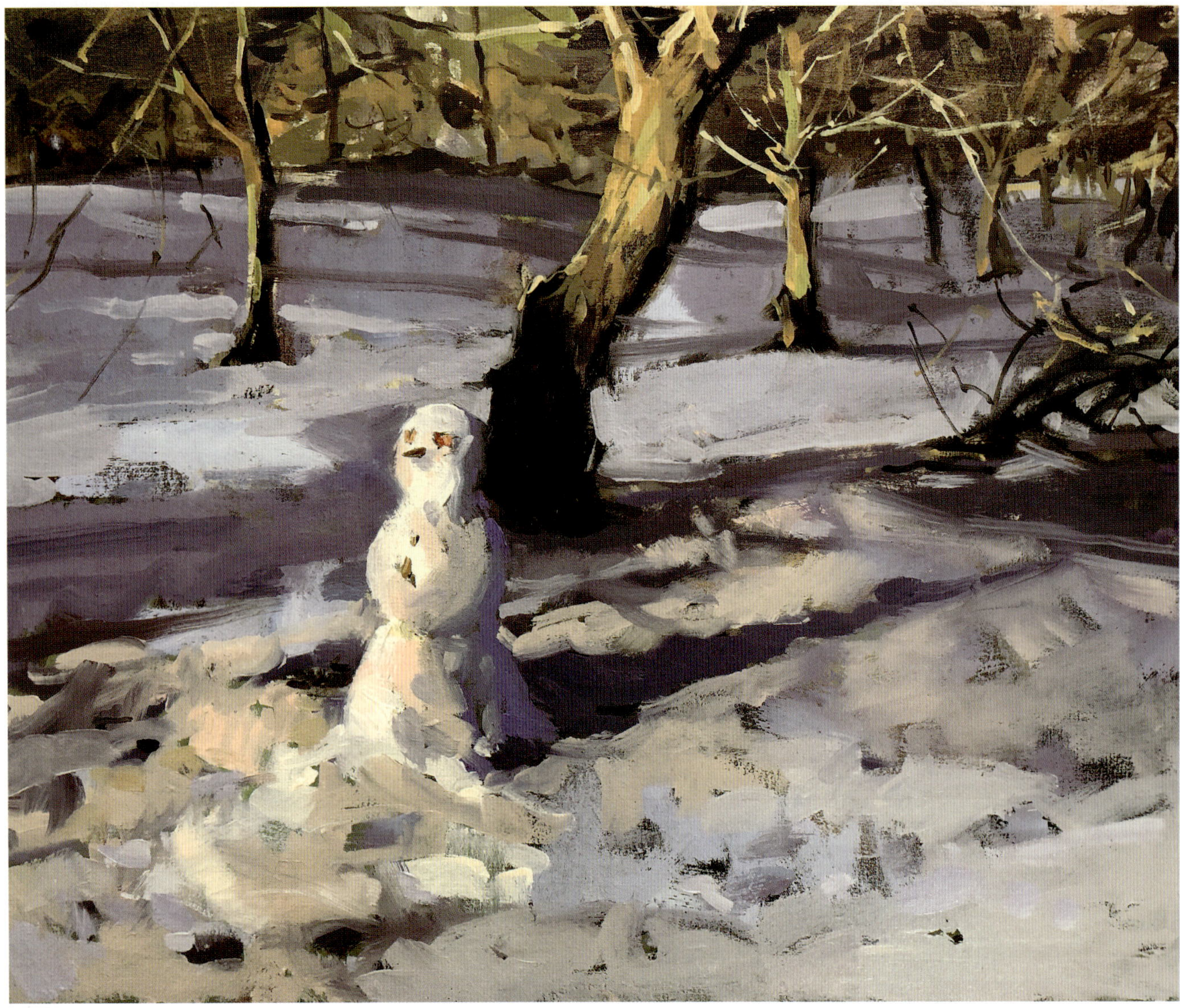

Extremes of temperature

People often wonder how I can paint outside in wintry conditions but it all boils down to having the right clothing and equipment and limiting the time spent outdoors. If you're venturing out with your paints into the snow, always wrap up more warmly than you think you will need to. Look for moisture-wicking fabrics such as merino wool and ski wear, wearing many layers and waterproof outer layers. A thick cosy hat and warm sturdy boots worn with a couple of pairs of thick socks are essential. I paint wearing fingerless gloves and a flask of coffee keeps me warm and cheery. I really do find that when I'm in a heightened state of excitement I don't notice minor discomfort at all. For me, painting in snow is such a treat.

I prefer cold to heat actually, as you can be well layered up to deal with it! Having always lived in England I can find extremes of heat difficult to handle. When preparing, do all you can to avoid suffering from heatstroke. The things that help are having plenty of water to drink and shade. I stand under a large umbrella which has a reflective silver coating on the outside.

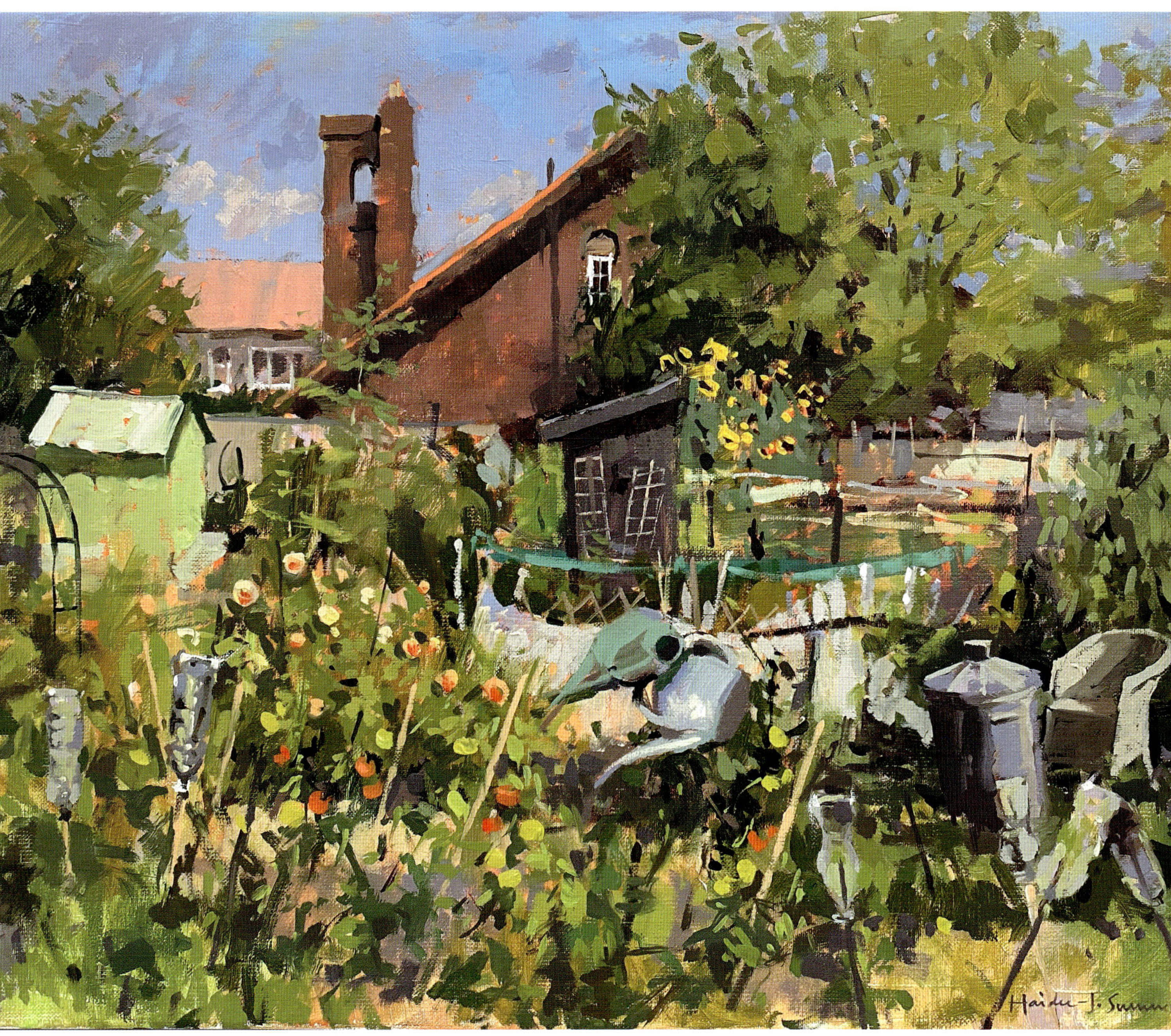

Peter's Allotment, Streatham
51 x 40.5cm (20 x 16in)

This was painted for a commission on one of the hottest August days following three hot dry summer weeks. My painting hours were from late morning onwards, and there was no place I could escape from the sun while still getting a view of this allotment garden.

During the afternoon the thermometer reached 35°C (95°F) – without the flannel trick I don't think I would have been able to carry on painting for half as long!

I have also used frozen ice packs to help keep cool in extreme heat: I stand barefoot on those for as long as they stay cold. A flannel is useful, too. Every so often you can wet it , wring it out over your feet, splash your face and head with water and then go back to painting with the wet flannel draped around the back of your neck.

Painting around people

Going incognito

You may find it a little intimidating to take your paints out to a public place, but rest assured that you're not alone if you have ever felt inhibited by the fear of being watched and judged by passers-by.

It can be difficult to get into a state of flow and focus on your painting when you're nervously looking around you waiting for the next approach from an interested stranger – but what if it was possible to go unnoticed? Working discreetly with a small pochade box can be the perfect solution, and it makes the most portable kit too.

With a small wooden pochade box and the paint already squeezed out on the palette beforehand, I have found it possible to work sitting at tables in cafés without anyone raising an eyebrow. If you enjoy people as a subject matter, what could be better than to get yourself a really small pochade box and make use of all the freely-available subjects out there at events, parties and cafés? If you can be discreet with your glances, they won't even realise that they're the subject of a painting.

Being a considerate artist

It almost goes without saying, but you need to have the utmost consideration and respect for the places where you will be working, and for the people around you. Do recognize that a café or pub is a business, and the owner might not want you to be taking up a table for a long stretch of time. I would only paint in such a situation for an hour or less, and of course order some refreshments while I'm there. If you are at all unsure about whether you should be painting in a location, always ask for permission in a friendly and polite way before you begin.

On a similar note, I wouldn't dream of using turps or any solvent with any smell whatsoever to work inside buildings. You needn't use any solvent at all for a short painting session like this: you can wipe your brushes as you need to on a rag and then take everything away to clean up elsewhere. You could also consider using water miscible oils to allow you to rinse with water rather than solvents.

Business Lunch, Cinco Lounge
25.5 x 20.5cm (10 x 8in)

I positioned myself next to a window when I painted this study so that I could see my palette and panel clearly, though I still had to adjust to looking into the relative darkness of the café.

If a scene catches my eye with a few key figures, I focus on plotting and painting them in first – and quickly, as they could up and leave at any moment.

Hartlepool Art Gallery
30.5 x 23cm (12 x 9in)

I couldn't resist making an oil sketch when I visited this fabulous gallery situated in a Victorian church. As is often the case with interiors, the lighting situation was extremely complicated, with natural daylight coming through stained glass from different directions, along with various types of artificial lighting. I had to keep screwing up my eyes to make sense of what I was seeing.

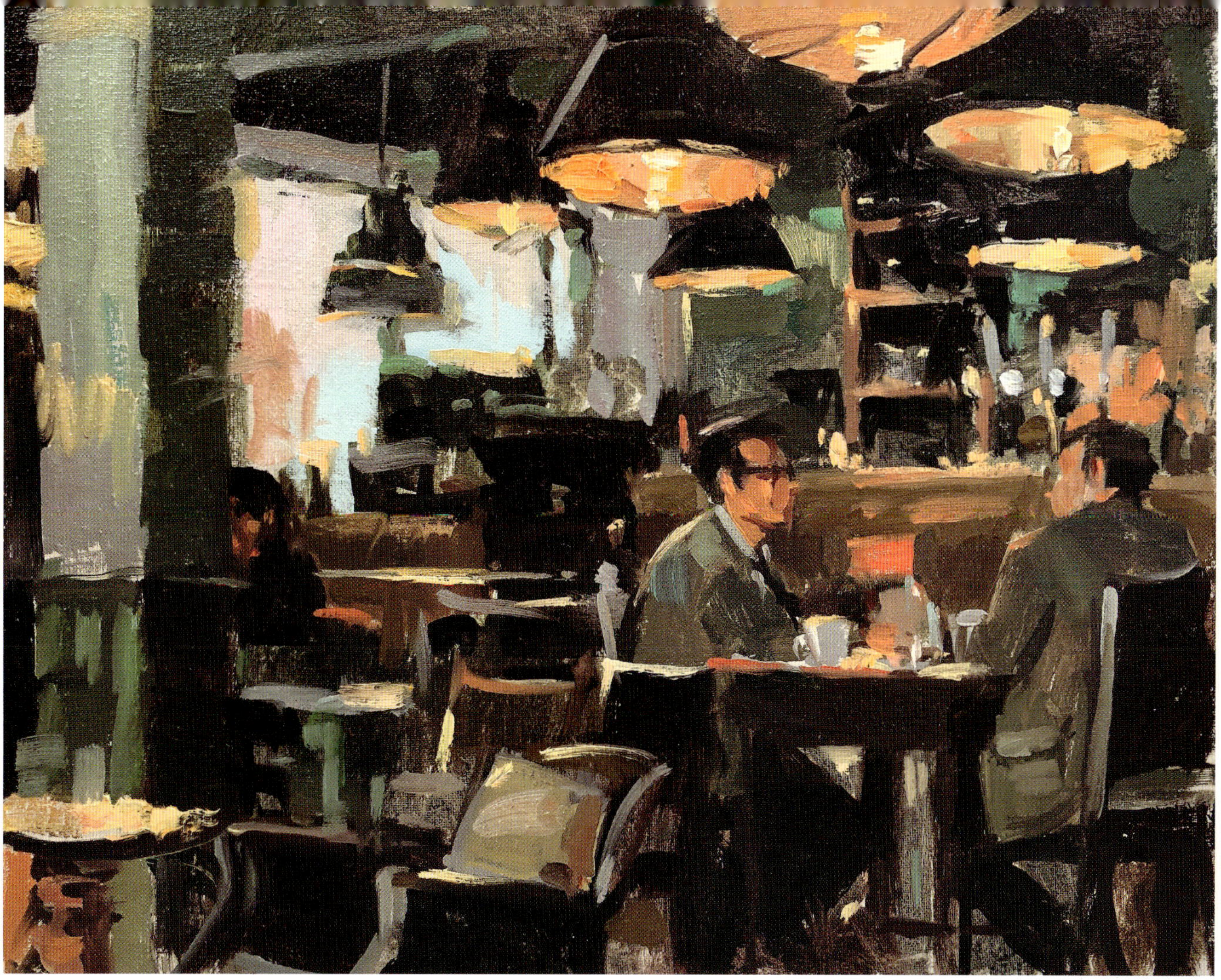

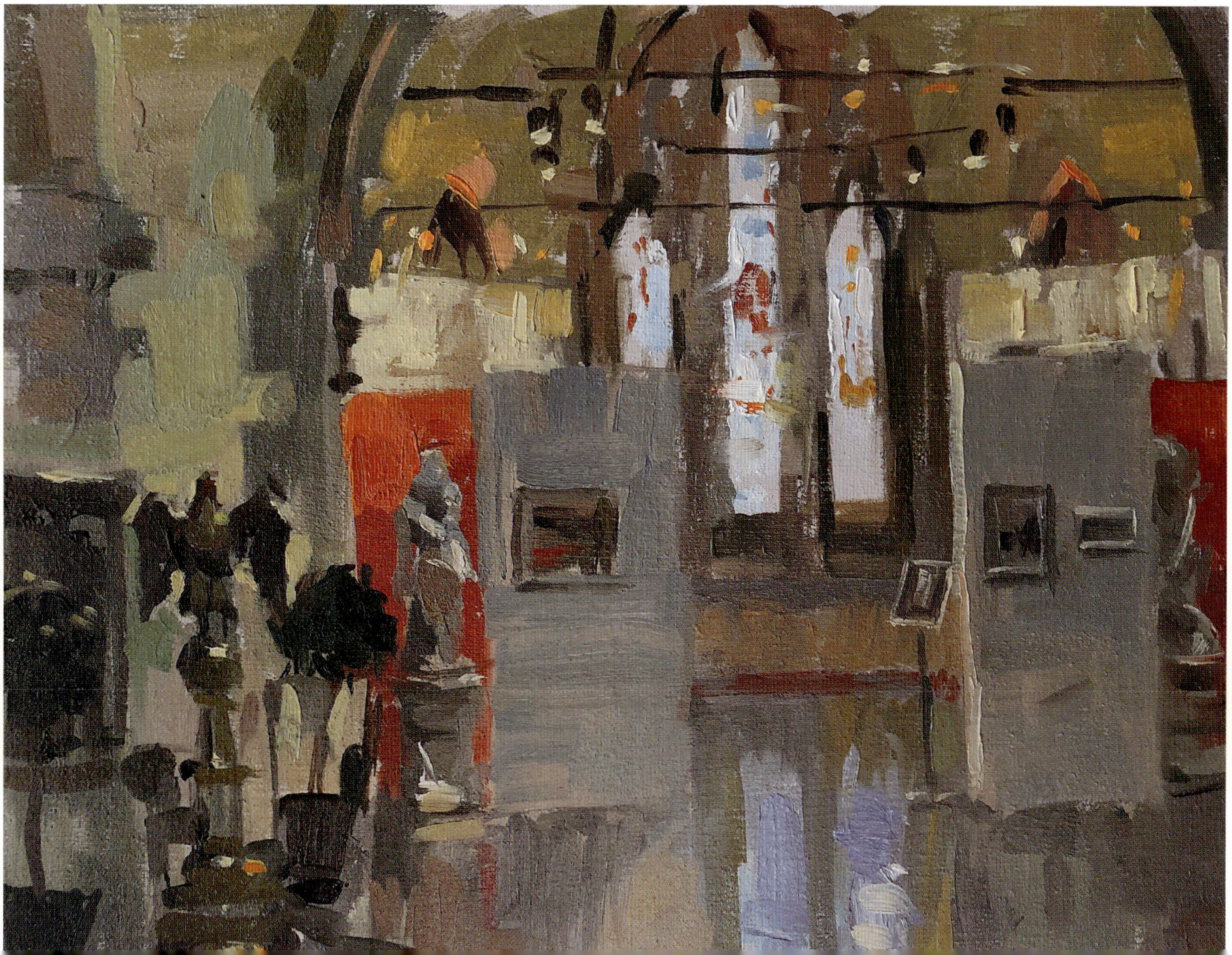

People and pochade sketching

The small format and minimal equipment involved in pochade sketching will allow you to rapidly capture ideas and impressions, making it ideal for working both discreetly and with limited space: great when sketching people in oils.

You may find that accuracy of drawing or planning a compelling composition fall by the wayside while sketching rapidly in oils, but that's okay. What you lose in that aspect you will gain in decisiveness and the resulting freshness of the brush marks.

All in all, I try to take a curious and interested approach, rather than having expected outcomes for these little oil sketches. I have the equipment all ready to go so that if I'm inspired by some interesting shapes, an effect of light, or the mood and feeling of a place, then I can get cracking straight away and capture the essence of the scene with a minimum of fuss.

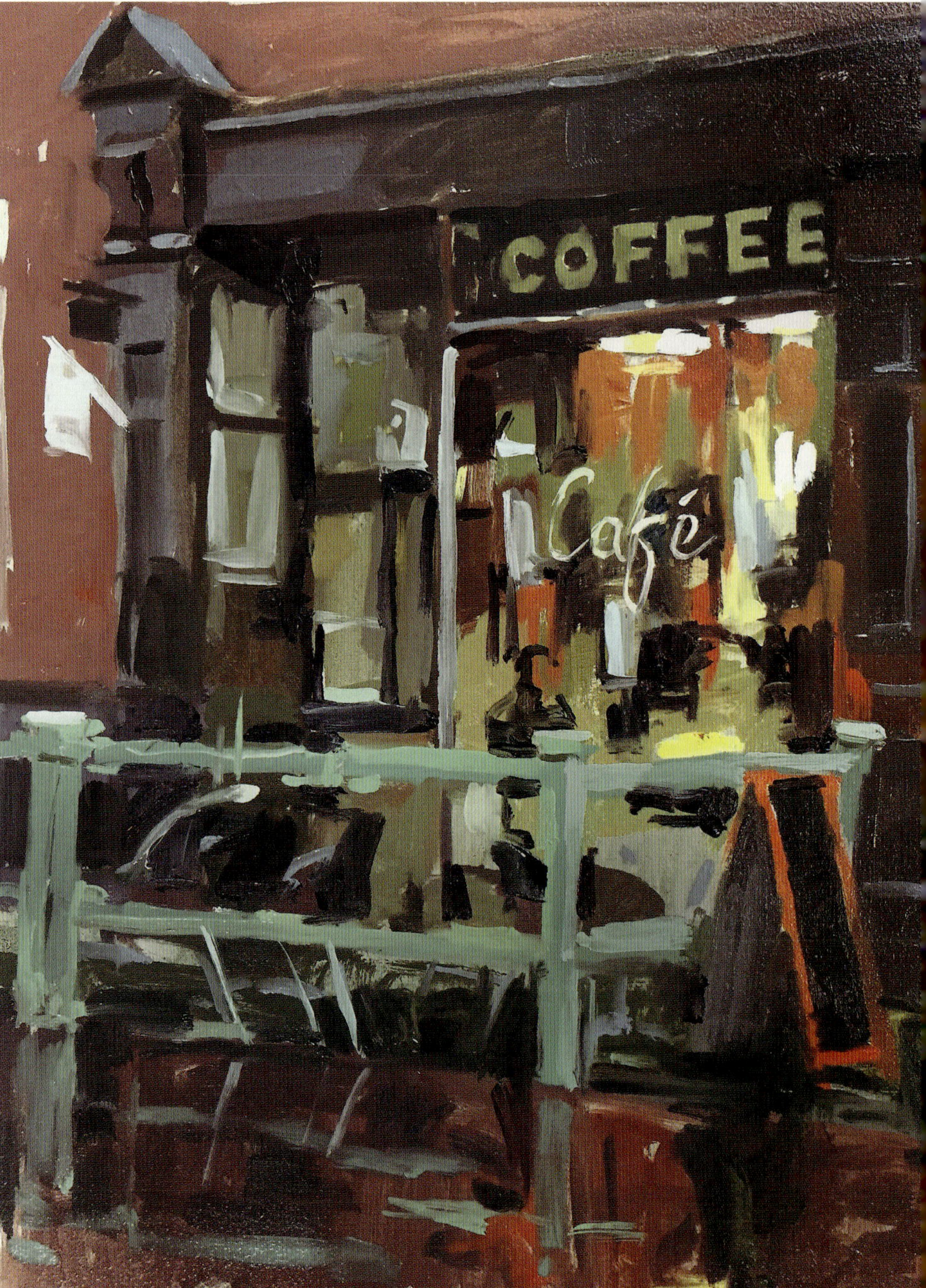

Coffee Shop, Friar Lane
25.5 x 30.5cm (10 x 12in)

I painted this oil sketch of a café looking through a window on a dark and rainy November day.

Adjusting your kit

While you are saving weight by using a pochade box rather than an easel, it follows that you will want to streamline the rest of your kit too, taking a minimal range of brushes and colours with you. I like to have short-handled brushes with me when using my smallest boxes because I am often seated while doing little sketches. If working inside a café or a busy building, I find that being seated is more discreet and attracts less attention than standing to work.

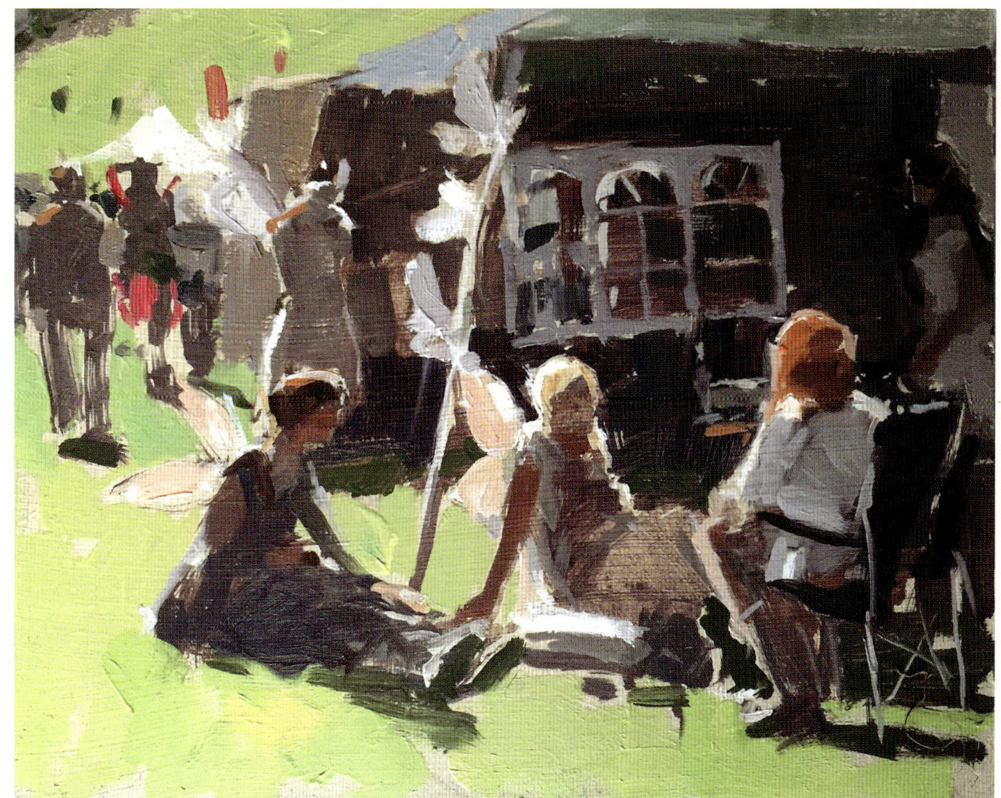

Fairy Festival
25.5 x 20.5cm (10 x 8in)

Lots of people were sitting around on the grass enjoying the sunshine, so these fairies didn't even notice they were being painted while they chatted.

Of course, people are constantly on the move, even while seated, and you just have to do the best you can to get a believable sort of solid figure down.

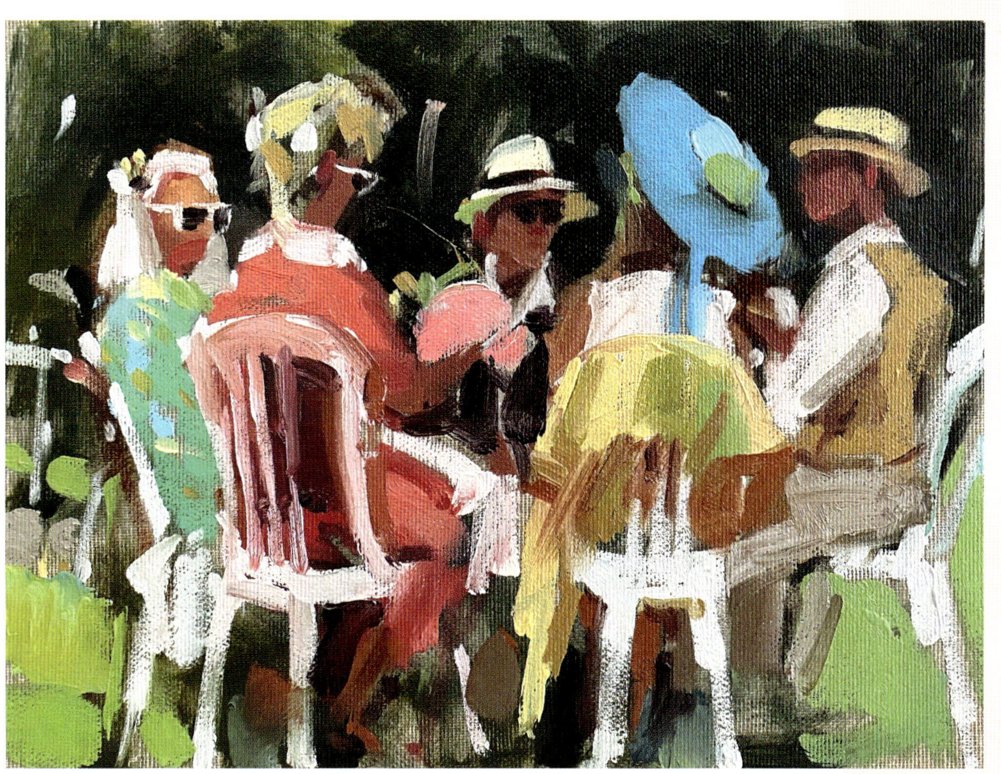

Putting on the Blitz
24 x 18cm (9½ x 7in)

A group of dandily dressed friends, who I was able to paint discreetly from a nearby table while enjoying a party atmosphere with live music at a 1940s re-enactment festival.

I love being able to paint while listening to live music, it's one of the best plein air scenarios!

Painting people in the landscape

The only way to truly improve your skills is to tackle those areas of painting that you find the biggest challenge; and an area that we often avoid is adding figures to our landscape paintings. Sometimes artists consciously don't want their paintings to be populated, because they feel it allows the viewer of the work to inhabit the scene exclusively. Certainly that's a valid way to look at it, if that's your preference. In my experience, however, a lack of figures in a painting is often simply down to the artist lacking the confidence to tackle them.

There are rural landscape scenes where you can certainly get away without adding figures, but if you are painting a market or street scene where one would expect to see lots of people, your painting is going to look strangely deserted – even eerie – without any. What's more, the addition of figures to an otherwise 'empty' landscape can add so much value: not least, they give everything in the painting a sense of scale. Including a few relevant figures will create interest and add meaning – and also help any viewer of the painting to picture themselves within the scene.

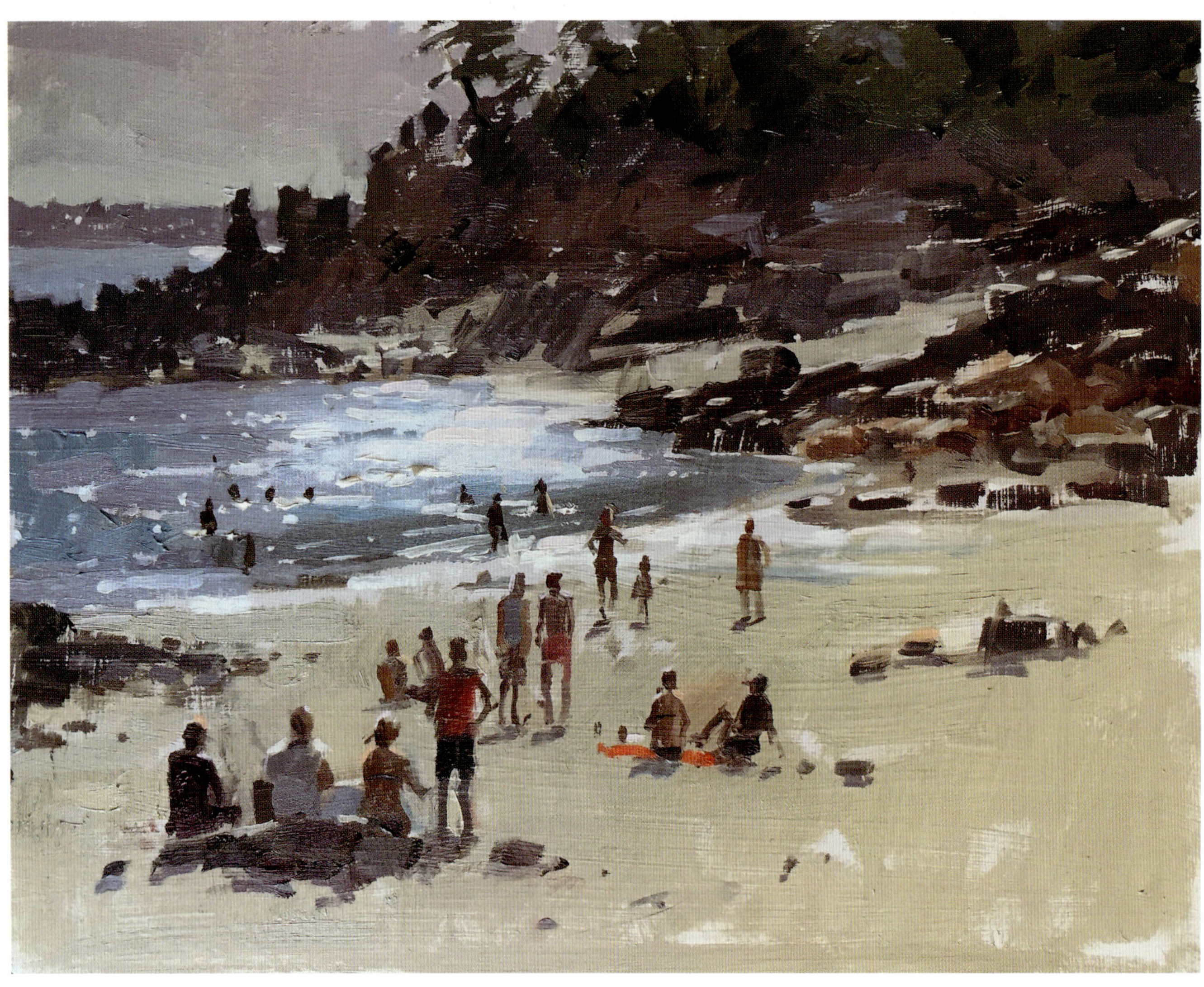

▲ *Beach study*
25.5 x 20.5cm (10 x 8in)

A quick alla prima beach study like this calls for rapid execution, and this lends a sense of liveliness and movement to the painting. I have dealt with many of the figures as simple silhouetted shapes, adding colour here and there to suggest clothing. The figures closest to me also have head and shoulder highlights. This extra detail gives us a huge clue as to this being a sunny rather than overcast day, as do the shadows on the sand.

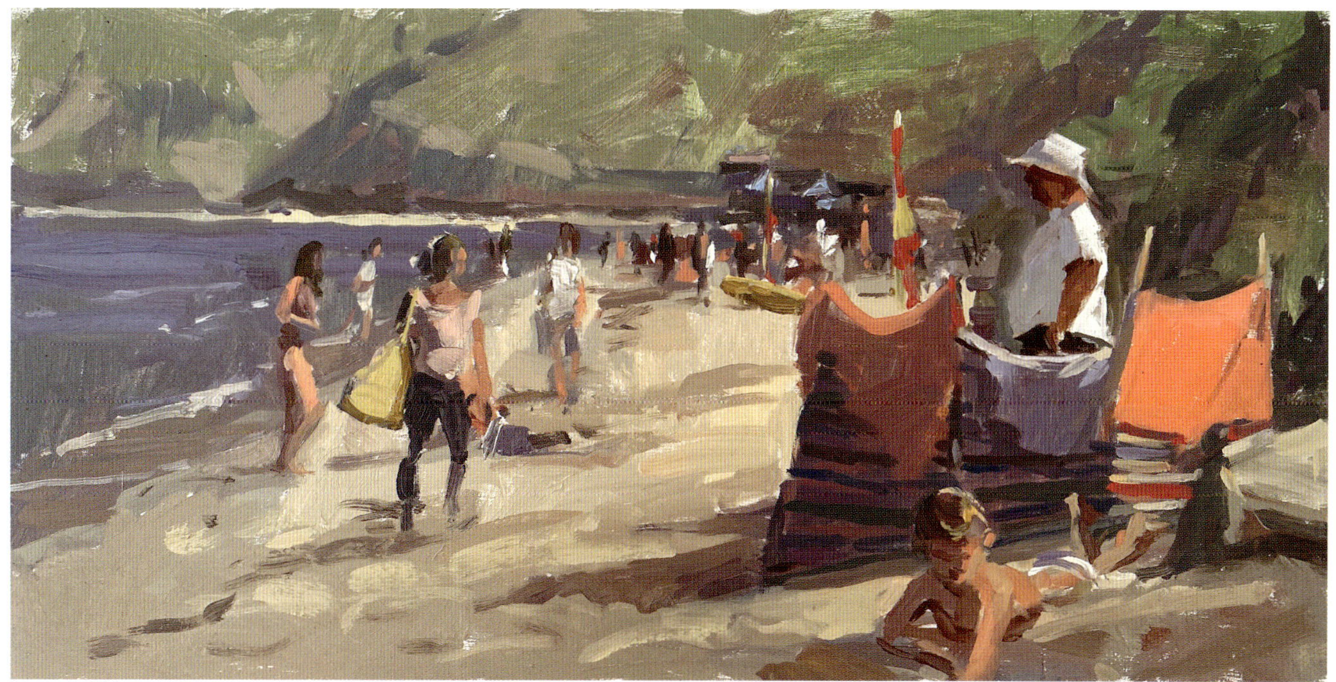

The biggest challenge when painting figures in an outdoor setting is to have them looking natural and as though they belong in that space. Have a look at other landscape paintings that successfully contain figures. To work convincingly they will be positioned well within the scene, having the right scale in line with their surroundings and, importantly, have the right proportions. A common mistake made by beginners is having the head too large in relation to the body, making the figures look clumsy and childlike.

Runswick Bay Beach
30.5 x 15cm (12 x 6in)

Another rapid beach study, in this one I had a change of scale to deal with, between people close to me, those in the middle distance and those further away, which are very loosely suggested with some dark, light and warm mostly vertical marks. You don't need to 'get it all in' for us to understand that we are looking at people. You will be amazed at how little you have to 'say' in the painting for your viewer to understand.

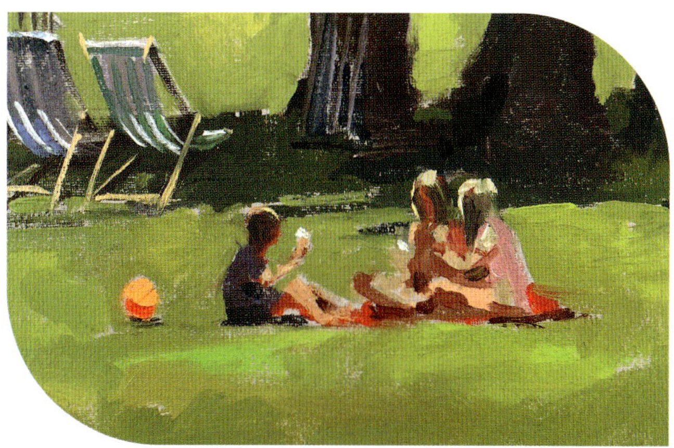

Detail of children eating ice creams

I was painting in a public park, looking out to sea, when I saw a group of children sit down for a few minutes to eat ice creams on a picnic rug. I squinted to pick out the essential value shapes and how they fitted together. I tried not to see them as children, but rather carefully observed the abstract shapes they formed as I tried to paint what I noticed quickly and decisively, with as few strokes as possible. I find that having different brushes to use for different colours is essential in a fast capture of figures from life. I love how abstract these marks are up close, and how it falls into place to become children sitting on a rug as you step away.

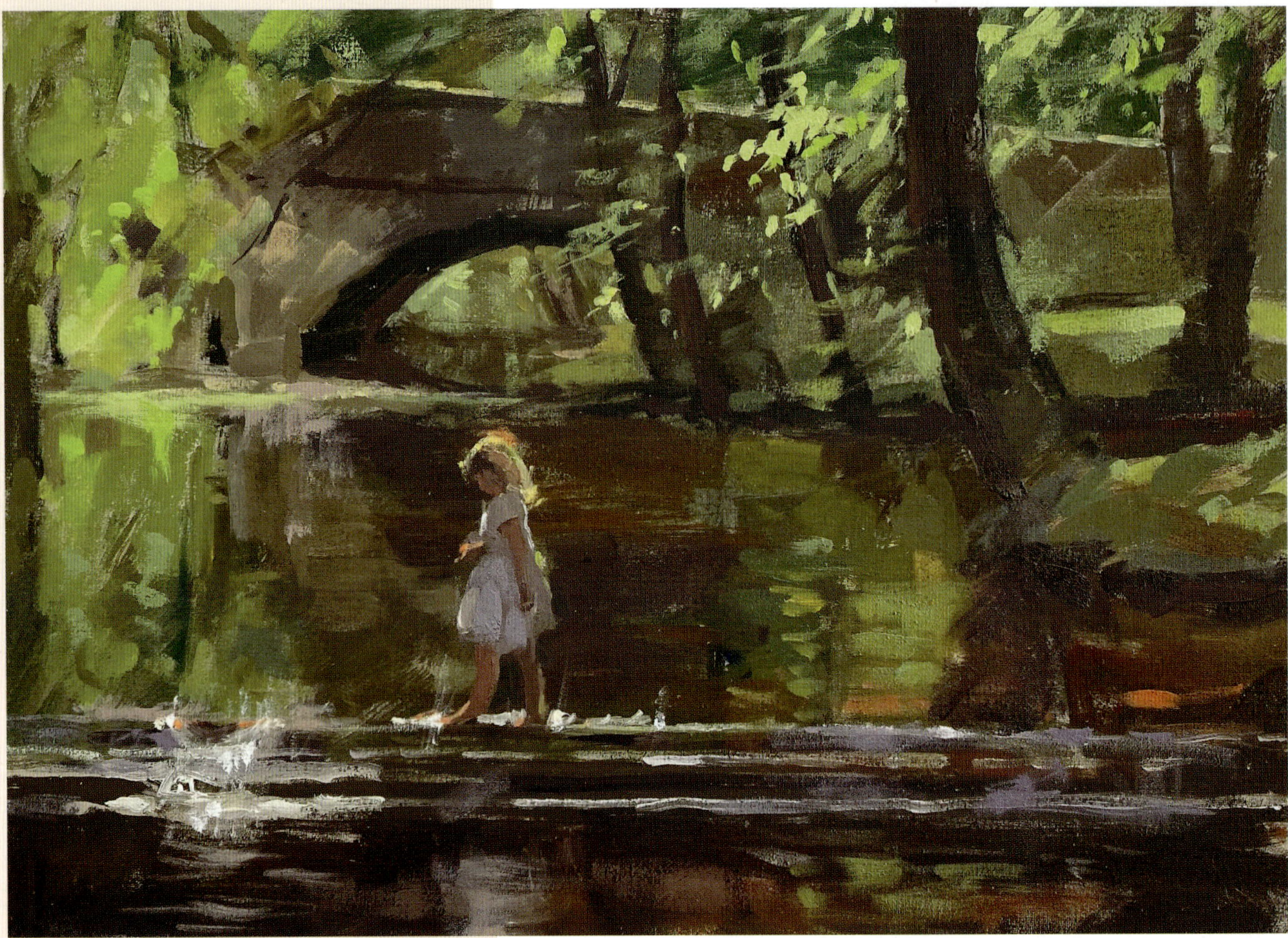

Eden Crossing The Weir
35.5 x 25.5cm (14 x 10in)

One of those golden plein air moments, when you happen to be in the right place at the right time. I was standing painting in a lovely cool spot by the water on a hot day, contemplating adding some ducks to my painting when the daughter of a fellow artist and friend started to walk across the weir.

The girl walked back and forth a few times so I had multiple chances to observe her in a similar pose. I would have been happy with this as a study of the bridge and river but the presence of the little girl adds so much meaning and interest to the scene. In fact, the painting becomes all about her. Try holding your finger over her to see how the painting would look without her in it.

Sketching figures

The more experience that you have in observing and sketching figures from life, the more believable your figures will be in your paintings – and so, as with everything, practice is key. The best way to practise is to get out and about with your sketchbook and draw figures from life as often as possible. This will hone your observational skills and you will get to learn crucial parts of painting people: their proportions; the way they move and sit and carry things; how the head fits into the neck; and how the neck joins the shoulders.

Go to places where people sit around for a while such as train station waiting rooms and coffee shops. You only need a small sketchbook and pen, and most people won't even notice what you're doing.

When sketching figures from life, try to do it by massing in tonal shapes rather than drawing with outline as this better represents what we do when we are painting. Progress from 'sitting targets' to sketching people who are walking about and moving. At first it may seem impossible, but you will quickly get faster and better; able to use just a few marks to capture a quick impression of the pose. Don't worry about not being able to get a complete figure down, or about your sketchbook page consisting of scattered body parts. It's far better to have a lone but well-observed leg than to not have bothered getting your sketchbook out of your pocket at all.

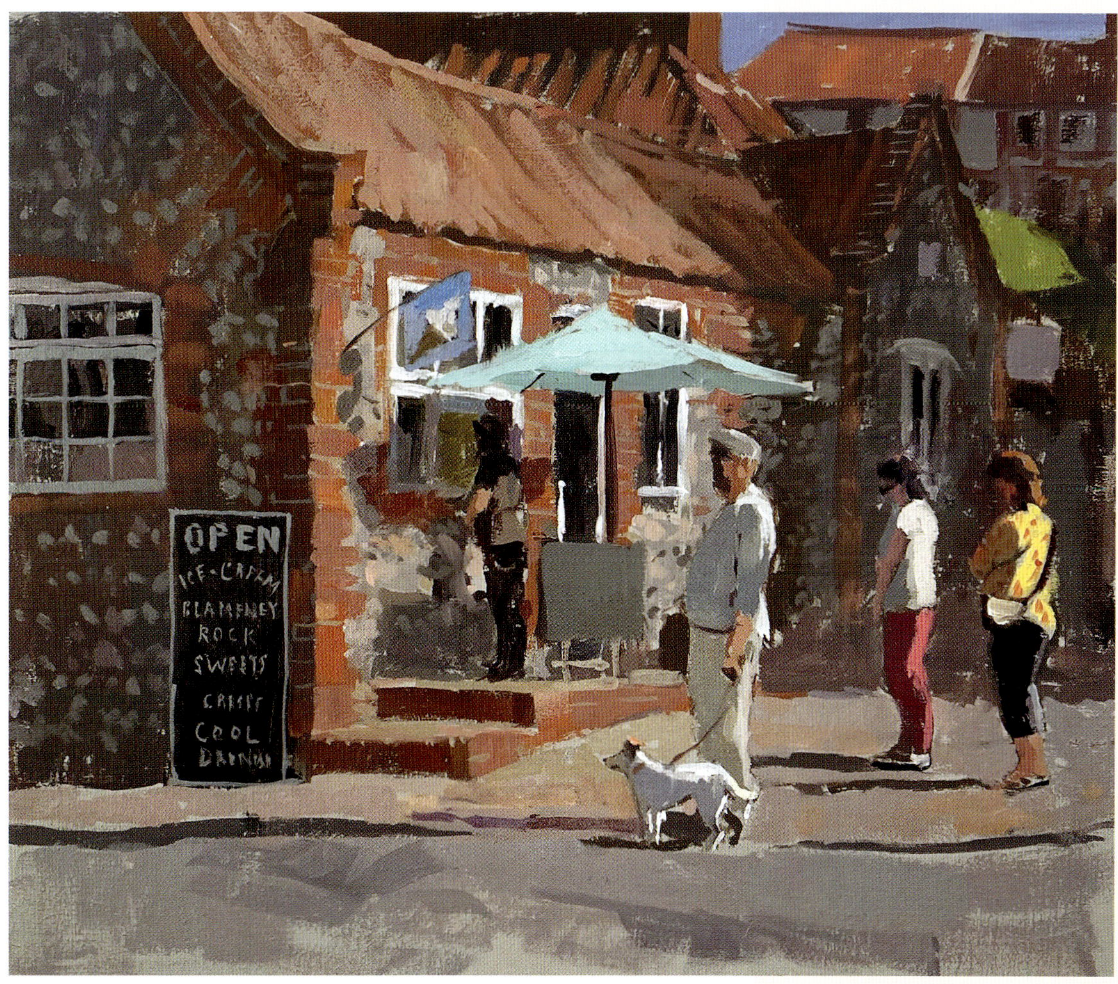

Ice Cream Queue at Blakeney Quay
33 x 28cm (13 x 11in)

I was attracted to this scene for the wonderful parasol and the lovely flint Norfolk buildings, but as a queue started to form, it became a great opportunity to observe some figures in the landscape. Notice how important overall shapes and values are, rather than details such as facial features.

When it comes to painting, your figures need to be simplified and incorporated naturally within the landscape; not treated as separate entities. There's a tendency to deal with figures in a special way or think that they require more detail – far from it. We need to be able to see them simply as patterns of light and dark, no more or less important than any other shape in the painting. Forget details such as facial features, and squint right down to see the necessary dark and light shapes. Ideally, from the beginning of the painting, treat your figures just as any other shape.

I scout for the possibility of including a figure or a group in the early stages of a painting, because it can be tricky to introduce a drastic change of value or colour on top of wet oil paint. Wiping off that area first can be a solution, but not always practical: when you're trying to get a figure down from life, time is of the essence. People don't keep still, even when seated.

The figures in my paintings often end up being combinations of different people I have observed, rather than a snapshot of one person. I may start with a general shape of an observed figure, but refine the stance and clothing using other people in a similar position. As a result, one person in a painting can be a hybrid made up of two or three passers-by. If you're painting with artist friends, you might ask one to hold a pose for ten minutes or so, which can feel like a real luxury when you've been trying to capture people on the fly.

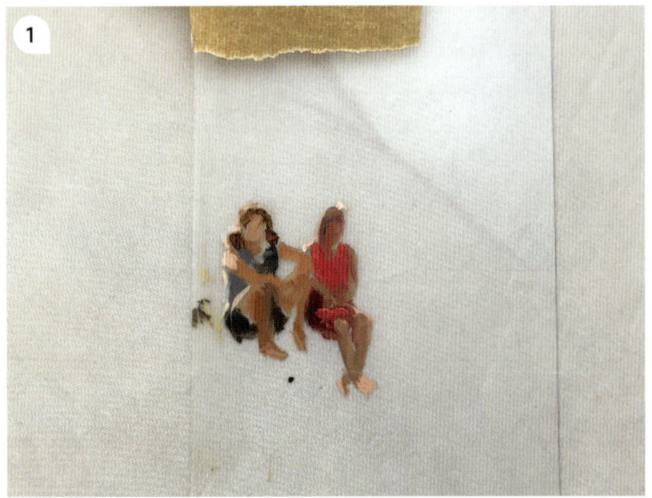

After removing the acetate from the painting, you have the freedom to move the figures around and try different ideas without risking the painting in any way.

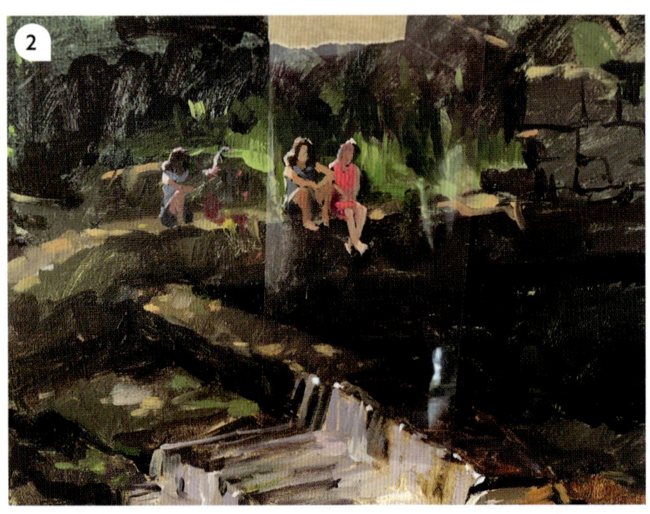

Adding figures to your paintings

I'm as guilty as anyone of painting a scene and being so engrossed in the complexities of the subject that I'm not even aware of the people passing by in front of my eyes. In such cases I'm not averse to adding a figure or two in the studio later, but if you choose to do this, you have to carefully consider their scale, appropriateness and especially how they would have been lit.

The technique shown here gives you a bit of a safety net, allowing you to experiment with whether and where to add figures to a finished painting before committing yourself. It's very easy to wipe the paint off the acetate and start again if you need to.

Dappled Light at Crowden Weir was painted in a beautiful spot in the Derbyshire Peak District. When I got it back to the studio I was really pleased with how it looked but felt that a couple of figures could add a really nice focal point and a spot of bright colour.

I checked back over my photos from the day. While there was nothing suitable in there, a couple of snaps of a family crossing the river with their dog did give me an idea of the size the figures would need to be within my painting. I thought that two girls seated on the far side of the river would do the trick, so I looked through my reference images for seated figures and made a little sketch of two that worked well together.

1 Once the painting surface is dry, cut a small piece of acetate sheet and tape it in position where you want the figures to be. Paint the figures directly onto the acetate, then peel away the acetate along with the tape and try a few different positions.

2 Once you are happy with the placement and the way the figures look, use the masking tape to re-secure the acetate a short distance from where you want the figures to sit, and begin to paint the figures onto the canvas, using the practice one as a guide from which to work.

3 Refine and detail the figures, then carefully remove the acetate to finish.

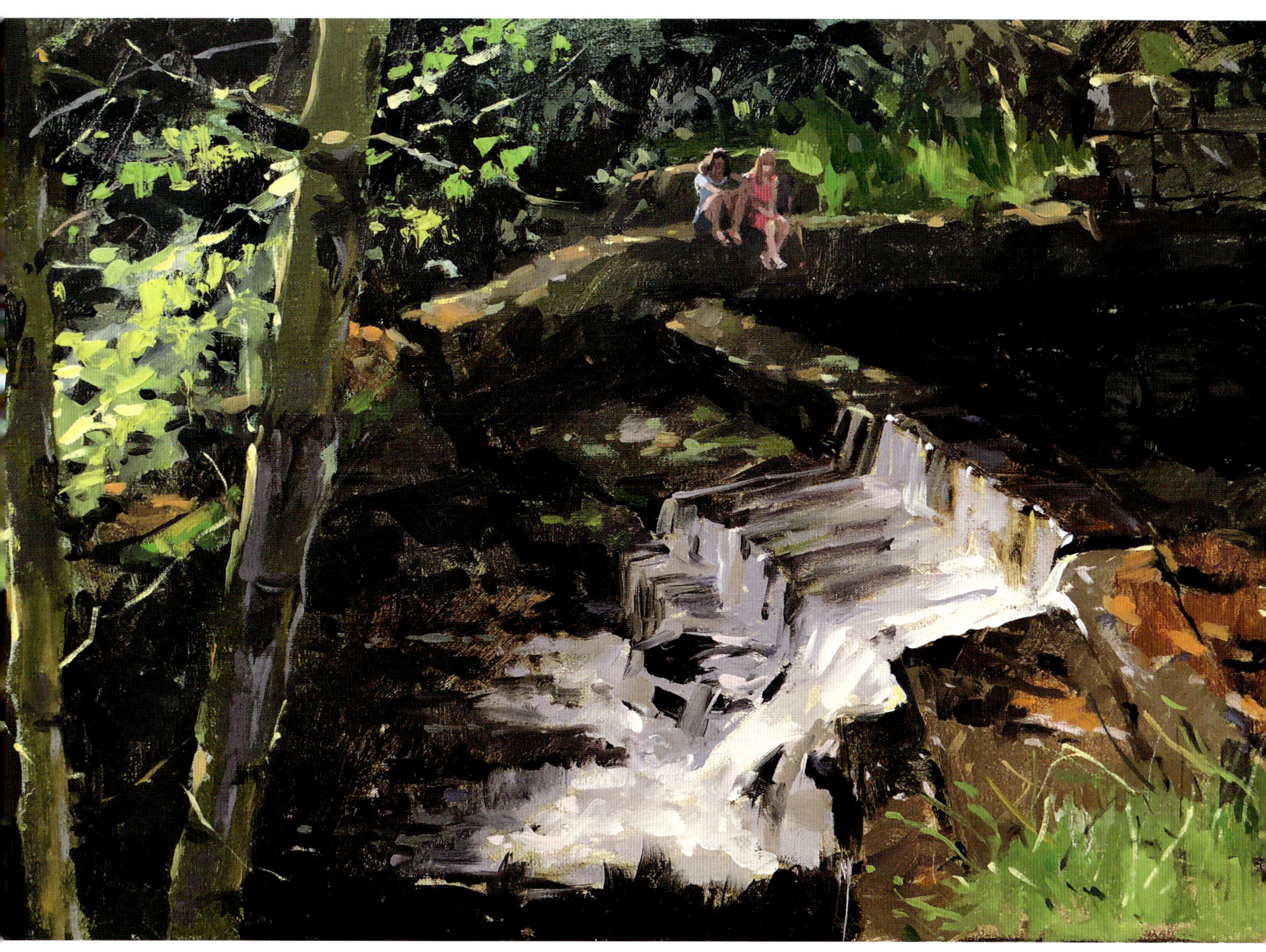

Dappled Light at Crowden Weir
46 x 30.5cm (18 x 12in)

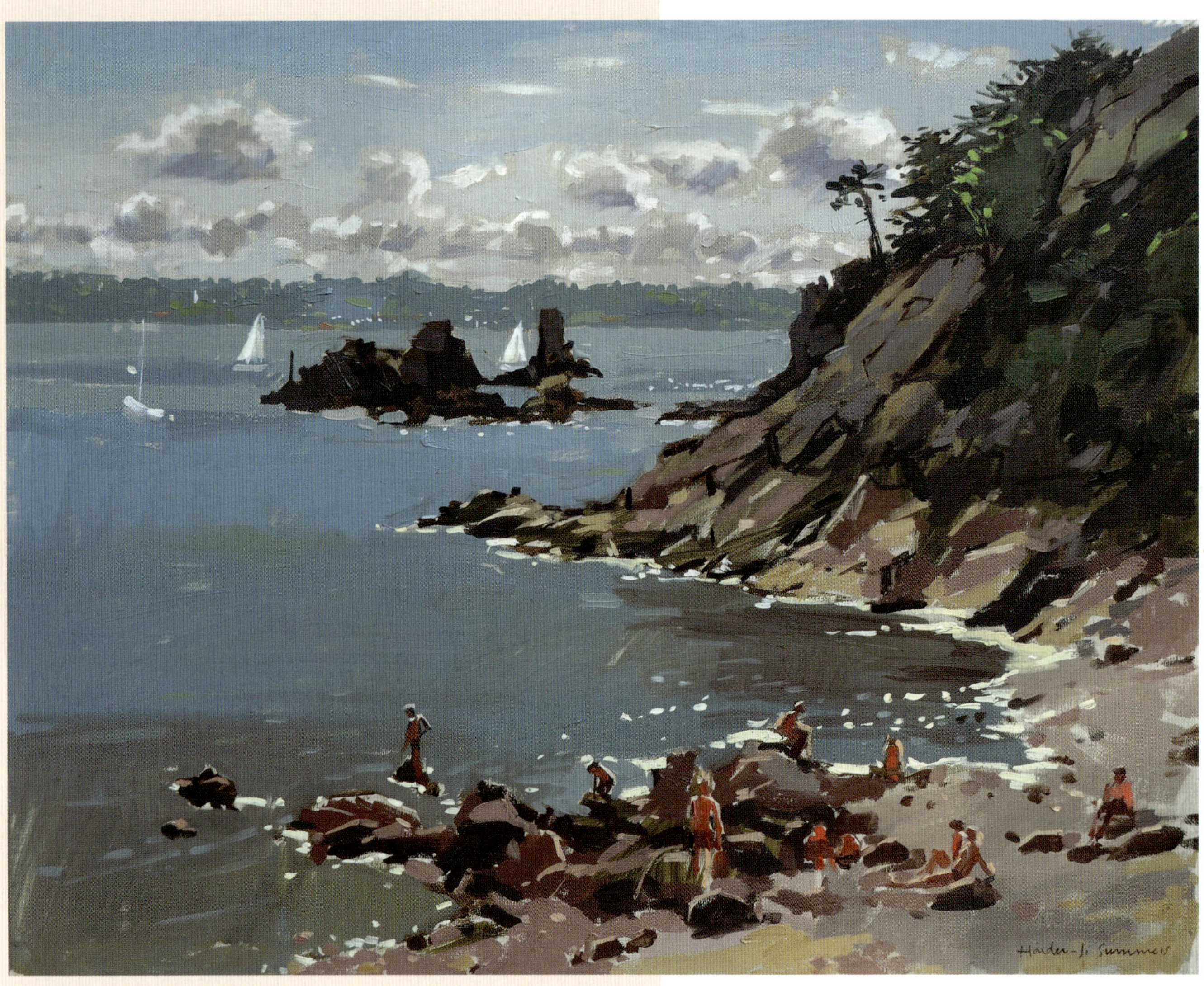

Evening at Guerzido Beach

46 x 35.5cm (18 x 14in)

A larger beach painting from a summer evening on the Île-de-Bréhat in France. I was standing at a higher vantage point, looking down over the beach. This gave me both a fantastic view of the sea towards the hazy mainland across the water, and a high horizon line. I aimed to capture some of the beachgoers enjoying the last rays of the sun in as economical a way as I could.

Nobody stayed still, so I had to see a shape and try to freeze it in my short-term memory just long enough to get it down. The figures are mostly painted in the same warm red-brown, with touches of a light value here and there where the sun strikes shoulders and heads.

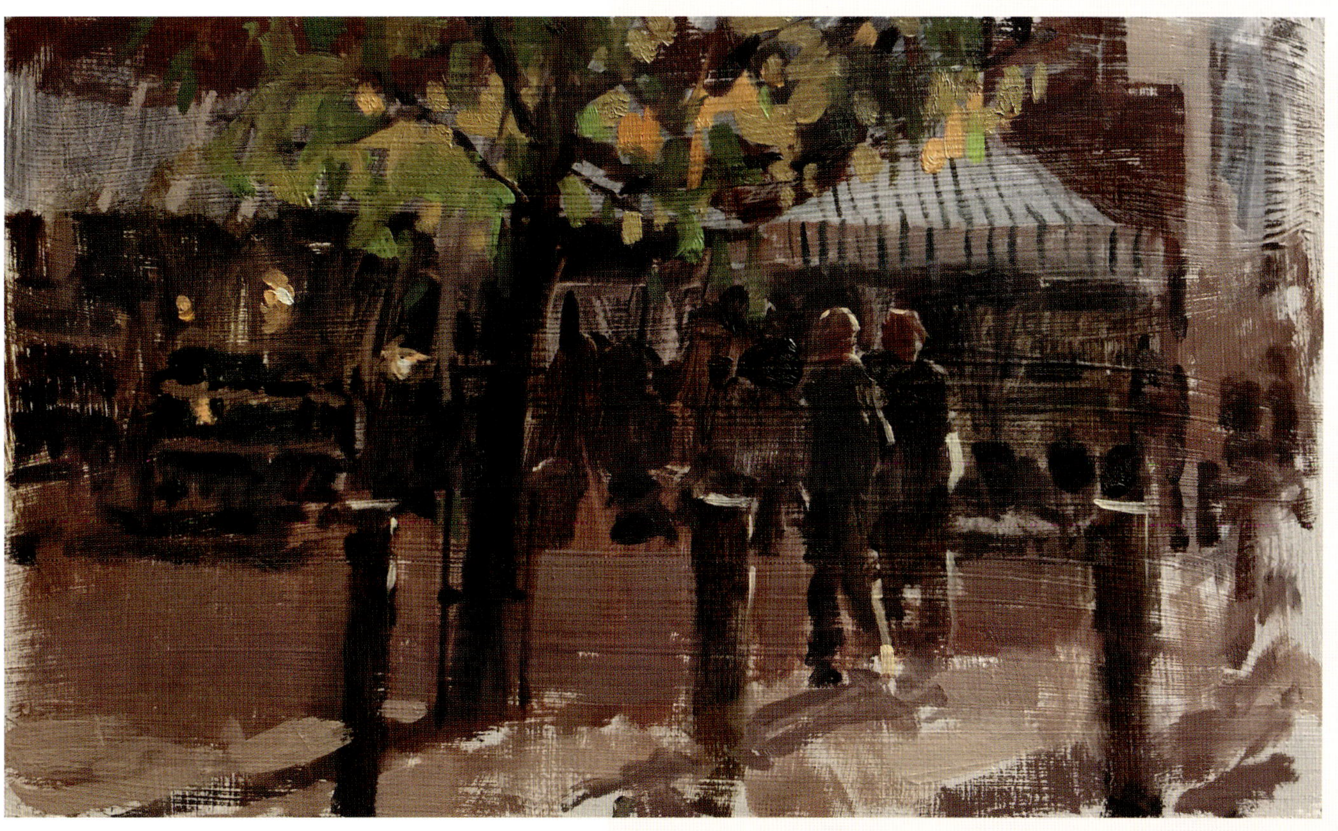

Autumn Market, Lincoln
23 x 12.5cm (9 x 5in)

I perched on some steps with my little antique pochade box on my knee for this one, trying to catch something of the atmosphere of the low sunlight ebbing away and the warm artificial lights glimpsed inside the shop windows.

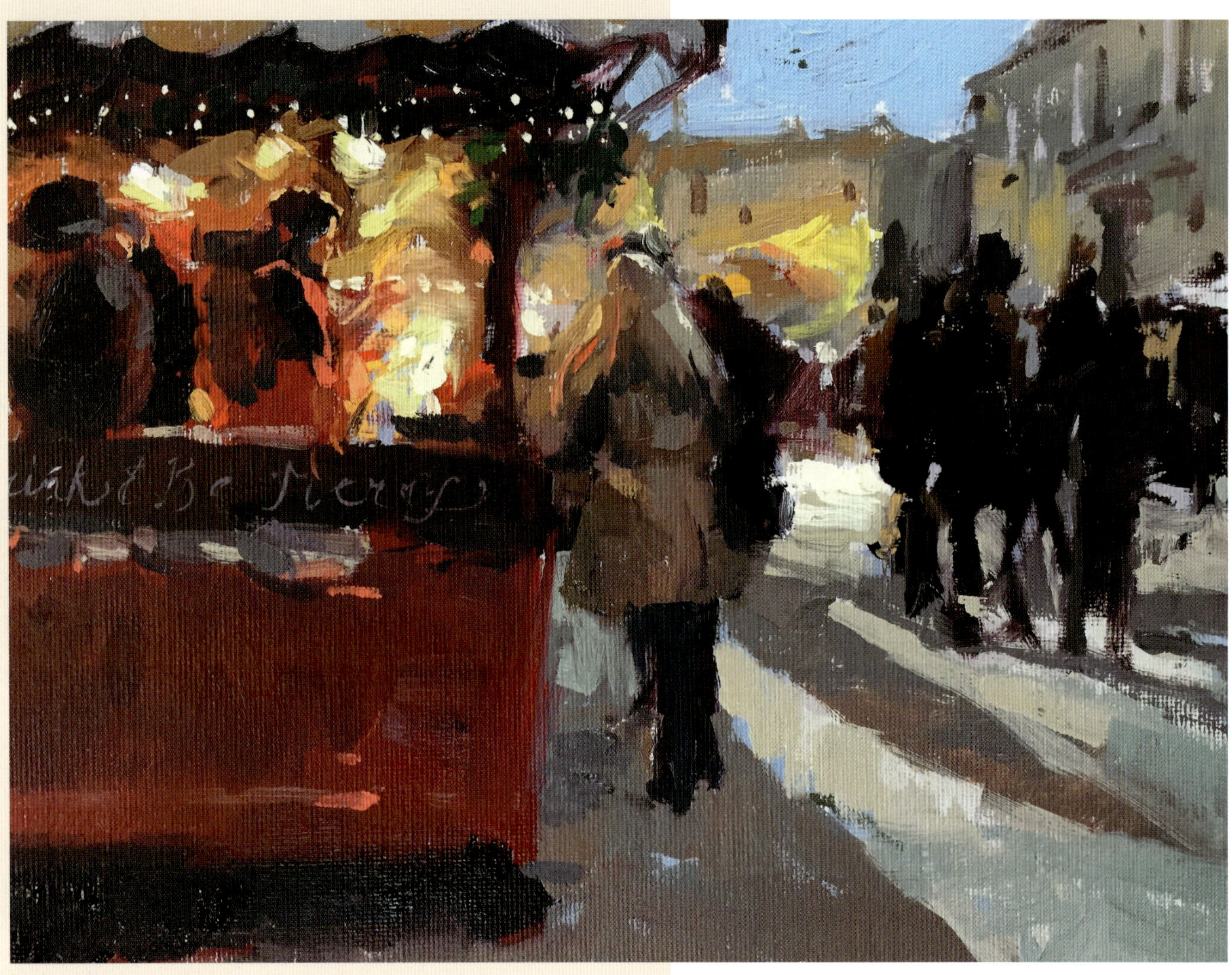

Mulled Wine Stall
30.5 x 25.5cm (12 x 10in)

I tried to rapidly capture an impression of the ambience of the Christmas market: the lights, music and busyness. On the right-hand side, I've used a single dark colour to suggest a whole group of figures in one silhouetted shape. There's very little information given, yet we 'see' a group of figures quite easily.

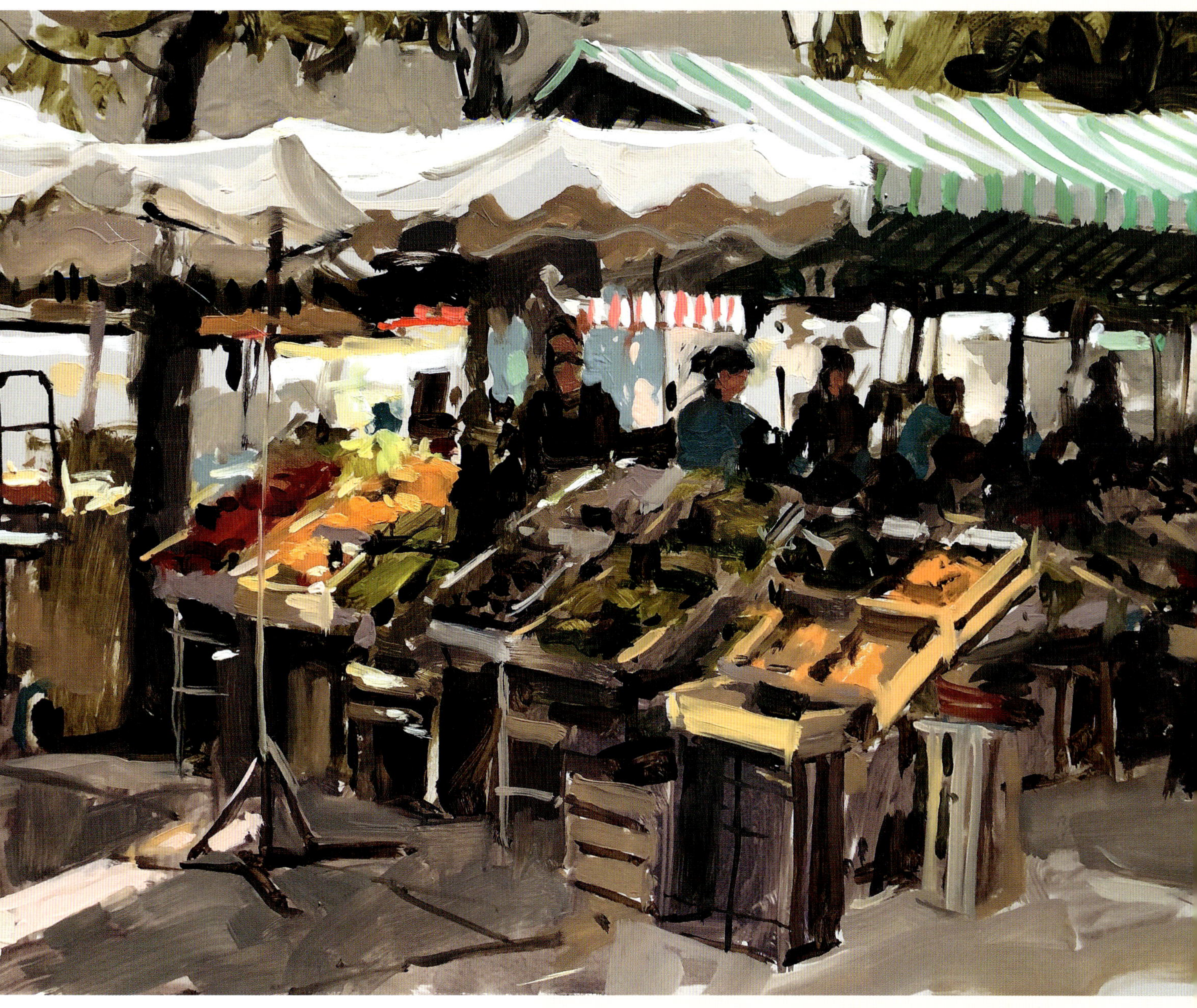

A Glimmer of Sunlight, Nice Market
30.5 x 23cm (12 x 9in)

After torrential rain for much of the morning, I was happy to see the sun shining again.

A market place is one of those scenes which would look strangely deserted if painted without any people in it. As with Mulled Wine Stall, opposite, I was able to make the figures simple silhouettes because they were seen underneath the market stall canopies, against the backdrop of the sunlit buildings behind.

Outdoor portraits and figures

Rather than observing figures from afar, your preferred approach may be to interact directly with people while painting an outdoor portrait or figure study. This is my absolutely favourite genre, and I relish every opportunity when someone is willing to sit for me to be painted outside. I am particularly in my element with a costumed figure, and love the additional narrative aspect of these types of paintings.

Painting people outdoors is an intense and absorbing experience that can take its toll on artist and model alike, so do consider how comfortable everyone is and allow for regular rest breaks. When setting up a model outside, it's a good idea to try to arrange as even and constant a light source as possible, perhaps choosing an overcast day or positioning the sitter underneath a large awning or tree.

As with all other subjects, squint to simplify what you are seeing and identify the dark and light shapes. After a brief colour block-in, I work more particularly on the figure because I know I'll have a bit more time to go back to the surroundings when the model is taking a break or has finished posing. If you are going to take reference photographs, remember to take these at the beginning.

At first you will need to identify the colour of the light that's hitting the subject. If it's a cool, diffused, natural daylight, look for correspondingly warmer shadows. If your model is positioned out in direct sunlight, there may be a warm light hitting the planes which face the sun, while the planes turned away appear cooler. In the deepest shadow parts, for example inside ears and nostrils, look for warmth again.

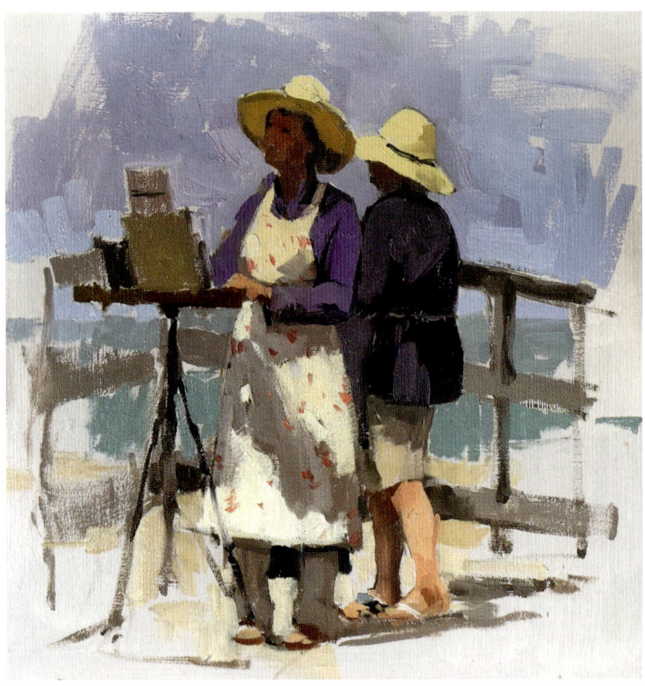

Painting Holiday, Île de Ré
20.5 x 20.5cm (8 x 8in)

Two of my lovely group on a painting holiday, both called Angela. If you spot a subject like this you can't procrastinate, because you don't know how much time you'll have with models who don't realise they're being painted.

It was a sunny day and this painting has a whole range of tonal values from dark to light. Compare how dark the tonal value of the face (shaded by the sunhat) is to the leg that is being lit by direct sun.

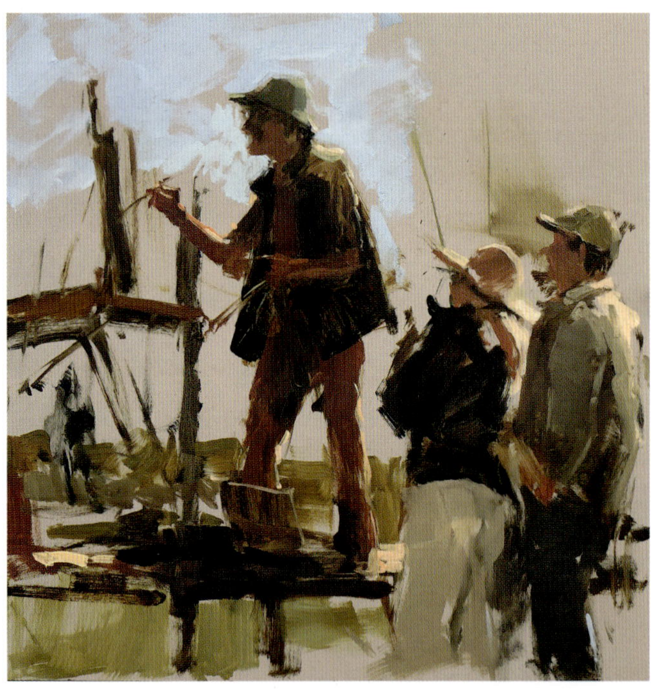

David Curtis Painting at Morston Quay
25.5 x 25.5cm (10 x 10in)

This was a very rapid sketch made while the artist David Curtis ROI RSMA was demonstrating at Morston Quay in Norfolk. I only started it when his painting was well underway, so I didn't know how much time I would have. Sometimes the fastest of paintings have the most energy and success; and this one really captured that special moment.

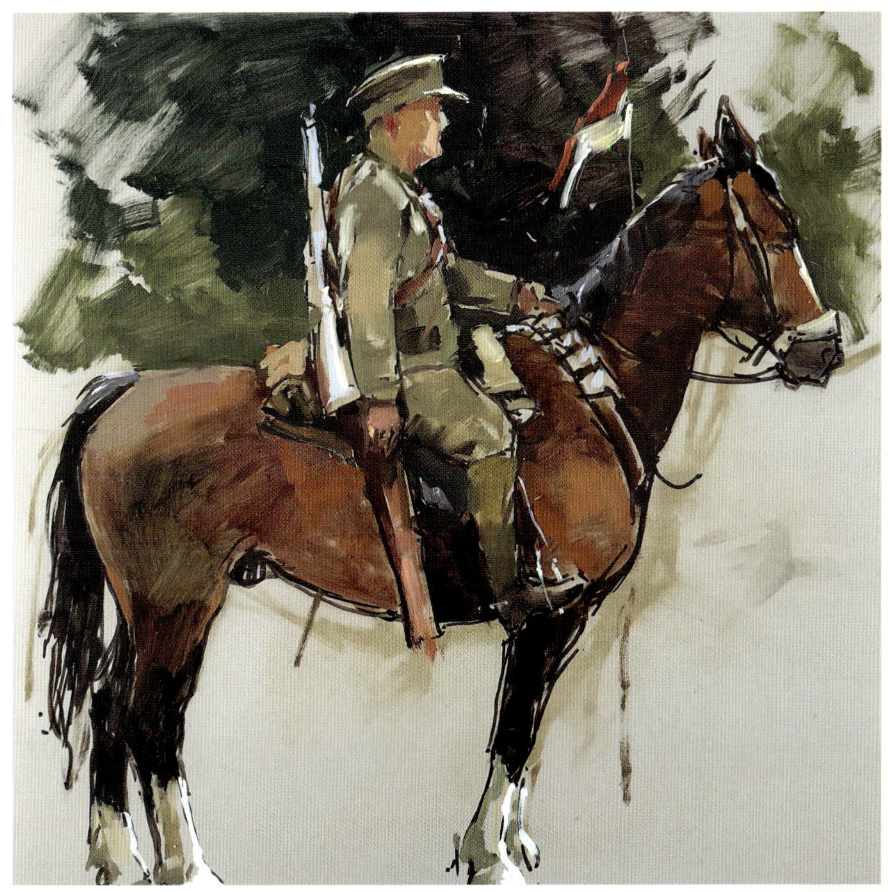

On Patrol
30.5 x 30.5cm (12 x 12in)

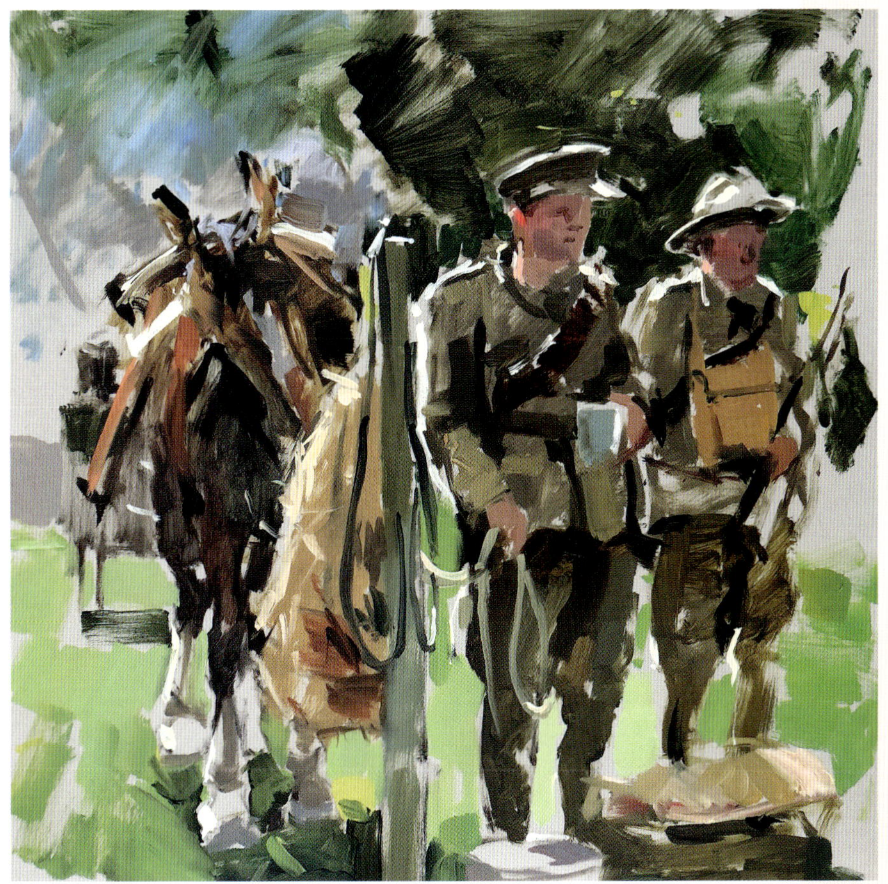

Tea for Two
30.5 x 30.5cm (12 x 12in)

I painted both of these small pieces at an event for a group of artists hosted by the Munnings Art Museum at Castle House, former home of artist Alfred Munnings, war artist and one of England's best-loved painters of horses.

The museum had arranged for a historical re-enactment group to recreate a small First World War field camp scene for us on the lawn of the museum. It was an intense and stimulating few days and I very much appreciated the chance to paint the horses as well as the costumed figures.

Realism, warmth and a convincing finish

A common mistake is to paint flesh tones too cool and with too much added white. As a consequence, the colours become chalky and the skin looks deathly. As a viewer of the painting we can't believe we're looking at a living person with blood moving around beneath their skin.

To avoid this tendency, the best advice I can offer is always to look for the warmth in the shadows, and consider using warm tints when mixing colours for skin. Steer away from using titanium white for making colours lighter and use instead warm whites, Naples yellow, pinks, flesh tints and warm greys.

It's not the facial features that are necessary to make a convincing figure in a painting – it's better to look for the light and shadows planes which show the form of the head. Even in my portrait of Gus the farmer, which is quite a large

painting, if you look closely you'll see I haven't painted his eyes. Instead you can see just the shadow colour which describes the sockets where the eyes are situated. Don't be afraid of using strong colours and dark values for skin, especially if there is strong sunlight.

Look out also for reflected light, which can be warm or cool depending on the surface the light is bouncing from. You may notice reflected light underneath your model's jaw or face from coloured clothing. If you observe it, then do add it to your painting – but don't let it compete with the planes which are receiving direct light. Keep a broad view of your values and make sure the reflected light stays in the shadow group. The key is to keep comparing values across the subject as you work.

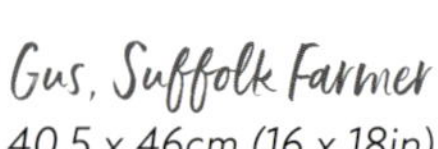

Gus, Suffolk Farmer
40.5 x 46cm (16 x 18in)

Sitting on the steps of a shepherd's hut in his traditional smock, Gus made a really good model. He was holding a crook and a model lamb. I used a rather ambitious size of canvas for a two hour session, but I continued to work on the greenery and hut after Gus had finished modelling.

I really struggled with the colours and values of the white smock in the shadow. I got there in the end with lots of squinting and constant comparisons between areas. All the time I asked myself questions such as 'How dark is this bit compared to the highlights here?', 'How dark is it compared to the skin in shadow?', 'Is that bit warmer or cooler than that bit?'

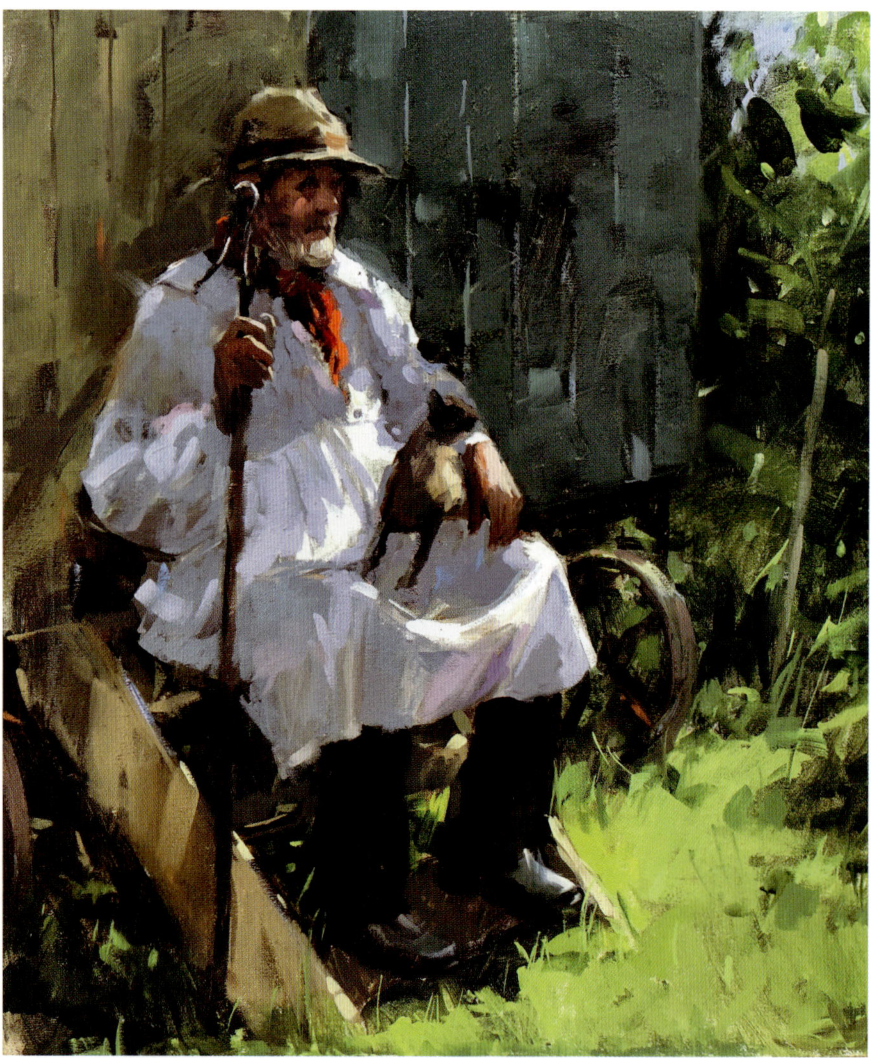

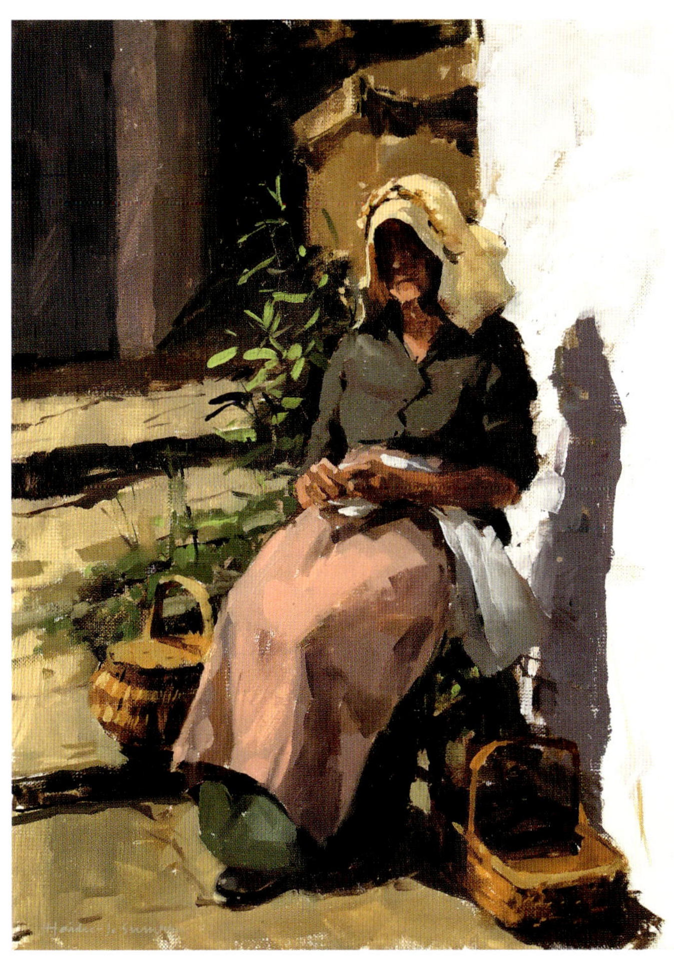

Jane Verrill, Staithes Fishing Heritage
30.5 x 40.5cm (12 x 16in)

I am hugely inspired by the work of the Newlyn and Staithes school of painters of the nineteenth century, when artists such as Laura Knight and Stanhope Forbes took their easels out into the fishing villages to paint the local community at work.

I had the opportunity to work with a group from a model wearing the traditional Staithes bonnet and apron. Not only was the group of artists painting on the same streets as our painting heroes, but our model Jane descends from a Staithes fishing family – and some of her family members had previously known and been painted by Laura Knight herself.

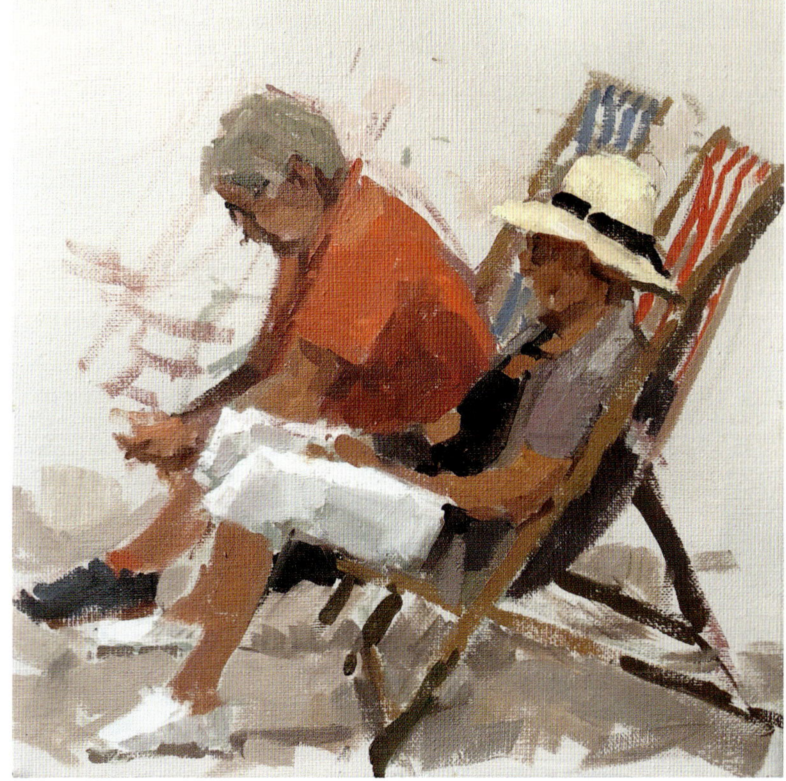

Tom and Pat at Sidmouth
25.5 x 25.5cm (10 x 10in)

While teaching a workshop at this seaside town, and looking for a subject with which to end the day, I spotted this brother and sister sitting on deckchairs looking out to sea. Fortunately they were happy to stick around a little while longer while I painted this demonstration sketch. The people you meet and the stories you hear are such a fulfilling part of plein air painting.

Exploring further: working in the studio

Not all the plein air paintings that I bring back to the studio are good enough to be framed and exhibited. Much as I try to win the battle there and then on the spot, sometimes I run out of time or otherwise have difficulties getting the painting resolved. These 'works in progress' then languish around in various stacks in the studio waiting for further action. There are various approaches you can take:

A Finish it off This approach is usually best when the artwork needs only a few additional touches.

B Start from scratch At the opposite end of the scale to finishing them off, you might choose to work over the whole thing with oil primer to make a clean slate.

C Use it as an underpainting I love the opportunity to work directly on top of failed paintings with a new subject, because you can incorporate colours from the first painting that you would never have thought to add otherwise.

D Experiment If I can't see a clear route to success but think that there is some potential with the painting, it is ripe for experimentation, which may or may not lead to a finished version.

It's a good idea to get into the habit of appraising your work back in the studio and, if you're not very happy with a piece, have a think about what you might do to improve it. You might simply start a new studio painting based on it, using the en plein air experience to inform your work and help you avoid making the same mistakes.

When I'm working from life I tend towards using a whole range of values. Sometimes I later wonder if a more successful effect of the light could have been achieved with a different approach: using colour contrast rather than relying heavily on value contrast, for example, or giving the painting a different key through use of a different value range. This food for thought gives me cause for further exploration in the studio. I might change the colours in a painting, remove or add elements such as figures, or perhaps simplify an area that has become confusing or cluttered.

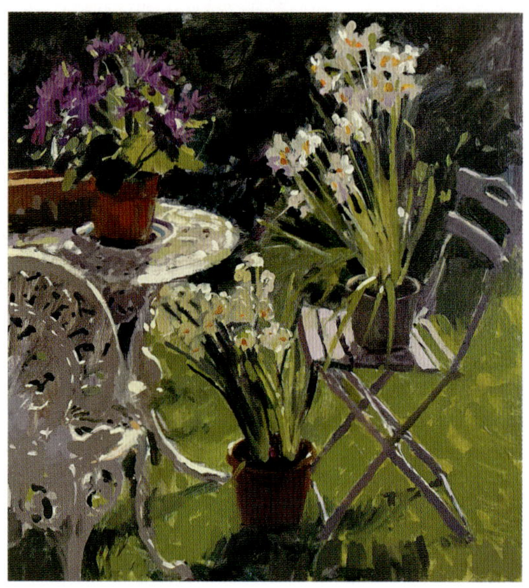

Morning Light, Narcissus - plein air version
33 x 35.5cm (13 x 14in)

I really enjoyed painting this, but when I got it back inside the studio the darks were a lot darker than I realized and I was disappointed with it. I decided to try a new version in the studio with a narrower band of tonal values to see how that worked out.

Morning Light, Narcissus - studio version
28 x 30.5cm (11 x 12in)

Showing the strong effect of the sunlight without using such a wide band of tonal values meant needing to be more creative with colour. I put a lot of violet into the shadow areas, and changed the colour of the flowers in the pot to pink to help them stand out from the background. I think this version is a lot fresher and not overworked, although it lacks some of the depth of the original.

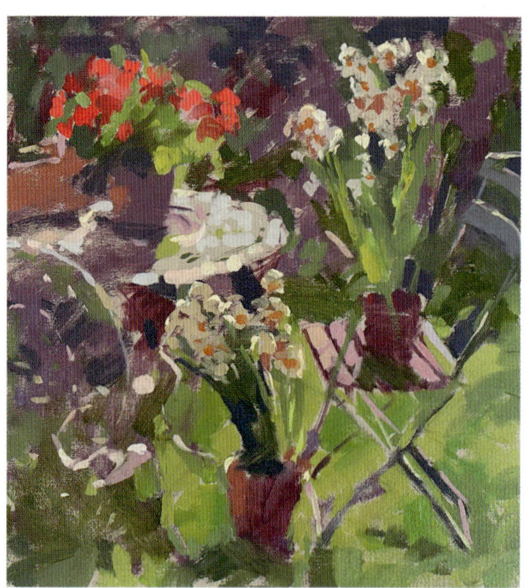

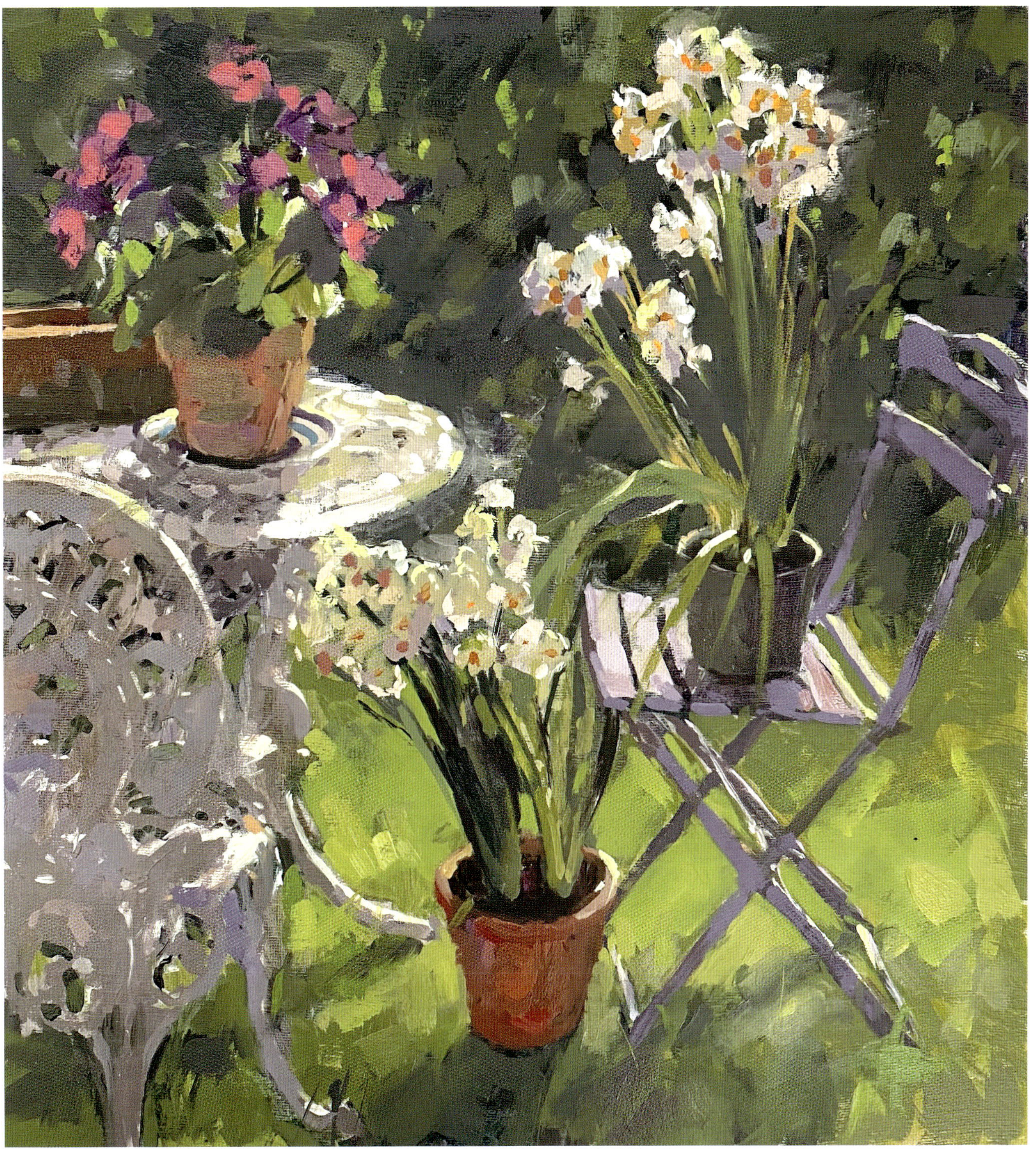

Morning Light, Narcissus
33 x 35.5cm (13 x 14in)

This is the final piece of the puzzle, the plein air version modified in the studio with the lessons learned from both the original painting and the studio version.

After painting the studio version I decided to rework the original because I wasn't happy to call it finished and frame it. The main changes I made were to alter the background greens and also the sunlit grass using slightly lighter values. I also used lighter values for both the terracotta pots, and again changed the colour of the flowers on the table.

Taking a second look

When you are in front of the subject, it's easy to become a bit of a slave to what's in front of you. To avoid this, I've started to work more in the studio from my plein air pieces, and if you want something new to try now that you are familiar with working en plein air, this is an approach to bear in mind. I find that, in looking at the painting with a critical eye away from the subject, I can access other parts of my memory and imagination by asking myself 'What does this painting need?'

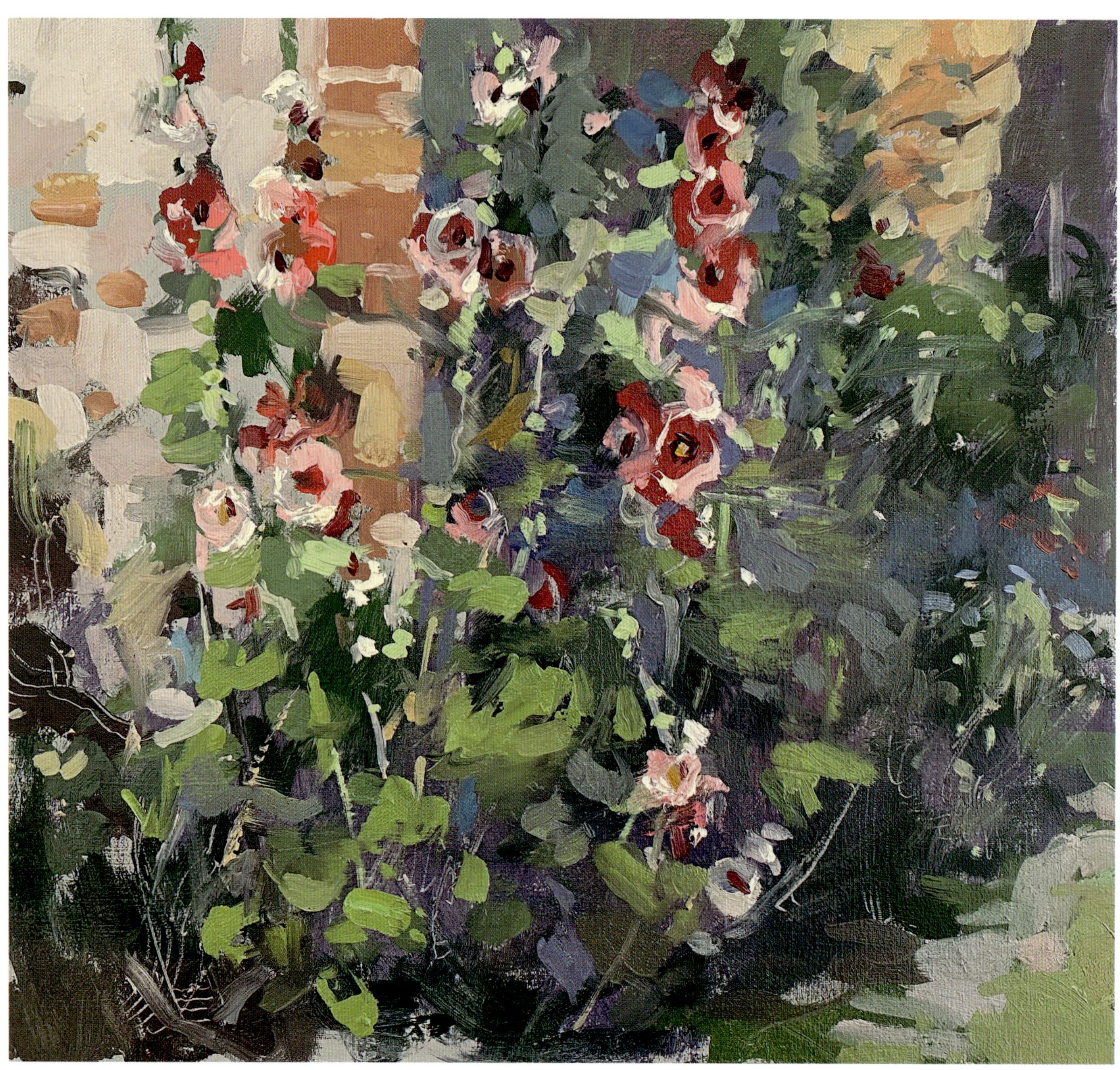

Norfolk Hollyhocks
28 x 25.5cm (11 x 10in)

Developing *Garden Chairs*

Started en plein air in the garden but abandoned, I picked up this painting a couple of years later to try to take it further.

1 Working intuitively, without any reference photographs or sketches, I began to add apricots, greens and violets to enrich the colour palette.

2 Employing my knowledge of the chairs – I've often painted them – I wanted to add a dappled light effect, using a white tinted slightly with pink and apricot. I also incorporated a cooler violet on the chairs and warmed up the shadow on the ground underneath the table.

3 I wondered if the feeling of warm sunlight could be better expressed with more use of pink, which would contrast with the green of the bright grassy area. To this end, I lightened the values on parts of the chairs and then cropped a thin strip off the top for a more interesting composition – I had felt that the foreground gravel strip across the bottom and the sunlit grass across the top had previously been too equal in size.

Going further

Garden Chairs is just one example of a painting that I've picked up recently to develop further. The notes above explain how I developed it – but this isn't necessarily the end. You can continue adding layers and developing your work as you wish. Perhaps this isn't finished yet, but it has certainly moved on.

I really like the thought of exploring memory and emotion and moving away from what is seen. In the future I might like to evolve more in terms of the merging of abstract and figurative elements in my work, and being engaged with the painting away from the subject seems a good direction to explore – a lesson I would never have found without working en plein air.

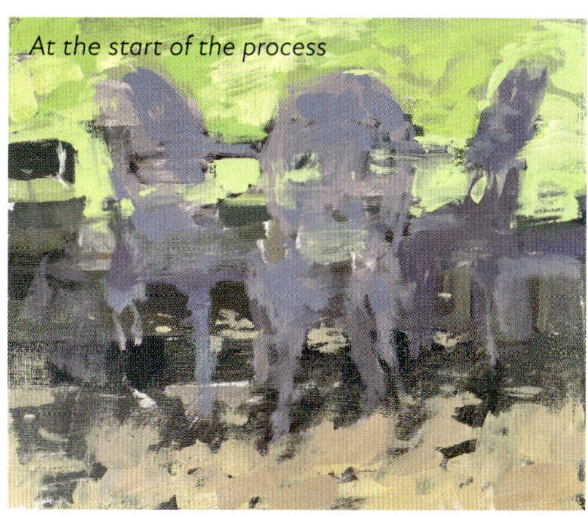

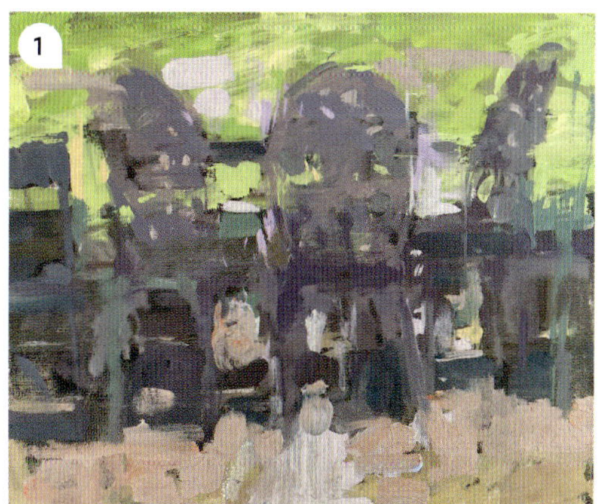

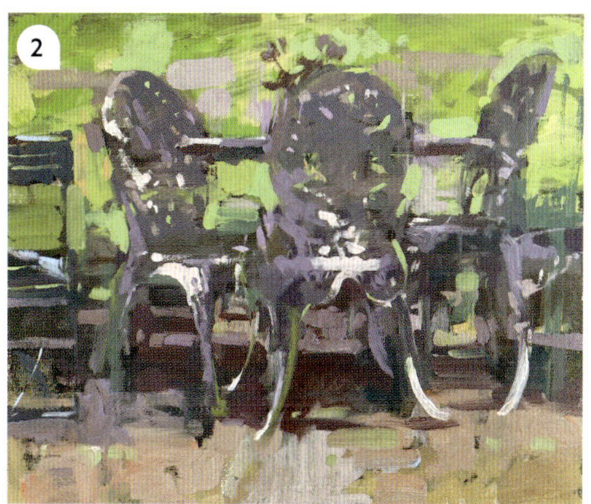

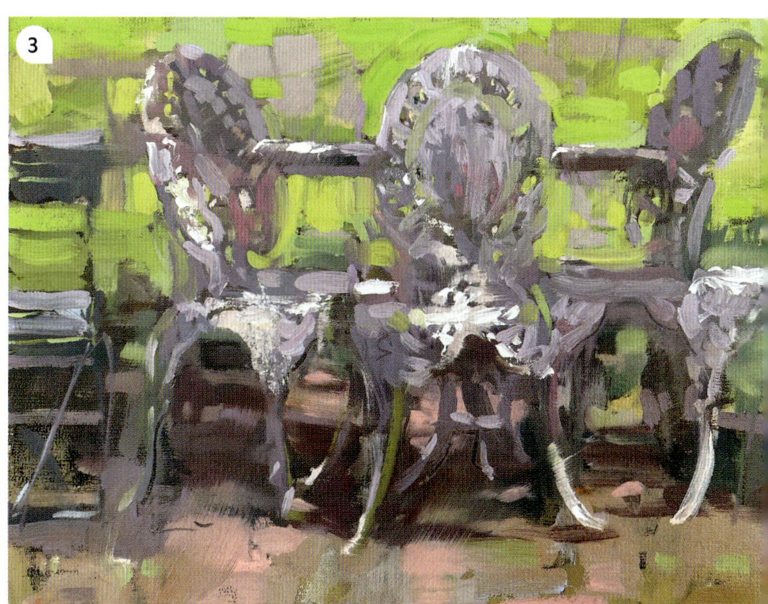

Afterword

I hope this book has given you plenty of inspiration and advice for getting outside to paint with oils. I've focussed my practice on painting en plein air for the last fourteen years and it's given me so many wonderful experiences I never would have thought possible. I wanted to write this book to encourage more artists to get outside and paint, as there's nothing to beat combining your love of painting with being immersed in the great outdoors.

As I've been writing this book we've been going through a worldwide pandemic. Although widespread travel has been off the cards for most of the past year, I've still been able to paint outdoors, although my activities have frequently been restricted to my own garden and immediate neighbourhood. I would say that being able to get outside to paint during this time has been essential to my emotional wellbeing.

Plein air painting is the biggest challenge for a painter, and also the best way to accelerate your learning. With greater challenges come greater rewards, and I hope that, like me, you get addicted to the thrill of facing difficulties head-on. Don't worry about whether you have any natural talent, a little persistence and determination will take you a long way.

I'll leave you with these words sung by Billy Ocean, which I think are the perfect motto for a plein air painter: 'When the going gets tough, the tough get going'.

> **'** Only those who will risk going too far can possibly find out how far one can go. **'**
>
> **T. S. Eliot, 1888–1965**

Pearls of wisdom for the new plein air painter

1 You will forget to bring your brushes with you, at least once.

2 You will arrive at your painting spot encumbered by every size and shape of painting panel – except the one you need.

3 You will meet many members of the public who have an auntie who paints.

4 On finding a promising spot in town, a large vehicle will immediately park in front of your easel, blocking your subject from view.

5 If knocked off the easel, your finished painting will always fall face down – especially when painting on the beach.

6 Cows will try to eat your equipment.

7 Brushes seem to vanish into thin air – you can never buy too many.

8 You can never wear too many layers.

9 You will wish you had stopped sooner.

10 You will make new friends and have funny stories to tell.

11 A dog will decide that your tripod leg makes a suitable urinal.

12 The tide will catch you out; you will quickly learn to wade while juggling all your equipment and footwear.

13 You may well accumulate an unseemly number of pochade boxes.

14 A sweet comment from a child can make your day.

15 A dog or seagull will carry off your lunch. When this happens, just think 'could be worse: could have been a bear'.

16 A small amount of viridian or cadmium red, which has seemingly come from nowhere, will only be noticed after making its way onto your sleeve, shoe, car seat, nose and carpet.

17 It's perfectly normal to experience every emotion during the course of one painting – I hope you like rollercoasters.

18 Remember: no struggle = no progress.

19 Before you set off, if you think that your backpack is too heavy – it definitely is! Repack and take out some items.

20 You may laugh, you may cry, but at the end of the day you'll be glad you braved it!

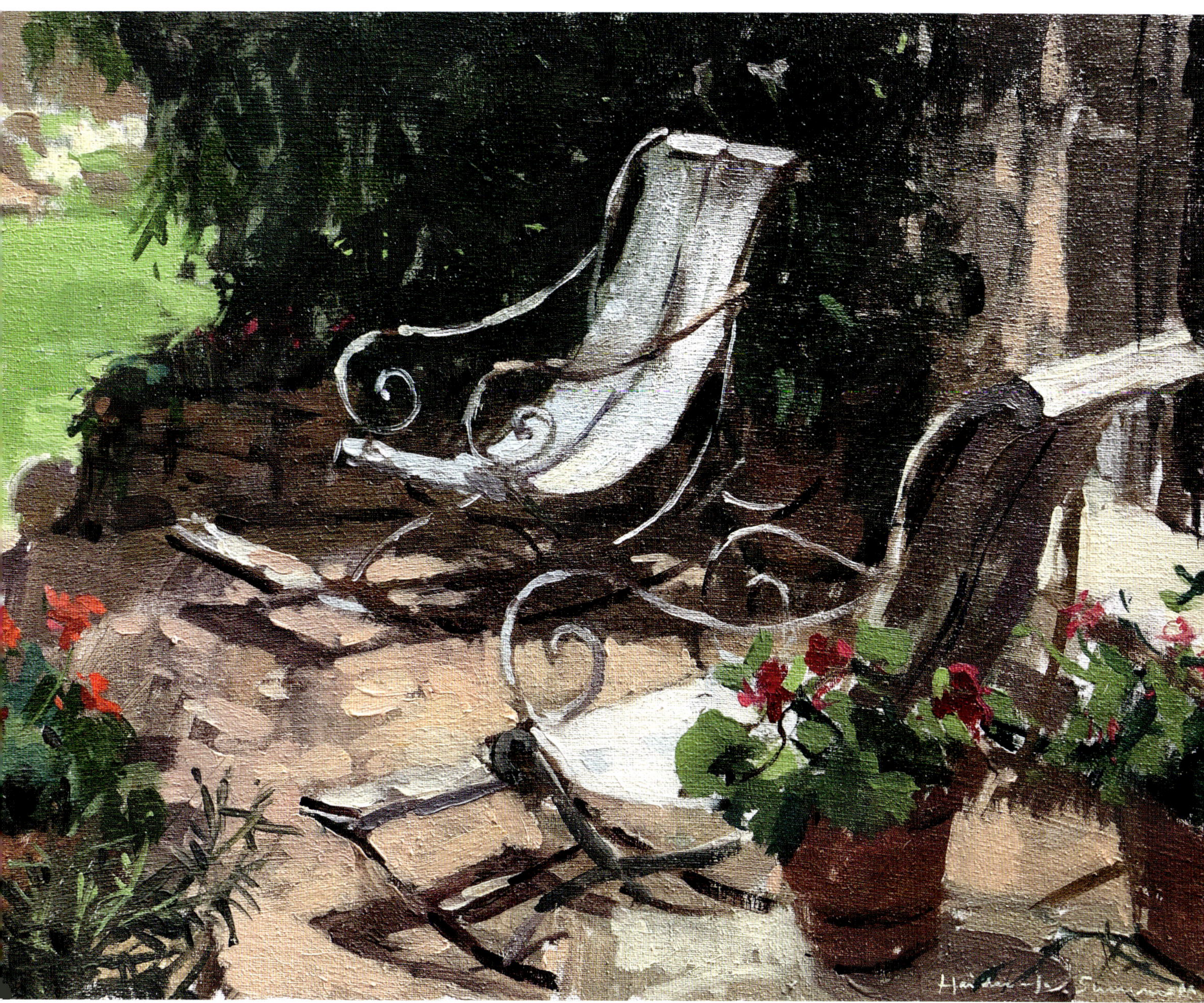

Rocking Chairs on the Terrace
30.5 x 23cm (12 x 9in)

Index